Sisters in Spirit

AFRICAN HISTORY AND CULTURE

SERIES EDITOR

Peter Alegi, *Michigan State University*

African History and Culture is a book series that builds upon and expands Michigan State University's commitment to the study of Africa. The series features books in African history, anthropology, sociology, and political science, as well as interdisciplinary studies, works on the African diaspora, and digital scholarship.

Sisters in Spirit

CHRISTIANITY, AFFECT, AND COMMUNITY BUILDING IN EAST AFRICA, 1860–1970

Andreana C. Prichard

Michigan State University Press | East Lansing

♾ The paper used in this publication meets the minimum requirements of
ANSI/NISO Z39.48-1992 (R 1997) (Permanence of Paper).

Michigan State University Press
East Lansing, Michigan 48823-5245

Printed and bound in the United States of America.

26 25 24 23 22 21 20 19 18 17 1 2 3 4 5 6 7 8 9 10

LIBRARY OF CONGRESS CATALOGING-IN-PUBLICATION DATA
Names: Prichard, Andreana C., author.
Title: Sisters in spirit : Christianity, affect, and community building in East Africa,
1860–1970 / Andreana C. Prichard.
Other titles: African history and culture.
Description: East Lansing : Michigan State University Press, 2017.
| Series: African history and culture | Includes bibliographical references and index.
Identifiers: LCCN 2016027499| ISBN 9781611862409 (pbk. : alk. paper)
| ISBN 9781609175221 (pdf) | ISBN 9781628952926 (epub) | ISBN 9781628962925 (kindle)
Subjects: LCSH: Universities' Mission to Central Africa—History. | Anglican Communion—
Missions—Africa, East—History. | Christian women—Africa, East—Social conditions.
| Christian women—Religious life—Africa, East.
Classification: LCC BV3530.P75 2017 | DDC 266/.367—dc23 LC record available at
https://lccn.loc.gov/2016027499

Book design by Charlie Sharp, Sharp Des!gns, East Lansing, Michigan
Cover design by Shaun Allshouse, www.shaunallshouse.com
Cover image is "Elderly returned Mbweni Schoolgirls. From left, Agnes, Kate, Mary, Emily, and Ester." From "Miss Jones' Girls," *African Tidings*, February 1907.

Michigan State University Press is a member of the Green Press Initiative and is committed to developing and encouraging ecologically responsible publishing practices. For more information about the Green Press Initiative and the use of recycled paper in book publishing, please visit www.greenpressinitiative.org.

Visit Michigan State University Press at *www.msupress.org*

To my family: Mom, Dad, Ian,
Erin, Oliver, and Patrick.

Contents

Acknowledgments

One of the greatest myths about writing is that it is a solitary occupation, a lonesome pursuit, something done locked away from the world. The process of writing this book was anything but; I was sustained and encouraged by a network of people and institutions. In fact, much like the spiritual community discussed in the pages that follow, this physical book both is the product of and engendered a great many connections and relationships—some intellectual and some professional, with a great many others based in friendship, comradery, faith, curiosity, family, and love—all of which span generations and continents.

The heart of this book is in Zanzibar and Tanzania, and would not have been written without the cooperation and engagement of colleagues and friends there. The Right Reverend Maimbo Mndolwa, Bishop of Tanga and Dr. John Kabudi generously provided contacts as well as intellectual and professional support. Mama Salma, Asha, and Salma welcomed me to Arusha with an intensive—in every sense of the word!—introduction to Kiswahili and to Tanzanian culture. Omega Ray is a patient, good-humored, and wise teacher. I am grateful to Mama Rashidi and to Diana Carvalho and her lovely family. Hellen Didas was a kindred spirit far from home. Irene Mashasi, Amina Iddy, Tom, and Robert assisted with research and translation. In Zanzibar, Mama and Baba Zeyn (Ali Aboud Mzee and Khadija binti Issa) and their children charmed me in many ways, not least of which was their spirited work for the 2008 Obama campaign.

Parishioners of former UMCA churches and descendants of UMCA congregants generously shared with me their memories, perspectives, and ideas. I am humbled to offer them my gratitude here: Margaret Amani, Joseph Apiuwa, Philip Baji, Margreth Philipo Bendera, Margaret Bartlett Carere, George Chambai, Margaret Chilumba, Agatha Joyce Chilunda, Father Amani Chitemo, Zainabu Dhahabu, Angela Charles Diwi, Charles Diwi, Edina George, Father Simon Habils, Matayo Hassani, Cecila Hemedi, Alfred Hemedi, Agnes Paulina Heri, Mama Juma, Leila Henry Kaleza, John Keto, Mary Rafael Kigo, Dorcus Kijazi, Lillian Kiondo, Tom Kwetukia, Monica Livinga, Marion Grace Lucas, Mary Diwi Lugendo, Prisca Emile Lutakamale, Steven Chambi Makala, Grace Makao, Joyce Mhando Mapunda, Sophia Herbert Masewa, Christine Mbaruku, Frank Mcharuru, Reverend Mathew Mhagama, John Mhina, Maria Petro Mhina, Basil Mkate, Irene Bartlett Mkoka, John Peter Mnyambu, Stella Mnyambu, Judith Atanasio Mokiwa, Frank Mselemu, Mary Muhina, Esta Musa, Mary Mvungi, Violet Namala, Christopher Njema, Florence Njema, "Mzee Nyangi," Chief Justice Augustino Ramadhani, Bishop John Ramadhani, Bridgeth Ramadhani, Alice Salimu, Veronica Milly Sambila, Philipo Magembe Sekomba, Basil Sembano, Agatha Semhando, Harold Semhando, Vicar General Elias Sengano, Mzee Simpindu, Jane Sudi, Mzee Sudi, Peter Sudi, Phoebe Suri, Nassur Tajiri Ali, Alfred Tandau, Margaret Tandau, Margaret Waimu, and Josephine Wakati. Some people, such as Bibi Miriam, Mama Kate, Francis the Choirmaster, Tom, Auntie Phoebe, Father Mathew, Bibi Miriam, Mama Joyce, and Mzee Christopher, wished to be known by first names. Sisters of the Community of the Sacred Passion and of Chama cha Mariamu Mtakatifu generally wished me to employ pseudonyms. I appreciate their contributions, as well as the contributions of those interlocutors wishing to remain entirely anonymous. This book belongs to all of them.

Some relationships forged in East Africa spanned continents. While in East Africa and since, I enjoyed the friendship of fellow travelers: Alisa Alano, Jim Brennan, Marita Ebil, Bre Grace, Josh Grace, Amy Jamison, Priya Lal, and Rachel Taylor. The staff at MS-TCDC are phenomenal and I've been honored to work with them.

Back at home, my colleagues at Northwestern helped me produce a dissertation. I thrived in the company of wonderful fellow graduate students: James Coltrain, Jesse Eaves, Erik Johnson and Noah Blan (the Power Tri), Pamela Khanakwa, Nate Mathews, Tom Rudczynski, Andrea Ferber Seligman, Marygrace

Tyrrell, Zachary Wright, and many others. I owe much to the faculty and staff in Northwestern's History Department, to the staff at the Melville J. Herskovits Africana Library, and to the folks at the Program for African Studies. I am also grateful for Jeanne Herrick, Renee Redd, Angela Johnson, and Elizabeth Pardoe. David Schoenbrun has an enviably endless supply of creative, stimulating questions that allowed me to see my work and others' in a new light. He is patient, kind, and generous with his feedback. Jonathon Glassman was a demanding and rigorous advisor, and I owe him as much for enduring my stubborn tenacity as I do for his insightful, incisive, and challenging scholarly instruction. Jon's scholarship is sensitive and thoughtful, and anything that is good in these pages is due to his mentorship and guidance.

Friends in Evanston and elsewhere provided a network of support, acceptance, and love that made all the academic work possible during those years. The Bahr family, Cindy Hogan, and Caroline Jevon were the best neighbors, and Heather, Chris, and Ella Ward were a great surprise upon my return from Tanzania. Sarah Holcomb and Brett Holcomb have been a treasured anchor in my life, as have Jim Steen, Marcie Steen, and Tori Steen—bear hugs, margaritas, and fierce, loud laughter are some of their many gifts. Erin-Marie Legacey, who from the first day of graduate school has been the merriest of traveling companions on this harrowing journey, believes so strongly in her friends that failure seems impossible. Hayward Kwit embodies the perfect balance of wisdom and whimsy—she is an amazing woman, a terrific mother, and a true friend.

My faculty and staff colleagues in the Honors College at the University of Oklahoma are dedicated teachers and incredibly decent, hardworking people. Rich Hamerla and David Ray fought for me when I needed it. Friends and fellow writers elsewhere on campus have made this an intellectually stimulating and emotionally supportive environment: Noah Theriault, Miriam Gross, Dan Mains, Kimberly Marshall, and Emily Rook Koepsel are great writing buddies. Ronnie Grinberg, Marc Levine, Jessica Pearson, and Erika Robb Larkins have been wonderfully supportive academic partners-in-crime and cherished friends. Alex Edwards, Becky Weintz, Francesca Winter, Danielle Theriault, Karen Colwell, Callie Morreau, Mairead Todd, Sam Stalcup, Alecia Shannon, Beatrice Williamson, Jennifer Whitner, various yogis and CrossFitters, and many, many others put the "home" in Oklahoma. Julia Ehrhardt is a fierce supporter, a model teacher, and a great friend. Carolyn Morgan paved the way for female scholars at OU, and I rely on her advice, mentorship, advocacy, and friendship daily. Sarah Tracy is a treasured friend, a keen reader, a superior mentor, and a role model in many ways. Her presence and encouragement kept me in the game and pushed me (carried me?) over the finish line.

I received a great deal of help with the research for this book, and it came in various forms. In East Africa, staff and faculty at the University of Dar es Salaam, Kivukoni College, St. Mark's Theological College, Minaki College, the Anglican Church of Tanzania, COSTECH, the Tanzania National Archives, the American Embassy in Dar es Salaam, and the Zanzibar National Archives were critical to this research and aided me in myriad ways. In Britain, archivists and librarians at Rhodes House at the University of Oxford, as well as at the School for Oriental and African Studies at the University of London, the Shropshire Archives, and the British Library granted me access to countless documents and were generous in their assistance. Yoland Brown was of particular help in Shropshire. Reverend Mother Superior Philippa CSP of the Community of the Sacred Passion granted photography permissions. Chapter seven previously appeared in the *Journal of African History*. I am thankful for my student research assistants from the University of Oklahoma: Oscar Enriquez, Jacob Henry, Kierstan Strachan, and Kellie Reidlinger. The VPR and the Vice President and Provost Kyle Harper have also provided support. The cartography lab at the University of Wisconsin, Madison created the maps included in the introduction. Lucy Gardner Carson provided valuable editorial assistance.

Our work is only possible because of the work of others, and I am also indebted to Caroline Bledsoe, Neil Kodesh, Laura Fair, Karen Tranburg Hansen, Kenda Mutongi, Elizabeth Prevost, Lynn Thomas, and Luise White. I owe Pamela Scully and Clifton Crais my career in African history, for they opened my eyes to Africa and to the fascinating stories that we can tell about the past.

Then there were those who literally helped me put these words on the pages that follow. Several writing groups have welcomed me into their ranks—some formal, some informal; some in person, others online (#GraftonLine); some long-term, others short-lived. "Writing coach" doesn't begin to describe how fundamental Michelle Boyd was to this project, and to my work and sense of academic self more generally. Emily Callaci, Kathryn de Luna, and Rhiannon Stephens read every word of this document, many several times over. Without their insightful feedback, critical challenges, encouragement, patience, and friendship, this book would not exist.

Fellowships and grants from several programs at Northwestern University, including the Department of History, the Program of African Studies, The Graduate School, the Nicholas D. Chabraja Center for Historical Studies, the Office of

Fellowships, and the Residential College Program, as well as an NCAA Post-Graduate Scholarship and a Fulbright-Hays DDRA supported this work. The University of Oklahoma provided funding in the form of the Junior Faculty Fellowship program, the President's International Travel Fellowship, the Faculty Improvement Grant, as well as time to write through the Honors College Research-Intensive Leave program. Additional financial support was provided from the Office of the Provost and the Vice President for Research, University of Oklahoma.

I am indebted to the many anonymous reviewers who took the time to provide thoughtful and constructive comments on different versions of this manuscript, and on work that has appeared elsewhere. Peter Alegi and the staff at the Michigan State University Press made this dream a reality.

My family has doubled in size in the time since I last wrote acknowledgments, but the love and support I've received has grown exponentially. My parents have always been blind to the possibility that I might not succeed—in this and all other endeavors—and deaf to any worries I voiced along the way. I often wondered at their faith in me; when I couldn't see what they saw, I used their resolve to plod forward. My brother, Ian Prichard, is an amazing man, and has given us the equally amazing Erin and Oliver. They are models of love, self-sacrifice, respect, kindness, and long-term, mutually sustaining friendships. Lincoln Prichard is the loyalist friend and my favorite distraction. In Patrick Schlecht I have found a place to call home.

Introduction

In January 1898, Beatrice Muyororo and Petro Kilekwa were married in a small but festive ceremony on the grounds of the Universities' Mission to Central Africa's (UMCA) Mbweni station on the East African archipelago of Zanzibar. The wedding took place in St. Mary's Chapel, a quaint building with a rounded, beehive-like brick nave and a three-story bell tower. Covered in a fragrant bramble of wisteria, bougainvillea, and honeysuckle vines, perpetually in bloom thanks to the tropical climate, the chapel was but several hundred meters from the rugged white coral coastline—this made it a breathtaking setting for the young couple's nuptials. Many of the UMCA's British mission workers likely attended the event, dressed in their stiffly starched and impractically white dresses and suits, as did the many African clerics and congregants who loved the couple and wished them well. Petro's classmates from the mission's Kiungani Theological College, as well as friends that Beatrice had known since she was a small child, probably also joined the celebration.

Born into the Yao ethnic group from the Lake Malawi region of Tanzania, Beatrice arrived at the mission in 1881 at the age of two or three as a refugee from the Indian Ocean slave trade.[1] Many of Beatrice's classmates ended up in the mission this way, kidnapped by slave traders from their inland villages and marched in neck yokes toward the coast, clinging tightly to their mothers' hands until separated by the whims of traders or by death.[2] Bound for plantations along the East African coast or for servitude further afield in Arabia, India, or Oman, Beatrice and eventually hundreds of other men and women in her same situation were intercepted by the British navy and entrusted to the care of the UMCA. The UMCA was a British Anglican mission founded by abolitionists to work among refugees from the Indian Ocean slave trade. The mission was an outgrowth of a revival movement within the Church of England; its founders were determined to recreate the church abroad, and they established stations and schools on Zanzibar to train their new dependents as evangelists.

Missionaries placed Beatrice on the mission's rural station at the Mbweni *shamba* (farm) several miles from Zanzibar's Stone Town, where she attended the Mbweni Girls' School and lived in its dormitory under the ever-watchful eyes of a British "lady" missionary. She was from the earliest accounts a star pupil: by thirteen or fourteen, Beatrice was reportedly "very good tempered, and always had a smile on her face." British missionaries regarded her as a success story, praising her religious spirit, her industriousness, and her domestic skills. Beatrice showed some promise as a teacher and, after leading small lessons for the younger girls at Mbweni, was promoted in 1893 to the role of pupil-teacher. At first, a report on Beatrice's career noted, she seemed to find "the new work very trying, and did not like to assert her authority." "I do not think she has ever been very successful in keeping a large number of children in order," the missionary continued, "but she has constantly used her influence with individual children when naughty, and by private talks made them see reason, and helped them to do better."[3] Indeed, on balance it seems that Beatrice was sufficiently prepared to assume her role as the wife of a traveling preacher when she married Petro in January 1898. After their wedding, mission administrators sent Beatrice and Petro to Masasi, a UMCA diocese in southwest Tanzania, to work as evangelists.[4]

When the Kilekwas moved to Masasi, Beatrice brought with her a wide complement of wedding gifts, including "plates, cups, mugs, a jug, teapot, spoons, ladle, enameled basin and saucepan, some print for a dress, and some colored handkerchiefs,"[5] which were provided with the hope that her daily performance of simple domestic tasks would transmit Christian values to neighbors and onlookers. These accoutrements of a proper, civilized Christian life were not the only, nor the most important, evangelical tools that Beatrice brought with her from Mbweni, however. Rather, the personal and spiritual relationships that Beatrice had cultivated at

UNDATED PHOTOGRAPH, FROM "A VISIT TO THE HILLS BEHIND KOTA KOTA," *CENTRAL AFRICA* 31, NO. 361 (JANUARY 1913).

FIGURE 1. Reverend Petro Kilekwa, his wife Beatrice, and their three boys.

Mbweni were templates for new relationships she would forge with students, protégées, neighbors, and new inquirers. These relationships not only served as Beatrice's evangelical tools, but they also were fundamental to the consolidation of a diverse, multigenerational network of African UMCA congregants that spread from Zanzibar to the mainland of Tanzania and Malawi between 1860 and 1970. The community that these ties produced and maintained was one that existed in the interior lives of the community's members, and can best be understood as an "affective spiritual community."

I developed the concept of the "affective spiritual community" to describe and better understand communities produced and sustained by a circuit of emotional feeling and spiritual connection. Women such as Beatrice and her colleagues, as well as the network and broader community they produced and of which they were a part, can both be understood as an affective spiritual community. In this book, I explore the process by which African adherents used a sophisticated evangelical repertoire—a shared emotional and spiritual subjectivity; daily, embodied performance of a set of commonly held, though always negotiated, values; and constant movement between mission stations—to build community. The UMCA's female lay evangelists built a unified community between 1860 and 1970, a period that stretches from the days of some of the earliest Western outposts in East Africa, across the colonial period, to the earliest days of Tanzania's independence, and across unconnected lands. I examine the construction, the content, and the resilience of the ties they forged, and follow the relationships as they radiated out from Zanzibar, throughout the Tanzanian mainland, and across generations.

Beatrice's personal life and career, and in particular her moves in the years after leaving Mbweni, elucidate the ways in which the unique affective dimensions of the lives of the UMCA's "sisters in spirit" produced and sustained an encompassing, multigenerational spiritual community. At Masasi the Kilekwas found a flourishing mission center, which was run largely by other African Christians trained at the UMCA's schools on Zanzibar. Settled by a contingent of British UMCA preachers and freed slave adherents late in 1876, the Christian presence in the area grew quickly. In 1898 the four-station complex that included Masasi, Miwa, Chiwata, and Mwiti boasted a total of 1,412 adherents. In the same year there were eleven schools scattered over the district, with 489 students enrolled.[6] As Beatrice's missionary "mother" had hoped, one of those eleven schools was in fact exclusively for girls.

The girls' day school at Masasi was run by Rose Muriezai, who was the wife of the African priest Barnabas Mtaula and was one of Beatrice's dearest friends from

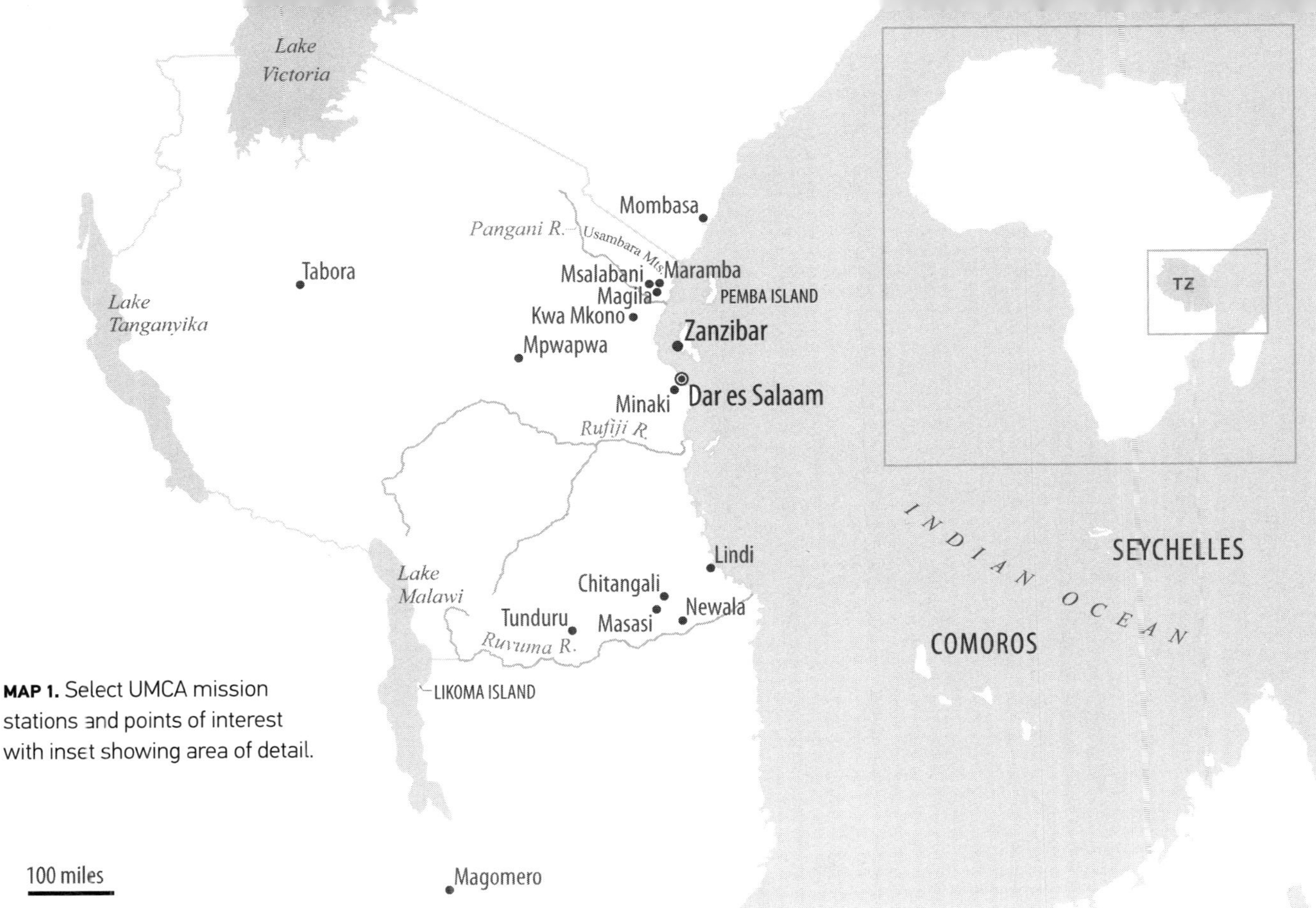

MAP 1. Select UMCA mission stations and points of interest with inset showing area of detail.

MAP PRODUCED BY THE CARTOGRAPHY LAB AT THE UNIVERSITY OF WISCONSIN, MADISON.

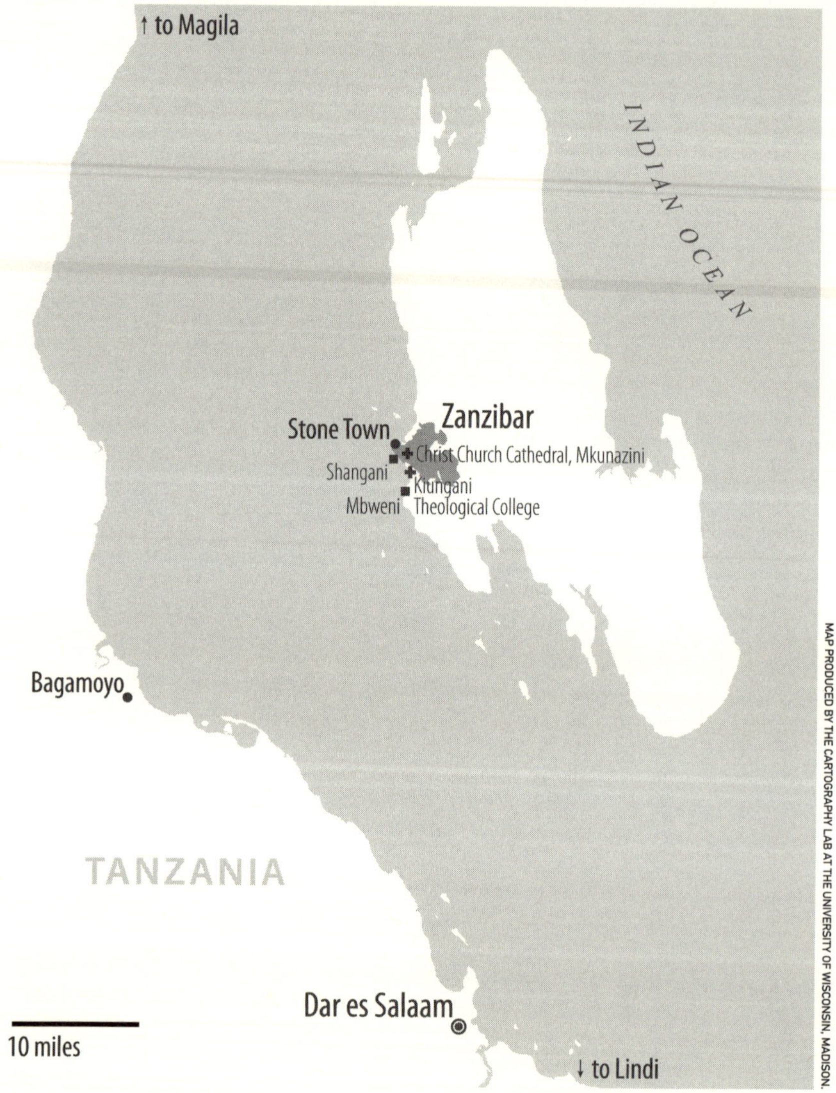

MAP PRODUCED BY THE CARTOGRAPHY LAB AT THE UNIVERSITY OF WISCONSIN, MADISON.

MAP 2. Significant UMCA sites on Zanzibar and the adjacent East African coast.

Mbweni.[7] Mbweni's British "lady" workers had praised Rose as one of the "best and most useful pupil-teachers," a "bright, clever girl, with deep religious principles, and . . . a real missionary spirit."[8] In this they made a good pair: not only had the women always been "great friends,"[9] but they also both looked "upon teaching as the great object of their lives," which was a trait missionaries believed would "be the means of leading others to Christianity"[10] once stationed together. This, of course, was the pair's essential task as Christian teachers: educating Rose's fifty-two female pupils was the key component, UMCA adherents and workers believed, in creating a "a race of intellectual Christians."[11] By "race," British missionaries were referring to the nineteenth-century sense of the word as a civilization bound and defined by a shared set of cultural values, rather than as a discrete and immutable category defined by geographical origin or heredity, as it is regarded today.[12] Beatrice and Rose would have approached their work with Masasi's young women with this concept in mind, assisting in the development, expansion, and consolidation of a new Christian civilization (or "race") in East Africa based on values they absorbed while at Mbweni.

The strong friendship Rose and Beatrice forged at Mbweni was based on the time they spent together as pupil-teachers, a sense they were set apart in their engagement in a common intellectual and religious endeavor, and their shared religious beliefs. They were both also members of the Guild of the Good Shepherd, the UMCA's professional development organization for female teachers. The guild, like the UMCA's theology more generally, encouraged members to "feel the power and help of mutual intercession and of prayer," and promoted special ritual and devotional practices as a means of instilling and sustaining a spiritual and a sensual or embodied connection between teachers, and between themselves and their students.[13]

The affective and spiritual bonds Rose and Beatrice forged at Mbweni were also undoubtedly strengthened by the situation at Masasi. It is true that the UMCA presence in Masasi was relatively strong and the number of adherents grew every year, but as preachers, teachers, and community leaders, the Zanzibar-trained couples were distinguished from their followers by virtue of their educations and positions within the church. Further, they were not "of" the people they were brought in to recruit, lead, and serve. Though Barnaba Mtaula was from the area (the son of a local chief) and Petro Kilekwa had spent about a year in Masasi in 1896,[14] neither Rose nor Beatrice was familiar with the land or its people. Cultural customs and language barriers complicated their immediate integration into the community. Since they did not speak the local language, they were left to communicate with each other in English or Kiswahili (neither of which was a native tongue) and with their followers either through an interpreter or silently, through the embodied performance of daily rituals. Rose and Beatrice's domestic routines—which included a particular wardrobe and style of dress, a favored floor plan for the house and compound, very precise laundry and cooking methods, and theories about child-rearing, for example—immediately marked them to passersby as Christians. These quotidian acts of civilized or "practical" Christianity, as historian Kenda Mutongi has called it, set them quite apart from their "heathen" neighbors and left them with an often overwhelming sense of isolation.[15] There was also outright resistance to the church's work, and to its agents. For example, in 1905 an uprising against the mission caused Rose and her scholars to flee the mission compound. She recalled working furiously to continue the students' Christian learning while in exile. Of her attempts to hold the intellectual and spiritual community together in the face of external threat, Rose wrote, "We are trying to keep our scholars together," despite having "no books here, but we teach them what we can remember of the scriptures, and we make them write with a stick on the ground."[16]

In this environment, far from the church's civilizational and spiritual center at Zanzibar, bonds with old friends, the presence of fellow believers, and proximity to those with whom the "native" evangelists shared cultural and religious practices were a comfort and a source of strength. Rose and Beatrice invested in relationships with other Zanzibar-trained Christian couples living near them, and they maintained ties with both their former home at Zanzibar and their friends in other parts of the mission. In this way, they engaged in the process of weaving together a spiritual community, one that crosscut and superseded other affinities. Their marriages, kinships, and friendships breached ethnic divides and bridged the wide geographical spaces of the mission's lands, all in the service of producing a "race of intellectual Christians."

Evangelists' affective and spiritual connections undergirded the expansion of the burgeoning "race" or civilization. When the Kilekwas left Masasi in 1899 for Likoma, an island in Lake Malawi, for example, they brought news of the Mtaulas and the Majaliwa clan with them, as well as gossip from their recent tenure at Zanzibar. While stationed at Mtonya they found Eustace Malisawa and Augustine Ambali and their wives Amy and Mabel, all of whom were Zanzibar-trained refugees from disparate parts of eastern Africa. These friendships sustained them, and reinforced the spiritual, intellectual, and emotional connections that united

UNDATED PHOTOGRAPH, FROM "MISS JONES' GIRLS," *AFRICAN TIDINGS* 16, NO. 208 (FEBRUARY 1907).

FIGURE 2. Elderly returned Mbweni schoolgirls. *From left:* Agnes, Kate, Mary, Emily, and Ester.

them. After several years near Lake Malawi, the pair departed for a six-month leave in Zanzibar; the bonds they had formed at Mbweni years before endured, pulling them home. Beatrice looked forward to seeing her friends and their missionary "Mother" Caroline Thackeray, and she in turn was so anxious to see Beatrice and the Kilekwas' young children that she personally paid for their journey.[17] Petro recalled their return to Mbweni as "everything we could wish for. In truth we were at our home."[18]

Connections like these among Rose, Beatrice, Amy Malisawa, and Mabel Ambali, and their friends and adoptive kin at Zanzibar, extended throughout the mission. The network of UMCA women knit together a larger affective spiritual community through their daily performance of a set of commonly held values; through a shared emotional and spiritual subjectivity; through their inherent mobility and constant movement between stations; and through the extension of new personal and spiritual connections. This community spread from Zanzibar to the mainland of Tanzania and Malawi, incorporated many ethnolinguistic groups, and encompassed several generations.

Efforts to build an affective spiritual community took place against a backdrop of the campaign to end the slave trade, the transformation of the East Africa economy, widespread Christian evangelism, and the consolidation of colonial rule. Individual congregants pursued opportunities for enhanced security, professional careers, and religious journeys alongside the broader changes happening around them, and engaged with these developments in patchy, uneven, and gendered ways. The UMCA was in many ways like other, better-known mission organizations, such as the London Missionary Society (LMS) or Church Missionary Society (CMS), and shared with the CMS mission at Freretown and the LMS mission in Sierra Leone a particular focus on ex-slaves and refugees from the slave trade. These similarities give the trends identified here broader applicability. This denomination's unique theology, the demographics of its adherents, and this work's focus on affective relationships, on the other hand, offer a new set of understandings for the history of religion and Christian missions in Africa, the creation of ethnicities, and the development of cultural nationalisms.

While resonating with other histories, this study offers an exceptional lens into the way the UMCA's particular theology and the social circumstances of adherents' lives combined to produce intimate, affective spiritual relationships between female lay evangelists that united the church across ethnic and generational boundaries. These understandings come through a focus on the lives, work, and personal relationships of the UMCA's sisters in spirit. They are examined in a series of vignettes and a set of historical snapshots of the lives of the UMCA's female lay evangelists, stories that reveal these women at work and at home as individuals and within the context of broader networks. The intimate scale of this study was intentional, for "thick description and studies of local processes can contain clues to large causation."[19] The voices of individual African women provide access to the interior lives and intellectual contributions of female actors. They also shed light on arguments about the development of some of the grander narratives of intellectual and political change in the long twentieth century—for example, on debates about the development of racial thought, the power of the unseen world to create political change, the articulation of national/ethnic boundaries, and the rise of cultural nationalisms.

Background and Scope

The men and women of the British UMCA were in East Africa specifically to work with Africans like Beatrice, all of whom were refugees from the Indian Ocean slave trade. These British missionaries were part of a broader trend among mid-nineteenth-century evangelicals, who spread out across the continent to work with ex-slaves and refugees from the illegal yet ongoing slave trades. Founders of the Church Missionary Society (CMS) mission at Freretown, Kenya, and the London Missionary Society (LMS) mission to Sierra Leone, as well as missions in southern Africa, also created missions explicitly to work with freed slaves. Both the LMS and the CMS had stations in what is today Tanzania by 1885. The French Holy Ghost Fathers began their work in Zanzibar with freed slaves but moved relatively quickly to Bagamoyo, where the remnants of their work can still be seen today. The White Fathers, members of a French society devoted to work in Africa, began work in 1879. Mission work expanded after German conquest. The Holy Ghost Fathers and the White Fathers expanded their work into the interior, whereas the CMS moved largely to Uganda and the LMS handed their stations over to the Moravians and withdrew. Several German missions quickly filled the void, including Roman Catholics, Benedictines, Lutherans, and Calvinists, all split among different mission organizations.[20] While the missions represented a wide range of denominations and theological approaches to what they called "conversion," they generally employed similar approaches to evangelism: they built schools and trained catechists, and encouraged believers to abandon old beliefs and practices.

What distinguished the UMCA from the other mission organizations setting up shop in East Africa in the latter half of the nineteenth century was their theology. The founders of the UMCA were sympathetic to the Oxford Movement, a reform movement within the Church of England that sought to address the Church's failings through a revival of the Church abroad. These Tractarian reformers (so called for a series of tracts published in Oxford and further afield announcing their philosophy and doctrine) hoped to cultivate among their new adherents a "Native Clergy." This group included ordained African men and their trained wives who acted as partners or "helpmeets" in evangelism; UMCA clergy hoped that the new adherents would lead the church in Africa and take responsibility for growing its membership. In fact, the British missionaries drew parallels between the UMCA's "Native Church" and the Israelites' reestablishment of Zion after Jerusalem's destruction. Similar to God's "chosen people," the freed slaves who had found redemption and salvation in the teachings of the UMCA would constitute the core of the new church. African clerics and their helpmeets would spread the news of Christ through evangelization and proselytization, performance of faith, and the quotidian work of Christian living.

As UMCA missionaries envisioned it, Africans from throughout the mainland would flock to this new Zion, ethnic distinctions would be eliminated, and African Christians would unite into a single spiritual community. As it had been in Isaiah's prophesies, missionaries and adherents alike imagined that they would help grow an East African "nation of worshippers of the true God of all peoples and tongues."[21] Because of their faith that Christian women alone were responsible for engendering—both biologically and ideologically—the spiritual community, church officials placed the majority of the evangelical burden on these generations of female adherents. Between 1865 and the 1960s, missionaries and African church leaders attended assiduously to the academic, cultural, religious, and moral educations of the UMCA's African women, and as a result of these attentions, UMCA-educated women came to embody the principles, practices, and ethos of the mission's particular brand of modernizing Christianity.

The group of women I term "sisters in spirit," and whom I follow in their pursuit of spiritual communion, does not include *all* of the UMCA's female adherents. Rather, I am concerned only with the subset of the mission's congregants who, through their daily performance of a certain set of values, evangelized to new believers on the frontiers of the mission. These women did so generally in three different ways. First, there were women like Rose and Beatrice, women who were trained as schoolteachers and clerics' wives to formally assist the church in its evangelical endeavors. They were not trained in theological colleges like their husbands, nor were they ordained clerics (the UMCA did not include women in the official church scaffolding), but they were an absolutely fundamental component of the mission's evangelical strategy. Second, I also follow the stories of women who were not trained as teachers or clerics' wives, but who otherwise assumed roles that were acknowledged by the church as part of the mission's official evangelical campaign.

This second group included educated women such as nurses, nuns, Sunday school leaders, and heads of Mothers' Union chapters, women who assumed positions that were widely recognized as educative, organizational, or instructive.[22] Finally, women who considered themselves to be UMCA congregants and were educated in schools run by the UMCA, but did not have professional, official, or even often acknowledged roles within the church's evangelical structure, also fall within the moniker "sisters in spirit." Taken together, these women can productively be thought of in a manner similar to Feierman's "peasant intellectuals"[23] in that they assumed social positions of mediation or translation; they were individuals who did work or in particular moments engaged in activities that were absolutely vital to the mission's domestic and quotidian evangelical efforts, and consequently to the spread of the church's ethos through congregations and across generations.

Whether or not all of these women saw themselves as a group set apart (although there is reason to believe that many of them did), a collective affective subjectivity did bind them together, and it allowed them to advance a network of believers through space and time. Orphaned refugees raised as siblings in the mission's dormitories on Zanzibar, for example, maintained intimate emotional and spiritual bonds after moving to disparate stations on the mainland with their husbands; as they knelt daily to pray, as they sewed dresses and embroidered vestments just as the missionaries taught them, and as they traveled great distances to maintain schoolgirl friendships, they continued to imbue a diverse spiritual community with meaning. Women like Beatrice and Rose claimed that even while separated by hundreds of miles, kneeling every day at the same time to recite the Lord's Prayer or to meditate upon the quarterly Thanksgivings and Intercessions offered by the UMCA Prayer Union allowed them to feel close to home.[24] To be sure, their membership in this spiritual community was as salient as others' belief in their own ethnicity or race. Bound together through intimate relationships of affective spirituality, the "series of nested circles" that constituted the UMCA originated in the private domain of the intellectually and spiritually formative spaces of Mbweni and the performative and constructive spaces of the Christian home.[25] The network extended to the social realms of congregations, to formal and informal women's organizations, to extended kin and social networks, and finally to the heart of the public sphere.

The UMCA's sisters in spirit used the emotional ties of affective spirituality as a tool to extend the reach of their community. They established sewing circles and mothers' unions to teach inquiring women how to raise Christian children; they formed intimate relationships with "heathen" foster daughters and with schoolgirls who showed dedication and promise; and they performed the daily acts of Christian living—such as laundry, cookery, fashion, and house design and appointment—for curious passersby and neighbors. Their extroverted performances and attempts to maintain the relationships forged in the church constitute a phenomenon akin to what Benedict Anderson has described as the modal journey of the religious pilgrimage. Sacred capitals came to have meaning only when the constant flow of religious pilgrims from otherwise distant and unrelated locals moved through areas such as Rome, Mecca, or Benares—or, in this case, Zanzibar. The unification of people of disparate geographical and cultural backgrounds in a place like Mecca was incomprehensible "without an idea of their community in some form. The Berber encountering the Malay before the Kaaba must, as it were, ask himself: 'Why is this man doing what I am doing, uttering the same words that I am uttering, even though we cannot talk to one another? There is only one answer, once one has learnt it: 'Because we . . . are Muslims.'"[26] And so, too, for the UMCA and its mainland communities, the idea of a community comprising Makua, Bonde, Makonde, or Oromo, freed slaves and mainlanders, sons and daughters of local big men and some of East Africa's most marginal, was inconceivable without the idea of a united spiritual community.[27] The reality of imagined religious communities—which were not just imagined but also "actually existing social contracts"—depended profoundly on these "countless, ceaseless travels" of the religious adepts, such as the Kilekwas, Mtaulas, Majaliwas, and their many colleagues.[28]

Affective Spirituality

A host of recent work on affect in Africa illustrates that engaging affect with knowledge and transmissions, ways of knowing through embodied being, and gendered subjectivities with the senses allows us to tell fundamentally new stories about religious ideas, political change, and intellectual history.[29] Being attentive to affect as an analytical category and as an archive is not the same as telling the history of a single emotion. Rather, it signifies a field wider than "emotions," for it includes "feelings, emotions, moods, sensations, and the like."[30] If affects are similar to the contagious nature of a yawn, a smile, or a blush,[31] we can productively imagine certain aspects of the lives of the sisters in spirit as being similarly contagious, productive, and constitutive of an affective spiritual community. This term, as I employ it here, builds on a much older definition of "affective spirituality" as an embodied experience of Christ's passion to suggest instead a circuit of emotional feeling and spiritual connection among individuals within a faith community.

In its traditional usage, the term "affective spirituality" indicates a form of Christian piety centered on the "compassionate devotion to the suffering of Christ."[32] The Medieval Church was particularly vigorous in its promotion of this form of devotion, employing a wide range of evangelical methods to promote a "widening of the contemplative net, calling more and more of its children to participation in the compelling experience of Jesus' suffering." During this period, sermons from the pulpit, exhortations from a dais in the marketplace, and treatises or pamphlets read in one's own parlor became increasingly concerned with Christ's suffering, eliciting in many Western Christians highly emotional responses to His torment and misery. For many early modern Christians in the West, the imagery of Christ's suffering called forth within the faithful certain feelings and bodily responses—uniting them, for example, in a "paroxysm of grief"—changing them inwardly and outwardly, and uniting them in a shared community of feeling.[33]

This shared community of feeling among sixteenth- and seventeenth-century Western Christians is what historian Barbara Rosenwein has termed an "emotional community." Emotional communities are, Rosenwein writes, "precisely the same as social communities—families, neighborhoods, parliaments, guilds, monasteries, parish church memberships." Each emotional community has its own "system of feeling," a particular way the community and the individuals within it "define and assess [what is] valuable or harmful to them"; how they evaluate others' emotions; the "nature of the affective bonds between people that they recognize; and the modes of emotional expression that they expect, encourage, tolerate, and deplore."[34] Attention to such communities as they existed in the past—to the embodied response to the Passion, for example, or to the expression and management of singular feelings such as love, fear, anger, jealousy, honor, or passion—allows scholars to better understand political relationships, relationships of the living to the spiritual world, community-building processes, and many other forms of historical change.

The network of discontiguous UMCA congregations that spread throughout Zanzibar and the adjacent mainland between 1860 and the 1960s can also usefully be thought of as an emotional community, one bound together by networks of affective spirituality. These networks were built in part on something resembling the medieval understanding of adherents' embodied, sensuous, emotive, and heartfelt devotions toward Christ through the Passion. In the context of late-nineteenth- and early-twentieth-century East African UMCA communities, the term "affective spirituality" also refers to the way in which affect and affective relationships and performances gave shape to the UMCA community across space and time. The affective and emotional dimensions of this community were rooted in missionaries' Tractarianism, which emphasized slow revelations of the Gospel through daily practice, and a preference for the teachable disposition of small children. The UMCA's Tractarian inheritance also taught that the way of knowing the truth was not merely intellectual—it was embodied and felt rather than reasoned; practiced and experienced rather than taught. More measured than their physically effusive forebears and disinclined toward lavish sentimentalism, Tractarians did, however, emphasize the relationship between mysticism and ritualism expressed by the ancient church fathers, and they valued the importance of an embodied, emotional spirituality.[35] To be sure, Africans have long engaged the affective and the spiritual, and there has been great attention paid to the embodied spiritual practices of Africans. Spirit cleansings and other rituals have long been part of Africans' ecstatic experience.[36] Rather than a charismatic leader inspiring deep faith (or fear) in the ancestors' return, or embodied spirituality serving as an expression of other concerns, individual UMCA sisters in spirit cultivated deep and resonant relationships among themselves and within the community. The lives of the UMCA's sisters in spirit illustrate the development of the affective networks and circuitry that made this community possible.

Once the first generations of African adherents began to proselytize, similar bonds grew up between African evangelists and adherents on the mainland, and between "native" teachers and their protégées throughout the mission. These intimate spiritual relationships manifested themselves in many ways. For example, in exile from lifelong friends, fictive and actual kin, and their missionary "mothers," and often isolated from other Christians, female evangelists like Rose and Beatrice felt homesick, isolated, bored, and nostalgic in their new homes. Rather than retreat from these emotions when they experienced them, many succumbed. To mitigate their feelings, they invested in personal relationships with congregants and inquirers through teaching associations, groups for clerics' wives, and in the fundamental model of the teacher-disciple. In so doing, the UMCA's female evangelists transformed homesickness, nostalgia, and alienation into powerful evangelical tools, which both sustained and extended the UMCA's community of affective spirituality.

As with all moral communities, the UMCA was an arena of constant debate.[37] The affective dimensions of the lives of women without "official" evangelical positions in the church shed light on the different pathways toward shifting, controlling, or manipulating virtue and identity. For example, women living on the Mbweni *shamba* in the 1920s debated the acceptability of particular forms of love, romance, sex, and marriage. A series of abortion scandals, and the events and relationships that produced those pregnancies and framed them as debate-worthy, reveal African congregants' views on the nature of racial and ethnic thought, and of accepted and acceptable behavior within the moral community. Individuals struggled to define the collective essence of an institution or group, the moral economy in which they lived. On a daily basis, believers sought to define the spiritual and cultural contours of the community—on the one hand through chastity and self-sacrifice, and on the other through romantic love, secrecy, and the particular use of language. UMCA congregants' shared consciousness and common devotional practices were unifying elements, actively tying together their community of believers. Affect, then, was a central component of UMCA congregants' spiritual lives, and the ways in which they transmitted their cultural and civilizational values to new inquirers living on the frontiers of the mission. Taken together, then, in the context of late-nineteenth- and early-twentieth-century African mission communities, the term "affective spirituality" describes the way a shared emotional and spiritual subjectivity was produced.

Affecting Histories of Mission

I was initially drawn to the UMCA as a subject of study by the mission's connections to the development of anticolonial nationalism and national identity in Tanzania, not by an interest in affect as an analytical category. Indeed, the UMCA was known for its important role in Tanzanian history; the African men who graduated from the mission's Kiungani Theological College (later Minaki) were central to the development of anticolonial nationalism and national identity in Tanzania.[38] Yet, as scholars lament, history says little about the role the mission's women played in these same processes.[39] The few details my early reading offered about the lives of UMCA women, however, were tantalizing. In particular, I was intrigued by the fact that the wives of the first generations of the UMCA's African clergy all attended the mission's Mbweni Girls' School. Theological students made an explicit point of searching for wives at Mbweni, even going so far as to ask missionaries to play matchmaker when they alone were not successful in their pursuits. Clerics from the mainland sent their girlfriends and fiancées to Mbweni for training because, as one missionary recalled of a conversation with two Kiungani graduates, "they did not want wives only to cook for them—they wanted wives who were educated, who were able to enter into their own ideas and aims and interests."[40] What was going on at Mbweni that was so special, I wondered, and what were the girls' "own ideas and interests"? In what ways did UMCA-trained women contribute to anticolonial nationalism and to the development of national identity in Tanzania, if any? Beyond that, in what ways could focusing on the lives, work, and relationships of the UMCA's women tell new stories about the UMCA, and offer new understandings about Tanzanian history, about the history of Christianity in Africa, and about some of the broader narratives of the nineteenth and twentieth centuries?

The same issues that constrain historians of women and gender working across Africa, and in other parts of the world, also shaped my early attempts to write a history through the eyes of the UMCA's female adherents: namely, the relative paucity of written sources by or about women. To be sure, much has been accomplished in terms of innovative strategies and methodological approaches in women's and gender history, and scholars are greatly indebted to the pioneering work of historians of women and gender, but the accepted stories of the spread of Christianity and the development of communities in the colonial world remain male-dominated. Indeed, colonial and national histories generally have tended to make the political actions and intellectual histories of women invisible and to "disappear" their contributions.[41] This lacuna is in large part a product of the available sources.

Sources from the precolonial and colonial eras are a product of the past in two different ways. On their most basic level, they are the ephemera of specific events, perspectives, and processes. On a deeper level, however, precolonial- and colonial-era documents, and the archives from which they come, derive their very shape and nature from the taxonomies that governed missionary and scientific exploration and colonial rule.[42] Missionaries and colonial officials "knew" the world around them in particular ways—ways that had much to do with religion,[43] with civilizational hierarchies, and with patriarchy. These ways of knowing the world shaped how documents were produced, what they contained, and how they traveled through the bureaucratic apparatus. As such, Ann Laura Stoler argues, colonial archival documents are also "active, generative substances with histories,

... documents with itineraries of their own."[44] Written documents, and the archives in which they reside, allow governments—and also missionary organizations—to carry out their projects of routinization, legibility, and control. Archives and documents also produce—or, more precisely, allow scholars to produce—histories with particular shapes and concerns.

Sources produced by the UMCA's sisters in spirit or those that speak directly to their lives, and academic histories about these women or women like them in other contexts, thus do not exist in the same way they do for their male counterparts. The UMCA had a unique interest in women's lives and work and was perhaps more attuned to the goings-on of their female congregants than other missionary enterprises. Female congregants also sometimes wrote about their experiences, but those contributions were often edited or otherwise mediated by UMCA missionaries.[45] In general, however, the extant records were composed by and reflect the concerns of the organization's British male leadership and by male African clerics.

Moreover, it is to the so-called "national" archives, which postcolonial governments inherited from the colonial state, and the archives of missionary organizations, to which Africanists and others first turn when writing about colonies or specific churches. These archives are, however, deeply affected by the concerns and frailties of postcolonial governments.[46] Multiple, abrupt changes in state power, economic constraints, and deliberate attempts to obscure past events have damaged the archives, as have the postcolonial governments' relative lack of concern with categorization, classification, and preservation.[47] It is not only documents produced after independence, or other records pertinent to the postcolonial period, that suffer. Just as the Tanzania National Archives (TNA) contains few accessible materials relating to the origins of *ujamaa* ideology or postcolonial foreign relations,[48] the number of UMCA documents that are tangible and accessible by researchers are markedly fewer than the listing guides suggest. Years of underfunding and neglect meant that as I began my research into the lives of the UMCA's female lay evangelists, request after request for files that John Iliffe, Anne-Marie Stoner-Eby, and Justin Willis had once used in their work on the UMCA went unfulfilled.[49]

As many scholars of Africa and of women are left to do, I began to explore the "shadow archives" of the British presence in Tanzania, and had serendipitous finds in several "tin trunk archives."[50] Diaries of British nuns helped to flesh out stories about young African probationers, suggesting the ways in which emotions such as fear and discontent, striving and aspiration shaped their decisions for a celibate life. Love letters an African Anglican priest wrote to his fiancée, which I found tucked in a glass-fronted cabinet in a small library outside of Dar es Salaam, compared their budding romance to the dawn of Tanzania's independence. I conducted oral history interviews that, despite their notorious difficulties, shed light on the ways congregants related to the developments of the twentieth century.[51] Elders from former UMCA congregations set their comments about the grand narratives of decolonization and nationalism within the context of their affective spiritual relationships.[52] I took these insights and read "against the grain" and "between the lines" of the colonial and missionary sources not initially written with attention to women. My extensive reading of UMCA documents, of the occasional sources authored by women, and of secondary literature on Tanzania and Christianity in Africa over the past decade provided context for the stories that emerged, which told a strikingly nuanced picture of the affective and emotional dimensions of the lives of the UMCA's female lay evangelists.

As I learned even more about the women I came to refer to as "sisters in spirit," I was impressed by the friendships they forged at Mbweni, and by how they maintained them after moving with their husbands to stations on the mainland, all in a time when reliable communication was lacking and movement over a distance dangerous. It was clear that women in particular used the affective dimensions of their lives—their friendships and mentor/protégée relationships, emotions we would call homesickness and loneliness, and their romantic affairs—to create and police the boundaries of a community of believers. The UMCA's female lay evangelists embodied a particular form of emotional and spiritual subjectivity to spread their faith across ethnolinguistic and cultural boundaries, and through time. Finally, I was struck that the particular theology of the UMCA was not only unique, but that it seemed to potentiate these connections by fostering a spiritual intimacy between adherents living and working at stations so far from one another.

At the heart of this book are stories of individual sisters in spirit whose daily lives and work produced the UMCA's pan-ethnic and intergenerational affective spiritual community. Histories of affect, and particularly those using affective dimensions of people's lives to tell broader stories, comprise a relatively young literature.[53] There remains a certain experimental nature about the methods and the sources historians use to explore the affective dimensions of life. Of course, this has been true of African history and anthropology since the 1950s.[54] *Sisters in Spirit* thus relies on traditional "objective" sources as well as more "subjective" sources to access affect, which I then use as an analytical tool rather than a research topic in its own right. Drawing the voices of African women out of these sources was possible for several reasons: I recognized the "common sense" that shaped the archives, I was familiar with the social structures and the realities that shape women's lives, and I was able to see their intersection with the contours of Tanzanian and sub-Saharan Africa. This approach contextualized the scattered ephemera, and allowed their voices to speak some of the choices and dilemmas female congregants and others on the frontiers of mission work across the continent faced.

As I began to explore the affective dimensions of the lives of the UMCA's female adherents, it became abundantly clear that not all UMCA actors, and indeed not all colonial actors, were "acting in the same theater."[55] Previous scholarship, and particularly Tanzanian historiography, tended to portray the rise of the modern nation-state and its attendant nationalisms as an inevitable result of the transition from empire. The accepted narrative focused on men involved in the institutionalized bureaucracies, on "proto-nationalist" organizations, and on the political parties that inherited the colonial state.[56] It soon became clear that the concerns that motivated politically connected Anglican men in the 1940s and 1950s were not the same concerns that motivated their female counterparts in the 1860s and 1870s. Women like Beatrice Kilekwa, Rose Mtaula, Amy Malisawa, Mabel Ambali, and others among several generations of UMCA-educated African women did not live their lives in a way that matches the outlines of the established historiography or the accepted institutional chronologies. They lived their lives untidily, led by hopes and dreams, expectations and obligations, in a bid to make the most of their circumstances. They moved and they traveled, they sinned and they repented, and they loved and they lost, sometimes with an eye toward the emerging political community, although oftentimes not. To be sure, their lives were the product of a historical moment that was focused on building an entirely different type of moral economy: the first group of women to join the UMCA did so on June 25, 1865. After having been stripped of their affiliation with their home communities and reduced to the status of slave, they were "rescued" from a slaving dhow by sailors in the British navy.

While the nation-state of Tanzania eventually became a beneficiary of the pedagogical, emotional, and spiritual labors of the UMCA's sisters in spirit—as the final chapters in this book illustrate—UMCA adherents initially came to see themselves as part of a deterritorialized affective spiritual community that catered to different needs entirely. When the first cohorts of female adherents joined the UMCA, they did so with little choice in the matter and employed locally resonant strategies designed to reduce their inherent vulnerability, forging familial relationships and imputing kinship with their new patrons and with other members of their new community. In part because of the theological teachings of the missionaries and in part because of the demographic realities of the Zanzibar mission stations and those that developed on the mainland, these affective and kinship (both real and fictive) ties were pan-ethnic and intergenerational. The expectations of British missionaries and their particular labor practices enshrined these relationships as fundamental to the mission's evangelical work, and they came to constitute the heart of the UMCA's affective spiritual community. Focusing on the ways in which these relationships of affective spirituality came to influence strategies of evangelical expansion *and* the ways they influenced the boundaries of the community tells an entirely different story than that told by looking only at the UMCA's men, and by viewing the traditional sources in the same way. The story of the sisters in spirit is one in which the notion of community was deterritorialized; in which spirituality, ritual practice, and affective relationships created networks between geographically disparate congregations; and in which people applied old values to new circumstances.

Cultural Nationalisms

Looking at the affective dimensions of the lives of the UMCA's sisters in spirit offers new insights about the role Christianity played in forming communities. In particular, their stories help us better understand the link between Christianity and the development of cultural nationalisms in Africa. Previous scholarship argued that ethnic identity was the most important identity to emerge from Africans' engagement with Christianity and the vernacular Bible. Christian education, as well as missionaries' and adherents' understandings of Christian doctrine and scripture, has been credited with the reification, consolidation, or "invention" of certain ethnic categories (such as Yoruba) during the colonial period.[57] In this literature, ethnogenesis and the development of cultural nationalisms are directly related to the way in which the Bible conceives of—and biblically literate people imagine—humanity as broken into "nations" and "peoples" to which the church must speak directly.[58] The Yoruba, whose path from liberated slave community to ethnic group Peel details in *Religious Encounter and the Making of the Yoruba*, are a classic example of the historiographic connection between missionization and the development of cultural nationalisms. Efforts to train Africans in their mother tongue—and the missionaries' work in general—were based on the premise that "the Yoruba" were a group that could and should be spoken of and to.[59] The CMS missionaries envisaged an ethnolinguistic nation and, keenly aware of the formational potential of their language work, succeeded in creating one. Over time, Yoruba cultural nationalism came to constitute a major strand of anticolonial nationalism in Nigeria.

In contrast to this West African example are ex-slave mission communities that comprised individuals from a range of ethnolinguistic backgrounds. Perhaps the best-known of these is the CMS project in Kenya.[60] Here, congregants' status as former slaves, rather than their ethnic background, provided an element of unity. Few were able to escape their status as social and political inferiors in the post-abolition period. Their story as a community largely ends around 1900, and there were no substantive efforts to carry the project to create a pan-ethnic communion into the twentieth century or to new areas.

The UMCA's first four decades were in many ways similar to those of the CMS, but several factors combined to produce an expansive, unified community that extended through several generations. Similar to the CMS, by the time the UMCA's Bible men and women established their station at Zanzibar they had abandoned all hopes of working on behalf of a particular ethnic group, "people," or "tribe."[61] The missionaries of the abolitionist UMCA set their sights on the spoils of the Indian Ocean slave trade, targeting freed slaves who hailed from communities throughout the mainland, including from what are today Malawi, Mozambique, and Congo, as well as Tanzania.[62] Several factors provided a different outcome for the UMCA. The lack of a lingua franca among their adherents led the missionaries to settle upon Kiswahili—East Africa's language of trade—as one of two languages of mission officialdom (the other being English).[63] Among later cohorts of adherents—such as those who came to the mission as non-Swahili-speaking adults or those to whom the mission evangelized in their home villages on the mainland—the British missionaries had to balance their anxiousness to bring the scriptures to Africans with their very Tractarian desire to re-create Zion in East Africa. Evangelists struggled with the vernacular until inquirers could operate sufficiently well in English or Kiswahili. Because language among the UMCA's diverse communities was not a singular vernacular, the quotidian embodied transmission of a particular brand of Christian femininity through affective relationships became a language that *all* community members could understand, helping to solidify this civilization or "race" of Christians in a way that individuals speaking different languages could never be.[64] The idea of community that circulated among UMCA female lay evangelists, church officials, and adherents was not bound to a particular ethnicity, nor did it emerge from the standardization of the vernacular and the subsequent translation of the Bible into the vernacular. Rather, adherents' identity emerged from and was bound to a culture of Christian living and spiritual affinity.[65]

As this study illustrates, the UMCA's founders encouraged their adherents to think of themselves as a distinct "race of intellectual Christians," the core of a new Zion. Individuals from throughout East Africa found community with the UMCA, and extended those ties across ethnolinguistic boundaries and unconnected lands. The day-to-day work of the UMCA's sisters in spirit made this possible, as did the relationships of affective spirituality that grew up among them. Clerics' wives and fiancées from across the mission moved with their husbands to attend classes at St. Cyprian's Theological College, learning to speak each others' languages as they sat sewing on a missionary's veranda. Young Christian women married across ethnic lines, seeking refuge with the church when their families grew angry. African clerics and their wives worked to adapt mission teaching to fit more closely with local customs. In these cases and others, women used quotidian, embodied performance of ideas, emotions, and affects as a way to transcend linguistic barriers. As a result, the pan-ethnic spiritual community that existed on Zanzibar in the 1870s and 1880s—contemporaneous with the CMS mission—still existed in the minds of believers living in geographically disparate communities nearly a century later. This outcome stands in stark contrast to the outcome of other missions across the continent, such as those of the White Fathers, the LMS, etc. In this book's sixth chapter, I illustrate how UMCA African nuns in the 1940s and 1950s invested in the community as a new form of family and security, and the courtship between a highly educated aspiring teacher and cleric explored in chapter 7 illustrates that bonds of affective spirituality were the foundation through which they understood, conceptualized, and contributed to the new nation-state of Tanzania. The social position of a community built by ex-slaves had been greatly elevated by their own work in establishing new social hierarchies, and offering ideas that were picked up and improvised upon by people engaged in building a new nation.

Gendered Intellectual Histories

The affective dimensions of the lives of the UMCA's sisters in spirit also offer new understandings about ways to access the intellectual histories of African women. There is a conceptual gap between the vigorous attention to the stories of gendered subjectivities on the one hand, and intellectual histories in Africa on the other.[66] To be sure, concerns about the lack of gender history that plagued earlier generations of feminist historians and historians of gender have largely disappeared, and the field of African intellectual history has recently undergone a resurgence. These new histories of ideas and thinking, however, rarely explore the gender dimensions of the biographies of intellectuals or their thought formation, attend to women's contributions, or make moves toward remedying gender inequity in the field.[67] The questions scholars of intellectual history generally ask about knowledge, transmissions, and sensibilities are about men or male-dominant spheres, and are thus implicitly about masculinity.[68] Weaving together gender, emotions, and thinking allows scholars to access intellectual histories of spaces that are often highly gendered, of gendered forms of knowledge, and of the domestic.[69] Building on this historiographical concern with the intimate relationship between the intellectual and the affective, this book explicitly engages affect with knowledge and transmissions, ways of knowing with embodied being, and gendered subjectivities with the senses.

The female lay evangelist's embodiment of Christian civility and femininity, as well as her relationships of affective spirituality redraw the boundaries of what we consider to be "intellectual" and what we consider to be "politics." Intellectual work cannot be conceived of as merely written or spoken, but is embodied and performed, transmitted through affect and spiritual connection.[70] Thus, rather than consider the erasure of women and femininities as inevitable, or rather than write women back into history and rehearse deeply entrenched "androcentric nationalist narratives," scholars must shift the definitions of "politics" and "intellectual" to include the domestic, embodied performance, and affect. The UMCA's sisters in spirit and the affective dimensions of their lives offer a way to rethink intellectual histories, the production of racial thought, and national imaginations.

Attending to the affective dimensions of the lives of the UMCA's sisters in spirit allows us to see the novel ways in which they contributed to debates about the development of racial thought against a persistent backdrop of religious competition. To be sure, women's bodies continued to be sites for the struggle for moral authority. However, while some Africans argued over the length of women's miniskirts as a way to impose values and exert control over women, for example, the UMCA's sisters in spirit themselves policed community boundaries through their quotidian performance, their embodied ritual, and their affective relationships.[71] The UMCA's female adherents used emotions such as love, lust, moral outrage, and shame to police linguistic and racial boundaries. The alarm or inconvenience of "improperly" conceived pregnancies drove adolescents to seek abortions, and a mixture of what we might understand as fear, shame, horror, self-interest, and ambivalence caused scandal over a Christian granddaughter's sexual dalliances with a local Muslim man. Such moments allow us to see the novel ways in which the UMCA's women contributed to the ongoing struggle over community perpetuity and the articulation of spiritual and racial boundaries.

Christianity

Historians have been relatively reluctant to discuss the spiritual components of Africans' engagements with mission churches, heeding warnings about the myriad instrumental and material motivations for affiliation.[72] Yet, individuals' stories can make it harder to ignore spiritual and religious motivations.[73] The lives of the UMCA's sisters in spirit require that we take religious faith and the power of the invisible world seriously, and that we trace their very real effects in the lives of its followers. Forces in the invisible world, such as spirits, ancestors, God, a shared spirit or consciousness, have real power—as real as the blush of new romance between lovers, or the long arm of the law that causes police to issue parking tickets.[74] This book centers the unseen world of affects, spirits, and religion; takes it seriously as acting in the realm of the real and as having real power; and therefore treats the religious and political in the same frame.[75] Attending to the unseen world, to affect and the spiritual aspects of religion, thus opens up avenues to see the formation of new subjectivities and of new forms of affinity and affiliation, such as the "sisters in spirit" whose embodied performances of Christian values potentiated a unique, inclusive spiritual community that crosscut and superseded ethnic affiliations. Indeed, rather than identify as Digo, Yao, Bondei, Makua, or Galla, for example, individuals who joined the mission prioritized a shared Christian civilization. By adopting a certain style of dress, by living in square houses, by speaking English and Kiswahili, and by carrying prayer books in their pocketbooks, congregants worked to bolster, sustain, and advance the values of this community. As the UMCA's female lay evangelists in particular taught embroidery and literacy; as they performed companionate, monogamous marriage for new inquirers; and as they complained about their "heathen" neighbors, they forged a new type of subject, one who deliberately set herself apart by using her faith in the power of the unseen to build a very real community.

As the lives of the sisters in spirit became entangled with the broader changes that characterized the colonial period, their instructional, spiritual, and emotional labors came to incorporate more than just the UMCA community, but to incorporate the emergent nation-state of Tanzania and to take on more explicitly political dimensions. Several explorations of the theological or doctrinal elements of precolonial political movements and of the political resonances of indigenous spiritual movements offer productive models,[76] but few studies have illustrated the ways in which Christian theology shaped individuals' engagements with politics, on a local level or a national level.[77]

Finally, while there is a growing secondary literature on African female Christians and their experiences in, and contributions to, church and national histories, African women are still underrepresented in the historiography. Historians of mission have long emphasized the need to explore African church leaders, adding African voices and perspectives to the history of African Christianity.[78] Few have done so, and even fewer have looked explicitly at female church leaders or attended to gendered dynamics.[79] *Sisters in Spirit* offers a history of African Christianity that foregrounds the quotidian, embodied work of unofficial female evangelists. Their gendered experiences as women are fundamental to this analysis, and also to the shape of the church itself. It was women's gendered vulnerability that shaped the way in which the first cohorts of African women engaged with the church, and that underwrote the ties of patronage and dependency that constituted its evangelical strategy. Women cultivated ties of affective spirituality with British missionaries, with other women on their stations, with new inquirers, and with spouses, and relied on those ties when they moved to the mainland and to remote stations. Women relied on affective relationships to help them hem the boundaries of the community, to allow celibate women to serve as social mothers, and as a way to engage in an explicitly Christian way with the budding national community.

■ ■ ■

The work of the UMCA's sisters in spirit offers new ways to understand the processes by which Africans engaged with the changing world around them over the course of the long twentieth century. The story of Beatrice Kilekwa brings into stark relief the networks of affective spirituality that persisted to define the lives of congregants living one hundred years later. Just as Beatrice drew on these networks to help her make sense of her move to Masasi, the Anglican teacher Rose Furahani drew on similar ideas to help her and her partner negotiate their role in the new nation-state of Tanzania. The love letters she and her fiancé exchanged illustrate that individuals applied values and lessons from the UMCA's affective spiritual community to new circumstances, reasserting the importance of longer-standing spiritual affinities and religious values in new times. By the 1960s most of the missionaries the Furahanis and other UMCA adherents knew had departed Tanzania, taking with them much of the mission infrastructure. While the Anglican Church of Tanzania (the official body that comprises both former CMS and UMCA congregations) remains popular in southern Tanzania, the UMCA pulled out gradually over the course of the 1960s. UMCA-trained teachers and clerics were well represented in the ranks of anticolonial nationalists and in the early years of the new government. For all their educational prowess, the early involvement of UMCA-trained men in the transition government, and their expectations about inheriting the postcolonial state, their power was largely eclipsed in the years following independence. Many of their core ideas and values, however, live on in the inheritances of former UMCA adherents and in the work of the UMCA's African nuns, for example, hinting at the contingencies of history.[80]

CHAPTER ONE

Tractarian Beginnings

Theology and Society in Britain and East Africa, 1830–1865

At forty-four years old, Dr. David Livingstone had spent the past fifteen years traversing nearly one-third of Africa and working to combat the slave trade by bringing news of the Gospel to the "dark continent," all while documenting its people, flora, fauna, and geography. He wrote home about his adventures, and British newspapers and church organizations published his edited field notes to rave reviews. Britain in the 1850s was a milieu given over to exploration and improvement, and Africa, seen by many as exotic, pagan, and deadly, as well as debased by slavery, Islam, and a host of other troubling social ills, seemed to cry out for redemption.[1] The "simple large-hearted hero" thus quickly became the subject of national fascination. The 1857 publication of his book *Missionary Travels and Researches in South Africa* only further galvanized his fame. On the book tour through Scotland, Ireland, and England, he was feted and cheered wherever he went.

Livingstone, a Presbyterian, set foot on African soil for the first time in 1841. He was supported by a stipend from the London Missionary Society (LMS). The LMS was founded in 1795 as a project designed to incorporate several small interdenominational groups working toward the same end. A product of its time, it grew quickly into something that was large and ambitious.[2] By 1818 it was largely Congregationalist, rather than interdenominational as its founders had imagined; this became even more pronounced as Presbyterians and Episcopalians began to found their own missionary societies.[3] Livingstone was inspired to join the mission when his father, who attended the Nonconformist independent Hamilton Church, showed him a pamphlet on medical missionaries in China. The younger Livingstone had long shown an interest in medicine and rural flora and fauna and was immediately drawn to the prospect of traveling overseas.[4] Livingstone had received some theological training at university and spent more time learning Latin, Hebrew, and Greek, but that was not enough even for the relatively undemanding society; they deemed him unfit at first application to be a missionary because he "lacked fluency in prayer and the conduct of worship." It was also not clear how well he knew the Bible. After several months of additional study, he eventually passed the LMS examination and headed to Bechuanaland.[5] Although Livingstone considered himself first and foremost a missionary, and remained dedicated to the cause to the end of his life, he had many other interests and did not limit his work to spreading the Gospel. Indeed, Livingstone made for a rather unusual missionary. He was, as the LMS saw it, often distracted from God's work by exploration, commerce, natural history, geography, and anthropology. Frustrated by his tendency to confuse exploration with evangelism, the LMS ultimately withdrew their support. Livingstone, however, saw no such conflict of interest. He believed that pursuing such a wide range of activities was a mutually reinforcing endeavor. In his view, nothing short of the simultaneous introduction of "commerce, Christianity, and civilization" would save the African body, mind, and soul from the evils of slavery, heathenism, and barbarism.[6] The "Three C's" were the only way to eradicate, Livingstone believed, "such absurdities from the minds of these poor people."[7]

Livingstone and the Birth of the UMCA

The son of a deeply religious traveling tea salesman who grew up in the tenements of the industrial periphery of Glasgow, Livingstone was in many ways a personification of the broader trends of which his participation in the LMS was a part. His childhood tenement home abutted a park, the private garden of the estate manager's large residence. Positioned firmly between the urban and the rural, Livingstone experienced the "contrast between the stark tenement and the verdant countryside, the laboring poor and the new rich."[8] This dichotomy was the result of the recent rise of the lower middle classes, a result of the Industrial Revolution.[9] Modest upward mobility and the acquisition of respectability, coupled with the rise of European modernity, produced the eighteenth-century preoccupation with "civilization"—a word that had only recently made its appearance in English.[10] The newly salient differences between civilization and savagery characterized the moral dichotomy between the working class and the middle/upper classes, all of which became wrapped up with a series of what Nancy Rose Hunt calls other "semantic polarities": "white/black, clean/dirty, lady/woman, home/empire, masculine/feminine, urban/rural, public/private."[11] Rather than directly critique the failings of the lower classes at home, Britons began to look overseas to the heathen "other" of the dark continent, using their plight and presumed barbarism as a point of comparison for the rising working classes and the "dark satanic" populations at home.[12] Domesticity, moral authority, and Christian virtue gained a "civilizing function reaching far beyond the threshold of the home," causing believers and middle- and upper-class Britons alike to look beyond themselves and into the homes of new colonial subjects and missionary objects.[13]

This preoccupation with civilization also became bound up with commerce in the later decades of the eighteenth century. In the 1780s the Clapham group, a collection of high-minded, upper-middle-class Anglican evangelicals with strong commercial connections, began to adapt this secular ideology to serve Christian morality. They argued that the advance of civilization—one of the goals of commerce, as current thinking had it—would be far better served through legitimate commerce than one based on "illegitimate" slave labor, and far more profitable, too. Moreover, they imagined it would help spread Christianity. Over the next twenty years, the Clapham group also invested in the missionary enthusiasm growing in Britain, and began to extend the rhetoric of civilization to evangelical societies.[14] Largely unconcerned with commerce, missionaries *were* concerned, however, with civilization—with square houses, straight streets, and sensible shoes, as well as reading and writing and eating with forks. These ideas became ever more intertwined in liberal evangelical circles with hopes for Great Britain's commercial success as "a divine goad to both economic and religious proselytizing." While "civilization, Christianity, and commerce" was by no means an official or explicitly stated missionary strategy, it had by the 1830s become a catch phrase widely used to describe the overseas evangelical imperative, and an ideology that underwrote countless expeditions to the continent.

Inspired by the "Three C's," Livingstone thus remained in the field, proselytizing Christianity to the benighted heathen, recording the natural geological features of the continent, detailing the foreign customs of the "primitive tribes" he encountered, and working tirelessly to abolish the slave trade. The "unmitigated horror" of the nineteenth-century slave trade was of particular concern to Livingstone, and to the British public, who responded to his stories of brutality with generous financial support. Although it is true that the British had several antislavery treaties in place by the time of Livingstone's journeys, in a deeply ironic twist the number of Africans involved in slavery on the continent had only increased over the century.

The conditions in which many Africans were living shocked Livingstone. In the interior of the continent, he reported passing village after village that lay burnt, empty, and deserted, ravaged by the trade. Their inhabitants, the people who had planted and tilled the ground and the children who had played among tall maize stalks, had been bound and carried away as slaves. He wrote that he saw women chained together by a yoke made from a tree trunk, fastened in the front with a rough iron bar. As they walked, the weight rubbed their necks and shoulders raw. On Zanzibar, he saw a great slave market where hundreds of Africans, boys and girls, men and women, were sold as animals into what he imagined was lifelong captivity and shame. He was haunted by his assumption that for every living slave who arrived in port, seven or eight died on the journey. In eastern Africa, he saw slave owners who seemed to forget that their slaves were even human, calling "the animal to do this or that," and cursing them as if they were but a "race of a dog." The experience tormented him, and in 1871 the man who was trained as a medical doctor offered this poignant commentary in his journal: "I am heartsore and sick of the sight of human blood."[15]

The devastation that so affected Livingstone was the result of a recent and rapid uptick in slaving over the course of the eighteenth century. Whereas the slave trade on the Atlantic coast of Africa had grown from the fifteenth century to a peak in the eighteenth century, in the areas that are now Kenya, Uganda, and Tanzania the slave trade had been insignificant before the late eighteenth century. The dramatic rise in the trade in slaves in East Africa was the result of two major and interwoven economic developments. First was the expansion of the slave-plantation complex into the Indian Ocean, which occurred by the final quarter of the eighteenth century.[16] Plantations on the Mascarene Islands, including Mauritius and Reunion, as well as on Zanzibar required vast amounts of slave labor; Omani Arabs in the Persian Gulf also demanded East African slaves as domestic laborers, plantation laborers, and sailors.[17] The Industrial Revolution spurred its own demand: the need for vegetable oils to lubricate the machines of industrializing economies turned traders on to East Africa's coconut and sesame oils, and they imported copal, a wild resin used to make coach varnish.[18]

Before the advent of these demands for particular raw materials from East Africa, Zanzibar and the neighboring mainland coast had relied on a totally different set of crops and different style of agricultural labor. Subsistence cultivation, not commercial trade, was the primary livelihood of Swahili-speaking people—at least until the final third of the nineteenth century.[19] People living along the Swahili Coast had fostered commercial ties with the Indian Ocean world for centuries; their trade included exports of rare luxury goods such as ivory, rhino horn, tortoiseshell, and coconut oil, and imports such as cloth and porcelain. They also exported slaves, who were bound for the Middle East and to French plantations on the Mascarene Islands. But before the mid- to late nineteenth century, slaves constituted only a small portion of the trade. And within East Africa itself, slaves were generally seen as personal dependents rather than as chattel. They performed a variety of duties and inhabited a variety of roles, including autonomous peasant, professional soldier, domestic servant, concubine, or trusted counselor; slaves were rarely valued only as forced field hands.[20] Indeed, African slavery has largely been idealized as what scholars refer to as "open" or "absorptive." Slaves were by definition socially marginal, and in an "absorptive" system were sometimes able to reduce their marginality, or even able to eliminate it altogether. This occurred over the course of several generations as masters absorbed slaves into their own communities and kin groups.[21] This would soon change dramatically after the mid-nineteenth century.

The second of two economic factors that fundamentally altered the nature and scope of slavery in East Africa during the course of the late eighteenth and nineteenth centuries was the European abolitionist campaign. It was not until British abolitionists began to call for "legitimate" trade goods, such as those previously mentioned, that the trade in slaves took on such great importance. In 1807, the British passed legislation that effectively outlawed Britain's central role in the slave trade. Then, between 1815 and 1831, a series of Anglo-Portuguese anti-slave-trade treaties outlawed Portuguese trade north of the equator. This had the effect not of stopping slaving, but of merely pushing procurement further to the south—both in western Africa near Angola and on the eastern Swahili Coast. Additionally, the British negotiated the first in a series of abolition treaties with authorities at Zanzibar. Taken together, these "abolitionist" treaties reduced the price for slaves, thereby encouraging people to find new local uses for slave labor. A move designed as an abolitionist intervention had the paradoxical effect of increasing the total number of slaves captured each year within East Africa.[22]

Beyond the two economic factors that spurred the expansion of the trade are several other factors that altered the nature of the slave experience itself. The nineteenth century was a "particularly bad time" for African slaves, in part because in many places masters that had once engaged with slaves in relationships of patronage and dependence were instead treating them as chattel. In responding to growing market demands, masters had to find new uses for slave labor and thus subjected their slaves to much more severe forms of slavery by forcing them to produce agricultural commodities such as cloves, coconut, grains, and sugar.[23]

Another factor in the transformation of the slave experience was the simultaneous, and in fact interrelated, increase in the ivory trade. The relatively frivolous European demand for ivory combs, billiard balls, and piano keys, which increased over the eighteenth and nineteenth centuries, pushed the East African ivory frontier—and the destruction and devastation that attended it—further and further into the African interior. The demand had already decimated sources in India and elsewhere, and the soft ivory of East African elephants was particularly alluring for the finer products then in vogue. Ivory traders in the areas that are now Tanzania and Kenya had for centuries passed their goods from hand to hand from the interior to the coast along a series of interconnected, short-distance trading routes. The demand for ivory in the nineteenth century was so steep, however, that individual traders and the occasional small hunting band were insufficient. These longer-standing small-scale suppliers were largely replaced by a system of caravans that traveled thousands of miles along three main routes from the interior, as far as present-day Democratic Republic of Congo, to the coast. Slaves staffed these caravans, and were also added to the caravans at their origin in the interior. The warfare necessary to secure coastal caravans access to the routes also allowed trading entrepreneurs to kidnap and conscript slaves who would perform the backbreaking labor of carrying the ivory to the coast. The advance of the ivory frontier left catastrophe—in the form of infectious disease, loss of life, the decimation of the elephant population, and economic collapse—in its wake.[24] It was an ironic cycle of events that dramatically altered the nature of the slave experience in nineteenth-century East Africa: a "boom in legitimate trade induced masters within Africa to work their own slaves harder, the spread of imported firearms gave trading warlords the means to capture more slaves more efficiently, and the

European naval blockades depressed the price of slaves in coastal regions that had once specialized in their export, making slave labor an attractive investment for growing numbers of entrepreneurs within Africa."[25] The effects of commercial and political policies devised by European missionaries, merchants, and politicians as a means to salvation were in actuality devastating to individual Africans.

Livingstone and other abolitionists were not wholly unaware of these developments. These men attributed their cause not to European intervention, but to the barbarity of Africans themselves—something that further confirmed the missionary civilizing enterprise. Seeing this "barbarism" firsthand made an impression on Livingstone. Back in England during the fall and winter months of 1857, Livingstone encountered sympathetic audiences. He encouraged members of Britain's elite universities to follow his example and plant missions in Central Africa with the express purpose of stemming the hemorrhage of slaves. A generation of British abolitionists had argued that Christianity and commerce would free the African, and now Livingstone was offering a practical program by which to realize this goal. His audience at the December lectures in particular, which included hundreds of undergraduates and their faculty, were in a unique position to assist, he argued. The movement, he told them, needed "men of education, standing, enterprise, zeal, and piety."[26] Due to the intellectual, emotional, spiritual, and physical demands of the task at hand, its pioneers "should be the ablest and best qualified men, not those of small ability and education."[27] Students and faculty, who listened to the sermons with rapt attention, responded by cheering "as only undergraduates could cheer," and resolved to found a missionary society to carry out the work Livingstone had begun.[28]

With members of Oxford and Cambridge Universities rallied to his cause, Livingstone moved supporters toward establishing the organization that would become the Universities' Mission to Central Africa (UMCA). Yet, for all his celebrity and charisma, Livingstone was perhaps a man better suited to rallying interest than organizing intervention: despite the resounding enthusiasm that attended Livingstone's travels, no further steps were taken toward a missionary society, and no committees were formed until late the following year. The fire kindled by Livingstone's visit to the universities might have died away entirely were it not for the 1859 visit of Robert Gray, Anglican Bishop of Cape Town and Metropolitan South Africa, to Cambridge. Gray rightly sensed that despite "a great interest felt in Africa," momentum for a missionary society was flagging. He used the occasion of his invited terminal lecture to offer "fresh impulse" for a mission to Central Africa.

This time, Gray reported, "the idea took—a committee was formed, and the thing started."[29] Founders settled on a name for their society—the Oxford and Cambridge Mission to Central Africa—opened subscription lists, distributed circulars, and arranged for a series of public meetings to determine the objectives of the mission.[30]

With trademark enthusiasm, Robert Gray took a leading role in organizing the infant mission. Naturally, he began almost immediately to guide the structural development of the society in a way that fitted with his own theological persuasions. Like most of the organization's earliest members, Gray was an Anglican. More specifically, he and many of the others were High Church Anglicans who aligned closely with a revival movement within the Church of England known as Tractarianism. In general terms, the universities' mission would look like many mid-nineteenth-century missions. It had a modest goal of establishing at least one station in the region broadly defined as "Southern Central Africa," which would be supported by annual subscriptions from the public for the next five years. Representatives of Cambridge and Oxford Universities were dispatched to "open communications" with other British universities, in the hope that they could expand their pool of supporters and workers. Finally, the association would send a team to include six clergymen, a physician, and a number of trained craftsmen to the continent itself.

The High Churchmen's theological proclivities, however, also required the small party to have "a bishop at its head." Sending a bishop without a flock or a diocese was a move of which many established missions disapproved, and that immediately marked the new mission as different from its predecessors. Henry Venn, the secretary of the competing Church Missionary Society, regarded the plan for sending a bishop as a "fanciful notion" that was likely to end in nothing but trouble for the mother church. Others thought that appointing a bishop to an undeveloped diocese would inevitably create "petty little sees," and that it had the potential to "lower the episcopal office." The British state, too, was concerned that the Church of England was consecrating bishops in areas outside of her domain. Was not the consecration of a bishop in a territory outside of British control essentially equivalent to a claim over that territory? And was it not in the best interest of the state to avoid moves that would lead the state toward more annexation of "backward and expensive lands"? contemporaries wondered.[31]

The mission's founders, on the other hand, felt strongly that the expedition should be led by a "missionary bishop" who could plant an entire church and who would bring all the leadership necessary for it to function independently. Their model for this new type of mission body was the bishop of New Zealand, George Augustus Selwyn. Bishop Selwyn was also a High Churchman who chose to apply the denomination's belief in the apostolic succession in the mission field in a very literal way. High Church Anglicans considered bishops to be "apostolic men" who should not be above doing the hard work of evangelism and church-planting themselves, like the first apostles. These men were not afraid to dirty their hands with God's work, unlike the British Protestant "grandees" who rode in carriages and mingled with royalty, "churchmen of dignity and smooth hands." Selwyn epitomized the High Church's ideal of the popular bishop. He arrived in New Zealand, "navigating his little boat through the Melanesian islands, wearing seaman's clothing, sleeping in the open, cooking his own meals, hauling on cables, digging with his spade, jumping ashore upon islands where no white had landed before, landing without knowing whether he would be greeted by curiosity or a bludgeon."[32] The Cambridge and Oxford mission sought their own Selwyn, someone who could be dispatched as an "evangelist-in-chief." The organization's preference for a "missionary bishop" was not a mundane matter, the result of a simple choice between a bishop on the one hand and a board of directors, similar to those that oversaw field operations in most established mission organizations, on the other. Rather, placing a bishop at the head of the new mission was a fundamental theological declaration that would shape the operations and tenor of the mission through its duration. In part, this decision meant the mission was better able to respond to the vagaries and vicissitudes of life in the field, of which there were many. This decision also embedded within the mission a spirit of evangelism, something that pervaded the work of the UMCA's clerics' wives and teachers and shaped their relationships with colleagues, protégées, and community members.

Tractarianism

In making this matter of church leadership the sine qua non of the infant mission, Gray and his colleagues also firmly established their new mission society as an heir of the particular iteration of High Church Anglicanism called Tractarianism. So called for a series of epistles published between 1833 and 1841 under the title *Tracts for the Times*, the ideology was a product of a revival movement within the Church of England. The Oxford Movement, named for the movement's birthplace and its founders' place of residence and work, first gained footing at Oxford in the 1820s, when many of the university's High Church Anglicans began to express discontent at the state of religion in England. Some among the Oxford community saw in the eighteenth-century Church of England widespread corruption and somnolence, and believed that Anglicanism had been debased by Erastianism—the supremacy of the state over the church in ecclesiastical matters—liberalism, and a rash of other troubling "-isms," such as materialism, utilitarianism, rationalism, scientism, latitudinarianism, evangelicalism, Methodism, and "aggressive anti-Popish Protestantism."[33] Further, the reformers believed that the Church of England had been meeting the country's most recent period of rapid and radical change—defined, as they saw it, by industrialization, urbanization, accelerating population growth, the erosion of traditional social norms, and the undermining of social structures—with "intransigence, conservatism, inflexibility, and lack of understanding." The structure and organization of the church were "archaic, its social and political ideology was outmoded and there was a lamentable absence of insight and vision," these dissenters argued.[34] Unease over the church's decay helped to sharpen Tractarian theology, and the Oxford Movement became a rallying cry to revive the Church of England.[35]

Redemption of the Church of England would come, the Oxford Anglicans postulated, not in doctrinal innovation but in a return to the principles of the universal Catholic Church, before it was divided in practice in the late fourth century. In other words, they saw the Church of England as a doctrinally sound, though increasingly lax, expression of the church catholic.[36] *Their* catholic church was to be "faithful in doctrine and ethos to the church of the fathers, in origins and authority absolutely independent of the kingdoms of this world." What distinguished this new church from Roman Catholicism is that it would not be led by the pope, but guided by an apostolic succession of bishops.[37] Tractarianism was a clarion call to the Church of England to rally around former conservative, traditional values; it was thus both a product of the age in which it arose and a determined effort to "turn back the tide of history."[38] In contrast to most Anglican missions of the mid-Victorian period, which were to some extent influenced by what became known as the Oxford Movement, the UMCA was a self-consciously Tractarian mission from its inception.[39]

The same forces that gave rise to the movement influenced its spiritual temper. While the Oxford Movement was at its core a spiritual revival, contrary to many contemporary dissenting groups its leaders were not necessarily interested in doctrinal invention or innovation; rather, the movement's leaders were interested in returning to the church of antiquity and its principles. Tractarians privileged the inheritances of "ancient" Christianity, such as asceticism and ritualism, and sought holiness "through self-denial and mortification of bodily and worldly appetites." Tractarian asceticism manifested itself in a restatement of the monastic and contemplative ideal (which would become a hallmark of the mission's British workers, as well as some Africans), as well as in "strict notions of prayer, alms-giving, fasting, the ideal of poverty, voluntary retirement, repentance, and penance."[40]

Members of the Oxford Movement were also influenced by the Romantic response to the Enlightenment. Leaders' embrace of Romanticism was spiritually liberating for Oxford's Anglican High Churchmen, who moved away from their old devotional practice because it was "cold" and "formal." Reformers instead came to identify more with the religious feeling and "heart religion" associated with evangelicalism, and as the movement progressed, Tractarianism became marked by a more "emotional and ecstatic spirituality." Reformers expressed a unique willingness to "learn from the 'primitive,' the unsophisticated, and the unfamiliar," and stressed a "reverence for the sublime, the mysterious, and the awe-ful." The relationship between mysticism and ritualism expressed by the ancient church fathers also resonated with the Tractarians, and they emphasized the importance of an embodied, emotional spirituality.[41] This embodied, emotional spirituality would become a hallmark of the mission's evangelical process, forming the basis of the relationships of affective spirituality that lay at the heart of the multigenerational network of Mbweni's female lay evangelists. An embodied, emotional spirituality was itself a powerful evangelical tool, inspiring Mbweni's former schoolgirls not only to maintain the relationships and lifestyle they had developed at Mbweni, but to re-create their experiences in their new communities.

Tractarianism was inherently missiological, and reformers were immediately faced with the question of how to bring new members into the fold. Particularly challenging was the need to balance the heightened emotionality of Tractarian Anglicanism with the ancient belief in revealed meaning. "Revealed meaning" in this context is the belief that there was more to the Bible, and therefore Christianity, than its literal meaning—the longer one practiced Christianity, the deeper one could venture into the religion's truth. One had to earn this deeper meaning, however, through a gradual mastery of the more basic elements of Christianity. The answer was an inheritance from the ancient church—the doctrine of "reserve" in communicating religious knowledge. Tractarians' understanding of the notion of reserve or "economy" is based on the *disciplina arcani*, a theological principle of the ancient church, which urged restraint in the timing and means of imparting religious knowledge. Tractarians' embrace of this ancient philosophy stemmed in part from their aversion to newer methods of evangelism, in which the "preacher forcefully declared the holiest and deepest mysteries of the Christian religion before crowds in the effort to secure conversion." Rather than mimic what they considered to be contemporary dissidents' "irreverent" behavior, Tractarians sought to follow the example of the apostles and "begin with milk in order that the hearers may grow up and later receive meat."[42] Those invested in the principle of reserve attacked the "unreserved and indiscriminate application of strong evangelic language to Christians who might be in the infancy of their growth" and counseled "an adaptation of imparted revealed truth to the capacities and understanding of the receiver."[43] Tractarian spirituality, wrote one historian of the movement, "disliked what was flamboyant. It shrank from religion in the market-square. It was not fond of seeking publicity . . . They were quiet men [who] stay away from too much traffic with the world and say [their] prayers."[44] Proselytizers from the UMCA would not, in other words, preach from a pulpit in the town square, converting new "believers" on the spot, and counting their success in numbers of new adherents.

According to Tractarians, the right way to promote truth was through slow revelations of the Gospel through ritual and practice and through the "formation of moral character by habit."[45] Intellectual learning, though important, took a backseat to other modes of experiencing God. Tractarians rejected the "presumptuous turn of mind, the reliance on intellectual ability, supposed to result from instruction addressing itself to the intellect alone" that accompanied the Enlightenment in favor of allowing the soul to grow slowly "into apprehending Calvary by doing right, by allowing grace to sanctify."[46] Conversion was to be achieved through a change in "conscience, not logical reason . . . ethical judgment rather than the argumentative judgment." It was not that learning was unimportant, but Tractarians believed that "true learning consisted of more than mere cultivation of the intellect. The prerequisites for the reception of the truth of the Gospel were not intellectual attainment or rational enquiry, but the simplicity and teachable disposition of little children."[47] To anticipate my argument, this was a fundamental component of the missionaries' strategy—they intended to work among children and teach them the fundamentals of Christianity through daily practice. While their focus on children became untenable, they retained a focus on quotidian practice and embodied performance. This theological particularity was the very trait that allowed the mission to incorporate such a diversity of ethnic backgrounds; allowed congregants to build intimate, affective spiritual relationships; and allowed evangelists to knit a network of believers across discontiguous lands and through several generations.

To Tractarian reformers, the way of knowing the truth was not merely intellectual—it was embodied and felt rather than reasoned; practiced and experienced rather than taught. Tractarians' stress on the limitations of human reason and intellect in perceiving religious truth led them to focus instead on the "sacramental principle." There are, argued Tractarians, "deeper moral truths that [lie] above and beyond nature, in the unseen world" that cannot be reached with speech or reason alone, but must come to be known through allegorical understanding. Sacraments and devotional rites are meant to reassure followers of the mystical realm of being, to the other "modes of being, operation, presence, extension, continuance, growth, production, union, incorporation, besides those we are permitted to discern in the visible creation." Reformers thus recalled certain sacraments for inclusion in Tractarian devotional practice as a way of assisting the faithful "in realizing Divine contemplations."[48] While this meant that in practice Tractarians received Christ on their knees and made the sign of the cross, it also meant that cultivating quotidian habits, performing embodied knowledge, and living out Christian principles were central to the Tractarian evangelical repertoire. It also means that the founders' Tractarianism resonated for more than a century in the work of the UMCA's multigenerational network of female lay evangelists.

Theology and Abolition

The Oxford Movement's call for a revival of catholicity within the Church of England and a remaking of the church abroad was, again, inherently missiological. This doctrinal mandate for missionary outreach coincided in the 1850s with the imperatives of an age given over to exploration, redemption, and improvement—these two reform movements coalesced to ultimately produce the UMCA.[49] The circumstances that potentiated the mission were unique to the time, for up to this point, the religious philosophy that drove many Protestant missions overseas was a millennial discourse that glorified contemporary Western culture as the most enlightened path to salvation, and emphasized conversion of the world as a means of ushering in the millennium of peace, happiness, and plenty that adherents believed would herald Christ's return to Earth.[50] Such eschatological—or end-of-the-world—beliefs were closely connected to secular moral philosophy that arose from the Enlightenment. Further, in the years after the American Revolution, the British saw a need for some "basic adjustments" to their overseas policies and began to look toward India and Africa. After the mid-eighteenth century, however, imperialism, secular humanitarianism, and economic policy further incited church organizations to turn their attentions overseas.

Overseas missionary organizations founded in and after the 1850s, and in particular the organization that became the UMCA, were influenced by moral secular philosophy as much as they were by religiosity. During the late eighteenth century, Europeans adopted a secularized version of Christian charity and came to believe that "human misery was not only an evil: to some degree it was a preventable evil." This inspired a new faith in the importance of "progress" and a renewed hope for the improvement of the human condition. The post-Enlightenment ideal that the rights of one man were the rights of all men, and that "human progress should be shared by all," further aligned secular humanism and the values of Christian charity.[51] In the late eighteenth century, the British came to believe that men and women, particularly British Christians, could remove the evils of the world they saw around them—such as slavery, barbarism, heathenism, polygamy, and poverty.[52] Particularly after the Napoleonic wars, Britain's overseas humanitarian urges became emblematic of national virtue.[53] Britons saw few of these social ills at home and took pride in their own civilization and culture. This sentiment led to the "easy assumption that the good life was possible only within the framework of Western culture," and that "civilization" was the panacea to the world's ills. Indeed, the British people's deep faith in the moral virtue of spreading Western civilization was deeply entrenched in mid-nineteenth-century national identity. Both missionary and secular reformers rallied behind the cause of carrying the light of "civilization" to the "dark places" of the world. "Civilizing" Africa would satisfy moral obligation, stimulate economic growth, and secure commercial profits for those involved in the African trade.

Britain's theological, humanitarian, economic, and fledgling imperial interest in Africa focused first and foremost on the abolition of the slave trade. A new interest in the plight of all men caused Europeans to see, many for the first time, the suffering on the African continent caused by the trade in slaves, the horrors of the Middle Passage and other routes, and the brutality on both African and New World plantations. Despite their own hand in the transformation of the slave trade and their unremitting consumption of the products of slave labor, when abolitionism gained popularity in England, British humanitarian reformers shifted their rhetoric to characterize Africans as barbarians in need of salvation. Citing what Europeans understood as long-standing institutions of slavery on the continent and Africans' apparent willingness to trade in slaves, European humanitarian reformers constructed an image of Africans as a different sort of man than Europeans—they were "'fallen men,' degraded by their savagery and by the equally savage Christians that carried out the slave trade." If slavery and the slave trade caused African barbarism, then abolition was the cure. Britain, the self-proclaimed leader among nations, claimed an ethical right to work against the slave trade and, by extension, "a moral right to intervene in Africa for the sake of carrying civilization to the barbarians."[54]

The imperatives of a time given over to humanitarianism and abolitionism and the clarion call to reestablish the church abroad coalesced in the Tractarians' mission to Central Africa. Part of the responsibility of Christ's Holy Catholic Church, "particularly that pure and reformed part of it established in this Kingdom," reformers argued, was to "make our pure part of His Church the means of informing all that are in ignorance, and of reforming all that are in error." In a series of sermons laying out a blueprint for a Tractarian approach to overseas evangelism, George Augustus Selwyn had once likened Britain's missionaries to the patriarch Abraham, the man who "of all the characters of Scripture, [is] the one best adapted to be the guide and example of the colonist." If Britain and her Tractarians were planning to "claim the stewardship of Abraham to be the Father of many nations," it would not be enough to tend to the heathen at home, but they must both "attack a citadel close at hand, and to advance against an enemy in the field."[55] The universities' mission embraced these values with a fervor unparalleled in earlier missions and began their new endeavor "committed both to missionary outreach and to the principles of the Oxford Movement."[56]

Building a "Native Church"

Tractarian philosophy mandated that the fledgling Oxford and Cambridge Mission to Central Africa would be both self-sustaining and evangelical, for, as Isaiah's prophecies told them, a true Zion in East Africa would only come through the work of the faithful themselves. Founders envisaged a church that was "native in the true sense of the word: the church of the people of the land, irrespective of European influence, and adapting itself to the special circumstances of the race and the country in which it exists."[57] In reality, this meant that the missionaries were pushing for a mediated form of Christianity—one they considered neither too "European" nor too "African," but which would incorporate habits of Christian living in a way that would resonate with the local culture. The new mission was not the only organization to doubt the universal applicability of the "Three C's." Indeed, missionary planners were beginning to see that "civilization" could mean something different to everyone who used it. For the Tractarians, their emphasis on quotidian performance and revealed meaning permitted the natural integration of certain local forms of expression and some longer-standing African practices into the new church. While "civilizing" Africans was important, Tractarians conceded that the day-to-day realities of African life made some behaviors and accoutrements of Western culture impractical. For example, the starched, high-necked dresses that defined Victorian respectability back in Britain seemed unfeasible in the muggy and dusty equatorial climate. While rarely stooping to forego the buttons and frills themselves, female UMCA workers would dress their charges in the cheaper and less maintenance-intensive *kanga*, or cloth lengths, popular in East Africa at the time. Missionaries were convinced that "a native ministry which relied on European customs, and was asked to accept the definitions of either England or Rome," would never be a success in East Africa, because "European customs and definitions were the result of a history and circumstance in which Africans did not share."[58] In contemporary terms, theirs was a relatively progressive approach to cultural change—other missions required a far more strict adherence to European values.

The idea of creating a "Native Church" was, however, not unique to the UMCA. No missionary society could possibly send enough workers to lead the new church, and many felt the best way to ensure its longevity was to train Africans to preach and as administrators. How this worked in practice was not consistent across missionary organizations. In 1874, for example, the Church Missionary Society (CMS) undertook the care of slaves freed near Mombasa, Kenya. The station was staffed in large part by individuals the CMS referred to as "Bombay Africans." These Christians were Africans who had left the continent as children, and who were then liberated during the 1850s in the Indian Ocean and in port cities of southern Arabia and the Persian Gulf before being turned over to the British municipality in Bombay. After brief stints living with European families in the colony, they were collected into an "African Asylum." There they adopted biblical first names and the surnames of their missionary caregivers, dressed in the contemporary British styles—women with ankle-length, shirtwaisted dresses, leggings, long sleeves, and collars, hair straightened and pinned in a bun behind their heads; men dressed in trousers and coats, often with vests, cravats, high collars, boots, and felt hats. They embraced European language, education, and habits.[59] Throughout the continent, missions employed the strategy of catering a message to local conditions. And, to be sure, the process of translation in and of itself could produce nothing other than churches that were inherently "native" in terms of belief and understanding. The process of learning about Christianity and determining its social and political performance was "a series of collective and contradictory acts of creation."[60] Despite this, many organizations in Tanzania in particular changed their tack after German conquest in 1914, in particular by encouraging converts to abandon old beliefs.[61] Even then, however, the UMCA would not adopt the *Volksmission* strategy of converting societies from the top downwards as a unit by adapting Christianity to the society's "distinctive culture."[62]

As their Tractarian values would suggest, the mission's earliest cohort of workers also believed that a successful native clergy, and indeed all African Christians, were best cultivated from childhood. Religious knowledge was something most successfully revealed over time, and shepherding adult Africans to Christ, missionaries realized, would require an abrupt and fundamental shift in morality—from "barbarism" to Christianity—and the renunciation of forms of authority with which they had lived their entire lives. Although the British Tractarians were content to let some native institutions and practices continue, they thought that most adult Africans lacked the capacity to transform their lives of sin and moral depravity to lives of godliness. On the other hand, they thought African children had not yet succumbed to the moral depravity that characterized their parents, and that they therefore possessed the capacity to be better Christians.[63] They were, in other words, a blank slate—or, as one missionary at the CMS station in Mombasa put it, "clay for the potter."[64] In a decided departure from the biological racisms of the day, missionaries saw their young adherents—be they freed slave children, orphans, or youths who were entrusted to the mission by their parents or who boarded at the mission's schools—as having been spared the "heathen" influence of their families and communities, leaving them open to a more full acceptance of Christ.[65] As one mission worker explained about the differences between children and adult former slaves, "the children because they have never been slaves, loose [*sic*] this failing of their parents [their "heathenism"] and are far superior to them and are better Christians (as far as man's eye can judge), sharper ie: more intelligent."[66] Children were malleable and impressionable, and their capacity for learning was untainted by years of barbarism and savagery. This preference for work among children was supported by Tractarian doctrine that, as we have seen, was based on the idea that the prerequisites for the reception of the Gospel were "not intellectual attainment or rational enquiry, but the simplicity and teachable disposition of little children."[67] The mission's orphans and other children would, in the missionaries' ideal world, grow slowly into the moral disposition required of Christians and come to embody the virtues and values of modernizing Christianity.

The belief that the British, with the Oxford Tractarian reformers chief among them, were uniquely qualified to re-create the church abroad while simultaneously ushering in a new type of church underwrote the mission's endeavors from the start. Inspired by their abolitionism, the founders of the UMCA imagined that their "native congregants" would be former slaves, refugees from the slave trade, and slave traders. Sure in their religious calling, officials saw biblical parallels at nearly every turn. In general terms, officials would be, as Selwyn put it, the "true children of Abraham, the fosterfathers of many nations," guiding "wretched troop[s] of slaves" from throughout East Africa to Christ.[68] More specifically, there were obvious parallels between the triumphant return of the Israelites to Jerusalem as the founders of God's new kingdom on earth and the redemption of Africa's heathen slaves for the work of Christ in East Africa. And indeed, UMCA officials turned in particular to the text of Isaiah time and again when speaking of their own chosen people—the freed slaves, their descendants, and other adherents among whom they would work. The Book of Isaiah offers a compelling tale of sin, judgment, redemption, the unifying power of the love of God, and shared religious identification. The account of Isaiah's prophecies to the Israelites opens by recounting the prophet's chastisement of the Israelites for the heathen practices of many among them, such as disbelief in God's word, superficial worship without true piety, idolatry, ungodliness, immorality, and a "want of honesty and uprightness" and "of humanity and compassion." Isaiah warned the Israelites of the urgent need for confession and atonement, and presaged the destruction and calamities that would befall them should they fail to do so. Their refusal to repent ultimately led to their destruction at the hands of hostile nations, the plundering and wasting of the land, and their exile from Jerusalem. The city was left in ruins.[69]

Isaiah's message was not complete, however, because the Israelites' trials and the destruction of Jerusalem were in fact what ultimately permitted their salvation and redemption. Isaiah prophesied that God, in His grace, would offer "redemption to His helpless people, for whom no one pleads, and who have so little of their own to recommend them."[70] He would then heal the "outward and the spiritual wounds" of the faithful and penitent among His people, which they had received as a result of their disbelief and exile. As they returned home safely through what was once dry and wasted land, they would experience the miracle of God's favor, for where menacing dragons and jackals once roamed was an oasis, verdant, rich in bloom and color.[71] The faithful among the Israelites would return to Jerusalem, which God had also restored, as "a purified, glorified people of God." As a nation they would constitute the core of the new Church of Zion, the "centre of God's kingdom on earth." The new spiritual nation would be "the foremost witnesses of the message of salvation to the whole world" and it would be them to whom the heathen would "join themselves in order to share in [the Kingdom of God's] blessings."[72] Gentiles from every quarter would flock to Zion, constituting a "cleansed, glorified, and blissful Church" where "distinctions of race were to be abolished," and the community that emerged would be unified above ethnic and linguistic differences.

The universities' mission so closely aligned with the stories in the Book of Isaiah that the archbishop of Canterbury spoke on the lessons in the spring of 1889 to commemorate the organization's twenty-eighth anniversary. In commemoration of the mission's progress in "winning . . . Eastern Africa for Christ," and of the role mission supporters believed the organization was playing in reviving the Church of England, the archbishop delivered a sermon in which he recalled for parishioners the Israelites' glorious return to Jerusalem and the subsequent rebirth of the Church at Zion.[73] Laced with poetic imagery and evocative biblical allusions, the sermon was doubtless designed to elicit listeners' sympathy in the form of financial contributions and pledges to join as missionaries:

> The vision of Isaiah did not fade from the prophet's sight when he had but seen the serpent homes transformed into sweet pastures. He saw the way of holiness, the new highway of nations, engineered by man, for man. Our maps of to-day exhibit to our sickening sight "what man has made of man" in hard lines and geographic colours. They show us the depopulated territories, the slave stations, the routes of those ghastly caravans. The prophet speaks of a morrow, when the highway shall be there, the way of holiness, and no ravenous nor unclean soul be found there; but new processions . . . shall stream along it, the redeemed of the Lord returning and coming to our Sion [*sic*] with songs and everlasting joy upon their heads. That is the mystical epic of the day and of the day's work you have begun.[74]

According to the archbishop, the UMCA's Native Church was in fact the epitome of Isaiah's vision. He would ask his congregation: Could "Isaiah himself have had present to that divine imagination of his a more perfect fulfilling of his image?" Analogous to the Israelites' desert were the East African freed-slave communities, recently ravaged by the spiritual and physical destruction of the slave trade. Here "the victims of the old serpent lay strewn, crushed and starved anatomies from the slave-show," and they were but "fed up for crueler servitudes and nameless degradations." To the minds of the British UMCA workers, the Africans' salvation and deliverance from their figurative exiles, their sins, and their spiritual depravity came not directly from God himself, but through the knowledge of Christ offered by British missionaries. English men and women, "afired [*sic*] with love and energy," brought together Africans "of all peoples and tongues" keen to confess and atone for their sins, and to pledge themselves as Christians.[75] Africans willing to abandon their "heathen" practices—their ignorance of God and practices of idolatry and polygamy, for example—were consecrated as the core of the new church. As in Isaiah's prophesies, at the core of the new African church was a community of penitent faithful; the cathedral they had built at Mkunazini, Zanzibar—at the very site of the old slave market about which Livingstone had written—was itself Zion. There, in the ruins and depravity of the slave market, "there are their houses, their friendships, their industries, the discipleship, their choirs, their sacraments."[76] Slaves from communities throughout East Africa came together at Zanzibar in spiritual union, constituting a spiritual nation as diverse as Isaiah's Zion.[77] These new African Christians, the foundation of the Native Church, would be the messengers of salvation throughout East Africa. According to the archbishop, by the time of his sermon in 1889, UMCA congregants had begun to realize Isaiah's prophesies. African evangelists had carried God's message from Zanzibar "far away to the south" to the "great settlements of the Rouvuma [*sic*]," and expanded God's kingdom "far away to the west [at] the vast waters of Nyassa"—in other words, from Zanzibar to the mainland, and across Tanzania to Mozambique and Malawi. Under the banner of Christ, "farms and villages are growing with all the energy of free labour dawning on peoples who once dreamt of nothing between lifelong idleness and toil under the scourge," along with schools offering "their minds the first glimpse of the great secrets of knowledge and self-restraint and power."[78] In the sermon, the archbishop drew upon much-longer-standing discourses of religious and ethnic unity within the mission community, discourses formed in the Tractarian move toward missionization in the 1850s, to make his point. Indeed, these same discourses were at play nearly three decades earlier, when church officials were preparing the first party of missionaries to enter the mission field. As they did so, they looked toward Central Africa with the longer-standing Tractarian discourses of religious and ethnic unity, of building a Zion in East Africa, as encouragement.

Toward Africa

In what would prove to be a rather ignominious start to their "grand scheme," on November 1, 1859, the Home Committee named Charles Frederick Mackenzie the first bishop of the new mission. No longer simply the Oxford and Cambridge Mission to Central Africa, the organization was now called the Universities' Mission to Central Africa (or UMCA) in honor of Dublin and Durham Universities joining the cause. At thirty-four, Mackenzie was "young, healthy, and determined." He was also a devoted High Churchman who was "keenly receptive" to the founders' Tractarian designs for the mission.[79] Although in his younger years he had showed "very little great intellectual ability," Mackenzie was apparently not lacking in diligence, tenacity, or hard work, because he eventually flourished at Cambridge. A vocation for theology ultimately led Mackenzie to pursue ordination. In his late twenties Mackenzie heard an "unmistakably clear" call to mission work, which he pursued as the archdeacon of Natal, South Africa, in 1855.[80]

Thus, when he assumed the helm of the UMCA, Mackenzie was a "reasonably experienced Africa hand."[81] In Natal, Mackenzie was initially responsible for an urban congregation at Durban. The posting was less than ideal, not least of all because the congregants battled him and each other over the direction of the church and the tenor of its services. He found solace in his work among the "Kaffirs" outside of Durban, and was greatly relieved when in 1856 he was released from "his harassing charge" and placed instead at Pietermaritzburg. The following year he received what he had long hoped for—a rural posting. It was in the rural areas of Umhlali, forty miles north of Durban, where Mackenzie did the bulk of the work that would soon recommend him for the bishopric of Central Africa. The archdeacon split his time between the central station, a military encampment a short ride away, and two more distant stations, growing the number of churches served from the central station to four and meriting the addition of another priest to the diocese.[82] In letters to family and friends back in England, Mackenzie reported that his happiness living with his two sisters in Kaffir huts was constant, even in the face of "floods, vermin, and poisonous reptiles." And indeed, for four years Mackenzie did God's work with a "zeal and cheerfulness" that firmly established in the minds of colleagues his "true missionary spirit."[83] In early 1859 Mackenzie made plans to return to England for consecration as coadjutor bishop for the Zulu country. When the appointment fell through, Mackenzie returned nonetheless, arriving home without employment. Mackenzie's return to England was serendipitous, for the UMCA's Home Committee had just begun the search for a bishop. Home Committee members were impressed by his résumé and experience in the South African mission field. Mackenzie's reputation for "muscular swashbuckling Christianity," however, seems not to have been immediately worrisome.

Mackenzie's enthusiasm for planting a church in Central Africa was unbridled (a trait that would ultimately prove to be much to the church's detriment). In 1860 Mackenzie wrote to the bishop of Oxford, Samuel Wilberforce, that "we are more popular in the country, than any other mission ever was, I believe."[84] Mackenzie's robust faith, his time spent in Africa, and the timing of his return seem to have instilled in administrators an elevated sense of confidence with regard to the upcoming mission. The party's imperfect preparation for the task was, in hindsight, evident as early as before their departure. Even the most important detail—where they would settle—was a "matter of perfect indifference," so eager were the missionaries to begin their work. They had left the matter of a station location to David Livingstone, on whose countless travels and work in the mission field the party would soon learn they relied much too heavily. In March 1859, Robert Gray had written to Livingstone to tell him of the universities' determination to begin work in Central Africa, and to ask Livingstone's advice about the most suitable field for these men. The decision was difficult for Livingstone. In his view, the Shire Highlands of modern-day Malawi "needed colonists and not just an isolated group of missionaries, who would be able to do little about the serious problems which would face them there." He feared, however, that if the news got back to London and the Foreign Office that this was not a suitable area for missionaries, plans for a colony there would also be tabled. So, in October 1859 Livingstone wrote to invite Mackenzie and the UMCA to settle in the Shire Highlands. We know that Livingstone saw the invitation as somewhat risky, but he did not at the time know how great a risk the UMCA would undertake.[85]

The party responded immediately and set a departure date for the following October. The timing of the invitation left little time to gather much useful knowledge of the communities among which they would be living, of the language, or of the local politics. Ignorance in each of these subjects would prove a disservice in the months ahead. Further, few among the missionaries who accompanied Mackenzie had field or travel experience. Several were not temperamentally suited to the realities of mission work.[86] Despite the party's rather lackluster preparation, the team nonetheless had the "confidence to go forth on this mission." They fancied themselves, in the words of the new bishop, "a small body indeed amongst the mass of heathenism."[87] Trusting that they had all they needed in God's blessing, the party departed after a solemn farewell service in Canterbury Cathedral on October 4, 1860. Mackenzie's parting words echoed the solemnity of the service. "I am *afraid* of this," he wrote, for "most great works of this kind have been carried on by one or two men, in a quieter way, and have had a more humble beginning." Perhaps Mackenzie feared that the excitement and focus that attended raising funds and recruiting workers obscured their more practical preparations for the field. Whatever the reason, he had cause to be afraid.

The party set sail for Cape Town on October 6, 1860. There the missionaries tackled bureaucratic details, such as Mackenzie's consecration, and convened with Livingstone to make their way to the mission site. Livingstone had selected a spot along the Shire River near Lake Nyasa, in modern-day Malawi, which was not where the party had initially expected to work. After a two-month journey into the Congo mouth of the Zambezi and its smaller tributary, the Shire—a journey that was marred by mounting evidence that Livingstone had misled them—the party reached their destination in the spring of 1861.[88] Rather than the verdant, fertile lands Livingstone had promised, the rolling hills and wide plains were dotted with rocky protrusions and were devoid of any crops, apparently hostile to cultivation. Equally inhospitable were the local inhabitants. The party encountered from the first only widespread instability and insecurity. They passed heavily fortified villages, which shielded people who were concerned only with their own safety. One record of this journey tells of Bishop Mackenzie entering his new diocese carrying his shepherd's crook in one hand and a shotgun in the other.[89]

The failure of the first UMCA station at Magomero has been recounted elsewhere, but the broad outlines of the story offer context for understanding the mission's dramatic change in focus—both ideological and geographical—that followed their initial foray to the heart of the continent.[90] It is also an example of the ways in which the UMCA, and indeed other missions, set out with a goal in mind but were thwarted by their lack of historical and political context, poor language skills, and the overconfidence that often attends good intentions. It also demonstrates, as we will see time and again in the pages that follow, the ways in which African initiative, creativity, and societal roles and frameworks shaped the nature of the work the mission accomplished. In the case of the UMCA, by the time the mission party arrived at their new destination, it had become painfully clear that they were ill-prepared for the social and political realities that awaited them. While en route to the Shire Highlands, a chance encounter with a passing slave caravan provided the missionaries with the opportunity for which they had long dreamt, that of liberating slaves from their "Arab" captors. Burdened now with eighty-four dependents, whom they guarded with guns and arms, they appeared to locals not as the "liberators" they saw themselves to be, but as slave traders. Hasty and uninformed political alliances, as well as a propensity to take up arms, put them at odds with large swaths of neighboring communities. The missionaries were absolutely unable to discern local politics, and were betrayed by the mutability and fluidity of the ethnic identities they thought were decisive. Their apparent ignorance and naiveté about agriculture, despite their protestations that they had come to work the land, baffled locals and caused concern about their true intentions. They had intervened in local markets, offering their imported goods in exchange for slaves or interest in the church, to such an extent that they destroyed the economy and stripped the land of surplus food. By November the missionaries were in dire straits: they had lost the support of their primary local ally, were hosting more than two hundred dependents on a peninsula devoid of crops and the promise of food, had run out of supplies, and were effectively at war with their neighbors.

Early the following January, while on an armed raid to "free" captives from neighboring tribes who they believed were trafficking in slaves (such expeditions were leading their neighbors to believe that they were, in fact, also trading in slaves), Bishop Mackenzie fell ill from exposure and diarrhea. Poor weather and flooded rivers delayed their progress toward home, and the party lost their medicines in a canoe accident. Mackenzie's health failed, and he died on January 31. When the team returned to Magomero without their bishop, it became obvious that the mission settlement was doomed. While they were gone, the famine had intensified, and was further aggravated by an outbreak of amoebic dysentery. Adherents absconded in search of greater security under other patrons. In April, unhealthy missionaries, a dwindling congregation, and increasing local insecurity confirmed the missionaries' fears: their experiment was over.[91] Those who remained from the settlement at Magomero built a new settlement near the Shire River, where they waited for nearly a year for their new bishop, intent only on survival. The experience at Magomero left many among the UMCA bitter "beyond all possible expectation," but it did not weaken their resolve to host a mission in Central Africa.[92] All agreed, however, that there would be some changes.

Zanzibar

After the shocking news of Mackenzie's untimely death in the highlands of East Africa reached England in 1862, the Home Committee wasted no time in consecrating a new bishop. The Reverend William George Tozer, a vicar in Burgh-cum-Winthorpe, Lincolnshire, assumed leadership of the mission on February 2, 1863. Tozer was, according to his friend and colleague Dr. Edward Steere, a man who "shrinks from nothing and succeeds in everything."[93] The new bishop would find himself drawing on this enterprising nature many times in the months and years ahead. Tozer sailed immediately for South Africa upon appointment and immediately undertook the several-hundred-mile trek to the mission, arriving in the Shire Highlands on June 26, 1863.

In the dry lands of the Shire Valley, Tozer found a flailing mission. Four of the original members were dead, and two he immediately deemed medically unfit to serve. There was little food to be had, the surviving population was at war, and transportation and navigation on the surrounding rivers were untenable. Tozer saw no future for the site and closed it immediately. Thinking it best to cut all ties to the area, Tozer refused to accept responsibility for the mission's dependent men, women, and children and left them unmoored in the still-volatile region—an ironic move for an abolitionist mission.[94] The UMCA would start fresh elsewhere.

Tozer proposed the island of Zanzibar, which sits about twenty-five miles off the coast of Tanzania, as a location more centrally located, closer to sources of food and other supplies, and, as mission sources recall, altogether more "civilized."[95] This did not sit well with mission administrators, neither those back in England nor those left alive in Malawi, despite his assurances that it was a place "where the good seed might be sown and reared and whence by another route the Great Lake might be reached." Continued resistance notwithstanding, Tozer closed the mission and left the continent for Zanzibar with his party in tow on August 31, 1863.

Although the UMCA formally established a mission station on Zanzibar in 1863, it was not until late in 1864 that the organization had its first African congregants. The first five congregants were all young boys and were a gift presented by Sultan

UNDATED ILLUSTRATION, FROM "ROUND ABOUT THE CATHEDRAL," *AFRICAN TIDINGS* 5, NO. 78 (APRIL 1896).

FIGURE 3. Sketch of the Cathedral at Mkunazini, Zanzibar.

Majid, the Zanzibari head of state, as a token of his support for the greater abolitionist cause. The first female congregants would not arrive until halfway through 1865. It was due in part to theology and in part to circumstance that the mission grew so slowly in its first few years. As their Tractarian roots dictated, the UMCA's intention was never, as Dr. Steere put it, "to bring in such numbers as that we might be overwhelmed by a mass of heathenism, but to try to give a Christian tone to our first scholars, and then to bring a few, time after time, so that they might catch the rising spirit."[96] And indeed, after acquiring the first five adherents in 1863, Tozer explained in a letter to his sister Helen that he was determined to "creep rather than walk." He therefore "declined having for the present any addition made to our little group of boys, who thus far are very satisfactory," and pledged that only once "these five are taught something and got into order, we can very well take more."[97] Female congregants were not at the time a possibility anyway, for there were as yet no female workers at the mission. Victorian decorum and the Tractarian emphasis on ritual learning meant British "lady" workers would be the best teachers for young female adherents.

Mass conversion campaigns would not have been possible either. First, the Tractarians' long-term theological goals precluded the quick, mass conversions of adults and focused instead on growing the Christian spirit in uncorrupted children over time. Moreover, the political environment at Zanzibar was not conducive to large-scale campaigns. Sultan Majid and the island's Muslim majority generally tolerated the mission, as long as they kept their proselytizing "to slaves and infidels" and left professed Muslims alone. It took little more than a death sentence leveled against a Muslim man who listened to Steere's vernacular street preaching to convince the missionaries that large-scale conversion campaigns would not be tolerated in Zanzibar.[98] Small-scale proselytizing did inspire some few congregants from the local Chinese, Hindi, Goanese, Indian, and European expatriate communities; however, African "converts," both slave and free, were scarce.[99] D. Y. Mills, a prolific missionary author, could recall but a single case of a local freewoman who came to the mission expressly for Christian teaching, and even she was not new to Christianity but had been exposed to the Gospel while living as a child near a Church Missionary Society station in Uganda.[100] In general, the local Zanzibari community responded to the mission's advances with about the same passing curiosity they afforded other foreign faiths espoused by travelers and settlers introduced into their cosmopolitan society.

On June 25, 1865, however, the UMCA's first two British female missionaries arrived at the Seychelles en route to Zanzibar. The 155-island nation situated northeast of Madagascar frequently served as a way station for travelers from Europe to the African continent, and for British navy cruisers policing the Indian Ocean for slaving dhows. In fact, at least as mission legend would have it, the arrival of the British "lady workers" coincided with the very moment a British cruiser docked in the same Seychellois harbor after a battle at sea with an Arab slave ship. On board were several hundred slaves who had survived a dramatic rescue by British mariners from the illicit slave dhow. To commemorate the arrival of the UMCA's "lady workers," Sultan Majid presented Tozer with fourteen of the children on board HMS *Wasp*, to add to the five boys he had given to the mission in September of the previous year. The gift included nine girls and five boys, and constituted the advent of the UMCA's ministry to women.

CHAPTER TWO

From Slaves to Christian Mothers

Developing a Doctrine of Female Evangelism, 1863–1877

When the HMS *Wasp* docked in the late Seychellois spring of 1865, the young Kate Kadamweli was among the nine girls who disembarked into the waiting arms of the UMCA's new British lady missionaries. Kate's disembarkation from the *Wasp* was the start of fifty-three years as a congregant with the UMCA, during which time she worked as an assistant teacher, trained as a nurse and tended to patients in the mission's hospital at Mkunazini, married, bore children, and mentored countless inquirers. Over her long career with the mission, Kate turned to the church to weather abandonment by her husband (also one of the mission's first African adherents) and the death of a daughter. Her faithfulness through trial inspired the authors of mission sources, who counted her as one of the mission's stalwarts and featured her time and again in UMCA publications and propaganda. Missionaries celebrated her "nice, modest, staid behavior," and congregants remembered her as "the dearest woman that ever was."[1]

When Kate arrived at the Seychelles, however, the achievements by which she would be remembered were still years in the future; in June of 1865 missionaries simply saw her as one among a group of "tiny young things" lined up on the deck of Her Majesty's Ship, awaiting redemption from a host of social, spiritual, and physical ills. Steeped in the rhetoric of nineteenth-century abolitionism, the missionaries

UNDATED PHOTOGRAPH, FROM "MAMA KATE. AN AFRICAN SAINT," *AFRICAN TIDINGS* 17, NO. 225 (JULY 1908).

FIGURE 4. Kate Kadamweli as an adult, Mission Hospital, Mkunazini.

who met Kate and her eight female companions at the HMS *Wasp* identified that day in June 1865 as their "liberation" from slavery. Not only were the girls being physically and legally emancipated, the missionaries exulted, but they would also now be free to escape the more esoteric cruelties and degradations that slavery entailed. Chief among these was the spiritual ignorance in which slaves lived. Free from the grips of heathenism—or worse, Islam—Kate and her companions could serve God according to their own judgment and win souls for Christ.[2]

Whether she had been enslaved for one month or several years, the moment of Kate's "liberation" probably passed her and her fellow refugees unnoticed. As a young girl from the mainland, Kate would have been wholly unfamiliar with the rhetoric of abolitionism, redemption, and liberation with which the missionaries approached their work, and could not have imagined such lofty implications in her physical transfer from an Arab dhow to a British ship that June day. The concept of an autonomous individual, free to choose in such black and white terms between salvation and damnation, was not something that Kate would have had the cultural vocabulary to understand. Rather, the East African system of patronage and dependency—the lens through which Kate would have seen her situation—is usefully imagined in terms of relative degrees, rather than in the stark terms of black and white so often associated with the plantation economy of the American South.[3] It is not likely that slaves whom missionaries "redeemed" in mid-nineteenth-century East Africa understood themselves as having secured any sort of "freedom." Instead, Kate would have seen her arrival at the Seychelles in a much more practical and mundane manner—as a transfer from one master to another.

The circumstances unique to East African women in the mid- to late-nineteenth century shaped how Kate engaged with her new masters. In much of precolonial Africa, women were in legal terms perpetual dependents. A woman's relationship to male kin, such as a husband, uncle, brother, or father, secured her status within a community. Without such rights, women lacked access to, and representation in, judicial processes and were highly susceptible to transfer, forced marriage, pawnship, enslavement, or other forms of exchange.[4] Women were also relatively easy to assimilate into domestic society through these same processes. The instability of the late nineteenth century left women even more vulnerable to transfer and enslavement than normal, and women quickly outnumbered men in the slave trade. When met with such extreme vulnerability, women did what their social standing demanded they do, which was to construe relationships as familial, to impute kinship, or to forge relationships that drew them into closer personal relationships with known protectors. And by 1865, missionaries were well known as powerful patrons and protectors in whom Africans imagined pathways toward alternative networks of support and valuable opportunities to create a range of new kinship ties—both real and imagined. Kate, then, would have seen these new masters as potential avenues to form a range of familial and kinship relationships, perhaps with the missionaries themselves or with other congregants of the mission.

The predisposition of East African women to forge familial relationships and to impute kinship ties dovetailed in many ways with the expectations of British missionaries. The mission's Tractarian ideology and related desire to hire only single British ladies with no children of their own led to a tendency among the UMCA's female workers to also approach their work through the idiom of kinship and family. These familial relationships and the (real and fictive) kinship ties that bound missionaries to adherents, and adherents to each other, came to constitute the heart of the UMCA's affective spiritual community. Yet, the missionaries did not fully understand the extent to which their new adherents' vulnerability shaped their relationships and the particular ways they invested in the UMCA community. The lack of overt conflict between the missionaries' assumptions and the refugees' expectations masked the subtle yet significant difference between them—a difference that would shape in unforeseeable ways the nature of the mission and its work, wresting control away from the missionaries in ways they could not have envisaged.

We Must "Decline Any More Single Women"

Although there were only nine girls in Kate's cohort from the HMS *Wasp*, their numbers grew quickly over the UMCA's first decade. By 1873, ten years after Kate and her shipmates were incorporated into the mission, the UMCA stations at Zanzibar boasted thirty-two women on the rolls.[5] By 1875 the population of female scholars alone had more than doubled to fifty-nine, not including women too young or old to attend school.[6] The girls' school, the bishop noted, was increasing "in even a larger proportion than that for boys."[7] The numbers overwhelmed the new Bishop Steere to such an extent that he knew "not how to turn."[8]

The influx of arrivals to the mission in the early 1870s—what missionaries would soon characterize as a crisis—can be explained in several ways. Perhaps the most immediate reason was an 1871 agreement between the mission and British consul Dr. John Kirk. Administrators had long harbored hope that Kirk's relationship with UMCA founders and workers, as well as his Anglican faith, would help grease the bureaucratic wheels in their search for adherents. Late in 1871, Kirk flexed his diplomatic muscles and secured a series of informal agreements that granted the UMCA first right of selection on all the children freed at Zanzibar, the Seychelles, and Aden.[9] While exclusive access to the orphans and other children liberated under

Kirk's domain virtually guaranteed the mission a steady stream of recruits, Kirk's offer came with a problematic caveat. Struggling to find homes for adult *mateka* ("captives" or "booty," i.e., slaves), Kirk granted the mission exclusive access to orphans and other freed children *only if* the mission would also accept adults.[10] In a letter to the bishop of Winchester, Kirk revealed the political calculations behind this offer. He suspected Tozer would feel that while adults were not the mission's intended audience, they would nonetheless be an advantage because they could provide labor on the mission's estates. The prospect of a permanent work force might be enough to convince Tozer to "accept a few of an older clap than he has hitherto admitted."[11] Were this true, it would only reinforce the similarities between slave owners and missionaries in the minds of redeemed Africans.

The second factor that caused an uptick in arrivals to the mission was an 1873 anti-slave-trading agreement. Britain finally succeeded in pressuring the sultan of Zanzibar to legally abolish all slave shipments by sea that year. While the seagoing trade in slaves may have been illegal, it was not illegal to hold or employ slaves. In 1873, the British consul general John Kirk tried to persuade the sultan's governors (sing. *liwali*, pl. *maliwali*) in the slaveholding areas of the mainland of the benefits of enforcing the sultan's 1873 treaty. Kirk argued that trading entrepreneurs on the mainland might benefit from putting slaves to work performing "continuous labor" on their own estates. And put them to work they did; Arab settlers, Swahili-speaking townsmen, and their non-Muslim neighbors employed slaves to cultivate local plantations in record numbers. This was the local impact of the broader economic and abolitionist processes described in the previous chapter, which had the ironic result of naturalizing slavery in East Africa. Further, authorities implemented the 1873 decree slowly and incrementally; both smuggling and overland trade to coastal ports continued to flourish for many years.[12] This process of the legal but not practical abolition of slavery exacerbated tensions within the coastal slave system that had grown up over the nineteenth century, resulting in the intensification of political and military conflict on the coast. Slaves rebelled, such as in July 1873 when slaves on the Pangani River took up arms and left their masters en masse. Others escaped, rates of which rose with the intensity of disputes.[13] *Watoro* ("people who run away") sought succor with patrons deemed (for whatever reason) to be preferable, or shifted locations in search of different masters. Increasingly after the 1860s, the range of new patrons available to *watoro* or other unattached slaves included missionaries.[14] The UMCA was not the only organization to benefit from the treaties; diplomatic machinations surrounding the 1873 decree allowed other evangelical organizations along the coast to collect enough followers to launch viable missions in the region. For the Church Missionary Society mission in Kenya, the 1873 diplomatic mission of Sir Bartle Frere altered the course of what had been an unsuccessful campaign up to that point.[15] In relative terms the UMCA incorporated far fewer *watoro* than their CMS counterparts in Mombasa, who frequently found themselves at odds with local *waliwali* over the fate of *watoro* and other maroons who made their way to the Rabai and Freretown settlements.[16]

When presented with Kirk's proposal, the missionaries were ambivalent. Gone would be the days when missionaries could make their way slowly among periodic gifts from the sultan, masters, and other residents, as well as individual *watoro* (runaways), *mateka* (captive slaves), and local slaves. They would be forced to accommodate adults, whose very presence at the mission would introduce what the missionaries considered to be serious theological and practical issues. Would the distractions that attended adult Africans outweigh the advantages of a virtual corner on the market of refugee children? they wondered. Adults were challenging cases, raised without Christ and influenced for too many years by the heathen customs of the interior. Adults also had "indefinite powers of addition," which caused practical theological problems.[17] Space was limited, and the adult adherents were as yet imperfect Christian parents. Despite their discomfort with admitting adults, first right of selection of liberated children proved too enticing for the missionaries to pass up. The mission accepted Kirk's proposal and begrudgingly welcomed all *mateka*, both young and old, into the mission. This would prove to be a much larger concession than they had imagined at the time, however, for although missionaries predicted in 1878 that the slave trade was "practically at an end," *mateka* and *watoro* would continue to arrive at the mission for more than thirty years to come.[18]

The third factor that accounts for the influx of refugees to the mission in the early 1870s—and accounts in particular for the disproportionate number of women on the mission's rolls—was the gendered dynamics of slaving. In general terms, single female refugees like Kate and her eight female companions on the *Wasp* constituted a majority of the Indian Ocean slave traffic.[19] This was true for two reasons. First, in most African societies, single, widowed, or otherwise dependent women were most vulnerable to enslavement because they lacked a husband, brother, uncle, or father to represent them in any number of local judicial processes. Second, in the profit-driven wars and raids that were increasingly common in the late nineteenth century, women and children were generally captured and men were killed, fates that reflected the ease with which women and children could be absorbed into a lineage or community.[20] Female slaves from local plantations also sought patronage with the UMCA in relatively large numbers, increasing even further the number of women and girls for whom the mission was responsible. All of this suggests that the gender balance of the day of Kate's adoption—nine girls and five boys—and of the overcrowded situation at the mission's Zanzibar stations of Shangani and Mkunazini, was less a reflection of mission policy or priorities than of broader trends in nineteenth-century Indian Ocean slaving. In fact, so entrenched were these trends that the gender disparity would continue to shape the mission for years to come. In 1877, for example, one mission worker reported that he was in charge of "fifty more women than men" at Mbweni and that, therefore, he must "decline [to accept] any more single women" from the consulate.[21]

Kate and Fayida

While Kate Kadamweli eventually came to symbolize for the missionaries and the UMCA propaganda machine the archetypal adherent, the story of her arrival at and incorporation into the mission is far more mundane. In fact, Kate's story and that of a young woman named Fayida mirror the arrival and incorporation stories of countless other female refugees and personify the broader trends that led to a gender imbalance at the mission. Told here, their stories offer two important insights pertinent to the development of the UMCA's affective spiritual community. First, their stories illustrate the process by which women in the first cohorts of UMCA adherents arrived at the mission. Kate and Fayida's journeys to Zanzibar illustrate how many others like them ended up at the mission's doors seeking succor, and the social structures and realities governing their lives, their understanding of the world around them, and their perceptions of the choices and decisions in front of them. Second, the context of the social systems and realities that governed the lives of Kate, Fayida, and others among the first cohorts of female adherents of the UMCA sheds light on the interior lives and expectations of the UMCA's female adherents. We see that the UMCA's British lady missionaries did not understand, and the mission sources misrepresented, much about their charges and the ways in which they approached their incorporation into, and lives within, the mission—these misunderstandings would fundamentally alter the nature of the mission's work with women.

Kate arrived at the Seychelles a young girl about whom we know very little. Kate's given name and her date of birth, for example, are lost to history. While we may never know what she was called by family and friends, it is not likely that Kate was actually the "tiny baby thing" Ms. Tozer and Ms. Jones recalled selecting from the group of children who disembarked from the Arab slave ship. Infants and toddlers were sometimes carried to the mission by their mothers, but Kate's mother seems not to have been with her at the Seychelles. It is far more likely that Kate made the journey from the interior to the coast by foot, walking under her own power. To do so, she would have been older than a "baby" and closer to the age of a young girl—perhaps seven or eight, or even an early adolescent. Malnourishment, tattered clothing, fear, and the painful subjugation of the previous months or years, however, may have made Kate appear younger than she actually was. Further, the paternalism inherent in the British "civilizing" mission presumed a childlike status of all East Africans. Ms. Tozer and Ms. Jones were likely falling back on an old trope, rather than reporting reality, when describing their newest charges.

Kate probably shared with her thirteen redeemed shipmates and congregants on the island several other characteristics, most notably their likely mainland birth. In the 1860s Zanzibar received large numbers of slaves from throughout eastern and central Africa, some of whom remained on the mainland to work for masters there, or became slaves on plantations on Zanzibar, Pemba, or other plantation islands in the Indian Ocean. An increasingly large percentage of the luxury trade into and out of Zanzibar during the nineteenth century consisted of slaves like Kate and the others rescued by sailors on the *Wasp*. Slaves were so valuable as status markers, historian Jeremy Prestholdt has argued, that "as much as Zanzibaris valued imported manufactures, they wanted imported people more."[22] Thus by the height of East Africa's nineteenth-century economic boom, human beings had become Zanzibaris' most highly valued and sought-after commodity. In the 1850s—fourteen years before the arrival of the UMCA—between ten and fifteen thousand slaves passed through Zanzibari ports every year.

It is impossible to say for sure whence on the mainland Kate came to Zanzibar, but the history of the slave frontier can offer a hint. By the 1850s the coastal Muslims who sourced many of the slaves that came through Zanzibar had established a permanent trade center at Tabora, and Unyamwezi became the traders' inland base. Caravan routes stemmed north into the interlacustrine kingdoms and west into the Zaire basin. By this time, the ivory frontier had receded, drawing traders further into the interior.[23] These central routes brought ivory and slaves from places such as Kigoma, along the lake border with what is today Democratic Republic of the Congo, or even from the DRC itself, as well as from Rwanda or Burundi, or near Mwanza, Musoma, or into Uganda. Given the demographics of the trade at the time Kate arrived at the mission, it is likely she made her way from one of these areas to the coast as a member of a slave caravan.[24]

Kate did not record a "redemption" story, but many other young women did. To be sure, even if a personalized account of Kate's journey did exist, gathering any "truth" from that record would have been a fraught endeavor. Recorded, translated, and published by missionaries, "receptive" stories present particular challenges to the scholar looking for "accurate" or "factual" accounts of the lives of refugees. Certain narrative conventions operate in accounts of slaves' lives as told by missionaries. Given that such accounts often served as fund-raising propaganda, and that missionary amanuenses heavily edited them, myriad alternative narrative outcomes are contained within and behind the stories that were eventually recorded. Indeed, the very act of seeking to "contain the 'native voice'" had the paradoxical effect of inscribing "a record of its presence and even its actual operation in the voices and narrative strategies of the texts themselves."[25] Although it is possible to argue that the voices of African congregants have been lost entirely in these "ventriloquized texts," when read against the grain these narratives can and do reveal some of the only traces of the otherwise-silenced voices of mission adherents. Other scholars working with recaptive life stories come to similar conclusions.[26]

The story of one Fayida (meaning "profit" in Kiswahili) sheds light on what Kate, and many of their fellow congregants, were likely to have experienced. Fayida related her own "redemption" story to mission workers in 1897, decades after both she and Kate arrived at the mission. When Fayida was young, perhaps an age similar to Kate, she lived in what was likely southeast Tanzania. The persistent insecurity from escalating slaving wars had already disrupted her family; her mother was missing—either dead or captured—and her father worked some distance from home. Fayida lived in the village with her sister and two remaining brothers. One day the small family heard rumors that a group of ethnic Magwangwara was headed toward the village, gathering captives to sell into slavery. The siblings spread scattershot through the open country surrounding their home, Fayida and her brother doing their best to hide. Unsuccessful, the pair was captured and joined a number of other men, women, and children in the caravan. Fayida, her brother, and their fellow captives walked for many days. Exhausted, she attempted to hide in a thick forest and escape, but caravan leaders spotted her and recaptured her. At the coast, the captors locked Fayida and the other children in a big stone prison house, where they bunked down in a shed on the roof. Here Fayida was separated from her brother—he was sold and never seen again. Fayida apparently remained behind, watching the comings and goings of other captives around her. Her captors were "horribly wicked," she recalled years later, and the remaining slaves "lived in misery and deadly fear."[27] One night, under cover of darkness, their abductors ushered Fayida and her fellow captive Panya—also soon to be a UMCA adherent—onto a waiting dhow.[28] There they spent several miserable days at sea—wet, sick, and hungry. Spotted by a British Navy cruiser, the dhow was stopped and its crew apprehended. With promises of food from the soldiers, the children bedded down along the water's edge and boarded the British ships in the light of day. Once on Zanzibar, the remaining slaves were held at the consulate until missionaries adopted them. Kate's experience was likely very similar.[29]

It is unlikely that Fayida and Kate understood their reception by the UMCA missionaries in the same way that the missionaries did, as the moment they gained their "freedom" or "liberation." Kate likely approached her "saviors" with, at best, the casual indifference of someone already familiar with the experience of being traded from one master to another several times in her short life. More likely, Kate and her shipmates responded to this move with fear and trepidation. The missionaries themselves even noted their new charges' sense of foreboding. They crouched on the deck "with no clothing save the narrowest possible strip of calico round their middles," recalled one onlooker in the sensational manner typical of mission sources, "with their hands clasped round their necks, looking up into your face with an expression of utter apprehension that something much more dreadful than even they had experienced, would surely come upon them, now that they had fallen into the hands of the dreaded white man."[30]

Further, Kate's existence among the British missionaries after her "liberation" would have offered few hints that her life had changed in any substantive way. Unable to communicate in either English, Kiswahili, or Kate's mother tongue, the missionaries would have packed Kate into the new ship bound from the Seychelles for Zanzibar without her consent. Soon after landing in Zanzibar, Kate would have been stripped of her old clothes and of her old name, signaling the birth of a new identity. Her new patrons would also require that she join the other African adherents in performing agricultural, manual, and domestic labor. Between these duties and the toll of the church bell for five-times-daily prayer, her days would have been highly regulated—just like those of coastal slaves. Marooned in this new environment, Kate and her fellow adherents would have done what any slave would do: rely entirely on the missionaries for shelter, protection, clothing, and sustenance. It is easy to imagine how in this context, the refugees' expectations of the UMCA missionaries would have been little different from their expectations of their previous masters. The term *watumwa wa balozi* ("slaves of the [British] consul") or *watumwa wa wangereza* ("slaves of the British") were colloquialisms that local Zanzibaris used to refer to *mateka* (captives) who lived on Zanzibar's mission stations, and their use in the late nineteenth century suggests that slave masters and missionaries were less distinguishable in the minds of Africans than either masters or missionaries would have liked to imagine.[31]

On that June day in 1865, however, Kate would have known nothing about the life that awaited her at Shangani. She would only have known what was immediately true, which was that she had recently been wrenched from her natal home, forced to walk great distances with little food, perhaps sharing in the burden of an ivory tusk, with people she did not know and who did not treat her especially well. She was now, apparently, under the guardianship of a new master, one with whom she did not share a language or the cultural repertoire to understand her new situation. Kate might have considered herself relatively lucky to have fallen at the doorstep of the Anglican mission, for the missionaries' offers of food, clean clothes, and other forms of protection suggested they were powerful patrons, and Kate may have heard rumors that missionaries were actively recruiting low-status clients. Some captives might have also understood that the missionaries represented new status hierarchies and avenues to access new forms of power emerging throughout East Africa in the latter half of the nineteenth century.[32] After all of this, she was very likely hungry, tired, and afraid.

Kate's uprooting, a tumultuous and lonely journey to the coast, and her likely confusion about the missionaries' intentions are important not only for understanding how East Africans came to be members of the UMCA mission community, but also for understanding the particular gendered experiences of female refugees incorporated into the mission in its first few decades. Kate, as we have seen, likely did not understand her arrival as a moment of "liberation." Rather, the ideology of paternalism that circulated in nineteenth-century coastal society—and which was similar to that of governing communities further to the interior—was in fact much more ambiguous. People called *mtumwa* or "slave" were in actuality one of several categories of subordinated client. The line between slave and free was really only distinct in the minds of society's most dominant members—slave masters and missionaries. And wherever that line lay in actuality, it was the result of struggle and remained in flux. Indeed, a slave "rarely rejected the language of clientele altogether but continued to search for a preferred patron-master."[33] Coastal dependents did not imagine their lives in terms of "freedom" or "unfreedom," but they sought instead to negotiate the best relationship of dependency possible.

For single women and girls, negotiating the best relationship of dependency possible often meant construing relationships as familial or imputing kinship. Again, despite localized variations in social practice, women in precolonial African societies were generally considered perpetual dependents. Without a husband, uncle, brother, or father accompanying her, a female refugee such as Kate or Fayida or countless other women whom the UMCA intercepted lacked access to the judicial process and to the legal and physical protections that relationships with a male kin would have provided her. When met with such vulnerability, women tended to construe relationships as familial, or to forge new relationships through the exchange of bridewealth, pawnship, or other forms of rights in person.[34] Vulnerable women sought protectors, offered them merciful expressions of gratitude, and felt a strong pressure to conform by forging, asserting, or claiming various kinship ties.[35] Crafting an alternative network of support was a strategy of survival that allowed a female refugee a way to reduce her isolation and vulnerability. Female refugees sought familial and kinship ties *not just* with members of new African communities in which they found themselves on the mainland, but wherever they were isolated from their kin group—including when they arrived in the care of the UMCA.[36]

Perhaps already calculating the ways in which she could reduce her vulnerability and intrude more forcibly into her new community, Kate traveled with the UMCA staff from the Seychelles to Zanzibar. If she was not suffering from the seasickness that routinely plagues voyagers who brave the choppy waters of the strait between Zanzibar and the Tanzanian mainland, Kate might have dared to look over the bow of the boat toward her new home. With every list of the ship, she would have caught a glimpse of a skyline nearly identical to the one that greets business travelers and tourists coming by dhow or ferry from the mainland today. Stone Town, built where the land juts out into a point on the island's long western side, would have offered Kate a breathtaking welcome. The shoreline is, as one contemporary observer described, "a fringe of large, and for the most part very stately, flat-roofed houses, looking as eastern-like as possible."[37] In Kate's time the buildings were new and crisply whitewashed, built to house some of the island's most important individuals, businesses, and foreign consulates. The massive yet simple homes of the island's wealthiest landowners, with skillfully carved wooden doors that exhibited "modest riches and subdued elegance," stood next to the Old Fort, what is today one of the oldest standing buildings in town.[38] The most imposing of the street's structures, the Beit al-Ajaib and the Old Dispensary, were not yet constructed, but the multistoried buildings with clock towers and opulent wood-carved balconies popular at the time would have been quite a sight for Kate to behold.

Depending on the route they took from the port to Shangani, the group may have entered the maze of houses and little shops that branched out behind the Old Fort. They would have walked past the pop-up stalls of lower-class merchants who sold fish and other species of seafood, freshly baked loaves of bread, the putrid-smelling durian fruit, and branches laden with the bright red, hairy fruit known locally as *shoki shoki* on the three-foot-high curbs of the white buildings, raised to allow pedestrians escape from the donkey-led carts and the floods of the monsoon rains. The travelers might have stolen glimpses through open wooden doors into the ground-level courtyards of the patrician homes, whose several stories spiraled up to rooms lavishly furnished with Persian rugs, Chinese pillows, ornately carved imported tables and chairs set with Asian or European porcelain, and walls hung with French mirrors and American clocks.[39] These were homes Kate might have entered as a slave, but her new life as a Christian would generally preclude mixing with town Muslims.

Once at the mission house in Shangani, with its wooden doors shut tightly against the heathenism and "Mohammedanism" of the outside world, Kate would have begun her slow transformation into a Christian. Before anything, Kate would have been bathed. In washing away any lice and fleas acquired on the long voyage from her home, the missionaries were also washing away remnants of Kate's past. Kate would have stepped out of the bath and into a pink dress and matching half-handkerchief, both physically and symbolically cleansed. Kate's redressing was part of the symbolic rebirth that slaves up and down the Swahili Coast endured each time they were sold, freed, or otherwise transferred. Had Kate or her companions been shifted to new patrons before, this would have been a familiar ritual. While perhaps not as extreme as the "horrible masquerade" that took place during slave markets, in which newly arrived slaves "were forced to wear a profusion of gold, beads, expensive cloths, sometimes even flowers in their hair" designed to make them look healthy and desirable on the auction block, new clothes were fundamental to this social remaking. This was true from the wealthiest Zanzibaris' clothing of their *wapembe* (decorated or adorned slaves), to the poorest Zanzibaris—some

UNDATED PHOTOGRAPH, FROM "THE CHILDREN'S PAGE," *AFRICAN TIDINGS* 12, NO. 168 (OCTOBER 1903).

FIGURE 5. Mbweni students. *From right:* Edith, Jessie, Harriet, and Irene.

of whom were themselves slaves—who clothed their new acquisitions in lengths of *merikani* cloth, to the missionaries, who offered their new adherents *merikani*, *leso*, and cotton frocks in various patterns stitched by church supporters at home. Redressing by an owner was a "graphic scene of domination" and a way to remove traces of their former lives and to mark them as members of the community.[40]

Part of a slave's symbolic rebirth was a new name. Slaves of all ages had received Swahili names that reflected the respective owner's hope for their collective future. Common among the UMCA's girls were Bahati, Faida, Mabruki, Baraka, and Heri ("fortune," "profit," "blessed," "blessing," and "happiness").[41] The ritual renaming after baptism was little different. In another step toward redemption, the little girl from HMS *Wasp* became Kathleen.

This symbolic rebirth was, of course, merely the first step in what the UMCA understood was a long journey into Christendom. The rest was a largely internal transformation that would unfold as the result of daily attention and learning by example. The ancient notion of "reserve" or "economy" that underwrote the

Tractarians' approach to evangelism meant that children and inquiring adults should learn about Christianity through slow revelations of the Gospel in ritual and practice. As we have seen, the missionaries were less concerned with the number of "heathen" they converted than with the quality of the religious instruction those adherents received.[42] The girls would "catch the rising spirit" only by living the faith, and would come to embody a distinctly African Anglican moral character over time. One day, missionaries hoped, they would have the wisdom to appropriately interweave Anglican principles with longer-standing African institutions and practices.[43] Over time, the missionaries would develop into a coherent ideology that privileged the Christian mother as the most perfect evangelist of this new way of Christian living.

And who better to teach these skills than the women whom social theorists imagined to stand at the top of the civilizational peak? Missionaries postulated that "English ladies" were "absolutely essential for the making [of] much real progress amongst the women of Africa."[44] The mission's belief that English ladies were crucial to success among heathen women was a product of mid-nineteenth-century British secular humanitarian thought and of the particularities of Tractarianism. Popular discourse held that British women had a duty and a unique ability to share their advantages and model their lives to their heathen sisters.[45] Through service abroad, European women could introduce a Western feminine ideal and a domestic agenda of Western modernity to indigenous peoples, embodying the new knowledge, technologies, and practices that were revolutionizing their own home societies.[46] Further, their shared womanhood meant that European women alone were capable of transforming heathen women; they alone, contemporaries thought, held the key to "opening heathen hearts to the civilizing influence of Christian love."[47]

British "Lady" Workers

In its approach to the evangelization of African women, the UMCA broke from the example of earlier overseas missions. Before the mid-nineteenth century, women were generally only permitted to serve in Protestant missions as wives of clerics and male staff. In addition to the manifold domestic duties required to maintain a mission station, mission wives carried the extra burden of the expectations of childbirth and child-rearing. Further, they were expected to help promote the evangelical work for which their husbands were responsible, and to assume the additional tasks of teaching schoolchildren and the local women the "skills of European domesticity." In some mission societies, a missionary wife was so essential to overseas work that recruiters insisted on providing bachelor conscripts with a "suitable companion" from among a pool of aspiring single female missionaries just prior to departure. Otherwise reluctant to send single women to the overseas field alone, home staff acquiesced only in the hope that the women would soon marry either widowers or bachelors already living in the mission field, relieving them from the labor and expense of returning home to acquire a wife, or saving them the disappointment of abandoning their work altogether.[48]

The paucity of women in the mission field changed mid-century. After the 1850s, Western women began pursuing professional careers to an unprecedented degree, which increased the number of women available for, and interested in, overseas mission work. Educated nineteenth-century women found foreign mission work to be very alluring. Between 1865 and 1910, the number of women in the mission field grew exponentially, and female lay workers soon outnumbered ordained clerics.[49] Particularly for single women, field service offered opportunities unavailable at home. Missionary work was a viable and socially acceptable alternative to marriage, and it allowed single women the opportunity to pursue careers that were less accessible in England, such as physician and teacher. Yet, while the movement of women to the mission field gave them an "independent outlet for salaried, professional work," it simultaneously "cast their mission field as a domestic sphere, exported patriarchal church institutions which marginalized women's formal religious authority, and projected a middle-class ideal of marriage and family life."[50] While the implications of this irony are explored in later chapters, it is sufficient for now to say that "women's work for women" became the catch phrase for British missionary activities from the mid-nineteenth century to the second decade of the twentieth century, when it functioned as both a justification for and a description of their work in the field.[51]

As a Tractarian mission, the UMCA from its inception offered devout, single Anglican women the opportunity to pursue a religious calling overseas. Indeed, although a recent historiographical survey of women in missions identifies the Edinburgh Missionary Conference of 1910 as the moment that Protestant women "develop[ed] an established professional identity which expanded beyond the private sphere," the UMCA seems to have considered its women missionaries to be professional members of the staff in the 1860s, well before its contemporaries.[52] As we have seen, Tractarians valued the ancient inheritances of asceticism and the monastic ideal of retirement from the world. Spinsters were idealized both as ascetics and as willing to retire and devote their lives to service. The UMCA's commitment to hiring only single women missionaries, rather than wives (or potential wives) for their male missionaries and clerics, meant that administrators could be selective about how a recruit's qualifications fit into the broader wants and needs of the mission. Perhaps more important for how the mission functioned in practice, a woman without any immediate kinship ties of her own—no husband, no children—was poised to invest fully in the Tractarians' emotional and embodied approach to evangelism. A confirmed spinster did not have a husband or biological children vying for her attention, and was therefore free to devote her time, emotional energy, and—significantly—mothering instincts to her African charges. The emotional availability of British lady workers for intimate affective relationships was central to the Tractarian evangelical strategy and to the filial nature of their relationships with their female charges.

Considering its female employees to be qualified professionals rather than simply "wives of" or temporary volunteers, the UMCA established and publicized minimum qualifications for employment. These minimum qualifications reveal much about the values of the mission and its expectations for the relationships of the British lady workers with their African charges. A woman's professional training, the strength of her religious devotion, and her personal character all constituted the evangelical repertoire from which Tractarian workers would draw while in the field, and mission recruiters carefully scrutinized each woman's credentials prior to conscription. Recruiters first urged aspiring female missionaries to consider carefully whether they had the religious devotion to see them through the challenges of the mission field. Overseas work was physically and personally demanding: death and chronic ill health from malaria or other diseases was common, return trips home for health care or to visit family were expensive and infrequent, and since the UMCA required their British employees to remain unmarried while serving, the female recruit faced the very real possibility of being the lone European woman at a remote mission station. Recruitment pleas thus specified among their qualifications "a real Missionary vocation, and a determination to give oneself up entirely to a life of religion and work."[53] UMCA recruiters and former missionaries alike were clear that all the work of the mission—the teaching, nursing, domestic, and industrial work—"need[s] to be done as a religious act, as an offering to God, as a way of helping on the whole work of the Mission: the spreading of the kingdom of Christ."[54]

Women secure in their religious commitment were reminded, however, that a "mere wish to be generally useful is not sufficient qualification." Rather, "ladies willing to offer their services should have had the training necessary to qualify them for the work they wish to undertake."[55] Nurses wishing to take up the mantle of Tractarian-inspired service, for example, needed "three years' hospital training" and "trained knowledge of midwifery" as well as dispensing. Recruiters urged prospective teachers to have classroom experience, plus time spent working with pupil-teachers, infant classes, or teaching Sunday school.[56] Further, recruiters stipulated that all women—especially those seeking only general domestic employment—should have "training in the womanly duties"; thus candidates were required to be competent in "cooking, bread-making, house-keeping, laundry work, needlework, [and] book-keeping."[57] Proficiency in "*all* that appertains to keeping a house nice" was important for two reasons. First, workers believed that "the health" and "nerves" of a mission station largely depended on well-cooked food and on the "order, punctuality, and peacefulness" with which European women could run field stations. Second, staffers argued that even if the new recruits "may not have to do the actual work . . . they are almost certain to have to train others to do it."[58]

The career headmistress of the Mbweni Girls' School, Caroline Thackeray, epitomized the mission's ideal of a professional staff member, and she surely underwent intense scrutiny to this end before being hired in 1876. A cousin of the English novelist William Makepeace Thackeray, Caroline Thackeray was born to an upper-class British family. At the time, personal wealth was a necessary requirement for mission work: upon announcing the small stipend given to clergy and lay members—£20 annually—Bishop Steere explained that "they who come to the work should either support themselves, or else that, having food and raiment, they should therewith be content."[59] And wealth was something Thackeray had. She paid for the construction of many buildings on the Mbweni campus herself, and funded her entire career at the mission, which stretched until her death, with personal funds. Wealth and class notwithstanding, Thackeray was a trained teacher. Charged with the task of running the girls' school, Thackeray arrived at Zanzibar via the boat carrying the mail from the Yemeni port of Aden on November 11, 1877.

UMCA recruiters judged the suitability of would-be workers not only on their professional qualifications, Tractarian-style religious devotion, and affinity for communal life, but also on a host of personal characteristics. A female missionary, for example, needed "a constant endeavour to bear and forbear; a determination to bear willingly, not grudgingly, the petty annoyances and discomforts and worries which are sure to be felt."[60] She needed patience, a sense of humor, and a sacrificing spirit. Thackeray, it seems, had all of these. She was reportedly "extremely cultured," but was also a "force to be reckoned with."[61]

Above all, mission sources detailed, the work "absolutely requires a person with something of the *motherly instinct* in her"; an interest "in teaching will not do alone."[62] Intimate, affective relationships that imputed kinship were absolutely fundamental to motivating missionaries' work in East Africa and in creating a sense of fellow feeling among members of the congregation. Cultivating a love for Christ was paramount to the mission's project, but the day-to-day efforts to that end were also emotionally charged. Beginning in the earliest days of the mission, the emotive component of female missionaries' work was essential to creating ties that bound young freed slaves to the mission. The UMCA's single lady workers and their parentless charges, many of whom they raised from infancy, formed intimate, lifelong bonds within the boundaries of the schoolhouse and orphanage, and many considered their young charges to be their very own daughters and sons. The UMCA's female workers often brought the youngest of the orphans into their homes and raised them as their own. This was particularly true in the years before the establishment of the refuge for adult former slaves at Mbweni, when parentless youths were placed with established Christian couples or families, and before the first cohorts of Africans were old enough to raise orphans on their own. Like most of her fellow women workers, for example, Miss Pakeman considered the girls with whom she lived to be her own daughters. Writing about the marriages of Kate Kadamweli and Mary Aliangu, who had arrived with Kate, Pakeman wrote, "I am quite proud of my married daughters who are winning golden opinions by their nice, modest, staid behavior since they attained to the dignity of married life."[63] As an unmarried, childless woman, it is likely that Pakeman did indeed consider Kate and Mary to be family.

The missionaries' own "mothering" of the freed slave girls and their descendants was also a model for the budding female evangelists. Writing about her own days in the classroom, Caroline Thackeray recalled how intimately teaching and mothering were tied: "I cannot imagine a more happy life than that of being 'housemother' and head-teacher in one, in such a school, if only the whole heart is in it."[64] Although the mission's preoccupation with cultivating female evangelists had underwritten mission practice long before, Caroline Thackeray made an explicit statement of this philosophy in 1898. Regarding the UMCA's approach to their female congregants, she wrote:

> It is not only as teachers, but as wives and mothers of the next generation of African Christians, that we have to look to them. As a rule every native clergyman and teacher is married, and what these wives of the native clergy and teachers *are* will affect the next generation of African women far more than anything else that is done in the Mission . . . because I am persuaded that as the mothers *are* so will the children be, and if we can train well these girls, it may make centuries of difference to progress in Africa.[65]

The African mother had "a natural and God-given capacity," Thackeray added. "Africa's future depends much in an earthly sense on her women," she wrote, "nay, in more than an earthly sense, for is it not the law of God's providence that the mothers of the next generation will have the greatest share in the moulding of it?"[66] If planting an expansive and unified church was the missionaries' goal, an investment in the mission's female adherents was the means through which they hoped to achieve it. They focused their efforts first on raising wives for the African clergy and on cultivating female teachers for marriage to other Christian-educated evangelists, convinced that a strong cohort of African female evangelists who approached outreach through an embodied affective spirituality was the key to extending the mission's influence throughout East Africa and to cultivating communities of followers.

As single women, the UMCA's British lady workers were well poised to turn their "motherly instincts" and emotional attentions to their new charges. Women who may have wanted families of their own but who never had the opportunity, and women who desired children but not a marriage, could find in the UMCA ready daughters. Single ladies could invest wholeheartedly in raising orphans, boarders, and adult inquirers alike from a state of spiritual and civilizational infancy to fully formed Christians. Without their own kin, the mission's lady workers devoted their lives to mothering good Christian citizens; especially in the first decades of the mission's work, British mission workers acted as both "mother and father" for hundreds of orphaned slaves the mission raised. Caroline Thackeray also considered graduates of the Mbweni School to constitute her "large family."[67] The numerous obituaries that Caroline Thackeray wrote about former pupil-teachers during her tenure attest to what the missionaries considered to be the strong and enduring bonds between pupil and teacher, mother and daughter. She lamented in an obituary for Blandina Limo, a former pupil-teacher, that "to me she was as a daughter, and her affection, and thoughtfulness, and interest in all that concerned me, made her few visits to the little guest-cottage on my *shamba* always a delight."[68] Many of the UMCA's female missionaries wrote home proudly that their young charges seemed to return the sentiment. One missionary described feeling "real sympathy with the young lady of 18 who, on being invited to superannuate herself [from school], remarked, 'far indeed be such a thought from me and what should I do with all my days? And are you not my mother? Why then should I wish to leave you?'"[69] On her deathbed, Sister Agnes's "daughters" are said to have implored their "'more than mother' not to die, but to come back to them again."[70] The complex social structures and realities that shaped the nature of refugees' incorporation into the mission made the expressions of filial love flow both ways.

The lady missionaries' willingness to act in loco parentis did not overtly conflict with the refugees' need for guardians, but it was also not precisely the same sentiment. Indeed, the missionaries themselves might not have understood the difference between a "liberated" refugee who was presumed free to make her own decisions, and a girl driven to forge familial ties and to impute kinship as the only means at her disposal to secure access to resources and protection. The distinction was slight but meaningful, and obscured differences that would provoke conflict not long down the road.

An Asylum for Freed Slaves

The broader historical trends and political agreements that presented the mission with adherents also quickly led to its overcrowding. Rather than drift from their theological moorings, the administrators redoubled their efforts to ensure that their youngest adherents were receiving the attention and guidance they needed to develop into civilized Christians. This was particularly true for the younger female adherents, a group about which the mission worried endlessly given the role they would have in shaping the next generation of Christians. Regarding the daily work that was supposed to instill Christian values in their young charges, one mission worker mused that if the UMCA's girls are "to prosper, they must have constant supervision. If you want a thing done you must insist upon it . . . after a struggle they accept a thing as inevitable and so do it."[71] According to officials, mission girls were blessed with little in the way of role models from older refugees who are "fed, clothed, and supplied with rice . . . of course they are as lazy as they can stand, and why not? Why should they work? They have got all they want."[72] Thus to insulate their impressionable young adherents from the influences of adult *mateka*, the administration separated the congregation and employed fallow farm land for the purpose of "disposing of liberated slaves."[73] Administrators designated the land the "Mbweni *shamba*," and in so doing ascribed a name to the eventual home to generations of female evangelists.

In theory, such an "asylum" would provide respite opportunities for adult refugees, many of whom were generally "quite unfit for work" upon their arrival. The proposed scheme for the *shamba* indicated that "all persons received on the estate will be required to work under the direction of the manager and will be fed, clothed, and lodged by the mission." Until they formed "regular" (by which Steere would have meant "Christian") marriages, "men and women will be lodged apart, each sex having its own house and separate meals." Once married, couples would take up residence on a "model farm," which was to be "planted out in a kind of village . . . each couple in a cottage with small garden."[74] Each couple would "have a house built for them with a plot of land attached, and will be allowed one day a week to work it for their own profit." In lieu of food and clothing, a couple could choose payments, which would increase with length of time and aptitude for work.[75] All persons living on this "model farm" were required to "conduct themselves according to the general rules laid down by the Mission." These rules aimed to instill a "general orderliness of life," which required "no theft, drunkenness, fighting, immorality, or bad language." Of course, they must also observe "Sunday, the chief Christian Holy days, and such attendance at Church and School as may seem desirable." Failure to maintain this "general discipline" would be met with "stoppage of payments and privileges, and in gross cases by the authority of the Consul General."[76] Missionaries intended that *shamba* residents, not just the farm itself, would serve as a model to the rest of the congregation and to local observers.

The adult refugees were not the only ones on the receiving end of the missionaries' matchmaking attempts. The true work of the mission, administrators believed, was "to train missionaries and only indirectly for the benefit of released slaves." This was best done by creating Christian families from two individuals raised as Christians since childhood. By 1874 this had already begun to happen. Steere reported that the year opened auspiciously with the New Year's Day wedding of Elizabeth Kidogo and Vincent M'kono, two of the mission's first adherents, both of whom had been incorporated as children. In 1875, there were several additional marriages "being negotiated between the elders of the respective schools." This number included John Swedi and his fiancée, and Francis Mabruki and his fiancée, our Kate Kadamweli. Francis, John, and John's fiancée had arrived with Kate at the mission in 1865. The mission's attempts at social engineering were so effective that their success surprised even Steere: "I have been greatly amused at the utter contempt of the elder boys for any girls not brought up by us; they treat the idea of looking for a wife anywhere else as utterly preposterous."[77]

These engineered, monogamous marriages were important not only because they were the foundation of the ideal Christian family. The Christian mother, missionaries believed, had an inordinate influence on the development of the family, and on all that family came into contact with. During the 1820s and 1830s, mission organizations became aligned, at least in the eyes of the metropolitan public, with the burgeoning antislavery and humanitarian movements. New theories of overseas evangelism, such as those discussed in the previous chapter, forged an explicit association between evangelical Christianity, civilization, and commerce—the "Three C's." Missionaries and the supportive public came to understand cultivating among heathens the benefits of Christianity, education, and Western ways of living as among the goals of imperial outreach.[78] Missionary propaganda portrayed the objects of evangelical outreach as savage, depraved, and ignorant, with their women debased by all manner of social ills. This was particularly troubling to Western missionaries because contemporary social theorists had convinced them that the place women held within a society was a direct indication of the society's advancement from a state of barbarism to civilization. Indigenous women's piety and conversion, as historian Susan Thorne has argued, thus became the "crucial precondition of any culture's salvation," for, once converted, women could change the whole moral system of a society. No longer the "corner-stone of heathenism," their influence shifted and they became "natural repositories of religious piety." As wives and mothers, Christian women made "the home a haven safe from worldly temptations and the family the critical unit of worship."[79] In order to raise the civilizational quotient of an entire society, missionaries focused their work on indigenous girls, who they believed were in "desperate need of moral rescue." Their salvation—and indeed their entire society's salvation—would come through domestic education and basic literacy training.[80]

Just as with Kate's introduction to the mission, it is likely that relationships between British lady workers and African female refugees were not as straightforward as the missionaries imagined them to be. To begin, most of the above statements were elicited for printed sources aimed at metropolitan audiences for the purpose of raising funds or other support. The relationships would therefore have been rendered in terms familiar to readers, and in terms that missionaries expected or imagined to be true. Further, even without Tractarian religious obligation and the practical necessities of raising orphans, the missionaries would likely have felt pressure from the freed slaves themselves to become in loco parentis. Among the older orphans and unaccompanied young adults from the first cohorts of freed slaves, previous experience might have taught them to depend on their new masters for all their worldly necessities and spiritual guidance. Younger orphans would naturally have sought comfort in the people who raised and tended to them from infancy. Women in general, we have seen, were motivated by their inherent vulnerability to form familial, kinship, and affective ties with their patrons, rooting them more firmly in their new community. Of course, this is not to say that slaves did not come to develop fond relationships with their female patrons, or that they did not think of the missionaries as pseudo-parents, for there is evidence to suggest that they did. Rather, it is to say that the relationships of dependence were expected, very real, and very powerful, but at times ambiguous.

CHAPTER THREE

Industrials and Schoolgirls

Bonds of Personal Dependency and the Mbweni Girls' School, 1877–1890

The "asylum" for freed slaves at the UMCA's Mbweni *shamba* grew much more quickly than missionaries had either imagined or intended. Between 1875 and 1880, the population of the *shamba* nearly doubled in size from 150 people to 260—the latter a number that did not even include schoolchildren. In 1881 alone, the mission received more than 155 slaves from British anti-slave cruisers.[1] These numbers, which were far higher than missionaries felt they were equipped to handle, were due in large part to the change in the East African export market, and to the ironic results of the string of legal resolutions the British and others enacted in an attempt to abolish the slave trade.[2] To many, it appeared that Steere's warnings about rapid growth outstripping missionaries' capacity to teach and transform were indeed coming true, and that there was no end in sight.

Rev. N. Forbes Capel, who arrived in Zanzibar as an eager new worker early in 1876, was deeply critical of the situation he encountered. A self-described "revolutionist," Capel's enthusiasm for his work was quickly dampened by the realities of life at Mbweni; after four months with the mission, he was overcome by what he called the "deplorable state of things on the *shamba*."[3] Capel's concerns about the state of the mission can be boiled down to two related points: first, that the sheer number of adherents taxed the mission's resources, and second, that the social structures and labor practices that were emerging on the *shamba* contradicted what the missionaries had imagined for a Christian community. The disproportionate number of women seeking succor at the already overcrowded mission was a particular area of concern for the missionaries, in large part because they believed women needed special attention and moral guidance, given the fundamental role they would play in the biological and social reproduction of the Christian community. Lack of attention to the women, missionaries reasoned, had begun to show itself in the nature of the relationships that were developing on the *shamba* grounds.

When, in early 1877, Capel's colleague Rev. E. Randolph accepted a group of fifty refugees to be housed at Mbweni, Capel snapped. In a spate of tersely worded letters to his colleagues, Capel listed the reasons the UMCA should refuse the new additions. It was not merely "a question of feeding and clothing these fifty slaves," Capel wrote, but "it is the immorality of herding together quantities of savages with next to no power of supervision either morally or spiritually to which I object." As it was, Capel protested, the mission was not doing nearly enough "towards teaching and caring for the poor people."[4] He argued that the missionaries had failed to instill in their adherents the most basic of Christian values of communalism, hard work, and self-reliance since "there is not the slightest pressure" from anyone in the mission "to make them help themselves." The only work the Mbweni residents seemed to do was that which was required to retain their rights to the land, lodging, and board the mission provided in exchange for labor, and nothing more. Even that paltry work they did with such reluctance, he insisted, that it was in effect "as much forced labour as West Indian labour used to be." Ultimately, Capel lamented, he could not see how the refugees were "being bettered. If tomorrow they were to change masters and Mohammed bin Ali were to take the place of Dr. Steere," he wrote, "I do not imagine they would know any difference, except perhaps that they would have rather more freedom . . . and be a little less discontented than they at present are."[5] "Knowing all this," he continued in a letter addressed directly to Randolph, "how can you seek to burden us with the care of fifty additional people? Have they no souls? . . . The past neglect of the people is already in my opinion, a shame and a scandal." He threatened to resign if the newcomers remained on the *shamba*.

Even more troubling to Capel were the social dynamics that had grown up among women at the *shamba*. The typical female student at Mbweni struck him, he lamented, as far from ideal. "Compared with their fellow country-women," Capel told the bishop, "the girls are being brought up as *ladies*. The result is that they are proud and stuck up, that they look upon work as a degradation." Even worse, he revealed, is that they "despise and revile the 'slaves' as they term them, on the *shamba*." And, when the young women of Mbweni married, they themselves tended to "keep a slave, and of course, do nothing—except gossip." "This may be African," he wrote, "but it is not Christian."[6]

Over the next ten years, the missionaries devised a plan to address both the overcrowding of the women's spaces, and what they characterized as the "non-Christian" social dynamics and labor practices. This plan comprised an investment in women's education in the form of two separate educational tracks at the *shamba*'s Mbweni Girls' School—one track for "Schoolgirls" and one for "Industrials." Far from bastardizing Christian principles, *shamba* residents were actually mapping the very lessons missionaries taught them about patronage and dependency onto the inherited ideologies of community and kinship that shaped refugees' engagement with the mission. Indeed, the UMCA's missionaries themselves pursued labor practices that were deeply hypocritical, but adherents saw in them valuable opportunities to establish affective relationships, to stitch together new kinship ties, and to embed themselves more forcibly and securely into the mission community. The tracked system of education enshrined, rather than eliminated, these labor practices and social dynamics among *shamba* residents and Mbweni graduates. The search for belonging, familial ties, and kinship networks characterized the nature of relationships first between refugees and missionaries, then between Schoolgirls and Industrials, and finally the evangelical relationship itself. As the *shamba* and in particular the Mbweni Girls' School emerged as the ideological and geographical heart of the mission from which evangelical and affective relationships migrated out over the next several generations, these relationship ideals underwrote their approach to evangelism on the mainland.

From *Shamba* to School, 1881–1887

The UMCA was not the only abolitionist mission struggling in the 1870s and 1880s. Rosters of missions across the eastern African coast swelled, the numbers straining resources and the diversity of new congregants taxing the plans and patience of administrators. In the Church Missionary Society's Freretown settlement in Mombasa, for example, arrivals of freed *mateka* overwhelmed the mission's capabilities.

The children were ill, the setting too new, and the missionaries too impatient. "The children we could easily manage," an exasperated missionary wrote, "but the adults are simply a lot of idle savages, and until they can be made to understand their position and our kind feelings toward them we shall have something to do to keep order."[7] The mission's lay workers, who were Africans educated at the CMS's mission schools in India and brought to Kenya for the purpose of educating new adherents, also frustrated the missionaries. The "Bombay Africans," as they were known, were a "continual clog and hindrance to the work," despondent missionaries asserted, complaining of their "idleness, carelessness, and shoddy workmanship."[8] Soon after the CMS established the Freretown settlement, slaves from Mombasa absconded, streaming into the station and begging for asylum. Whereas the Freretown missionaries could work with government *maliwai* to return runaways to their masters when the space got overcrowded, the UMCA's island location provided them slightly less flexibility to return Africans for whom they did not have room.

The Holy Ghost Fathers, one of four other mission organizations working in Tanzania and Zanzibar by the late 1870s, also worked with freed slaves and by the early 1880s had become dissatisfied with their approach. The Fathers did not produce a single serious candidate for holy orders and despaired of ever finding one among freed slaves. Their work often felt more like political machinations than evangelism.[9] The newer mission societies, including the CMS, the LMS, and the White Fathers, were eschewing work among freed slaves for work with discrete "peoples" further inland. These missions, the UMCA included, also felt the pressure of the Islamic revival happening along the coast during the late 1800s and early 1900s. The Quadiriyya brotherhood carried Islam further into the interior, extending the reach of Arab and Swahili caravan traders and leading to the first extensive acceptance of Islam by communities on the mainland.[10]

While official mission propaganda and missionaries' letters home described Mbweni in the mid- to late 1870s as "prospering" and "better cared for than ever before," private correspondence tended toward the more critical, and workers quibbled back and forth with what seem like endless complaints.[11] The appearance and cleanliness of the house and of the girls was "disappointing," they said.[12] The dining hall was "a dreadful hole, always as close and hot as it can be." With no ventilation, the room never cooled and "anything like fresh air is unknown."[13] The drainage from the roof to the girls' dormitory was so poor that in the rainy season the girls "generally sleep on a wet floor."[14] Things seemed to missionaries little better inside the schools. Even if the adult population on the *shamba* continued to decline, missionaries reasoned, failure in the schools would have been disastrous—the whole future of the mission rested on producing an educated Native Clergy. Capel spent a great deal of time "carrying proper order and discipline into the system of the girls' school" during his time at Mbweni because, as he pointed out, "tho we may live without carpenters, tailors or washermen, we cannot live without native teachers."[15] If things were not ideal at the boys' schools, the girls' school seemed to be in particularly dire straits. "After four months experience," Capel penned in yet another letter of complaint, this time to the bishop himself, "I am of the opinion that the school wants revolutionizing. The present system seems to me false." The female scholars were hard to train, missionaries complained in their logs and letters home. They were stubborn, they were insubordinate, and they were willfully disobedient, missionaries wrote. Responses from students indicated that they failed to see the relevance of their education: Nine-year-old Chela explained that she refused to attend classes because "learning is not property, I don't want to learn!"[16] To Chela, who was born into a society that valued people as the basis of wealth, and raised at a time when accumulating people was paramount, accumulating book knowledge must have seemed an implausible way to get ahead in life.

As someone new to mission work, it is possible that naïveté and misplaced enthusiasm had raised Capel's expectations and, once disillusioned, he painted a picture of Mbweni far worse than it deserved. Yet, Capel was not ignorant of the demands of *shamba* life—for nine years he had served as the UMCA's honorary organizing secretary in England, "generously and unweariedly devoting his whole energies without remuneration to the cause."[17] Part of his duties as honorary organizing secretary even included touring the mission's stations on Zanzibar in 1875. While there, he felt the call to service and shortly thereafter resigned his secretaryship for a life in the field. Capel was tasked with supervising the *shamba* and the girls' school. Not long after he assumed his duties, he came to see that everyday life on the *shamba* bore little resemblance to what he had envisioned.

In addition to his long list of complaints, Capel offered recommendations for reform. "I believe," he wrote, that instead of allowing what he saw as the gossiping, the "slave holding," and the otherwise lackluster moral development of the *shamba* girls to continue, "a better course would be to put out such big girls as are not wanted in the house, to work on the *shamba*."[18] In other words, what Capel was proposing was that the mission remove women made "troublesome" by their age, unmarried state, or other refusal to fit within mission expectations of their behavior from the schoolhouse and evangelical framework altogether. Rather than try to groom "rebellious" women into lay evangelists, the mission should instead remove them entirely from the physical spaces of the mission where learning and moral development took place. This, Capel believed, would allow the mission to keep the "scholastic element" and the cultivation of a native ministry "prominently in the front as of paramount importance" to the mission's work. "In my view, nothing is of equal importance with the scholastic element as leading to a native priesthood," including educating those whom he believed to be the more unsavory members of the mission's congregation.[19] What Capel proposed was a way for the mission to remain focused on the needs of the Native Clergy, without being burdened by the demands, individual personalities, contingencies, and expectations of individuals who did not immediately fit the mission's objectives.

Despite Capel's enthusiasm for reform, change was slow to come to Mbweni. And when it did, it took the fresh eyes of a new bishop and nearly a decade of repeated complaints by Mbweni's headmistress. Bishop Steere succumbed to a stroke on August 27, 1881, and the mission was "widowed" for just over two years.[20] The organization finally found a suitable leader in Charles Alan Smythies, also a Cambridge man. Before he was bishop, Smythies was the vicar of Roath in Llandaff Diocese in southern Wales. A former colleague there described him as having great "ability and assiduity" as well as "patience, tenderness and courage," and as having "labored to set free and teach individual souls"—all of which were traits Mbweni and the rest of the mission desperately needed. Smythies oversaw a flourishing mission. In 1867 the mission had sent its first evangelists to the mainland, where they established stations in the region of what is today Tanga and the Usambara Mountains.[21] In part to relieve the creeping claustrophobia, the UMCA sent fifty-five freed slaves from the *shamba* to the mainland at Masasi, an area inland and to the south of Lindi near the border with Mozambique, in 1876. They settled in the dry, rocky ground of southern Tanzania and continued the mission's expansion to the mainland. Removing the Masasi congregation failed to permanently relieve the population pressure, however. By 1880 the companionate pairs the mission had been so keen to see grow into nuclear families were beginning to realize what Bishop Steere had quipped were "their indefinite powers of addition": in those five years, the *shamba* had grown to include 230 adults alone, 200 of whom were married couples with 30 young children among them.[22]

As soon as Smythies arrived in Zanzibar in February 1884, he saw the "strain of over-fatigue" to which Mbweni's supervisors, Miss Thackeray and Miss Berkeley, were subjected. While some of the strain seemed to come from a lack of trained assistants, the bishop believed that the responsibility of keeping girls who were unsuited or undisposed toward teaching out of trouble until they married was the heaviest of the ladies' burdens. The pool of suitable young men for educated African Christian women was relatively small, Smythies lamented, because they could not marry either "Mahommedans or heathen." The only option missionaries felt they had was to remove young women whose behavior was "not satisfactory" from the house altogether, either to live in the single women's home and work in the fields, or to face excommunication. Thackeray did just this to an unnamed girl in 1885. By her very presence in the house she was "doing so much harm among the small girls," and she was thus banished to the single women's house at Mbweni, where she would be "quite out of the girls' bounds." Forbidden to even go near the school grounds, her education was over. The anonymous girl, although not befitting the ideal of a Christian girl, was apparently not so objectionable that she could not be put to work in service of the mission. Under the charge "of an older person in the single women's house" she did manual labor instead.[23]

The solution, as Smythies saw it, was not to battle with unmotivated, bored, or lackluster students in the classroom but to put some of the girls, particularly those who "shewed no capacity for the work of a teacher," under "different rules" and a different roof.[24] Separating the girls into teachers-in-training and "others" would not only solve their immediate behavioral and space challenges, he believed, but it had a host of other benefits. There was little need to go on producing teachers at the rate they had been, Smythies pointed out. "As yet the country is not prepared for the higher education of women," he noted; "all they need is a good elementary education. Even for teachers we have but a limited demand; we need enough to supply the places of those who marry and leave the school, but we do not find we can use any women as teachers elsewhere." Smythies was concerned not just about misdirecting the mission's resources by investing in women who were not prepared to make full use of the education, but also about the effect that an unnecessarily advanced education would have on a young woman's marriage prospects.[25]

Smythies's decision to separate future teachers and clerics' wives from those girls who were either unfit or undisposed to be either marks the tentative first steps toward realizing Capel's suggestions from an earlier decade. (Despite once claiming that a loss of faith in the mission would be "pretty much like cutting off my right arm," the reverend was not around to rejoice; he had resigned amidst concerns about the mission's future several years earlier.[26]) Smythies's solution hewed closely to Capel's in that it did not yet institutionalize an educative program for those who were uninclined toward teaching. It did, however, remove them from the schoolhouse and set them toward more domestically productive tasks. This new scheme began in 1885 with twelve girls who, at fifteen or so, were "too old to go on any longer in school" but desperately needed to be "out of the schoolroom, and free from school-girls' rules as much as possible."[27] The girls would "form quite a separate establishment" under the watchful eye of May Allen, a worker from Shropshire, England.

The daughter of an archdeacon, Allen grew up hearing her father's employer, Bishop Selwyn—the intrepid former bishop of New Zealand whom we met in chapter 1—preach the values of foreign service. The idea of outreach resonated with Allen, who trained as a nurse not because she particularly wanted to practice medicine, but because it was one of the few opportunities for women to "serve." Fresh out of nursing school, May Allen worked as superintendent of the Convalescent Home for Ladies in Scarborough. She would do much the same when she arrived in Zanzibar, initiating the first hospital work at the central mission house at Mkunazini. She also spent time in town, proselytizing to urban Muslim women who were confined to their homes due either to domestic obligations or to a combination of class and religious prescriptions that required elite women to observe purdah, or seclusion, during the daylight hours.[28]

Tending to the ill and recalcitrant seemed ample preparation for work with this "troublesome" group of women. Allen immediately arranged for the girls to occupy a separate space, which was essentially a shed with a *makuti* (coconut leaf) roof.[29] It was, as far as the missionaries understood, local "custom" for women to work on the land, and each of the twelve students received a grant of land that they would cultivate as part of their studies. The girls would "work all day in the garden and on the land round the house under an overlooker." These skills would be "most useful to them," Smythies reasoned, because "a husband often values his wife in proportion as she is good at helping him to cultivate his ground."[30] Anticipating some resistance from the new cohort of women, Smythies lectured them about the reasons behind his decision. As soon as children in England were old enough to leave school, he told the girls, they worked "because: (1) we had found out that the only way to be happy was to work; (2) Because it was the only way to keep out of sin."[31] Idle hands make the devil's work, world round.

This was little more than a temporary fix designed to meet the immediate needs of these twelve "troublesome" girls, and administrators longed for something more permanent. In 1885 Caroline Thackeray wished "more than ever" for "some

UNDATED PHOTOGRAPH, FROM "MBWENI PAPERS," *AFRICAN TIDINGS* 20, NO. 263 (SEPTEMBER 1911).

FIGURE 6. The Industrial Wing at Mbweni Girls' School.

outlet for those of our elder girls who are indifferent scholars—either from having come late into the house or want of capacity for books." According to Thackeray, "there will always be a proportion of such and they both form a very troublesome element in the school." Thus, she proposed that they might be "far better trained and happier for the two or three years before they marry in an Industrial Home, with rules and regulations in many ways different from those which suit a school."[32] In the end, missionaries adopted a more moderate version of Capel's proposal, choosing instead to separate women of schoolgoing age into two tracks: a track for Schoolgirls and a track for Industrials. The name for the latter derived from industrial schools in Britain, which were essentially vocational reformatories. In particular, the Industrial Wing was named after the Clewer Industrial School. Founded in 1852, Clewer was initially established as a refuge for prostitutes who wanted to leave the streets.[33] Rather than send women who were "given over to evil living" to a penitentiary for reform, as was popular at the time, they were put to work.[34] Some of the same assumptions that characterized the Anglican response to prostitutes also characterized UMCA missionaries' assumptions about African women. Plans were undertaken and the school was set to open in late 1887, about a decade after Capel's earliest complaints.[35] In offering a tracked system of education to its female adherents, the UMCA was not unique, as a wide range of missions recognized their adherents had different needs, skills, and personal capacities. Indeed, the UMCA already funneled their male adherents into different tracks for vocational and clerical workers. However, the labor practices at the mission and the particular vulnerabilities of women in late-nineteenth-century East Africa combined to produce a unique focus on personal relationships that underwrote the mission's expansion to the mainland.

Labor and Relationships of Personal Dependency

Ironically, Mbweni's tracked system of education was built upon, and in fact further enshrined, the very social dynamics missionaries had hoped to eliminate. The similarities between the missionaries' own labor practices and the relationships of patronage and dependency that their female refugees used as a pathway to intrude more forcibly into new communities and to reduce their marginality, point to one of the deepest paradoxes of the UMCA: namely, that although the missionaries were self-proclaimed abolitionists and some of the most notable critics of slavery, the mission itself relied heavily on African labor—including slave labor—to carry out its evangelical project. In a highly visible example, Bishop Steere was posthumously accused of employing slave labor to build the Slave Market Memorial Church at Mkunazini, a building intended to represent the "presumed affinity between Christianity and anti-slavery" and stood as a "home of freedom" for "all colours and races."[36] Steere had initially planned to have freed slaves build the church, but they did not possess the skills for the work he needed done. They thus remained largely confined to labor on the Mbweni plantation, where they harvested coral to be used in the construction of the cathedral walls. Instead, he employed skilled hire-slaves, including Hindu masons, who were of the highest class of manual laborers in Zanzibar.[37]

Missionaries rationalized this apparent contradiction in several ways. First, they argued that building the cathedral required a level and variety of skills that the mission's freed slaves did not possess. This was no doubt true, but it rankled members of the local British administration and staff in the UMCA's home office nonetheless. Second, although the slave trade was officially outlawed, the use of slaves as servants or laborers remained legal for British subjects outside of

British dominions. By 1888, it was finally illegal for British subjects to hire slaves through the slave master, but one could still arrange a contract directly with the slave herself.[38] And third, the missionaries believed in the biblical significance of labor and servitude. UMCA missionaries, like others of their time,[39] argued that the condition of slavery took away an individual's freedom to choose and removed their authority over their own body, stifling the development of any incentive for self-improvement or morality. Once freed, Africans could undertake wage labor, which the missionaries understood as having a host of other benefits. The UMCA's brand of Christianity was steeped in agricultural metaphors and allusions to church work as a way of serving God; missionaries commonly referred to themselves as "workers" or "labourers for the master's harvest." One freed slave described his journey from the slave trade to the mission with a similar trope: "I was going to be sold away to Pemba, but Jesus carried me away to be His servant, and now I am trying to serve Him." Missionaries also believed Christian wage labor taught the dignity of labor and encouraged better "habits" and "improvement." Missionaries argued that although the "Arab" slave owner "might not be as cruel as the English slave owner in the Americas, the absence of wages still hindered productivity and diligence." Labor also helped maintain efficiency and a social hierarchy.[40]

Ultimately, the mission approached the all-important question of labor more as employers attempting to understand and engage with particular local labor customs than as zealous abolitionists. While the missionaries realized that rejecting local customs outright was futile, they worked to produce Christian workers from within the mission itself.[41] This approach satisfied both their abolitionist and evangelical goals. Paradoxically, the UMCA's ambition to create a self-sustaining Christian labor force and community out of freed slaves essentially meant that while the new congregants had ceased to be "slaves" in the legal sense, they remained so in practice. As we have seen, the UMCA's congregants were often treated as slaves; it is also likely that they continued to see themselves as the subordinate partner in a relationship of dependency. Indeed, despite the missionaries' theoretical and theological commitments to abolition, the ideology of client slavery continued to regulate the lives of congregants on the *shamba*; they were known colloquially, as we have seen, as *watumwa wa balozi* ("slaves of the [British] consul") or *watumwa wa wangereza* ("slaves of the British"). *Mateka* would have been familiar if not comfortable with this relationship; freeborn mission Christians would have assumed these relationships to be natural, knowing no other way of life.

This complicated relationship to labor was not uncommon within late nineteenth-century British missions in East Africa. Indeed, historians have observed contradictions between Christian ideas of freedom and Christian ideas of labor throughout the continent. Africans on the Swahili Coast often thought of their missionary neighbors as yet another brand of trading chief or warlord, one who "competed for political hegemony by the time-honored technique of building up followings of slaves."[42] There are many examples of conditions that appeared, for all intents and purposes, to be slavery. Contemporaries regarded the working conditions in the Church Missionary Society (CMS) stations in Kenya, for example, as having surpassed the hardships of Swahili plantation slavery. Several scandals at CMS stations near Mombasa and on the central caravan route near Mpwapwa illustrate the often brutal working conditions many congregants faced. After watching a CMS worker cruelly beat an adherent for committing fornication, one Mombasa slave concluded that "it is much better to be the slave of an Arab than the slave of a European."[43] At Bagamoyo in the late 1870s, villagers worked twelve hours a day, five days a week for the mission, and received food, clothing, and a plot of land to cultivate in any spare time. Church attendance was mandatory, there was a curfew at 10:00 P.M., and no resident might leave the village without permission. Minor offenses were punished by "penances," more serious ones by imprisonment.[44] Indeed, "slaves who sought to escape a brutal master by taking refuge with the Christians were often disappointed to find that the daily mission regimen of work, prayer and corporal punishment was harsher than that which they had left behind."[45]

At the UMCA one found similar conditions. As Capel himself noted, the missionaries forced their congregants to work for the land they farmed, the clothes they wore, and the food they ate. Officials told newcomers where to live, whom to marry, and to whom they should pray. They punished people by withholding their payment and food, and when that did not work, by banishing them from the community altogether. African children and adolescents often worked as domestic laborers, a concession to the high costs of running a mission, which the missionaries rationalized as industrial education. Work included cleaning, cooking, collecting water, serving food, maintaining the grounds, and waiting on the missionaries. Failure to complete assigned tasks was an opportunity to teach discipline and to enforce the missionaries' vision of a Christian work ethic.[46] And, once on the station, the refugees remained outsiders without any social or kin ties on the island, except—and this is significant—for those with the UMCA missionaries who had settled them on the station. Missionaries did provide hope for some refugees, in that they could offer the sustenance and protection any powerful patron would offer in return for loyalty, as well as new familial and kinship ties. Refugees had many reasons to invest in the relationships of dependency, family, and kinship that the missionaries, and alliance with the mission community, offered.

Significantly, while UMCA missionaries used labor and relationships of patronage and dependency to create Christians, they objected when Africans tried to do the same. Capel watched the *shamba* women and determined that they "kept slaves," objecting to this behavior on the grounds that it was not "Christian." Yet the missionaries' complex theological understanding of the spiritual benefits of wage labor was often invisible to the *shamba* residents. By employing slave labor, by tightly controlling their congregants' daily labor and schedule, and by providing refugees with patronage and security, the mission blurred the lines between slave master and evangelist. It is thus not surprising that the congregants acted in ways that did not live up to what the missionaries believed they were preaching. By following the missionaries' lead, the *shamba* residents managed to create complex social hierarchies and relationships of patronage and dependency on the *shamba*—relationships that both mimicked those modeled by their Tractarian leaders, and resembled social structures and dynamics of the societies from which they had come.

The institutionalization of the Schoolgirl and Industrial tracks likely seemed to its participants to be a logical or natural outgrowth of existing circumstances, as they had experienced no other system. Pupils at the Mbweni Girls' School might have been even more willing to engage in this new system as they were unlikely to have imagined one's determination as an Industrial or a Schoolgirl as static or prescribed. Rather, drawing on inherited ideas of personal dependency, the Mbweni students were much more likely to have seen the missionaries' formally "tracked" educational system as fluid and contingent. Much like the status of coastal slavery itself, the Industrials' was a marginality that they imagined could be reduced to manageable proportions, eliminated altogether over the course of several generations, or remedied immediately by a calculated marriage, suitable adoption, or by imputing other forms of kinship.

In many cases, an African Schoolgirl patron might have seemed at least as desirable as a British missionary, or in many ways largely indistinguishable. Indeed, the same relationships of fosterage, mentorship, and fictive kinship that grew up between British missionaries and female adherents also existed between female adherents themselves. As early as 1871, church administrators began to place young female orphans in the homes of adult freed slaves whom they settled at the Mbweni *shamba*. These relationships were likely familiar to the participants, many of whom may have arrived to the mission as slaves via pawning or another form of temporary fosterage or exchange. Fosterage has a long history in many parts of Africa. Adoption, fostering on a temporary basis (including but not limited to pawnship), and various forms of support or investment in children by interested relatives, acquaintances, or clients allowed precolonial Africans to negotiate, between individuals and among communities, the rights and responsibilities that attend parenthood. Conventionally, relationships of fosterage in precolonial Africa had enormous advantages for guardians. Foster children could provide extra labor to an elderly couple or infertile woman, perform domestic or market chores, or take care of younger children or infirm members of the household. Foster parents could attempt to claim additional benefits such as access to certain social networks, or future benefits such as bridewealth payments or straight cash assistance. Such arrangements allowed prospective parents to reap the benefits afforded by children irrespective of any limitations placed on fertility by biology or the life cycle. The ability to cultivate foster relationships in the absence or felt paucity of biological children would thus have been particularly attractive to women. [47] Biological parents negotiated foster relationships in order to secure an apprenticeship for their child, access to social networks to which they themselves were not privy, or other social or religious training or guidance. Children entered foster homes for trade apprenticeships, to train in the domestic arts, and particularly in areas with large Muslim populations, for Islamic education with private teachers.[48]

Evangelical communities in late precolonial and colonial Africa relied heavily on fosterage as a tool for social reproduction. In CMS communities in Nigeria, for example, Igbo clerics' wives trained Igbo children in Christian living. In addition to raising their own children, missions encouraged young Christian wives to take in "a few of the children of other, aspiring families and train them about Christianity, sanitation, and the proper care of a 'modern' household." These children acted as "household help for their foster mother while gaining access to the Christian networks that could eventually mean school, employment with the colonial administration or, at least, an enhanced understanding of the new regime."[49]

UMCA adherents and mission workers cultivated similar relationships, first in Zanzibar and later within mainland communities. Kate Kadamweli, one of the first female adherents at Mbweni, participated in several such foster relationships with women the mission considered "wayward" or "lapsed."[50] Elizabeth Kidogo was one such "notorious bad woman" from the Mbweni *shamba* who spent the last few years of her life in Kate's home.[51] Other *shamba* women in good standing with the church looked after younger engaged women immediately before their weddings by acting as stand-ins for absent mothers, for those unwilling to participate in a Christian marriage, or for those the church deemed unsuitable parents. These foster mothers helped prepare young Christian women for marriage by helping to finalize their domestic or academic educations before the wedding, and worked to ensure chastity during engagements. Once a young Christian woman reached puberty, she was subject to a higher level of scrutiny from church administrators and their female interlocutors; if a Christian mother was not around to look out for the young woman's virtue, church officials called on certain well-respected women to look after her. Records from the 1910s affirm that this practice remained a valuable tool for decades. On June 30, 1919, Louiza Kachija apparently "reached puberty" and was sent by church administrators to live with one Rhoda Kemblu in the hopes that *Mama* Kemblu would watch over her until a suitable match was made. In another case, *Mwalimu* Louisa Numbi, the wife of an African cleric, mentored Mbweni student Fibi Salama in Zanzibar for some time before her wedding.[52] When it came time for Fibi to attend the church's obligatory pre-marriage counseling sessions, it was Mwalimu Numbi who attended as Fibi's guardian. Another young woman, Faith Naubri, attended the *shauri* with them, perhaps in preparation for her own marriage.[53] Fibi married Mkabi bin Majanja of Pemba on June 2, 1919, and they returned to Pemba to live.[54] Mama Logi, a member of the Zanzibar mission, took on a formal, paid position caring for Neema Heri, a woman "who does not want to be married."[55]

In the late 1880s, UMCA adherents, particularly those just entering the mission as refugees, might have been even more willing to engage in a range of relationships that offered them security, even if they seem undesirable to the modern-day reader. German commercial expansion on the mainland had just begun, exacerbating unrest and turmoil in some regions. Changing social and political relationships on the mainland might have made students even more willing to engage in a social hierarchy that they knew and that promised inclusion, rather than in one that was largely unknown.

The Mbweni Girls' School Industrial Wing

On Monday, November 21, 1887, the Industrial Wing of the Mbweni Girls' School opened to much fanfare. With the help of Archdeacon Hodgson, the girls decorated the walls inside and out with pennants left over from their celebration of Queen Victoria's Golden Jubilee five months to the day prior. There were palms and flowers, too, from Mbweni's gardens. The embellished white coral rag shone in the bright sun of that rainless day, which was a rare treat at that time of year. At four-thirty in the afternoon, as the sun was making its descent and the hottest time of day had passed, a procession formed at the girls' school. Mr. Allen, a British missionary, went first, followed by the Reverend Cecil Majaliwa. Cecil had become a dependent of the mission when he was rescued from HMS *Dryad* on June 1, 1871, at the age of six, but had quickly risen through the church ranks to attend Kiungani, the UMCA's boys' school and theological training college, and then Saint Augustine's College in England. When he returned to Zanzibar he was ordained as the first African priest of Tanganyika.[56] Epitomizing the mission's successes, Cecil took pride of place in the day's procession, walking in front of the bishop and carrying his staff. The British teachers and nurses followed Bishop Smythies. The "Native Christians" brought up the rear, proceeding in reverse hierarchical order: first came the new Industrials, in blue dresses with scarves and red *kofias* (hats); then the pupil-teachers and first-class girls, both wearing red chintz dresses with white accessories; and last of all, the head class from Kiungani.[57] The procession was far from somber, buoyed by the sounds of hymns and by the words of Psalm 67, recited as a prayer for the enlargement of Christ's kingdom:

> God be merciful unto us, and bless us: and show us the light of his countenance, and be merciful unto us:
> That thy way may be known upon earth: thy saving health among all nations.
> Let the people praise thee, O God: yea, let all the people praise thee.
> O let the nations rejoice and be glad: for thou shalt judge the folk righteously, and govern the nations upon earth.
> Let the people praise thee, O God: let all the people praise thee.
> Then shall the earth bring forth her increase: and God, even our own God, shall give us his blessing.
> God shall bless us: and all the ends of the world shall fear him.[58]

UNDATED PHOTOGRAPH, FROM "THE INDUSTRIAL WING AT MBWENI," *AFRICAN TIDINGS* 1, NO. 38 (DECEMBER 1892).

FIGURE 7. A group of unnamed Industrials at Mbweni, including the missionaries Ms. Key, Ms. Thackeray, and Ms. R. Berkeley.

As with Israel, if the Lord would bless the UMCA, the community might, in turn, be a blessing to the world.[59] The bishop said more prayers for the congregation to call all people to God, and the group recited prayers and sang hymns throughout the corridors and rooms. The first of two tea receptions followed. The Europeans crowded into one of the classrooms, where they socialized at tables, sheltered from the now setting sun. The children, eating fruit while they squatted on the verandah, would have watched dhows, silhouetted by the setting sun, glide past on their way from the Stone Town harbor. The second tea party was the next day, with all the teachers, married and single, and the Schoolgirls in attendance; the new Industrials were not invited to partake in sweets and biscuits consumed in their honor, for they were already ensconced in their new roles, cooking and serving behind the scenes.

The story of Fayida, who as we recall had arrived at the mission in April 1893 by way of HMS *Philomel* after a long trek to the coast with her brother, illustrates what might be thought of as the typical experiences of a young woman who found herself on the roster of the Industrial Wing. Fayida likely entered the Industrial Wing in 1895 or so, once it had been up and running for nearly a decade, and by a path that would have been common to those who preceded and followed her on the rosters. Early reports of Fayida were not flattering. Without the Industrial Wing she might have quickly been deemed a "troublesome element" and jettisoned from the school entirely. Indeed, workers reported that Fayida "gave a good deal of trouble at Mbweni." She was, they said, "what her bringing up made her—weakly, timid and deceitful, and occasionally given to terrible fits of passion." Having arrived at the mission at age ten or eleven, Fayida would have had memories of home, of a family who loved her, and of a traumatic dislocation from all that she knew. Speaking neither Kiswahili nor English, she was likely lonely, homesick, and scared. Pain and resentment no doubt fueled those early "fits of passion." After a year or so, however, she settled into her new life and began to flourish.

At approximately twelve years old, Fayida began to prepare for baptism. We cannot know for sure if Fayida's heart was changed, but it is easy to imagine that Fayida took stock of her situation and made a resourceful decision. By 1895 the UMCA was one among several options Fayida was likely to have known about—the fledgling hierarchies offered by the German colonial administration on the mainland and Arab masters on Zanzibar were others. Revolts attended the imposition of German rule, and individuals from many sectors of coastal society and of communities farther inland resisted. The encroachment of the German colonial presence further destabilized areas along the caravan routes, particularly after 1890.[60] After what she'd endured, life in the Industrial house was surely better than a life lived largely in the field, or in exile. Of course, Mbweni staff credited Fayida's engagement with the "main truths of our religion" and her mastery of the Creed, the Lord's Prayer, the Ten Commandments, and the simple Catechism for allowing "her real character . . . to show itself." "For sheer plodding," one lady missionary wrote, "I have seldom met her equal." She seemed to not care for reading other than religious tracts, nor really to be "clever enough at book-learning to make a school-mistress." The girl who seemed born for domestic work, with hands and arms that were "strong and delicate, that of a craftsman from shoulder to finger-tips," thus made her home among the other "domestics."[61]

Like the other girls without "an aptitude for teaching," Fayida would have taken up residence in one of the two dormitories that made up the second level of the long, narrow white house built of coral rock and lime that adjoined the school chapel and the schoolhouse. Less a bed than a mat, her sleeping pad would have been adorned with a patchwork quilt stitched by a ladies auxiliary group back in England, and with the cards or trinkets that her British patrons sent her. The dormitories were accessible from an outside verandah through the bedroom of a *Bibi*, or British lady worker, set up to double as a "guard post" to keep the girls in, young men out, and virtue intact. The upper verandah, which faced west toward the sea, offered "the prettiest views of Mbweni," which was indeed saying something as the entire site offers magnificent views toward the coast and setting sun. Above, the large flat roof often served as a dance floor on bright moonlit nights. Below, leading to five rooms, was the ground floor verandah, which was a popular spot for sitting and gossiping between chores or after a long day of work. One of the five rooms was a sitting room for the *Bibi*s, one a lamp room, and the third storage, where the girls kept their personal items and clothes.[62] The practical blue frocks the girls wore nearly every day hung on pegs or sat folded in cubbies. These dresses, stitched by mission patrons in England out of the very same material used for dresses worn in the British workhouses after which the Industrial Wing was modeled, were both cheap and durable.[63] The girls' white dresses would have been tucked away for special occasions, such as church holidays, Sundays, and weddings, safe from the red dust and coarse sand that was constantly tracked in by bare feet. The wing's two other rooms, both quite large in size, are where Fayida and her classmates would have done their laundry work, studied their lessons, and prepared and eaten their meals—all separate, of course, from the main house.

Safely out of the classroom and away from girls the mission considered to be the more serious scholars, Fayida and her classmates practiced, as UMCA adherents always had, Western habits of personal hygiene: washing with soap, wearing clothes, and keeping their living spaces clean and tidy. They were also expected to learn to value—even covet—certain material goods, such as their blue "working girl" frocks and the lace that bordered their special-occasion white dresses. By the time they descended the stairs for the day's lessons, they had transformed once again from slaves to the living embodiments of the "Three C's" that Livingstone and others espoused as the remedy for the slave trade. Becoming a Christian "does not simply mean a changed soul," one Quaker missionary living among the Maragoli in Kenya wrote to her parents, "it also means a changed life."[64]

As for classes, the missionaries' Tractarianism meant that the Industrial curriculum would be a mix of Victorian domestic values and what the missionaries believed to be "indigenous custom." As we have seen, the UMCA was determined to build a Native Church, an institution they defined as adapted to the "special circumstances of the race and the country" in which they worked.[65] In such a church, the essential core of Tractarian doctrine would remain intact, as would the movement's emphasis on, for example, sacramentalism, ritualism, and reserve. They sensed a need to compromise on the incorporation of certain forms of expression and of longer-standing African practices into the new church; for example, UMCA workers deemed asceticism, retirement, and the monastic ideal as unsuited to African life and thought it wise to permit African clerics to marry, for the purpose of growing the church—both biologically and socially. British missionaries were not prepared, however, to concede on the issue of polygamy, and they staunchly advocated for only monogamous marriages between two autonomous individuals. These concessions and adaptations were not fixed, but were sites for contestation over the ability to define the church's borders and to stake out membership within the church community, as we shall see.

The Industrial girls learned that cleanliness was next to godliness and developed a healthy respect for the value of clean clothes, for example, but they were taught to wash only "in native fashion." "Perhaps you will say, 'Why not teach them English ways?'" asked one missionary rhetorically about this plan. "But, you see, we have to look to the future. These girls will soon have to live in a native hut up country, and the cost would be great indeed to carry tubs, mangle, and all the plan required for an English laundry to a far-off station. But now these girls take a wooden tray to wash upon their heads, a bucket, and a charcoal iron, and they can go hundreds of miles up country and have all they require for this work." Clean clothes would prove their Christian virtue even in the far corners of heathen lands, and would set them apart from their less unsoiled neighbors. UMCA trainers also considered English cooking techniques to be impractical, unlike brethren at other missions. In the Belgian Congo, for example, Nonconformist missionaries working in the equatorial forest on the Congo River in the 1920s sought to make their station as much like their home as possible. Adherents learned to serve and to consume full three-course, European-inspired menus. When a new missionary sat down for her first dinner party with "natives," she was surprised that they ate roast meat with mint sauce, potatoes, peas, and rice. Criticizing the adherents' inability to use cutlery she wrote, "Of course it *was* a little difficult to convey peas safely to their destination by means of a fork, when you have never done it before . . . But with the assistance of a dessert spoon all went well." African Christians in the Belgian

Congo developed fine motor skills and even finer palates. When King Leopold II's son, Prince Albert, visited the same station in 1909, his experience with the landscaping, food, accommodations, and service was such that "one would truly think one was in England."[66]

On the other end of the spectrum were those like the London Missionary Society's eccentric missionaries J. T. Van der Kemp and James Read. The pair believed local custom was no hindrance to a Christian life, and even embraced it themselves. Read lived for a time "shoeless in a clay hut with a Khoekhoe wife, learned to like Xhosa sour milk, gave up bread, tea, and coffee when he could not afford them."[67] Van der Kemp, who advocated purity through renunciation and suffering, was often seen "without a hat, his venerable bald head exposed to the burning rays of the sun . . . dressed in a threadbare black coat, waistcoat and breeches, without shirt, neckcloth, or stockings, and leather sandals bound upon his feet, the same as are worn by the Hottentots." He even went so far as to "marry" (though "free" or "hire" might be more appropriate) a thirteen-year-old slave girl from Madagascar. It is likely that neither Read's Khoekhoe wife nor Van der Kemp's Malagasy bride cooked pot roast and green peas in a double boiler on the veld. Such impassioned embrace of local culture was not the kind of accommodation the Tractarians had in mind; indeed, UMCA missionaries advocated a middle road between Nonconformists in the Belgian Congo and the likes of Read and Van der Kemp in southern Africa.

Fayida's daily work, then, was a mix of laundry and ironing, sorting and pounding rice, collecting firewood, gardening, and cleaning. The purpose of her and the other Industrial girls' work was twofold. First and purportedly foremost, the Industrials completed their daily chores in order to learn to execute the quotidian domestic skills that underwrote a civilized Christian life. Mastery of all that constituted the "Victorian cult of domesticity" would make the Industrials good Christians, good models of Christian behavior, and good evangelists.[68] "Although these girls have not chosen teaching as their vocation," one missionary wrote, "we hope when they leave us and go to their own homes they will be a power for good in the world, by leading consistent Christian lives themselves and doing what they can to influence their neighbours."[69] Any good work could be transformed into God's work, and the girls and young women were encouraged to carry the spirit of God's grace with them wherever they went and in whatever task was at hand. Even without polished teaching skills, missionaries conceded, they could still set a good example and enlighten "their less fortunate sisters . . . for, as we say in Africa, 'among the blind the one eyed is king.'"[70] This would be especially true if they wound up living in areas where they did not speak the local language or share in local customs—the daily performance of these values was a language all onlookers could eventually understand.

Second—and perhaps more important to the missionaries and the Schoolgirls—the Industrials provided the daily labor that kept the schoolhouse running and the Schoolgirls free for more important intellectual pursuits. Thus the Industrials were responsible for cooking the midday meal, which was enjoyed by both their British instructors and the Schoolgirls. When not cooking or washing up, Industrials worked in the kitchen garden cultivating sugar cane, Indian corn, vegetables, and groundnuts, among other crops. Their training also provided them with some income-generating skills, such as laundry, mat plaiting, and sewing, which would help support them after school ended and they were no longer in direct service of the mission.[71]

The ironies implicit in the new track system of education did not end there. The new social hierarchy of the mission also resembled in many ways the conditions institutionalized under the so-called Poor Laws in Britain, which were codified in the late 1500s and reformed in the 1830s to include the system of workhouses for which the laws are known today. The missionaries would have been familiar with this system because poverty and unemployment were a central concern of 1870s bourgeois British society. These laws, a predecessor to the modern welfare state, offered relief to the very poor in conditions so rigorous that "no-one would voluntarily seek it in preference to work." Poor women suffered double injustices under this system, for they were largely considered "non-wage-earning dependents" and were treated not as autonomous individuals who had a capacity to contribute to family income, but as dependent upon their husbands. They were therefore not granted the opportunity, as it were, to pursue workhouse labor on their own, and to raise themselves and their families out of debt. It was not until 1871 that a labor option was introduced for women. Single women—such as those who were widowed, divorced, abandoned, or never married—became equal to men under the Poor Law: as "potentially recalcitrant members of the work force."[72] These women, the law insisted, had a duty to work. With that duty came, in theory, access to useful training in the workhouse. This legal provision was not widely implemented, however, lest it make the workhouse too attractive.

While poverty and charity incite sympathy, they also breed stigma. As much as upper-class, churchgoing ladies' auxiliary members in late nineteenth-century Britain might have sympathized with the plight of these women and offered them outreach and assistance, they did not empathize. Charities and upper-class altruists sought ways to distinguish the "deserving" poor from the "undeserving" poor and struggled to understand the true root of poverty, something that they believed did not reside within them. Indeed, after the 1830s the complete transformation of working-class morals and habits "became a central feature of bourgeois cultural strategy."[73] In the 1860s the "social problem" of poverty and unemployment remained seemingly intractable, and British philanthropists sought the "revitalization of existing ideas and practices, with a consequent emphasis upon the reform of working-class habits, the need for discrimination and organization in charitable giving, and the value of personal contact between the classes as exemplified by the persistent ideal of the home visitor."[74] Questions about the natural tendencies and inherent propensities toward indolence, laziness, or sloth remained as the stigma of pauperism and relief.[75]

The same ideology that motivated philanthropists of mid-nineteenth-century Britain to invest in the poor at home motivated others, such as the Tractarians, to look overseas. If Britain and her Tractarians "would claim the stewardship of Abraham to be the Father of many nations," it would not be enough to tend to the heathen at home, but they must both "attack a citadel close at hand, and to advance against an enemy in the field."[76] Just as their charity applied to Africans as a race, so too did their skepticism of African morals and habits. Perhaps nowhere was this more true than in the case of unmarried women who, in the eyes of the British workers, were beginning to show little capacity to excel at the one career the mission made available to them. To the missionaries, these women suffered the multiple indignities of being African, being women, and being incapable of academic work, self-reliance, and personal uplift. They were sent to the workhouse, where they, like the most privileged of Britain's female workhouse residents, could get useful training that, in theory, would lift them from their degradation. The Mbweni workhouse girls could not seem to escape the prejudices that plagued their British contemporaries, for they were essentially institutionalized, separated from the more "promising" segment of the Schoolgirls, and taught to live in service to others.

Thus ultimately, it seems that Capel's assessment of the girls' tendency to keep "slaves" was not too far off the mark. As illustrated above, these were relationships the missionaries themselves performed. Similar to their British contemporaries members of a society in which one could find domestic servants, both paid and unpaid, at every level but the very poorest—Mbweni pupil-teachers relied on others to complete the mundane domestic rituals of a civilized life.[77] This arrangement may not have been all that surprising to the young women involved, for two reasons. First, as we have seen, Mbweni's Schoolgirl/Industrial hierarchical labor system closely resembled both the system of client slavery from which many of the UMCA's congregants had fled, and the now-familiar master-servant relationship on the station. Young Industrials had every reason to invest in relationships of personal dependency that they believed would further solidify their membership in the UMCA community. Especially if the young women did not see these relationships as static, but as a way to reduce their marginality over time, they might have seemed a savvy choice. Second, some among the Industrial students may have also grown up in communities in which the more powerful men practiced polygamy. In these places, junior wives served senior wives, and older girls did what was asked in service of the extended family. An Industrial education allowed women to forge new kinship ties and family units, albeit in ways that were unfamiliar and surprising to British mission staff. When presented with choices on the *shamba* about how to live out one's life, not all women felt suited to the options missionaries presented to them. Faced with studying texts inside all day, a woman inclined toward farming or with a special talent in husbandry might have focused her attention on agricultural tasks instead. When she learned that she would have to lead Bible-study classes and recruit followers, a more introverted woman might have lost interest in her studies, focusing instead on cooking or making vestments for the clergy. A woman averse, for whatever reason, to marriage would likely have found ways to escape matchmaking for as long as possible, particularly that which might have paired her with the epitome of an African Christian man—the aspiring Native Cleric. Rather than seeking trouble for trouble's sake, women the mission deemed "troublesome" were more likely simply expressing themselves in a way that did not match the categories to which the mission had ascribed them. As the mission responded to these idiosyncrasies, it did so in a way that exacerbated stratifications that were already beginning to emerge on the *shamba* based on female congregants' own social positioning.

Mbweni's Schoolgirls

After Smythies removed the twelve girls from the schoolhouse in 1884, only the teachers-in-training remained. A young woman named Kathleen Mkwarasho was enrolled at Mbweni during this time of transition, and was chosen to continue on

UNDATED PHOTOGRAPH, FROM "IN SCHOOL AT MBWENI," *AFRICAN TIDINGS* 20, NO. 261 (JULY 1911).

FIGURE 8. An unnamed Mbweni teacher and her students.

in the teacher-training track. Like Fayida, Kathleen's experiences were likely typical of an Mbweni Schoolgirl in the 1880s and 1890s. Given that she appears on mission registers as a Makua, it is likely that Kathleen was born either in Mozambique or across the border in what is now southern Tanzania.[78] The girl who came to be known as Kathleen was probably either captured in a raid or else pawned by her family to creditors and never redeemed. She ended up, by what trials we shall never know, aboard HMS *Briton*, whence she was transferred into the care of the mission in 1874. Kathleen was baptized just six months later.[79] She must have been about three or four years old when she was incorporated into the mission, for she was counted among the "elder girls" in the 1886 school exams. She excelled on those tests, receiving commendation for her papers on the authorship of the Epistle to the Hebrews, the irrigation of Egypt, and the histories of Germany and Athens.[80]

With the opening of the Industrial Wing the following year, Kathleen would have become a "pupil-teacher." Dressed in the red Turkish chintz dresses that "betrayed a teacher," Kathleen and her classmates would have followed a strict curriculum meant to prepare them for their lives as clerics' wives at remote mainland stations.[81] Kathleen and her fellow pupil-teachers split their time equally between learning and teaching, spending one month with their books and the next in a classroom with younger students. Their studies might have consisted of Robert

Isaac Wilberforce's *Five Great Empires*, Andrew Jukes on the *Types in Leviticus*, and a little natural history. They often studied the Book of Acts, and had private lessons on the Gospel of Saint Matthew and other relevant pieces of scripture. Arithmetic, too, was on the lesson plan, although many missionaries believed it to be the school's "most deficient point" because "it is always a great difficulty with African children."[82]

In alternate months Kathleen and her contemporaries practiced their skills in classroom management and curriculum preparation. The elder girls were effectively teachers' aides, expected to "use their influence amongst the children to keep order, and see that the rules are not broken."[83] They learned how to construct timetables, "how to be prepared for the many difficulties that come to a person who has a fair-sized school, and has to teach it single-handed, with only such help as can be got from the children themselves." In addition to such concrete academic skills as reading, writing, and arithmetic, the girls worked to hone their skills at evangelism and proselytization. The missionaries tried at all times to "impress upon them that they must be kind and friendly toward heathen parents who do not see the use of education, having none themselves." And, most importantly, workers tried to help their students "look upon their work as missionary work." "I know," confessed Thackeray, that "one cannot put the missionary spirit into anybody's heart, but I think one may help to remove obstacles to its growth."[84] This idea, that teaching and working with parents was evangelical work, would continue to undergird the curriculum and training of the UMCA pupil-teachers for years to come.

Free from performing the mundane duties of civilized Christian life while the Industrials labored on their behalf, the Schoolgirls turned their attentions to their books and to shoring up their teaching, curriculum-development, and classroom-management skills. Relieved of the burden of domestic work, the balance of the Schoolgirls' days was little different than it had been for all adherents in the mission's early years. Indeed, for years, all of Mbweni's elder students received on-the-job teacher training. For example, Lucy Majaliwa, Cecil's wife, was grown, educated, and married by the time the tracked system of education at Mbweni began. Without a separate teachers' classroom and with no extra British staff, the only training Lucy received for her teaching career was what she could glean while supervising the lessons of the younger students. Lucy had "natural abilities and goodness," however, that allowed her to build a successful career as a teacher and cleric's wife. Kate Kadamweli received a similar education before the Industrial Wing opened. "From the first," Kate was "looked up to as head girl" by the others of her cohort, and thus it was little surprise that she was in charge of day scholars at Mbweni, and of supervising the young pupil-teachers who were over the lower classes.[85] When Caroline Thackeray arrived at Mbweni, she found Kate in the schoolroom "surrounded by girls, busy fixing the needlework which they were doing."[86]

While the Industrials prepared to do the work themselves, the pupil-teachers trained expressly to *teach* others the essential skills and behaviors of a Christian life. In their future capacity as teachers and mothers at remote mainland stations, the missionaries idealized the Schoolgirls as the mission's most important means of modeling and passing along the skills and domestic callings associated with Western civilization (as with many of the missionaries' plans, the realities of the pupils' lives would complicate this distinction). Just as the UMCA required their British lady workers to have domestic expertise before entering the mission, the mission desired its pupil-teachers to receive proper training in Western domestic skills. The theory, apparently, was that one ought to know the "rules" before they could be bent to accommodate the necessary concessions for African life. And, for the most up-to-date and sophisticated training, the mission sent some of its female protégées to Europe. The Industrial School at Clewer, England, offered a four-year course for women aspiring to be trained in the domestic arts. In 1885 Nena Chadisa and Neema Chande, two of the girls in the newly formed pupil-teacher track, left Zanzibar to enroll at Clewer for four years. At Clewer, Nena and Neema would have studied "all household-work, laundry-work, and cooking," skills that would "be of untold value in Zanzibar and on the mainland."[87] Such courses became popular during British rule, when formalized programs were established at industrial schools throughout Britain to attract girls from the colonies. Less formally, Thackeray took students with her to England when she returned for home leave. The girls helped in fundraising pitches and mission outreach events, but they also toured local homes and churches and took classes. Kathleen Mkwarasho went with Thackeray to England in 1882, and Keziah Shikalako was a senior pupil-teacher at Mbweni in 1893 when she traveled to Rome, where she took "lessons in church embroidery from a mistress trained in one of the great embroidery schools of the city." According to plan, she "so profited that she has lately been able to superintend the church embroidery class at Mbweni."[88] Mwalimu Keziah's embroidery class at Mbweni was, as we shall see, one of many classes in the domestic arts taught throughout the mission's lands. Central to the mission's civilizing rhetoric, the domestic arts were a gateway to rituals of a Christian life. The domestic arts were also evangelical tools women could deploy wherever they traveled with their husbands, whether they spoke the same language as new inquirers or not.

Travels with British missionaries to England and Europe were but one of the many ways in which the mission further inscribed in its future teachers and aspiring clerics' wives their privileged status within the mission. These moments also served to reinforce a sense of camaraderie between the British missionaries and Schoolgirls. And indeed, there were many similarities. The *Bibi*s and Schoolgirls lived together on the mission grounds, sharing a building that was separate from the women who worked for them. And they shared in the missiological burden, responsible for spreading Christianity to new generations of Christians. They were all well-educated, literate, sophisticated women who were creative about carving out respectable futures for themselves. Yet both the British women and the Schoolgirls had their futures circumscribed by the social and cultural realities of their separate societies; the missionaries were hemmed in by the professional realities of Victorian England, and the very category of Schoolgirl (and indeed Industrial, too) was only possible because of the persistence of relationships of dependency. Facing limited options, the missionaries and the Schoolgirls both sought to expand their respective domains as much as possible, always pushing the boundaries or creating new boundaries in a circumscribed world. Both marginalized in different ways, missionaries rewarded those who they understood to be most like them.

Kate Kadamweli, for example, was proving to be in all ways a model of modernizing Christianity. In school, she quickly became "the most advanced of all the girls in general intelligence" and was the best at needlework among her peers, sewing hems "quite respectably." Temperamentally, she struck missionaries as "being very truly religious, absolutely reliable and worthy of all the respect we could show her." Under Miss Jones's instruction at the girls' school, Kate grew to be a talented seamstress with an obedient and teachable disposition. She and several others taught by Miss Tozer, the late bishop's sister, were "distinguished by their peculiarly sweet accent and pretty manners" and carried some of Miss Jones's influence, or so it was said, in her gentility and capacity for conversation. She was a "real influence for good, and her life shone out bright and pure among her heathen surroundings." After leaving Mbweni, and being imminently "useful," she pitched in where needed around the mission's stations and ultimately became indispensable to the staff in Zanzibar Town. She was particularly kind and helpful to those who had fallen into sin, taking them into her house and nursing them when they were ill. She was, the hospital matron would say of her upon her death, "one of the most Christian women I have ever worked with."[89] In 1870 Kate married an African subdeacon from

Kiungani and became the mother of one biological and several adopted refugee children. In 1875, after a distressing stint on a mainland mission station during which she endured the death of a child and separated from her philandering husband, she returned to Mbweni. There, Kate took up teaching and became the school's first and only Head Native Teacher.

Managing Marriage

Integral to, and indeed the most important product of, the tracked system of education at Mbweni was the development of communities. The experiences of female Industrials and Schoolgirls at the *shamba* encouraged congregants to think of themselves as participating in several overlapping and intersecting communities: as part of a community of other Industrials; as set apart in a community of Schoolgirls; as part of a universal communion of Anglicans; as part of a spiritual community of African UMCA congregants; and as part of a single Christian nuclear family. Each of these communities was based on a series of relationships, forged through common experience and a shared investment in the community and its perpetuity. These relationships unfolded similar to what Dorothy Ko, a historian of China, has described as a "series of nested circles."[90] We can think of the UMCA's sisters in spirit as unfolding in concentric circles; the innermost circle can be imagined as that which was absolutely fundamental to the biological reproduction of the UMCA's community: the companionate pair, the unit on which all good, Christian, monogamous marriages—and the mission's evangelical strategy—were based.

As we have seen, African women were the crux of the mission's plans for biological and ideological reproduction, and faced—at least according to the missionaries—a range of potential evils should they remain unmarried.[91] Equally important was the nature of the marriage that ensued: British workers had in mind that their African congregants would pair off along lines drawn in the UMCA curriculum—Schoolgirls with male theological students (destined to be clerics and teachers), and Industrials with male congregants pursuing other careers, such as carpentry or working in the print shop. A rigorous matchmaking agenda that followed these specifications would, missionaries hoped, create a cadre of highly trained and educated evangelists who would spread out across the mainland and establish new congregations, setting a standard of African Christian civilization. British workers and African officials thus attempted to carefully manage the marriage process, hoping to control the nature of the emergent community, though having less success in practice than they desired.

When the UMCA's Mbweni girls, both Industrials and Schoolgirls, were "old enough to think of marriage," they were allowed to receive visits from male students on monthly "Boys' Sundays." Young lovers would sit on the verandas, feasting on all sorts of "native sweets and dainties" prepared for the occasion. If, for some reason, a mission boy could not find anyone to spend his Sundays with, he would employ a mission official to "write to one of the ladies in charge of Mbweni and state the case." The Mbweni teacher would then "either send me the name of one, or names of any of the girls who were not 'engaged' or were not put down as friend of anyone," or she would "send word asking the lad to call and see her when he went to Mbweni next time."[92] Fayida began courting a boy from the Industrial boys' home at Mkunazini not long after she arrived at the mission. He was, Fayida learned, prone to drinking, so she sent him away, pledging to not see him until she knew "he had been quite steady." She hinted that if he were to sober up, the young man might "hear from me again." And indeed, several months later, while spying through lilac passion-flower bushes at her young charge, Anne Foxley spotted Fayida, in a crisp new frock, leaning against a pillar next to a "tall, well set-up young fellow, who looked very well content with his position."[93]

While last we hear, Fayida's love affair was continuing "very happily," it is unlikely that any relationship would have continued long without the meddling hands of the missionaries. As single women with no children of their own, the UMCA's British lady missionaries were likely very keen to plot marriages and weddings for their "daughters" on the *shamba*. And, there was so much riding on these matches that strict rules governed courtship and marriage. Girls were not allowed to consider themselves engaged "until they [herself and her lover] have been 'friends' (*rafiki*) one year at least." If mission workers determined that the suitor was "in a position to marry, they are considered 'engaged' until the wedding can be arranged."[94] After a marriage was agreed to by the "elders" of each school, the wedding would soon follow. Officials actively discouraged long engagements because during a long wait to marry "there is almost a certainty of mischief resulting."[95] In a letter regarding marriages between mission adherents, Steere explained that the mission was "not dealing with the case of born Christians, or of intelligent thoughtful people, we are dealing with the case of heathens, unaccustomed to restrain their passions, and barely just beginning to comprehend the existence of a law and of self-restraint, and to get a glimpse of spirituality," and therefore, the mission should encourage among their Christians "marriage, openly and deliberately entered into" in the "hope of escaping innumerable and nameless mischiefs."

Although the girls were ostensibly given free range in their marital choices, mission officials had high hopes that "the boys who are teachers will take the educated girls, who can help them in their work." The pupil-teachers, after all, had been especially trained to "look forward, when they marry, to taking small isolated schools on the mainland" with their husbands.[96] Missionaries seemed particularly tickled when their matchmaking worked out. Take the marriage of Harry Nasibu and Emma Zalana, for example. Harry, or "Henry" as he first appears on mission rolls, was Kame by birth, presumably from the area near Morogoro. Mission logs indicate that Harry came to the mission straight from Zanzibar, perhaps as a runaway from an island plantation, in June 1873.[97] Emma, a Makua, arrived at the mission as a refugee by way of HMS *Flying Fish* on May 25, 1875.[98] She would have been a student at Mbweni before tracked education began, and was therefore prepared to be a teacher and encouraged to marry one. After graduating from Mbweni, Emma taught at a girls' school at Mkuzi, in one of the most beautiful villages in the Usambaras, where Harry was a teacher.[99] The couple returned to Mbweni for a time, and Caroline Thackeray wrote glowingly of the pair. Emma was clever, Thackeray noted, and had a great thirst for knowledge, something that did not seem to have "diminished during the years which have passed since her marriage, as she always seems delighted when here to share in any lessons of the pupil-teachers or to copy out any notes of lessons which we have done whilst she was on the mainland."[100] Harry and Emma's marriage was, at least according to missionaries, "a most happy and suitable one. Their house with its bookshelves and little table, always with signs of exercise books and pen and ink on it, looks completely like what one wishes a teacher's house to be, and they seem to spend a good deal of time comparing notes and looking at each other's work. Certainly her interest in her own work has increased rather than diminished since her marriage, and her house is also excellently kept."[101] They were, to the missionaries, a model pair.

But even under such intense scrutiny, things did not always work out as the missionaries imagined. Indeed, they soon found that "the course of true love will not always run in prepared channels," for it seemed that the African "teachers sometimes think a girl who has learnt industrial work will make a better wife."[102] Further, the ratio of male teachers to female was not always even, so "the native clergy and teachers look to the Industrials for wives when there are none to be found in the school."[103] Although most Industrials did not go on to be teachers, there were exceptions. For example, Beatrice Kilekwa's friend from Likoma, Mabel Macheka, married Augustine Ambali and went with him to Msumba, on the shores of Lake Nyasa, where she did "good work as a teacher." It was a challenging posting for the pair, Mabel explained in a letter to Caroline Thackeray, because "life in the midst of a heathen village was much fuller of temptations than at quiet Mbweni."[104] Sara Fatima, who married a teacher, was herself a "very capable 'dobi,' or laundress." Together the Amanis lived on one of the mission's stations in the Usambaras, where Sara helped teach in the girls' school and did laundry work. Additionally, as with the inherited social systems of patronage and clientship on which these relationships were based, the boundaries between the categories of Industrials and Schoolgirls were fluid, and one could move between them over generations, over the course of a lifetime, or through marriage, adoption, or by imputing other forms of kinship ties. It is unlikely that Industrials saw anything subversive or revolutionary in their decisions to marry clerics- or teachers-in-training, but rather saw it as one of a range of options available to them that would allow them to reduce their marginality. In the minds of the missionaries these arrangements were not ideal, but when seen through the lens of the missionaries' own actions and the safety and security offered by inherited social structures, marriages across professional tracks offered women the opportunity to intrude more forcefully into the community and into status hierarchies that resonated with them. This was particularly important as the mission expanded to the mainland, as evangelists moved between discontiguous stations, and as German colonial rule solidified on the mainland. The latter was a process that made day-to-day life on the mainland significantly more difficult for evangelists from Mbweni, both in terms of their actual work and in terms of straining their sense of connection to Zanzibar.

▪ ▪ ▪

Capel, who had abandoned the Mbweni mission for India in 1878, would have been surprised to learn of the mission's relative successes.[105] That two decades later the mission would be sending well-traveled, well-educated, companionate pairs to the mainland as foot soldiers in the campaign to spread civilized Christianity would have been hard for him to believe. That women like Kathleen Mkwarsho and Lucy Majaliwa would raise daughters and teach young women who would come back to Mbweni to learn and to teach, and that they would create networks of "former Mbweni girls" to sustain themselves and the church through the Tanzanian mainland, was surely far beyond Capel's 1877 imagination. What would not have surprised Capel, however, is that these successes came at a cost.

A series of ironies shaped the Mbweni *shamba* during the 1870s and 1880s. The number of slaves available for proselytization, for example, increased with abolitionists' efforts against the trade. The British women who searched for professional careers ended up reinforcing in the Industrial Wing the very system of circumscribed opportunity they professed to be leaving behind. And, rather than obliterate the master-slave relationship to which they were ideologically and theologically opposed, the missionaries enshrined it as integral to Christian life. The UMCA's labor practices demonstrated to refugees and freeborn adherents alike that relationships of personal dependency were central to the mission's efforts to build a new community. Particularly important to efforts to establish the new community, and to convince people to invest in it, were the affective elements of relationships of personal dependency. Whether it was British lady workers seeking relationships that mirrored the mother-daughter relationship, whether it was female refugees seeking to impute a range of kinship ties to intrude more forcibly into the community, or whether it was Industrial girls seeking husbands among the clerics- and teachers-in-training, affective relationships bound community members to one another. Gossip and ostracism, which Capel identified among his female adherents, were also forms of affective relationships that gave flesh to the community. As African evangelists spiraled out from the mission's heart at Zanzibar to the farthest reaches of the ever-expanding dioceses, these affective relationships bound them to each other and to their colleagues, friends, and loved ones who remained behind at Mbweni. And, as other options for affiliation and status competed with the mission for Africans' affections and allegiance—such as those offered by mainland communities or by the incursions of German conquest—these relationships strengthened their resolve and shaped their work.

CHAPTER FOUR

Networks of Affective Spirituality

Evangelism and Expansion, 1890–1930

In August 1894 Mwalimu Blandina Mwanbwanaa and her new husband, the Reverend Petro "Peter" Limo, departed Zanzibar for their mainland posting. In lieu of a honeymoon, the Limos headed to Peter's childhood home of Magila, in a region of northeastern Tanzania that lies just east of the Usambara mountains and close to, but not on, the coast.[1] The son of a local Kilindi leader, Peter lost his father during an uprising when he was just a boy. The elder Limo's death and the complexities of local politics spurred Peter to affiliate with the church, and allowed him to ascend quickly through the local ecclesiastical hierarchy and to become the "pick of the elite" in Bonde.[2] He was the first man from a mainland UMCA mission station to attend Kiungani, the UMCA's theological college in Zanzibar, and became a person of considerable influence in the church.[3] While a student at Kiungani, Peter met and courted Blandina, who was also an ethnic Bondei from northeastern Tanzania. Unlike Peter, Blandina had arrived at the mission some two decades earlier as a freed slave. The young woman was thus without any kin at all, except for the friends she considered "family"—that is, the British lady missionaries who had raised her and the other Schoolgirls.

The pair become engaged after perhaps three years of courtship, but they delayed the wedding date so each could pursue advanced studies in England.

Peter enrolled at Dorchester Theological College, and Blandina studied for a time at the Clewer Sisterhood's School for Domestic Education.[4] After their return, Peter's anxiousness to "have a really well-educated wife" caused them to once again postpone the wedding; missionaries believed that "more teaching" would be "profitable" for Blandina's future.[5] In the interim, Peter was ordained, and became the first freeborn mainland African to be ordained with the aim of returning to teach "his own people."[6]

As was the case with all Native Clerics and their wives, Peter and Blandina were to work together as a team at their station of Kwa Kibai, preaching to the nearby "heathen" villagers and ministering to local Christian families. It was their task to educate the children, and to perform the day-to-day work required for a fledgling outstation congregation. Peter supervised the construction of a house typical to the area—mud plastered over a latticework of wooden strips, with a thatched *makuti* (Kiswahili: coconut palm) roof.[7] The shape of the home, however, was atypical—square instead of round. The floor plan consisted of two bedrooms, a study, and a small chapel. The strange shape set the house apart from their neighbors' one-room huts, marking it immediately as a pastor's residence.[8] In their square home, donning their modest Western dress, and settled in their monogamous marriage, Peter and Blandina modeled the virtues of the Christian nuclear family for their neighbors at Kwa Kibai. There was never, one sympathetic missionary reported, "a happier couple, they were not only deeply attached but also were really companionable."[9] The Limos' work, their married life, and "the way he evidently talked with her about his own work and aims and ideas, how high a standard they showed, and therefore made to seem possible, to other African husbands and wives" that they, too, could live out the Christian ideal.[10]

Blandina's daily life at Kwa Kibai was defined both by the expectations of the mission and by the social realities of her new home. In particular, Blandina modeled the benefits of Christian education for her new neighbors. She focused on the younger generations of women first, setting out to open a girls' school almost immediately upon arriving at Kwa Kibai.[11] Both she and Peter believed strongly in the value of women's education; Peter, in fact, was known as "one of the foremost of the African clergy in advocating more and better education for *girls*."[12] The work was "very difficult," Blandina told some British friends in an 1895 letter, because the students "have not been taught anything for all their life." Much the same could be said of the local community, which, until Peter arrived, had "never heard anything about the Gospel." Blandina invested in relationships with local women, and even

UNDATED PHOTOGRAPH, FROM "OUR AFRICAN MAIL: HEGONGO," *AFRICAN TIDINGS* 12, NO. 160 (FEBRUARY 1903).

FIGURE 9. Padre Petro "Peter" Limo, his wife Blandina, and their child.

fostered young women in her home when they showed interest in Christianity but found their conversions threatened by something or someone at home. Because the UMCA's theology eschewed methods of evangelism aimed at mass conversion in favor of a system of education that emphasized slow revelations of the Gospel through ritual and practice, Blandina was largely restricted in her formal work with villagers to what she seems to have considered the somewhat remedial skills of reading and writing. In their early days at Kwa Kibai, Blandina was not even free to teach sewing to inquirers lest they leapfrog past the Christian virtues imparted in the instruction of less sophisticated domestic tasks.[13]

Blandina struggled in this work alone because none of the local Christian women were trained to help. Even her assistant, the wife of a local teacher, was—in Blandina's eyes—thoroughly unprepared for the work that needed to be done. *Mama Mwaimu* [*sic*], as she was known, was "no scholar; she cannot help me to do anything." Blandina was even doing her own cooking, she lamented, because she did "not trust anybody to cook as I shall like, so it is best to do it myself." Blandina had ample opportunity to instruct on the basics of Christian living, however, when a famine caused by a plague of locusts brought villagers to her home nearly every day, either "to beg for help or to borrow some money."[14] The evangelist might have found inspiration at this moment in the Book of Joel, which depicts a similar invasion of locusts. A mighty army of the insects, with the "teeth of a lion and the fangs of a lioness," left fields ruined and the ground dried up, the people grieving for the lost wheat and barley, and the cattle moaning. Yet as people turned to the church for help, God responded by driving back the horde with the appearance of horses and the noise of chariots; by providing grain, new wine, olive oil, and food to eat until they were full; and with a promise that they would never again be shamed.[15] As in the biblical story, Blandina and Peter used the famine to evangelize, welcoming new inquirers into the church, providing them succor, and helping them rebuild.

Despite the fact that their new home was "quite central for the Bondei country," and despite their growing relationships with local congregants and inquirers, the couple's academic, social, and religious distance from members of their new community, even those who professed Christianity, sometimes left Blandina and Peter feeling "quite alone."[16] The famine and the resulting exodus from the area only heightened this sensation. And even though the pair originally hailed from the greater Bonde region, they were (and largely remained) marginal to the broader Bondei community. Blandina, by some accident of circumstance—a debt, a family hardship, a kidnapping, or capture—had fallen victim to the slave trade at an early age and had spent little time in the area. Locals might have remembered her family's slave past and allowed it to cloud their interactions. Further, it is likely that if she had ever known Kibondei or any local customs, she was literate in neither by the time she returned as an adult. Peter's early and singular affiliation with the mission community had been a result of his lowly status in Bondei society; the same divisions that had assured his ascendance through the ecclesiastical hierarchy continued to mar local politics, resulting in continued tensions to which he was anything but immune upon his return to the area.[17] And while the Limos and the local UMCA staff successfully attracted some converts during the 1890s, the rate of conversions decreased with the establishment of the German administration and the arrival of settler planters during the same decade. The availability of new sources of patronage meant that the missionaries were no longer the most attractive patrons in Bonde. Christians of lowest standing in the church in Bonde sought out these new patrons, particularly when the mission refused to stand up for its followers against the nefarious tactics of German administrators and planters. Feeling frustrated and isolated, Blandina wrote a letter to her friends in Britain. With an undertone of loneliness she told them, "I do miss my Mbweni friends and companions, but I hope to get accustomed to the people very soon."[18]

Blandina's description of her experiences at Kwa Kibai betrays a sense of homesickness and nostalgia for the life and Christian community she had left behind at Mbweni. And judging from the writings of her contemporaries, she was not alone in yearning for a lost home. Rather than allowing their professional careers to be hindered, however, the UMCA's evangelical wives turned this feeling of isolation and nostalgia into a highly productive evangelical tool. Homesickness bolstered professional obligation, inspiring Mbweni graduates not only to maintain the relationships and lifestyle they had developed at Mbweni, but to re-create their experiences at Mbweni in their new stations on the mainland. With duty and longing as one, Blandina and her colleagues pursued evangelical careers on the mainland that actively maintained and extended the community they had left behind. Standard outreach campaigns and village visits, establishing schools, and the daily performance of Christian living produced new congregants in Kwa Kibai and elsewhere. Women like Blandina forged teacher-disciple relationships with local women, fostered inquiring girls in their homes, and held Bible studies, sewing circles, and lace-making seminars, drawing new congregants into the UMCA community.

To combat their sense of isolation and alienation, the Limos, like their classmates scattered throughout the mainland, also remained oriented as much as possible toward the religious heart of the mission at Zanzibar. The Limos routinely undertook the six-hour walk from Kwa Kibai to the nearest central station, where Blandina met to worship and socialize with Louisa Sehoza and Faith Kayamba, childhood friends from the *shamba*. The pair also returned "home" to Zanzibar frequently, like their colleagues Beatrice and Petro Kilekwa, and maintained a spirited correspondence with their Zanzibar-based teachers and friends, as well as with patrons in England. If the women in these early days wrote letters to each other, the letters have not survived. We do know, however, that many clerics' wives communicated with each other through their "mother" at Mbweni, Caroline Thackeray. She traveled frequently to visit her "daughters" and their families at their mainland stations, and brought news of the activity of their friends and classmates in other regions. She also published their (edited) letters in the UMCA's monthly circulars, *Central Africa* and *African Tidings*, and word traveled back to the wives themselves, many of whom were consumers of these magazines.[19] While in some spiritual communities congregants used the medium of the written letter to participate in "an imagined emotional community," Blandina, Peter, and their contemporaries used the daily performance of Christian values and the relationships born from this work to participate in, maintain, and extend the UMCA's affective spiritual community.[20]

Between 1890 and 1940, the UMCA's African female lay evangelists forged intergenerational and pan-ethnic relationships, including friendships, formal teachers' guilds, ad hoc gatherings for clerics' wives, and teacher-disciple relationships. An examination of the historical context of the mainland during the time these relationships were forged and maintained suggests that the consolidation of colonial rule and the First World War exacerbated the conditions of isolation inherent in the evangelical enterprise. The lives, work, and emotional, professional, and religious intimacies of women like Beatrice Kilekwa, Lucy Majaliwa, and Kathleen Mkwarasho—women who embraced and embodied the UMCA's particular ideals of prayer, ritual, scripture, secular and religious education, marriage, motherhood, and child-rearing that defined a UMCA Christian—translated these ideals to Africans living on the missionary frontier. These networks "worked," as it were, in sustaining and expanding the mission community because they played on the very real feelings of isolation, homesickness, and nostalgia and on the slightly alienating experience of mission work that was cultivated early in its history by British missionaries, and adopted by the first generations of African evangelists. Rather than retreat from these emotions when they experienced them, clerics' wives succumbed. To mitigate these feelings, they invested in personal relationships with congregants and inquirers through teaching associations, groups for clerics' wives, and in the teacher-disciple relationship. In so doing, the UMCA's female evangelists transformed homesickness, nostalgia, and alienation into powerful evangelical tools, which both sustained and extended the UMCA's community of affective spirituality across disconnected lands and through generations.

The Affective Networks of Mainland Evangelism

The UMCA community, particularly as it stood after the substantive growth of several mainland congregations in the 1880s, might usefully be thought of as what Barbara Rosenwein has termed an "emotional community."[21] "Emotional communities" are "precisely the same as social communities," but scholars' analyses attend to "what these communities (and the individuals within them) define and assess as valuable or harmful to them; the evaluations that they make about others' emotions; the nature of the affective bonds between people that they recognize; and the modes of emotional expression that they expect, encourage, tolerate, and deplore."[22] After the UMCA's expansion to the mainland, the community did not occupy a single physical space, but was rather a series of disparate physical places bound together and given life by bonds of affective spirituality, by the nostalgia for an idealized "home" at Mbweni, and by the yearning for the final home with Christ. The implicit emotional dimensions of the UMCA were rooted in missionaries' investment in the church's particular brand of Anglicanism, which first bound missionaries, and then their converts, together in an affective spiritual community. The emphasis placed in Tractarian theology on slow revelations of the Gospel through daily practice, and a preference for the teachable disposition of small children promoted a sense of spiritual, if not actual, kinship between missionaries and converts. The social structures and realities of vulnerability in late nineteenth-century East Africa led female refugees to invest in relationships as familial and to impute kinship ties when possible. Similar bonds of affective spirituality grew up between members of the same generation of congregants and between evangelists and converts, and teachers and protégées. In exile from lifelong friends, fictive and actual kin, and their missionary "mothers," and often isolated from other Christians, the UMCA's female evangelists seem to have experienced feelings of what we would call homesickness, isolation, boredom, and nostalgia in their new mainland homes. When these emotions mixed with a sense of professional duty, women like Blandina invested in evangelical outreach, expanded their social networks, and committed to maintaining relationships from Zanzibar.

Schooling, professional organizations, movement between stations, and the capacity for ritual practice to forge relationships between individuals and communities in diaspora created networks that sustained and expanded the UMCA. It is possible that in carving a united spiritual community out of "heathen" lands, the UMCA's freed slaves and mainland congregants also were influenced by historically long-standing strategies for constructing arenas of collective action and achieving social and political complexity. People living in discontiguous territories frequently came to think of themselves as members of a single clan, clan network, or kinship group by a process similar to one employed by the UMCA's female lay evangelists. Beginning in the fifteenth and sixteenth centuries, people living in Buganda (in what is today central Uganda) made important innovations in the realm of spirit mediumship. These innovations, spurred by particular agricultural challenges, transformed "previously territorial spirits into portable spirits capable of ensuring the health of disconnected groups of people." This process "drew upon the skills of itinerant mediums and lay at the core of clan formation." The movements of these itinerant mediums from shrine to shrine over discontiguous clan lands created "therapeutic networks" that brought together communities whose leaders had a diversity of skills and knowledge, thereby "forging a powerful connection between clanship, collective health and the composition of knowledge."[23] Scholarship on these "dispersed clan networks" of the distant Ganda past illustrates the capacity for "ritual practices to forge relationships among communities whose members did not necessarily share face-to-face interactions" and who lived in unconnected territories.[24] It is indeed possible that the process of building networks across dispersed mission stations was a strategy lodged in the historical memories of the UMCA's freed slaves and mainland congregants, retrieved and deployed in new and changing circumstances.

Networks across disparate mission stations can be understood to be given structure by affective relationships, in particular by terms we understand as homesickness and nostalgia. Historian Susan J. Matt glossed the contemporary American idea of homesickness "as the longing for a particular home," and nostalgia as "a yearning for home, but it is a home faraway in time rather than space."[25] The Swiss scholar Johannes Hofer first coined the word "nostalgia" in 1688 when he combined the Greek word *nostos*, "return to the native land," with *algos*, the word for pain. Used to describe what was then a "new disease that affected young people far from home," both glosses of "nostalgia" seem to fairly describe Blandina's sense of longing, isolation, and alienation. It is not purely coincidental that the emotions to which Blandina referred were also central to a genre of late nineteenth-century missionary writing that described the heroism, martyrdom, and self-sacrifice implicit in the lonely and slightly alienating experience of doing mission work. Literary tropes invoked in mission propaganda, fundraising calls, and organization-specific journals reflected—and often romanticized—the very real risks associated with mission work. Mainstream missionary hagiography of late nineteenth-century Britain implied that to be a "soldier" in Christ's army, one must accept "the possibility of death in the line of one's daily duty."[26] Obituaries of missionary women, which captivated audiences at home, glorified and valorized deaths that came in the act of self-sacrifice, duty, and service.[27]

It is not surprising, then, that the records of female evangelists' lives on the mainland highlight a similar longing for a sense of home, and a desire to, as Matt describes it, "bridge past experience and present conditions."[28] Indeed, the same British women who sent lonely letters home, penned obituaries of their fallen comrades, and wrote articles for missionary publications were the very same women who served as amanuenses for African congregants, edited their personal letters for publication, and encouraged them to write in the first place.[29] And, even for the women who wrote their own stories, told their own tales, or composed their own letters, they were unarguably influenced by the missionary-authored publications they read, and by the rhetoric of martyrdom, alienation, and self-sacrifice adopted by their missionary counterparts. As is the case with the voices of colonized women, their letters are extant, although fewer and farther between than scholars would like. Yet "even in the most unfavorable circumstances, the voices of the colonized subjects cannot be completely suppressed."[30] The echoes of their voices ring even louder when seen in the context of the isolation, alienation, and homesickness of African female lay evangelists at remote outstations on the frontier of mission at the turn of the century.

Two factors in particular shaped the isolation, nostalgia, and homesickness evangelists and other travelers experienced while away from the idealized center of the mission at Zanzibar. First, the ceaseless travels and lives of itinerancy that UMCA evangelists embraced as a natural part of their career path were inherently isolating. For the first generation of Mbweni graduates, marriage meant much more than simply the start of a new personal partnership and professional career. Marriage was a moment of rupture and dislocation, an end as much as a beginning. For many among the first generations of Mbweni students, Zanzibar was the only home they had ever known. They left behind the British women who had raised them, and they left their friends and classmates—all of whom had become like family. Moving to the mainland, they also left the relative comfort of the Zanzibar Christian community. Instead of generally sharing with one's neighbors a worldview and common enterprise, the priests and their new brides faced the possibility of being the only Christians for miles. The relative personal, economic, spiritual, and political security that congregants experienced on the *shamba* was replaced by the sense of isolation and instability that came with living among "heathen." Evangelists were rarely experts in the complex political idiosyncrasies of their new stations, and they often faced hostilities of unknown and shifting origins. Even for those who, like Blandina and Petro, were headed to a familiar area, their faith, language, and cultural affectations immediately marked them as "outsiders" or "other" to the local population.

Lives of itinerancy and dislocation were particularly challenging for women in the late nineteenth century, Africa being no exception. Whether it was white American women engaged in local and regional migrations, British female missionaries enlisting as "'soldiers' in the army of the king of kings," or African clerics' wives making new homes on the mainland, they were all subject to the conflicting demands of a particular brand of late nineteenth-century womanhood. On the one hand, even the most mobile of women had relatively limited control over their own movements. Where they lived and whether they undertook migration depended on the decisions of fathers, husbands, and bishops, as well as on powerful social ideals that constrained their professional options. On the other hand, women were still seen as inherently domestic, tied to the home by a mix of ideology and social organization. Americans moving westward and Britons concerned with colonial expansion understood that women and the domestic had an important role to play in sustaining and safeguarding the home front. As Susan Matt has observed, for women in late nineteenth-century America "these ideals of feminine behavior did not always sit easily together, for in such a scheme, women were to be defined by home but also willing to leave it."[31]

What was left for many women, then, was a tendency to idealize a particular vision of home as a "bulwark against the restlessness of the age."[32] Fundamental to this idealized vision was a public sentimentalization of domesticity. In missionary writings of this period, "feminine self-sacrifice/heroism was presumed to be a part of daily domestic living in a good and comfortable British home. The aim was to show that even extraordinary women had their roots in the commonplaces of human life."[33] The lonely, self-sacrificing "soldiers" of Christ's army epitomized a sense of "domestically based self-denial," and "glamorize[d] the essentially domestic drudgery that was supposed to occupy . . . the time of so many lady missionaries." African women, many of whom were freed slaves or of the generally marginalized population who tended to affiliate first with mission communities, felt this homesickness acutely. For American slaves in the late nineteenth century, their homesickness was "intensified by their lack of control over their own destinies and was a reaction not just to the fact of separation and distance but to their powerlessness in a brutal system." Indeed, psychologists believe that "those who cannot control their movement experience the feeling more than those who can."[34] As *watumwa wa balozi* (a colloquialism meaning "slaves of the embassy" or, more generally, "slaves of the whites"), UMCA congregants and their descendants remained circumscribed and marginalized, even on the mainland.

Second, the advent of German colonial rule, the consolidation of the British colonial administration throughout Zanzibar and in parts of East Africa, and the First World War intensified the homesickness, isolation, and marginalization already inherent in the work of African clerics and female lay evangelists living, working, and traveling on the mainland. British missionaries in areas of German East Africa continued to function largely unaffected by German rule until the First World War, and the UMCA—like other missions—expanded its work on the mainland during this time. While the British missionaries generally avoided political entanglement, individual African members of churches felt the change more acutely. In the 1890s the German government prioritized military security and political control, which it achieved through violence and by affiliating with African leaders. Collaborators shifted the balance of power in each region, and the balance of privilege, and some Christians left the church for the promises of new German patrons.[35] The administration imposed a tax in 1898, and demands for tax and labor were as unpopular in Tanganyika as they were elsewhere on the continent.[36] A series of natural catastrophes as well as an economic shift away from its former orientation toward Zanzibar were also challenging for Africans throughout Tanganyika, not just Christians. A locust plague followed by a drought in Bonde in 1894 and 1895 was experienced by UMCA adherents as the "famine that kills," taking the lives of people "like animals, two and two."[37]

It was not only UMCA evangelists who experienced the disruption and marginalization of the early 1900s; committed Christians throughout the mainland struggled with their own feelings of isolation and persecution, which were compounded by German rule. Adherents of the Bethel mission in Usambara, for example, fled to hilltop villages to escape the hostility of extended families, and the threats posed by alcohol and "coastal hairstyles," and by their own marginality. "They led a different life from their relatives," a descendant remembered. "They were regarded as *dead* by their parents and relatives."[38] Lutheran and Moravian missions encouraged their adherents, both explicitly and implicitly, to form communities separate and distinct from their heathen brethren.[39] During the last decade before the war came to East Africa, Asians began to move inland from their enclaves along the coast and were accompanied by an increase in white settlement. Land alienation affected Africans throughout Tanganyika, increasing tensions and further isolating Christian communities.

As news of the crisis in Europe reached Tanganyika and Zanzibar in June 1914, the very act of following the Queen's religion and outwardly sympathizing with her culture and customs became perilous for entire communities of UMCA adherents living in what was then German East Africa. Such danger doubly affected clerics and female lay evangelists who were already on the margins of mainland communities. As the war began, expatriate German officials quickly provoked and sustained full-scale war in East Africa in order to lure enemy troops away from more important theaters. This move epitomized Africa's colonial exploitation by turning the region into a mere battlefield. And indeed, with the resident German Defense force—which included Europeans and African *askari* (soldiers/guards)—already in place, Colonel Paul von Lettow-Vorbeck and his troops engaged in a ruthless guerilla campaign. In order to pull ahead on the battlefield, Germans and Britons both tightened control over their East African territories and increased demands on residents.[40] Famine and disease were commonplace, and fear predominated. Roaming armies looted and pillaged. Perhaps most dreaded was the Belgian Force Publique, widely believed by Africans and many Europeans to employ cannibals. Evoking bitter memories of Nyamwezi slave raiders, Belgian troops lived off the land and created unmitigated terror in the Tabora region.[41] For many UMCA congregants, especially those who had lived through raids, kidnappings, and the general instability of the slave-trading era, it must have felt as if the horrors of the slave trade were descending once again.

The war quickly disrupted British evangelical work in German East Africa. British missionaries of many denominations fled either to British regions of East Africa, to Zanzibar, or to Europe, abandoning their stations throughout the mainland. The Germans and their *askari* arrested many of those who remained, along with many African teachers, lay workers, and congregants. By December 18, 1914, the last of the UMCA's British missionaries stationed at Msalabani, the mission's largest station in Tanga region, were arrested; *askari* took African clerics and teachers to internment camps, where they would remain until the end of the war.[42] Male congregants were conscripted to work as porters and manual laborers, and unmarried African women were enlisted to "prepare and clean flour, rice, beans, etc." for German officials and troops.[43] By July 1915, one of the few remaining African teachers at Msalabani wrote of the period after the outbreak of war that "the people here are being very harshly treated now, the district is like a wilderness, there are hardly any people except women and children. The few men who are left have exceedingly hard service of porterage [*sic*], and are constantly beatne [*sic*], and if a man is known by the officials at Marimba to be a Christian his hardships are without expression, because they are known as the friends of the English."[44] Blandina Limo's husband, Peter, was forced into work as an overseer on the Handeni Road. By the end of the war, his right arm was paralyzed and he was deaf in one ear. A German official had treated him like an "animal," he said, kicking him and striking him in the head. Peter had also become "very poor since the war," he said. He returned to find "even my house and church was broken down."[45] Despite the work many African clerics like Petro performed in the hopes of keeping the churches open, there were congregants who left the UMCA. In Bonde, for example, after hearing on December 9, 1914, that twelve teachers had died in prison, there was widespread "mourning in the land" and "people despaired of further hope of seeing the others back." Congregants lamented, "there is no Christianity now—let everyone do as he likes," and retreated to the lush hills to fend for themselves.[46]

Although missionary absence and the difficulties of war dismantled many fledgling Christian communities and some stations lost congregants, the ordeal ultimately strengthened the UMCA. The war consolidated power in the hands of the Africans who remained behind, offering them responsibilities they otherwise might not have acquired.[47] Left alone at mission stations, African clerics—whose authority and decision-making power had for years been circumscribed by European control—were now in charge. To be sure, the UMCA's African clergy had by design more autonomy and responsibility than Africans in other missions; this was particularly true for Africans in charge of and in congregations at rural outstations. Yet the UMCA's Native Clerics assumed even more autonomy and authority during the war, and congregants who remained faithful to the church made tremendous personal sacrifices to keep their communities intact, if not flourishing. Samwil Mwenyipembe, for example, was on staff at an outstation in the Magila complex of missions when the war began. Left alone to tend to the spiritual and physical needs of a community that stretched several days' walk in all directions, Mwenyipembe assumed the responsibilities of his imprisoned colleagues: he performed services, repaired and maintained church buildings and farms, mediated between German officials and imprisoned church staff, allocated increasingly scarce resources to congregants and other remaining staff, and maintained the print shop. Along with these additional duties, Mwenyipembe requested and was granted limited permission to perform marriage ceremonies. Concerned that their unmarried girls would be conscripted into manual labor or worse, congregants had begun to arrange marriages under "heathen rites."[48] In December 1915, for example, a young girl named Masingano caught the eye of a German official stationed locally. Afraid of Herr Fischer, her relatives acquiesced and allowed him to pay 80 rupees in exchange for her. She remained with him until he fled at the end of the war.[49] Mwenyipembe's new authority would have prevented such matches in the future.

For many adherents—clerics, their wives, and lay congregants alike—the deterritorialized affective networks in which they were embedded gave them strength during deeply challenging times. So, too, did their awareness of, and investment in, their broader evangelical project. African church leaders—both male and female—were aware of their place within a larger, changing society, and of the role that they would play in shaping it. In 1908, Samuel Sehoza—a priest originally from the Bonde region—spoke to the Kiungani students about their theological responsibility. "People of Africa!," he addressed the multiethnic group in front of him:

> We were born in different parts and belong to different tribes, but we were all living in darkness and in the shadow of death. God led us through many hardships, by long journeys, through hunger and thirst, and even death, without our understanding that it was the good hand of our God upon us leading us in love. But today we understand the reason why we left home—today we have learnt and we know that Almighty God loved us, and when we were far away He remembered us. So when we think of our past dangers and our present prosperity, we give our thanks to God.[50]

Displaced from what they knew as "home" and seemingly alone in a foreign land, UMCA evangelists used a homesickness for Zanzibar and a longing for the relationships forged on that island as a powerful evangelical and community-building tool, as they had done for decades. This historical context illustrates that rather than having their marginalization mitigated over time, isolation and homesickness continued to be relevant emotions that women invested in professional guilds, ad hoc pan-ethnic groups for teachers' wives, teacher-disciple relationships, and intergenerational fosterage and friendships as a way to solidify and extend the deterritorialized affective networks from Mbweni across the mainland and through several generations.

Guild of the Good Shepherd and Guild of All Saints

Mission officials founded the Guild of the Good Shepherd in 1885 and the Guild of All Saints in 1887. Both guilds were intended to be professional development organizations focused on enhancing the teaching careers and "spiritual lives" of Mbweni's pupil-teachers, and of maintaining relationships between Mbweni's Industrials after graduation. The British missionaries who founded the guilds or attended their meetings wrote most of the records of the guilds that exist today. These records often include quotes from African members about their experiences in the guild, but as is often the case with the voices of African female lay evangelists, their responses are mediated by British translation or editing. Background provided by British missionaries, quotes from African guild members, and the broader context of the relationships between congregants and the structure of the mission suggest the particular reading of the guilds as mechanisms for both maintaining and forging spiritual and emotional connection, even across unconnected lands and through generations.

At its most local level, the first guild, the Guild of the Good Shepherd, offered pupil-teachers an opportunity for continuing education and professional networking. One guild leader recalled the lessons that she and others had imagined when they founded the guild: "Teaching is a high vocation and not to be undertaken lightly; that we must try to train our scholars' whole being, body, soul, and spirit, and not be content with mere head knowledge." In order to do so, she continued, "a teacher must teach by example as well as by work; that we must never do our work in the spirit of an hireling, but seek out our scholars with diligence, and take for our pattern the Good Shepherd 'Who lay down His life for His sheep.'" At guild meetings, officials led members in a short office, offered a series of standard prayers, including their eponymous Psalm 23, and sang hymns before concluding with a short sermon on the "duties and privileges of a teacher's life."[51] Holding guild meetings regularly at the guild's offices at the Good Shepherd Chapel suggested to members a certain physicality to the communion of Mbweni-trained teachers—it was a place to which women could come to be with other new clerics' wives, to catch up with friends, and to reconnect with their own former teachers. The very existence of a guild for Mbweni-trained teachers from multiple generations also suggested to its members that theirs was a community that stretched through space and time. The guild introduced teachers to other women who had attended Mbweni either ahead of or after them, expanding the UMCA's affective community by creating new social, intellectual, and religious intimacies. The content of these meetings, and the discussions that unfolded between individual women there, also illustrated to attendees that they were part of a single ideological community that shared in certain central tenets of mission theology and practice.

Special occasions, such as guild anniversaries, taught current members about the reach of the intellectual and professional genealogy rooted at Mbweni. For example, church officials used the opportunity of the guild's seventh anniversary in 1893, or "Good Shepherd Sunday," to remind teachers of the service of their late colleague Mildred Furahani. Mildred was the first Mbweni-trained teacher to start a boarding school on the mainland. Among other sacrifices for the mission, Mildred adopted ten "little girls" at a mission station where she and her husband, Martin, served, "providing for them entirely, the Mission clothing them only." Mildred's girls were, in the words of one missionary, "quite like a bit of Mbweni."[52] Mildred's story, and the guild leaders' public accounting of it, positioned current guild members within a longer-standing intellectual genealogy that began with such early Mbweni graduates as Mildred Furahani and extended several generations later to the girls whom she had clothed and educated. In bringing "a bit of Mbweni" as she called it to the mainland, Mildred and fellow guild members reproduced this ideological community there. In sharing Mildred's story, guild members not only reinforced their existence as a community, but defined the boundaries of it. Even in diaspora, teachers and students could reenact the Christian virtues and practices that defined both education at Mbweni and its graduates. With Mildred's attention and care, her adoptive children were more than just mainland inquirers; they came to embody the reproduction and extension of the UMCA's community to the mainland.

Formally, special guild retreats were an occasion for professional development, but UMCA teachers also benefited greatly from these opportunities to cultivate relationships with women in different cohorts at Mbweni, fleshing out their professional, personal, and spiritual networks. Every year or two, women and clergy who had served on the mainland returned to Mbweni to discuss their "experience of difficulties and trials of work on the mainland" in order to give "counsel to those young women who are going to work in distant places."[53] Such retreats offered practical information for the soon-to-be mainland teachers as well as for veterans, who could pick up new tricks of the trade, and also were an opportunity for experienced teachers to model the relationships that were expected of and possible for the next cohorts of teachers. European teachers recognized that among the returnees for these retreats, "the bond which began in their old class-room days . . . still holds, and . . . they love to meet and talk over the old times."[54] In so doing, returnees inaugurated new graduates into a much larger fellowship of teachers, and instilled in them the techniques and relationships necessary for building congregations and communities. These reunions also offered women the opportunity to make new connections that would sustain them during what was an inherently isolating and increasingly unpredictable political situation on the mainland.

While physical reunions were an important activity of the guild, of even greater significance to the extension and solidification of the UMCA's network of female lay evangelists was the affective spirituality of guild life. The "rules" of the guild were three: (1) to communicate with prayer for the guild once a month; (2) to say the guild prayer daily; and (3) to attend the monthly guild meeting. Guild founders hoped that participation would increase members' "sense of the religious character of the teacher's office [and to] encourag[e] intercessory prayer for one's scholars."[55] Guild officials also advised students to "set a good example to their scholars and to pray for them by name."[56] The guild's emphasis on the recitation of particular prayers was a meaningful tool in the maintenance of community, for the "guild prayer" reinforced to its practitioners their membership in the community, and reminded them of the particular practices, behaviors, duties, and tasks they had pledged to perform and uphold. Prayer for one's scholars was also an evangelical tool, a practice that bound teachers to their students and incorporated new generations of Christians into the UMCA's spiritual community.

Members also relied on the affective spirituality promoted by guild prayers to help them maintain their ties to Mbweni and to the UMCA community while in diaspora. When members left for work on the mainland, there was a celebration and service, with "special prayers and intercession for the teacher who is leaving." Teachers and clerics' wives carried this spiritual connection with them to the mainland, where they relied on their own prayers and the prayers of others to assuage the loneliness and alienation of life on mainland stations. Members often detailed in letters to Mbweni and to their guild colleagues "how much they feel the support of each other's prayers." Perhaps feeling unmoored in her new station, with no friends nearby and only a few Christians to worship with, one teacher found temporary solace on "Guild Day," when she knew that the guild's leaders and members would "be all praying for us."[57] Instead of falling out of touch once on the mainland, the traveling teachers came to rely on their membership in the guild as a "great bond of union." Indeed, prayer not only reinforced their ties to other members on Zanzibar and across the mainland, but it kept them bound to the civilizing influence of Mbweni. Daily prayer allowed guild members to seek refuge in ritual, reminding themselves of their training, of their duties, and of their commitments to their husbands, to the mission, and to God. Reciting guild prayers daily was also a way to bolster resolve and avoid the temptations associated with life on the frontier of the mission. Prayers offered a respite from the domestic drudgery of life as a cleric's wife, teaching grown women skills one had mastered as a young girl. Indeed, the prayer activated a particular emotional subjectivity shared (at least in theory) by all guild members. This was particularly valuable to women living and working on the mainland during the 1910s, when German political rule and the threat of war made movement and travel increasingly perilous. When physical travel to one's friends and colleagues was impossible, prayers and spiritual bonds provided comfort and sustenance.

Yet despite all this, we can imagine that guild prayer and the spiritual community it purported to uphold was only a moderately satisfying stand-in for a physical community. For women living in communities where they did not speak the language or have many confidants, we can imagine (and imagine we must, for no women's voices were recorded on this point) that consorting with friends or seeking the advice of colleagues would have been greatly satisfying. Newlyweds or women teaching for the first time might have liked to share their frustrations or concerns, to be heard, and to have someone to commiserate with. When famine or the encroachment of German troops brought fear and threatened physical danger, as happened in Masasi in 1905 and in much of the mainland in 1914 and 1915, women likely yearned for more tactile aid rather than simply spiritual comfort. Guild prayers were a Janus-faced tool: when one is homesick or lonely, prayer—particularly prayers written by the guild's British founders—could confirm one's isolation.

Based on the success of the first, mission officials founded a professional organization for the UMCA's Industrial girls. The Guild of All Saints was founded in 1887 and quickly grew to be twice the size of its sister organization. Founders imagined that, similar to the Guild of the Good Shepherd, the Guild of All Saints would "bind" the Industrials "to us and to each other." In keeping with the tracked system of education established a decade earlier at Mbweni, the "rules" for the Guild of All Saints seem intentionally less onerous than those for the teachers' guild. Perhaps church officials feared that less capable scholars would also prove less adept at living up to the expectations of the Guild of All Saints. Regardless, the All Saints "rules" encouraged women (1) to "try" to do "any work for God given them by the clergy"; (2) to "help" each other in sickness; (3) to say a short prayer for the guild daily; and (4) to communicate together on All Saints' Day and the Feast of the Visitation. Although few of the members of the Guild of All Saints had explicit teacher training, many of them ultimately married teachers. (Whom their Kiungani boys fell in love with was not, as we have seen, something the church had as much

UNDATED PHOTOGRAPH, FROM "MBWENI PAPERS," *AFRICAN TIDINGS* 20, NO. 263 (SEPTEMBER 1911).

FIGURE 10. Members of the Guild of All Saints, Mbweni.

control over as they would have liked.) Thus, although officials' expectations for the evangelical capacity of the Industrial guild were lower than for the teachers' guild, the women were still encouraged to attend church regularly, to "choose good friends," to "be very careful about their conversation," and to "try and draw others to lead a holy life." The Industrials were evangelists in their own right, for they were expected to invite "people from house to house to special services," to help with mothers' meetings, to meet for prayer, and to meditate and give advice on "the duties of wives and mothers." Indeed, membership in a guild might have been even more valuable to Industrial women, who could not fall back on teacher training or the cultivation the mission provided to clerics' wives.

Informal Training for Mainland Preachers' Wives

Whereas Mbweni's formal guilds bound Christian-educated, professional women together spiritually and emotionally across great distances around the turn of the century, the mission's theological colleges struggled with the challenges of initiating a very different type of woman into the ideological community. During the first several decades of the mission's work in East Africa, Zanzibar-trained evangelists left the island to establish schools and congregations on discontiguous stations throughout the mainland. As soon as the 1880s but increasingly so in the early 1900s, congregations and schools in the interior began graduating aspiring evangelists of their own. Mainland schools did not generally have the myopic focus of Mbweni in preparing women for careers as clerics' wives and teachers; thus, many of the women who graduated from mainland mission schools needed an extra element of education to prepare them for life as a preacher's helpmeet. They therefore often accompanied their fiancés or husbands to one of the several new theological colleges the mission opened on the mainland. While not formally enrolled in college, partners of aspiring clerics and teachers participated in what can be thought of as ad hoc support groups for mainland-born clerics' wives.

The mission founded Saint Cyprian's College in 1929 to augment the mission's attempts to increase the number of African clergy in southern Tanzania. Saint Cyprian's offered a variety of informal lessons, seminars, work experience, and individualized training, as well as community-building initiatives for wives and fiancées of theological students. The college, named after the African bishop and martyr Saint Cyprian, was located near the outstations of Saidi Maumbo and Namasakata, several hours' walk to the southwest of Tunduru, east of Masasi on the Lindi-Tunduru road. The spacious compound included a chapel, lecture room, and housing for college staff and students.[58] The UMCA had been evangelizing in the general area of Saidi Maumbo since Bishop Steere and a group of Mbweni congregants arrived in 1876 to establish an outstation, but the work had been slow. Kolumba Msigala, an ordained graduate of Kiungani, established the outstation at Saidi Maumbo in 1924. When Msigala arrived, there were "a few scattered Christians in the new parish" and he was largely doing "pioneer work" among the residents of the area. His work was productive: not long after his arrival, houses for two English nuns who had followed him from his previous posting at Chiwata were constructed; teachers were placed in new outstations; a dispensary—which soon became a small, albeit very basic, hospital—was opened; and a girls' school was added to the compound.[59] Thus when the college was founded, it complemented what was already a rapidly growing, ethnically diverse Christian center.

The Saint Cyprian's campus, a spacious plot carved out of a well-forested slope near Saidi Maumbo, was in many ways a microcosm of the diocese itself. The students came from stations and schools scattered throughout southern Tanzania, from areas as central as Tunduru and Masasi, and from outlying areas to the east and south. The aspiring clerics were members of several different ethnolinguistic communities, but all shared a general knowledge of Kiswahili and, in some cases, English. These men joined the college's British workers and African staff and their families on the hill; the families of teachers employed at the primary schools that were affiliated with the college lived nearby. Boys and girls from the local UMCA schools increased the bustle on campus, as did the mixture of other mission staff and congregants. And, of course, there were the wives of aspiring clerics or college staff, as well as local young women who were dating or engaged to theological students.

In keeping with the UMCA's theological approach, college staff believed that the most effective evangelism was through a well-matched, companionate pair of educated Christian workers. It was not enough to simply prepare a man for Holy Orders, they reasoned, but they must also attend to the partners of their aspiring clerics. The wives of Saint Cyprian's students, unlike many of the women in the earliest cohorts of Mbweni students, had generally received very little, if any, training before coming to the college. Except for women raised near a central school, many of the aspiring clerics' wives had not received more than a cursory primary-level education. Very few had spent much time outside of their immediate villages or attained much confidence in the Kiswahili or English language. Given their lack of education, lack of fluency in the languages of mission, and lack of experience around people with whom they shared little but a nominal identification as Christians, many wives felt isolated or lonely. One student explained that many of the wives felt "as if they had been brought here in a great flying machine, and when they look round for their fellows they don't see them."[60]

As a sign of their commitment to the role of women in the evangelical process, within a year of its founding the college had initiated a series of ad hoc measures aimed at increasing the general level of competency with the roles and responsibilities of a cleric's wife. Immediately the women learned (if they did not already know) how to read and write; they received religious instruction and were taught about ministering and parish visiting.[61] On June 18, 1931, the priest-in-charge began a series of lessons for the women "on one or two points in connection with their future position as Deacon's wives," which was followed by several lectures by Canon Kolumba on "certain aspects of the work a 'minister's wife' could do in her husband's parish.'"[62] In the 1940s the sardonically named Miss Wisdom offered regular talks to the students' wives, organized special retreats for "work amongst the women," and assisted a fledgling branch of the Mothers' Union.[63] The women, explained one of

Saint Cyprian's European teachers, were "carefully instructed in the Catholic faith; they are taught how to help their fellow Christians in the parishes to which they will go; and they are also instructed in any matters that may appeal to them."[64] They also had special retreats and quiet days, during which they practiced these skills and learned certain rites and rituals they would use in their work.[65]

The women were encouraged to practice their leadership skills, which they would need as clerics' wives among new congregations, by creating and rotating through official positions within the church. In April 1932, for example, the women of Saint Cyprian's formed a *chama* (Kiswahili: party or group) to run the church on Sundays. An *Mkuu wa Kanisa* (Kiswahili: Head of Church) would collect alms on Sundays and keep the younger children occupied while their parents worshiped. Two-week terms were effected so that many different women could rotate through the position; Rahel Nufunga was the first to shoulder the responsibility.[66] The women also learned the essential duties of clerics' wives, which they would enact for the daily running of their new churches and model for their new congregations. The same *chama* that created the position of *Mkuu wa Kanisa* also arranged for the wives of students to "help their husbands to decorate the altar with flowers, so as to learn how to do it, with a view to helping in that way hereafter in their parish." While such activities might seem mundane or even commonsensical to the modern-day churchgoer, they were not intuitive to women who had grown up on the very edges of the Christian frontier. Manual labor was required to build and maintain a proper space for worship, much of the responsibility for which fell on the shoulders of these young wives. The Saint Cyprian's logbook is flush with concerns about the structural integrity and appearance of the mud and wattle chapel. The students' wives were frequently recruited to perform both basic maintenance and more substantive repairs, as well as to prepare the chapel—the center of spiritual life at Saint Cyprian's—for worship: they were tasked with mudding the floor of the chapel with local black earth; to pack white earth sent from Chidya by a British friend of the mission onto the mud walls of the chapel, especially to decorate the inside of the chapel; and to do the seasonal structural "mudding."[67] Their "zeal" for this work was reportedly compromised only when they were attending to other duties, such as births and deaths.[68]

In addition to gaining competency in these skills, the act of performing the ordinary tasks of Christian living together helped the Saint Cyprian's wives to forge bonds of friendship and personal intimacy that sustained them while at the college. This communal work also illustrated for the women, and allowed them the opportunity to participate in the construction of, a particular ethos that underwrote the UMCA community: that of diverse, encompassing spiritual unity. To the church administrators in particular, the cross-ethnic immersion these women experienced was a valuable community-building tool. In 1932, for example, Mwalimu Gerard, an African teacher at the college, lectured the students and their wives about a troubling trend on campus. Rather than referring to teachers simply by their professional title, "Mwalimu," or their professional title and Christian name, such as "Mwalimu Gerard," for example, students tended to emphasize the ethnic distinctions among the class by referring to teachers by their professional title and their ethnic group, as "Mwalimu Mmakonde" or "Mwalimu Mmakuo." Mwalimu Gerard lectured the students, wives included, about the "necessity of unity among Christians," and called for a stop to fractious "tribal" politics.[69] The women's engagement in these everyday acts of Christian living, such as mudding the church, attending to births, and learning to sew, was one way of emphasizing the similarities between them and promoting their shared identity as Christian clerics' wives above all other affiliations, including ethnic. While we do not have records of wives themselves expressing such internal shifts, one church administrator described the changes that he believed they experienced over their time at the college: he saw "an enormous change in their attitude towards each other. They are learning to be sociable outside the tribe. School has brought them together: sewing on my veranda they have learnt to talk to each other. They are now very interested in each others' customs; they rock with laughter over their language differences."[70] This emotional connection between clerics' wives and their shared homesickness was vital in helping them establish a sense of community. Unlike Susan Matt's nineteenth-century immigrants to America, who were spurred by homesickness to invest in ethnic enclaves, organizations, and associations and to "recollect the past communally," the UMCA's clerics' wives used homesickness, a newfound sense of interethnic camaraderie, church teachings on ethnic unity, and their shared faith to create a new form of subjectivity.[71]

Teacher-Disciple Relationship

As we have seen, the UMCA's British missionaries—and in fact workers from missions throughout the continent—embraced the civilizing influence of British women missionaries as an evangelical tool, leading them to privilege an intimate teacher-disciple relationship. British women "could reverse the dangerous effects of a heathen lifestyle and instill a Christian character in young, unlearnable girls, at once elevating their self-respect and their material condition."[72] In missions that followed the model of the Native Church, young African women were educated and "empowered to enact change in their own society by evangelizing others."[73] Assuming the missionary role themselves, the UMCA's female lay evangelists followed their husbands to establish and serve at stations on the mainland, employing the model of the teacher-disciple relationship in their own evangelical efforts. These African women worked in homes, schools, and clinics to create the cultural institutions that would solidify their husbands' "official" conversion campaigns.

The first generation of African women educated by the UMCA at Mbweni transformed the teacher-disciple relationship from one between British civilizing missionaries and "heathen" Africans to one between two African women, one the embodiment of a compendium of Christian values and African tradition, and the other a mainland inquirer motivated by a host of complicated goals and desires. Kathleen Mkwarasho (the young Makua woman whom we met in chapter 3 just after she arrived at the mission on HMS *Briton* in 1874 from the general area of what is today southern Tanzania or neighboring Mozambique) was on the front lines of this change. Although Kathleen was a pupil-teacher at Mbweni, her evangelical career began in earnest after she returned from her trip to England with Caroline Thackeray in 1883 and married Nicholas Mkwarasho.[74] Nicholas trained in the mission's Industrial program and, after their marriage, volunteered to work in the print shop at the central station on Likoma Island in Lake Malawi, some five hundred miles inland from Zanzibar.

The pair undertook an arduous voyage by sea, up the Zambesi River to the Upper Shire River, and finally to the shores of Lake Malawi, where they boarded the UMCA's steamer and traveling mission station, the *Charles Janson*. Aside from the few other Zanzibar-trained teachers, the newlyweds were now largely among strangers on the island; it seemed "to them a foreign country full of people speaking a strange language."[75] Until they learned the local language, Nicholas was hampered in his outreach efforts. Kathleen, however, had the skills she needed to begin her work immediately. Each time the mission expanded to a new station or community, workers relied on the performative work of educated Christian women to bridge linguistic and cultural divides. Without a shared language or cultural practice, evangelists were forced to rely on their domestic skills, rather than on formal proselytization, to attract new followers. As we have seen, this approach

UNDATED PHOTOGRAPH, FROM "HOW WE KEEP SCHOOL AT LIKOMA," *AFRICAN TIDINGS* 4, NO. 74 (DECEMBER 1895).

FIGURE 11. Kathleen and her husband Nicholas at Likoma, standing at right, accompanied by two other teachers.

fit with the mission's Tractarianism: evangelists were theologically disposed to the "formation of moral character by habit" over an indiscriminate revelation of the core of the faith to inquirers.[76] A sense of obligation to her evangelical duty likely combined with emotions of loneliness or isolation, despite the presence of a few Zanzibar-educated Christians in the area, to spur Kathleen to reach out to her new neighbors in whatever way she could to increase the number of like-minded individuals around her.

Thus central to Kathleen's work, and to the work of other Mbweni-trained teachers building relationships on the mainland, was the ongoing practice and modeling of Christian living. The daily performance of particular "cultural politics and practices" for the creation and contestation of nationalist ideology is a "potent vehicle for inculcating and mobilizing" new forms of consciousness. This is especially true, she proposes, in areas where literacy (or, in this case, even a shared language) is not widespread.[77] Kathleen, for her part, would have had to live out the virtues of a Christian education and model the role of Christian motherhood that missionaries believed would expand the mission. In order to increase the size of her local community, to decrease her sense of homesickness and isolation, and to attend to her evangelical duties, she would have imparted to her students, disciples, and protégées the ideals that defined UMCA Christianity. In this the teacher-disciple relationship was the relationship at the heart of the expansion of mission through the reproduction of certain core values.

Immediately upon arriving, then, Kathleen began the difficult work of building up a girls' school, "hunt[ing] up scholars from the villages near Likoma station," and teaching local women in informal settings.[78] By 1892 Kathleen was single-handedly running the girls' boarding school.[79] In the rough stone and mortar schoolroom, Kathleen helped an ever-rotating staff of European missionaries teach English, Kiswahili, and the local tongue, Chinyanja, as well as the full syllabus of academic subjects, sewing, cookery, and, above all, scripture.[80] By 1902 Kathleen was the "Head Native Woman Teacher" at Likoma Central School, a position in which she would remain for the rest of her career. In this role Kathleen was responsible for the education of all of the other African women working at the school, as well as many in village schools.[81] She was, missionaries reported, a "good example of conscientious work to the young teachers, and of humility." Kathleen was deeply embedded in the local community; she led classes for the young woman "hearers" and "catechumens" and "did very useful work as a woman elder among the women."[82]

By 1906, Mwalimu Kathleen and the local mission staff could boast some four hundred names on the Likoma Girls' School roster (although the highest daily attendance was but 256). Kathleen's school was having a significant impact on the area: That same year, mission sources reported that the boarding school was smaller than it had been, largely because the students had been granted permission to sleep at home in their villages rather than at the school. The villages on the island, wrote the missionary, "are so much more Christian than they used to be, so that old objections to their sleeping at home do not now apply."[83] By the end of her career, there was "hardly a woman or girl at Likoma who has not been taught by her, and many others round the lake have learnt from her pupils."[84] Kathleen's daughters went through teacher training under their mother's watchful eye, and in 1928 Kathleen and two of her daughters, together with twelve other women, received government recognition for having served the mission for over twenty years.[85] Her British colleagues conceded that Kathleen so perfectly embodied the balance of the UMCA's Native Church that she was "indeed a 'Mama' to the Nyasa girls in a way we could not hope to be."[86]

Mission sources attribute the relative success of women's education in the Likoma area to an intellectual genealogy traceable to Kathleen and her training at Mbweni. Kathleen's influence remained strong in Likoma even after her death. In 1932, a report on the education of Christian women on Likoma credited the long history of women's education on the island to the "early pioneers" like Mwalimu Kathleen, who "herself bringing from Zanzibar a tradition of education as desirable for even mere womenkind, popularized it for ever in this island."[87] In the 1930s, the main Likoma school compound, with its airy classrooms and wide verandas, had room enough for the 391 girls on the books and sixty to seventy pupil-teachers. Five village schools educating a mix of boys and girls brought the number of women enrolled in schools at Likoma to between six hundred and seven hundred. Even the infamous Phelps-Stokes Commission recognized the firmly established tradition of women's education in Likoma; when the commission asked "how it was that the women in this part were so much keener on education than in some other parts of Africa," mission leaders credited the responsibility that women felt for educating the next generation of Christian mothers. The region's success in educating women was "because they themselves have been so very instrumental in their own progress, for in the early days almost as soon as one could read for herself she was used to teach others."[88] This habit of mentorship between teachers and protégées extended the intellectual genealogy traceable to Mbweni, rooting both female teacher and the mission deeper into mainland communities.

Intergenerational Fosterage and Friendships

Just as their Zanzibar-trained mentors had, the first generation of women educated by the UMCA on the mainland—women like Kathleen's disciples—eventually came to think of themselves as members of a broad, united UMCA community. Women were brought into the UMCA's deterritorialized affective networks through informal intergenerational relationships that grew up between not only teachers and their students, but also between foster parents, mentors, and young girls from the mainland. These relationships were yet another way that Mbweni-educated women living on the mainland after 1890 used affective spiritual ties to bridge enclaves of believers living on discontiguous lands, and to incorporate new generations of believers into the deterritorialized community.

A young woman named (perhaps pseudonymously) "Sikujua" (Kiswahili: "I did not know") was incorporated into the mission community through an informal, intergenerational fosterage relationship. The Kiungani-educated freed slave Paul Kangai returned to his childhood home near Chitangali, a village in what is now southern Tanzania, about five days' walk from the coast near Masasi, to take up evangelical work in the late 1800s. Here Paul met and befriended the Majaliwas. Soon after returning home, Paul learned that a woman he had known and loved before his capture, kidnapping, and life on Zanzibar was still living in the area. Kangai committed to finding her, and to marrying her. At the time the woman, Sikujua, was enslaved to a local man. She was not a Christian, and Cecil attempted to dissuade Paul from marrying her. She was "a heathen," he told Paul, "and you cannot marry a heathen." Enamored and undeterred, Paul developed a plan to buy Sikujua's freedom. Once he did, he took Sikujua to live with Cecil and Lucy Majaliwa and their children. Lucy was a freed slave who had been educated at Mbweni; she was not a regularly trained pupil-teacher, having attended Mbweni before the teacher track was established. The pair married in 1879 and eventually moved to Chitangali, where they very soon had the first of their eight children. Things at Chitangali were challenging for the Majaliwas. Cecil was reportedly intensely lonely and had forgotten his childhood language; he experienced anxiety and depression. "I am left alone in the midst of the heathen, he wrote, "like a cottage in the middle of a forest." Further solidifying their feelings of marginality, the Ngoni raid occurred soon after their arrival and forced them to hide in the bush for a month. Lucy pined for Zanzibar and longed to bring up her children in a "civilized" environment. Lucy Majaliwa was said to have taken "a deeply religious view of a teacher's work," and

UNDATED PHOTOGRAPH, FROM "A FAMILY GROUP," *AFRICAN TIDINGS* 6, NO. 97 (NOVEMBER 1897).

FIGURE 12. The Majaliwa family, minus Cecil. *Clockwise from upper left:* Florence, Agnes, Lucy, baby Bartlett, Mona, John, Eliza, Margaret, and Louisa.

filled her house even further with local young inquirers and children interested in the mission who were facing opposition at home.[89] While in exile from Zanzibar, Lucy's ministry to inquiring girls was likely another way to keep her spirits up and to extend the community of like-minded people around her, and her young daughters. In the Majaliwas' home, Sikujua would learn the faith and ways of a Christian. In assuming this relationship with Sikujua, Lucy reaffirmed her commitment to the continuity of the church and the perpetuity of the values and practices she herself saw as fundamental to living a Christian life. Indeed, the capacity to influence the nature of an inquirer's belief through quotidian practice was not only inherently Tractarian, but was also a prerogative women assumed when negotiating these intimate fosterage relationships.

As in Sikujua's experience, the UMCA's Christian women also assisted in raising young inquirers or mission school children with heathen parents, teaching lessons about religion and Christian life that the girls' heathen parents could not teach. Ajanjeuli Achitiano was one such girl. Ajanjeuli was born around 1883 in Chitangali. The Achitiano family was Makua, descendants of an elephant-hunting clan whose involvement with the ivory trade before the middle of the nineteenth century brought them from south of the Ruvuma River, in what is now Mozambique, northeast toward the coast to eventually settle in the Masasi district.[90] Bishop Steere's party had arrived in Masasi from Mbweni in 1876 and was slowly making advances among the local population; it was not for several years, however, that Cecil Majaliwa was able to convince the people around Chitangali to build a church.[91] One of Ajanjeuli's extended relatives, Barnaba Matuka—eventually Barnaba Nakaam, for his ascendency to a local titled position—affiliated with the church and attended Kiungani on Zanzibar as one of its first freeborn students. Ajanjeuli's parents were not among Majaliwa's early converts.[92]

Cecil's early support of young Ajanjeuli prompted the mission to connect her with a British patron who would support her education, and by 1890 she had enrolled in the village school. The updates Cecil provided to her patrons and the letters Ajanjeuli later wrote provide much of the information we have about her life.[93] In 1897, after a delay caused by her parents' insistence that she continue to perform what Cecil called "their wicked heathen customs" at home, Ajanjeuli was baptized and took the Christian name Agnes, reportedly for her sponsors from St. Agnes' School in Trimingham, England.[94] At some point Agnes's family moved and she enrolled in school at the Chiwata outstation under the tutelage of Christabel Matoka, an Mbweni-educated wife of a Zanzibar-trained deacon. At fourteen, Agnes was "delightfully promising . . . bright—clever so much above the average." Christabel knew that at Mbweni anyone "as clever at learning as Agnes" would have been promoted to the teacher-training track, but at Chiwata there was no such option and Agnes's school days were officially over. Not content to send her back to the village and, very likely, into an early marriage, Christabel promoted Agnes to the specially created position of pupil-teacher.[95] It was through these relationships with Lucy and Christabel that Agnes eventually committed to the church, in spite of her parents' resistance. Lucy and Christabel also introduced Agnes to the profession of teacher and to the idea of a companionate Christian marriage, providing her with an opportunity for both.

Lucy and Christabel were not the only two people looking out for Agnes. Barnaba Nakaam, a convert not only to Christianity but to the virtues of women's education, supported the mission's efforts to arrange marriages between its male teachers/clergy and educated Christian women. Nakaam was also determined that his nephew, Francis, should marry a girl who "was not only an educated Christian but a *mwungwana* (a freeborn person, as opposed to one who had been a slave)."[96] Agnes apparently fit the bill, and the match was made. The pair did not marry for several years, however, in part because Sapuli was preparing for Holy Orders at Kiungani, and in part because church officials were worried about Agnes's relative youth at the time of her engagement.[97]

Well before her marriage, Agnes had taken over the patron updates from Cecil Majaliwa. These letters, apparently dictated by Agnes but penned by an amanuensis in Kiswahili, reveal Agnes's longing to find and build a community, and to forge relationships with other Christians, women in particular. Soon after their marriage, the Sapulis moved from their home at Chiwata to the Mwiti outstation. Although she had moved several times before her marriage, Agnes was now a teacher and a cleric's wife, responsible for evangelism of her own. This appears to have been both an isolating and a challenging time for the new bride. For example, not long after their marriage, Mwiti's resident deacon, Kolumba Yohana Msigala, left for Zanzibar to make his final preparations for the priesthood, leaving Agnes and Francis alone at Mwiti.[98] Soon the couple took up the life of itinerant evangelists themselves, moving from station to station at the instruction of the church administration. Agnes recounted their movements for her patrons: "When we left Mwiti, we were sent to Luwatala after my husband was appointed to the work of a reader. We were 9 months at Luwatala, and now we have been sent to a place called Chilimba. Chilimba is a little hill at the foot of . . . the river Mwiti which is near the Rouvuma river."[99]

The very work Agnes and Francis were sent to Chilimba to do exacerbated Agnes's sense of isolation. Francis was on a mission to "try and restore those Christians who have fallen and who were lost without a shepherd." Those whom he succeeded in returning to the church were "obstinate and are angry at being told to repent," which did not leave the couple with many companionable neighbors.[100] While maintaining a professional relationship with her congregants, Agnes also looked to other evangelists for friendship, support, and companionship. In her letters, Agnes recounted what Benedict Anderson might call a "consciousness of connectedness" to other itinerant teachers.[101] "Many teachers are being moved to other places," she wrote, and "perhaps next year we shall be sent to a different place, we do not know."[102] In the mission field, the rituals of Christian life and the loneliness of itinerancy forged relationships among individuals and communities whose members did not necessarily interact face-to-face. In fact, Agnes's sense of belonging to the UMCA's spiritual community was so strong that it inspired her to pursue spiritual and personal relationships with British women.

In writing about Anglican evangelization in the late nineteenth and early twentieth centuries, the British historian Elizabeth Prevost has reported that British female missionaries became deeply invested in creating a sense of shared womanhood with their African disciples, a multiracial community bound by gender and religion. The Anglican missionary Gertrude King, for example, who served in the Ladies' Association (after 1894, the Women's Mission Association) of the Society for the Propagation of the Gospel (an Anglican mission organization) in Madagascar around the turn of the twentieth century, understood that for women the "deepest value of mission work" was "the spiritual connection that she had forged with African women." So, too, it was in Uganda where Dora Skipper of the Church Missionary Society was moved by the discovery of a shared womanhood in the mission field: she wrote of her first days in Nabumale that she attended "a lovely service this morning, a native communion. The church was full and it was so nice to feel the oneness of black and white as we knelt together."[103] Prevost states that through their work with African women, many missionary women ultimately "reconfigured their mission work as a medium for religious exchange with African women." This affective spirituality, in turn, created a "mutual space wherein British and African women interacted on a number of levels, infusing mission Christianity with a dynamic female religiosity which was capable of mediating divergent cultural and religious expressions, effectively blurring the sacred and the secular, European and African, Christian and non-Christian dimensions of the mission encounter."[104] Agnes's letters personally addressed her British patrons and friends in Kiswahili, rather than in Yao, a language that would have been much more accessible through the translations of returned missionaries. In maintaining a correspondence with her British patrons, Agnes Sapuli crossed cultural and racial divides to incorporate herself into a much broader communion of Anglican women.[105]

▪ ▪ ▪

Agnes died in 1918, but not before her daughter Rose Annie left Chilimba to attend boarding school at the central station at Masasi. Rose's departure was the intended result of the investment female evangelists made in affective evangelical relationships, and marked the start of another generation of women who were connected through education, itinerancy, and the affective spirituality of the mission.[106] Lucy

Majaliwa and her husband Cecil offer another example of the intellectual and affective lineage Mbweni graduates brokered. To maintain their ties to Zanzibar, and to provide their children with what they saw as an adequate education, the Majaliwas sent each of their children back to Kiungani and Mbweni as boarding students. Because of their parents' status in the mission, Florence Flower, Agnes, and Mona were placed among the small group of pupil-teachers in the Mbweni schoolhouse, rather than in the much larger Industrial Wing.

In addition to what they believed were the obvious educational benefits, the Majaliwas' decision to send their children to boarding school at Zanzibar helped the family solidify ties with families in other parts of the diasporic community of Christians. Each of the Majaliwa daughters completed teacher training and married a Kiungani student, men who envisaged careers in the church administration. Cultivating these ties with other families was not unlike the hopes for increased lineage ties, wealth and knowledge, and dependence that motivated Africans to forge marriage alliances in the precolonial period, and not unlike the strategies of imputing kinship and constructing familial ties that refugee women adopted as a means to incorporate more fully into the evangelical strategy. In the new context, however, the Majaliwas were using marriage alliances and the affective kinship ties that attended them to reinforce their bonds to other members of the spiritual community, and to embed themselves more firmly in the mission despite their distance from its figurative center.

Further, the choice of men with whom the Majaliwa family forged marriage alliances and extended kinship ties was significant. They were highly educated men who were destined to be community leaders, but who turned out to invest in the community-building project in a way wholly unlike that which the missionaries and their African congregants would have been likely to imagine at the time. Florence Flower married the Reverend Daudi Machina, a priest who would be active in local politics of the Magila area during the First World War. Her sister Mona married Daudi's brother, the Reverend Samuel Chiponde, the first African editor of the *Msimulizi* newspaper and a government interpreter involved in the African Civil Servants Association (ACSA). The UMCA-sponsored *Msimulizi* ("storyteller" or "narrator") was the first Swahili language newspaper, and the ACSA was an outgrowth of protests by Chiponde and two other progressive UMCA adherents to the chief secretary on behalf of forty African clerks regarding perceived discrimination in salaries, housing allowances, and leave arrangements when compared to their "Asiatic" counterparts. Agnes married Augustino Ramadhani, the senior head teacher at Kiungani. Ramadhani eventually became the head of Zanzibar's Christian community, and the leader of the Zanzibar branch of the African Association (AA). The AA was an intrareligious and intraethnic political organization that, together with the ACSA, preceded Tanzania's anticolonial nationalist organization, the Tanganyika African National Union (TANU).[107] Through their involvement in the soccer clubs, civil servants' associations, and other proto-nationalist organizations that coalesced in TANU, Chiponde and Ramadhani were among the earliest pioneers of modern nationalist politics in Tanzania. These early glimmers of strivings for self-rule by UMCA Christians were logical extensions of the concept of the Native Church, for they show how political innovators within the ranks of the Christian nation took the idea of the spiritual community and applied it to local and contemporary circumstances.

The homesickness, isolation, and marginalization inherent in the UMCA's evangelical diaspora to the mainland were compounded by the effects of the consolidation of colonial power and the First World War. At the end of the war, German East Africa became the British-mandated Tanganyika Territory, and UMCA stations on the mainland came under British administrative rule for the first time. In addition to a change in authority, the new government offered novel forms and definitions of status, authority, and prestige. For many Africans, our Mbweni congregants and their descendants being a clear example, the church community had always offered much more than spiritual relief, and this period was no exception. Many Africans in the interwar era saw the church as a way to develop the skills and other knowledge and technologies that would provide them access to these new opportunities. Literacy skills taught by British missions in English and Kiswahili looked as though they would be invaluable under the new administration. Clerical and organizational skills, as well as familiarity with British ways of being, also promised to offer a leg up.

As useful as they were for extending the church and uniting evangelists across time and space, the bonds of affective spirituality employed by the UMCA's female evangelists suggested certain limitations for their engagement with the rapidly changing world of late nineteenth- and early twentieth-century Africa. Indeed, there exists an irony inherent in their endeavors, which is that for all their earnest attempts to cross geographical, ethnolinguistic, and generational divides in service of a united spiritual community, the women profiled in this chapter were merely drawing new lines between "us" and "them." In forging strong and enduring ties between one another and across space and time, Mbweni graduates and their descendants were at the same time distancing themselves from the other communities to which they had once belonged.

As the UMCA's community spread across the Tanzanian mainland, the UMCA's affective spiritual community became more and more salient in the minds of its believers. The isolation, affective spirituality, and shared history that bound the UMCA's female evangelists to their old friends and their new congregants were powerful, integral parts of building a community. It was also an exclusionary force, one that served an important role in regulating the boundaries of the community and solidifying Christian identity. Indeed, the 1920s and 1930s UMCA congregants began to direct their pedagogical, spiritual, and emotional labors toward the creation of a specific brand of African "civilization," a form of cultural nationalism that grew increasingly salient as the colonial period progressed. Just as the community was defined by Christian modernity and a rich sense of supra-ethnic unity, the UMCA community was also defined by its congregants' race.

CHAPTER FIVE

Of Marriages and *Mimbas*

Minding the Borders of the Christian Community, 1910–1930

By 1910 a multigenerational network of Mbweni graduates, their daughters, their female protégées, and mainland-trained preachers' wives and teachers connected UMCA stations in Tanganyika, Zanzibar, and Malawi. Despite missionaries' repeated declarations that adopting Christianity would not require the inquirer to make "any very great outward change in his daily life," the examples of the female lay evangelists suggested to new congregants that there were certain habits and behaviors that would define them as Christians and distinguish them from their "heathen" neighbors.[1] Thus even in the most rural of these communities, it was becoming relatively easy to spot a Christian. African church officials dressed in Western suits; their wives donned utterly impractical long-sleeved, high-necked, lace-adorned white dresses. Schoolchildren wore donated cloth stitched into frocks or *kanzu* by either British volunteers or local seamstresses-in-training. Proselytes did the best they could to observe Christian standards of modest dress, which to the chagrin of missionaries resulted at times in what they considered to be highly questionable sartorial choices. A missionary in Likoma, for example, banned British patrons from sending dolls to the female boarding students because women tended to steal the doll clothes for their own wardrobe. This resulted in what the author lamented as the unfortunate fashion misstep of a woman "wearing a piece of bark cloth round her waist, and above was her doll's frock *tied around her chest*."[2] Congregants took pride in their well-appointed square homes; their "civilized" methods of dining and washing; their observance of prayer times and school attendance; their skills in sewing, embroidery, and lacemaking; and their literacy in English and Kiswahili.

Yet the values that united the community also obfuscated contentious questions about what, exactly, it meant to be part of the UMCA community. In the 1910s and 1920s, as disparate UMCA stations were beginning to cohere around the idea of belonging to a single Christian community, congregants were also directing their pedagogical, spiritual, emotional, and actual labors toward the creation of a specific brand of African "civilization." Congregants worked to define ideological, social, and biological institutions—and therefore to define and police the boundaries of the community. This chapter explores two cases in which UMCA female lay evangelists strove at particular moments to maintain the community's external boundaries. The women who directed action in these events were not trained as clerics' wives or as teachers, but in specific moments engaged in activities that were absolutely vital to the mission's domestic and quotidian evangelical efforts, and consequently to the spread of the church's ethos through congregations and across generations. Through the lens of a series of marriage and abortion scandals that rocked the Mbweni community in the 1910s and '20s, one can see how debates about love, romance, passion, and secrecy became a battleground for congregants' struggles to secure their membership in, and the longevity of, communities that would offer them security and stability in a rapidly changing world. At the same time, congregants also sought to monitor, hem, and police the boundaries of the spiritual community.

Twentieth-Century Change and Community Entrenchment

Since UMCA missionaries first set foot on the island of Zanzibar in the 1860s, several issues confounded the question of what constituted acceptable behavior for their flock—just as they had confounded similar discussions on mission stations throughout the continent. First, scholars of Christianity in Africa have shown that "conversion" to Christianity was not an act of surrender on the part of Africans or a "colonization of consciousness" by European evangelists, but rather that Africans adopted what they understood to be elements of Christianity into longer-standing ways of knowing the world. I say "understood to be" because such issues as translation, local epistemologies, and inherited beliefs about another world, for example, mediated between missionary intention and African interpretation. This was part of the ordinary development of Christianity worldwide; Christianity has only ever been what local idioms allowed it to be. Failing to see Christianity as a discrete category of human activity, African "converts" instead drew on both Christian values and preexisting ideas without distinguishing between them and with no sense of contradiction.[3] This was perhaps especially true for the UMCA's first cohorts of freed slaves, who saw the missionaries not as bearers of "the truth" but as a new kind of master with novel and often attractive ideas they could incorporate at will into their own ways of seeing the world. To further complicate this persistent dissonance between missionaries' intentions and congregants' interpretations, the UMCA's African spiritual community was becoming larger and even more diverse in the early twentieth century, cutting across colonies, ethnic associations, and civic organizations. In a multiethnic group of refugees with diverse cultural and linguistic backgrounds, this process was not straightforward; if the meaning of Christianity was not coherent among members of the community, then what constituted "proper" Christian behavior was never a foregone conclusion either.

In addition to the myriad possible interpretations of Christianity in local communities, the UMCA's well-intentioned plan to create a Native Church also confused the boundaries between the acceptable and the deviant. The UMCA's insistence on creating a "church of the people of the land, irrespective of European influence . . . adapting itself to the special circumstances of the race and the country in which it exists" caused seemingly endless debate about which local customs could be reconciled with the UMCA's Tractarian values, and which were inimical to Christianity.[4] These questions were especially important as African evangelists and their helpmeets were fanning out across the mainland, establishing outstations and congregations of their own. Administrators sought to legislate behavior through synods and church councils, although what behavior officials and community members actually accepted on a day-to-day basis was fluid and varied. Polygamy, for example, was something about which missionaries refused to negotiate. As one missionary declared, "Christianity demands monogamy or the single life for all."[5] Yet congregants like Hilda, the mother of a newly married Mbweni resident, sought to find balance between the church's instructions and her own personal beliefs. Hilda wondered, for example, whether it was apostasy if a congregant kept a mistress in secret.[6] She had, after all, recently advised her son that if he "kept to one [woman] only he would go mad!"[7] Or, was it only sacrilege if officials found out about the affair?

Finally, the destabilizing effects of the First World War and the political, gendered, cultural, and economic changes wrought by the consolidation of the British colonial administration increasingly gave rise to debates about acceptable behavior among UMCA congregants. When faced with these changes, UMCA congregants did as many before them did, which was to seek to embed themselves within communities in ways that would grant them access to the widest range of possible resources. Seeking further integration into particular niches of early twentieth-century East African society, Africans of all stripes continued to adopt or reformulate significant cultural practices to their benefit. For example, in the late nineteenth century, African Christians in a Church Missionary Society community in central Tanganyika found their marital lives and sexual behavior coming under increasing surveillance by church administrators. Rather than abandon the community, congregants employed the very legal categories authorized by missionary judges to "reframe arguments about property, marital deference, or work. By accusing their spouses of moral indiscretions, litigants reconvened the church courts in their favor."[8] And on Zanzibar, former slaves living in Stone Town who were not affiliated with the mission adopted cultural affectations that would allow them to identify as members of ethnic or racial communities—such as freeborn Swahili, indigenous islander, or Arab—that at different historical moments gained favor with the state.[9] As colonial Africans sought to integrate further into particular communities, they did not necessarily abandon or disavow earlier identities, but negotiated between often-competing communities and communal ethics in order to make the most effective claims possible on resources, rights, or opportunities. In the two cases explored below, women used inherited knowledge about abortion and longer-standing marital practices—which missionaries considered inimical to membership in the Christian community—as a way to make claims on membership in the UMCA. Women also imputed kinship ties with members of the local Arab community, a historically slaveholding and competing religious community, as a way to retain Christian affiliation.

As the 1910s and 1920s unfolded, congregants' struggles to integrate further into the mission community resulted, perhaps naturally, in increased attention paid to the institutions that sustained and perpetuated that community. In particular, congregants attended to institutions of social and biological reproduction—marriage, pregnancy (referred to by congregants and missionaries alike as *mimbas*), and child-rearing. UMCA congregants were not alone in their attentions to these institutions; scholars have shown that throughout East Africa, the interwar years were especially difficult for African women. New agricultural policies, deemed essential by administrators to the social and psychological reproduction of migrant wage-laboring men, affected women in particular. Confining women to their farms "served the interests of capital as well as of rural patriarchs, always seeking new ways to retain their authority over wives and daughters."[10] And toward the end of this period—for Tanganyika, 1925—the new British administration began to shift to politics of indirect rule.[11] British authorities deputized senior African men (irrespective of traditional systems of authority) to fill the positions of chief and to rule on their behalf. Colonial states established courts based on "customary law," which simplified practices that were in constant flux to the particular benefit of court officials, who were invariably senior men. Colonial officials and the new African chiefs quickly recognized a mutual interest in controlling women.[12]

Women, it seemed, were facing assault on all fronts. Throughout East Africa, for example, there was what scholars have called a "crisis in marriage." The changing colonial economy, particularly in rural areas, made it even more difficult for Africans to amass wealth in the traditional way. Young men had begun to move away from rural pursuits to occupations in the cash economy, and were often left without access to cattle or other customary tokens of bride-price. In western Kenya, for example, conditions were particularly bad. Young men who could not afford to marry turned to abducting young women with the intent to force a "marriage." Further, officials throughout colonial Africa were exceedingly concerned with the demographics of their colonies and congregations. The 1920s saw a preoccupation with women's fertility and fecundity among colonial officials who understood a constant supply of labor for public-works projects and settler farms to be one of their chief responsibilities.[13]

To be sure, attention to these issues was not only a product of the colonial administrations' concern with women's fertility and fecundity. In precolonial Africa, an abundance of land and a relative scarcity of people to work that land led to an investment in people as the basis of wealth. In some regions, human capital was valuable not just for working the land; individuals were also valued for their particular knowledge, personal capacities, or extended social ties. In the wealth-in-people model, leaders exercised power through building coalitions rather than by conquering, and through nurturing societies by investing in institutions designed to secure lasting relationships of mutual obligation. Communities acquired or incorporated an individual based on her capacity to add to that community in some unique way. In other words, strategic compositional processes and deliberate coalition building constituted the heart of many precolonial Africans' attempts to develop communities. The transfer of rights-in-people and other forms of wealth between lineages, communities, or other social units through marriage, then, was a widely recognized means of tapping new social networks, securing access to new resources, and complementing an individual's or a community's particular capacities or knowledge. It was also fundamental to individuals' attempts to compose communities in a manner that would ensure collective prosperity and perpetuity. Marriages were important not only for the social networks they cemented, but also for their reproductive capacity—something that was possible, too, though not often sanctioned, outside of contracted or in-process marriages. Victorian and Edwardian Britons, as we have seen, felt similarly about the natural and central role of women in the productive and reproductive labor of the nation. Reproduction, then, and the institutions that attended it—such as marriage, childbirth, and child-rearing—were at the very heart of communities' attempts at strategic composition and communal perpetuity.

Ultimately, then, congregants' reinvestment in the church community in the first decades of the twentieth century exacerbated debates that had been unfolding since the mission's founding: how best to create and sustain a Native Church and ensure its adherence to the mission's social, biological, and ideological tenets. At the heart of these debates were the institutions of communal perpetuity—marriage, reproduction, and child-rearing. Significantly, just because these institutions were important does not mean that parties or even individuals agreed on what constituted accepted or acceptable behavior in this respect. The essential tenets of community require "not only imagining but work; community had to be created and recreated on a continuous basis. Daily, face-to-face contact between residents, in their neighborhoods . . . during the course of work, or at places of worship was an essential component of this process of crafting social community."[14] The conversations within these encounters allowed members to hash out boundaries between the acceptable and the deviant, and to define—for the moment at least—the moral standards of their community. Longstanding debates about institutions associated with biological and social reproduction were exacerbated in the 1910s and 1920s by broader historical trends unfolding in the communities where UMCA mission stations were planted.

The hardships of war and the consolidation of British administrative rule in the early decades of the twentieth century led UMCA Christians in particular to reinvest in the church as one of the communities that guided their lives and directed their behavior. But they often did so in ways that surprised missionaries, leading to scandals and debates about community boundaries and acceptable behavior. UMCA communities on both Zanzibar and the mainland in the 1910s and 1920s were thus a milieu given over to debates about strategic compositional processes and communal perpetuity. Women and the institutions with which they were associated—marriage, childbirth, and child-rearing—naturally figured prominently in these debates. During the colonial period, African women throughout the continent were subject to two patriarchies: African men and European men. When debates about communal perpetuity raged during the second and third decades of the twentieth century, UMCA women faced a patriarchal regime: God and His proxies.

Women engaged with these patriarchies in ways and for reasons that surprised, and were often invisible to, men. As such, women appear in much of the primary and secondary literature as beings without agency.[15] As the cases below illustrate, however, women used inherited knowledge and female networks to secure the means to abortion and to cover their tracks; they brokered marriages and tested them out before tying the knot; and they pushed the boundaries of the community as a way to intrude more forcibly into it. In the events that follow, women appear as active agents, intentionally hiding from view, acting "offstage," and behaving in ways that were not always visible to male observers.

Reading Sex and Scandal

Gossip, rumor, hearsay, suspicions, accusations, allegations, and investigations into and about congregants' sex lives, relationships, and homemaking were registered in official records of mission organizations throughout Africa. As in the moments of scandal that constitute this chapter, church administrators recorded their reactions to alleged "sins of the flesh" in station logbooks, diaries, registers, and letters. In general, church officials maintained such records in order to create a historical memory of events on the station for themselves, for newcomers, for visitors from the home office, and for other officials. Scholars have observed that missionaries' compulsive need to keep records was also a method of gaining control over their adherents' conduct. By maintaining "catalogues of decisions made, sins disavowed, and judgments rendered," the authors of record books "reached outside the archives' walls and reformed Africans' real-life relationships." The entries in church registers, diaries, and logbooks served, on the one hand, as evidence of the promises that parishioners had made to the church, and as a means to call "errant parishioners before the [church] courts, asking them to live up to the promises they had made on paper." With this evidence, church officials "invited adherents to conform their lives to the book, to orient their behavior to accord with the mode portrayed in the record." And, Africans often played into Europeans' archetypes, signing their names to registers and confessing sins. They also used the same legal categories missionary judges had authorized in order to reframe arguments about property, marriage, or work to their own advantage.[16]

However just as often, as we will see below, Africans jettisoned this theater altogether and sought to keep their private affairs out of reach of the arm of the church. They were not always successful: news of salacious events bubbled to the surface, appearing in written records such as the diaries and logs of the Zanzibar station. In some cases, congregants sent letters to anonymously share news they themselves found to be scandalous. As is common with gossip, the logs' authors and the other participants were hazy on many of the details of the events. To be sure, pregnancies, botched abortions, marriages, and adultery can be at once very intimate and very public affairs, and are often highly consequential, rendering the accusations and truths that surround them all the more difficult to parse.

Before finding its way to the missionaries' logs, news of scandal would have circulated through the close-knit and overcrowded *shamba* community. In some cases, elder women called in to consult on the technologies of abortion might have told their husbands or friends the details of the house call, or a neighbor might have seen a woman known to be proficient in such knowledge visiting with an engaged woman who was suspected of spending time with other men. Mothers and other female relatives living in close proximity to a young woman would have known of a missed period, and would have been able to read the looks of concern on her face. A missing girl would have raised questions, and a grandmother would have explained her absence in different ways, depending on her audience. As missionaries and African evangelists and teachers went about their daily work, they came into contact with people with stories they were keen to tell for myriad reasons. The "bush telegraph" and "pavement radio" also transmitted rumor. Rumor is "carried by the oral culture of face-to-face encounters" but can generally remain "essentially anonymous and democratic." Adherents likely supplemented the intensely personal form of gossip in small groups with the relative anonymity of rumor, passed by letter, by speaking loudly as a missionary passed, or by a husband speaking for his wife's friend.[17]

Events do not become rumor-worthy scandals unless they shock, cause moral outrage, betray, hurt, or cause jealousy. Records of these moments are an opportunity for scholars to separate the epistemologies that "shock and scandalize" from those that do not.[18] In the cases documented here, love, lust, passion, and desire, among other emotions, can be imagined to have caused lovers to start affairs, and families to rally around their adolescents. Fear, shame, faith, and an investment in the community caused congregants to hide others' actions or to seek to expose them. While a complex array of emotions produced these scandals, emotions—particularly others', much less our own—are difficult to acknowledge, name, and record. They therefore do not appear in the official record as emotions per se. Their effects, however, do. Emotional debris appears in missionary logbooks, diaries, and reports as gossip and scandal. And among Anglicans on Zanzibar in the first half of the twentieth century, what consumed a great deal of emotional energy, and thus produced the most vociferous gossip and scandal on the missionaries' pages, seems to have been when Africans' and missionaries' ideals about the best ways to regulate the institutions of communal perpetuity—marriage, reproduction, and child-rearing—rubbed up against one another.

Throughout the 1910s and 1920s, British workers at the Mbweni *shamba* noted in the mission's logs an increase in the number and severity of scandals concerning women, marriage, and reproduction. In August 1913, for example, there was the scandal with Beatrice Nyasa. Beatrice had been living apart from her husband for some time when she gave birth to a baby girl. Until the baby was actually born, Beatrice denied both being pregnant and the accusations that she was having an affair with Cecil Duma, a fellow congregant.[19] Church officials were up in arms that Beatrice had had an affair and then lied about it and about the pregnancy. Then in January of 1917, the priest-in-charge noted that there had been "wrong doings" in preparing the *shamba*'s young women for marriage. Not only was there "evil bringing up of girls as regards betrothal," but there was "wickedness of the people and their being in league to hide up their sins." Missionaries found the situation to be so disconcerting that they threatened to sell the *shamba* if conditions did not improve.[20]

These "girl cases," as one colonial official referred to similar events, were not isolated incidents.[21] UMCA station diaries reveal other attempts by church officials to adjudicate their congregants' morality. In these books, and indeed in logs from mission stations throughout Africa, administrators recorded thefts, lies, betrayals, and many of what they considered to be their congregants' other varied sins.[22] Administrators also recorded the punishments they doled out. For example, an author of a Zanzibar station log wrote that a young Christian was "found guilty of [the] gross immoral behavior" of stealing Church vestments and other valuables. The young man was "dismissed" from the community, tried in a Zanzibar court, and sentenced to three months in prison.[23] In another case, one Evelyn Tatu was "caught stealing an enormous bunch of bananas" and was "sent . . . to court in the hope that the court would order her to be shut up as [a] nuisance."[24]

Nor, for that matter, were these cases restricted to the African members of the congregation (although those cases are primarily what concern us here). Missionaries and Africans alike were concerned with community reproduction at many levels, and policed the boundaries of the spiritual community wherever they felt it was needed. Church administrators were careful to keep scandals involving British workers out of the official record, but we do know of one woman whose Tractarian resolve to celibacy in the mission field did not hold. In October of either 1908 or 1909 (the handwriting in the diary is unclear), Miss Stevens, the manager of the boys' school at Kilimani, returned to England from Zanzibar on the October mail boat.[25] Although the official reason provided for her retirement was "urgent private affairs," a letter from Bishop Frank Weston reveals that she left the mission amid accusations of affairs with male African adherents. On the outside, Miss Stevens was a "lady leading a solitary life . . . very much engrossed in her school who stoutly maintains that her relations with the boys have always been proper and Christian." Yet Weston provided a litany of evidence against her: there was an "enormous body of public opinion that she is leading a bad life with boys"; a "charge of long continued bad relations with one individual," and the individual in question confirming an "intimate" relationship with Stevens; a "charge of a bad conduct with a boy, everything short of actual connection being witnessed"; and two accusations by boys that they "have been with her."[26] African adherents were clearly knowledgeable enough about the intricacies of the missionaries' decisions to remain celibate while in the field that they could mark her behavior as "bad" or "wrong," and saw her transgressions as significant violations against the morals of the community to bring to the attention of church leadership. It is also possible that they themselves felt violated, betrayed, or jealous by her choice in partners, or outraged and alarmed by what the offspring of such a union would mean for the nature and boundaries of the community itself.

The emotions that drove the transgressions, accusations, and confessions alike were complex. Attending to these emotions, and to the affective relationships that accompanied them, allows us to better understand the scandals that wrenched the *shamba* community in the first third of the twentieth century. Attending thusly also allows us to see where congregants were drawing the lines for inclusion or exclusion in the spiritual community, and the ways in which they went about patrolling those borders. We turn now to an exploration of scandal at two separate moments on the Mbweni *shamba* in order to shed light on how individual African congregants negotiated between the demands of concurrent, and often competing, community affinities. By focusing in on the affective, embodied, and emotional dimensions of particular events, we can understand how and why they became framed as scandals, and better understand what was at stake for particular protagonists. The first event is what I call the "1921 Mbweni Abortion Scandal." The scandal had its roots in events that played out on the *shamba* in August of 1919, but which came to a head more than two years later.

The 1921 Mbweni Abortion Scandal

In late August 1919, a young African mother named Olive "Lulu" Feruzi began to miscarry a pregnancy that, if carried to term, would have given her a second child. Family members took Lulu to the hospital in Zanzibar's Stone Town, where she presented with "great pain."[27] At the time of the miscarriage, Lulu was well known to church authorities from several events that had occurred in the months leading up to her hospitalization. The first concerned the woman's young son. On May 21, Lulu apparently "threw her baby down in a fit of temper." This was the "second or third time something of the sort" had happened, leading officials to believe that Lulu was "weak minded" and could therefore not "be trusted with a male child." The priest-in-charge of the Mbweni station ordered the boy removed from the home, to be raised by Mary Juma, the child's godmother.[28] On July 16, Lulu caused even more trouble for herself by running away from home for several days after a quarrel with her husband. Church officials were troubled by this pattern of behavior and lamented, "she has very little brains and it is impossible to do much with her."[29]

Lulu's behavior did not trouble church officials for long, however. Just five days after arriving at the hospital, she was dead. Suspicion began to cloud the circumstances of Lulu's death even before she was buried. The priest-in-charge reported that there had been "something suspicious about her death"; he and others close to Lulu suspected that some sort of *dawa* (medicine) had played a role. Appended to the final sentence of the entry, in parentheses and in Kiswahili, were the words *kuharibu mimba* (destroy the pregnancy). The notation was a suggestion in the written equivalent of hushed tones that Lulu or someone close to her had attempted to abort the pregnancy.[30]

Officials made no further comment about Lulu's fate until two and a half years later, when in November 1921 the priest-in-charge at Mbweni named Lulu in a group of *shamba* women known by their neighbors to have attempted to induce miscarriage. An anonymous letter handed to the priest-in-charge on his way out of church tipped administrators off to these alleged transgressions. Although he was not certain, the priest-in-charge claimed he had "a lot of reasons for believing" that Vera Tano had written the letter.[31] Such a claim was indeed plausible, as several months earlier Vera, an Industrial girl at Mbweni, had sought out administrators at Mbweni to confess that she had "sinned with Denys Thackeray and was with child." Confession was a brave move, as she was sure to know the consequences: Vera was "severely punished by her foster mother," summarily fired from her job with the mission, and forced to sit in the back of the church during services.[32] Equally bold was Vera's lover, Denys, who admitted his sins to the priest and declared his intention to marry Vera. The priest eventually consented, and even helped Denys secure *mahari* (bride-price).[33] Despite his forthrightness, Denys did not escape his confession without a beating.

The note the priest received five months after Vera's and Denys's confessions concerned Etheldrea Mabruki, an Mbweni congregant and age-mate of Vera's. If Vera did indeed write the letter, perhaps it was the very same sense of Christian virtue that initially drove Vera to confess her own and Denys's transgressions to the priest-in-charge, which once again motivated her to expose Etheldrea's failings. Or maybe it was jealousy at the possibility that Etheldrea could escape punishment for the same sins that, just months before, Vera had been held accountable for. Whether it was Vera or someone else who filed these strategic moral accusations, it is clear that the letter writer intended to raise the alarm about behavior he or she found reprehensible. The letter's author claimed that Etheldrea had a "*mimba* (pregnancy) by Samwil Musa but . . . the *mimba* had been destroyed."[34]

UNDATED PHOTOGRAPH, FROM, "MBWENI PAPERS," *AFRICAN TIDINGS* 20, NO. 263 (SEPTEMBER 1911).

FIGURE 13. The chapel at Mbweni.

The priest-in-charge was alarmed by the accusations. Determined to get to the bottom of the matter, the cleric recruited a female teacher from the girls' school and together they visited Grace, Etheldrea's mother. Initially Grace "absolutely denied the whole thing," but eventually she admitted that she suspected her daughter had not menstruated for at least two months. She revealed that this, coupled with the "strong rumors" that her daughter "had sinned," caused her to grow suspicious. She had arranged for a fellow congregant who worked as an *mkunga* (midwife) to examine Etheldrea. Despite the widespread suspicion about Etheldrea's condition,

Mama Mwajuma reported that nothing in her examination suggested that the girl was or had been pregnant. Still skeptical, the priest-in-charge took Etheldrea to town to be examined by the mission's own British nurses. Miss Winter and Miss Edwards determined "undoubtedly" that Etheldrea was "ruined" and that "recently she has been pregnant but is no longer now."[35] Despite this evidence, and likely out of fear, shame, and a sense of privacy, Etheldrea and Samwil continued to deny the affair, the pregnancy, and the alleged abortion.

A lack of evidence might have stalled the investigation and compelled church officials to drop the matter, just as they appear to have done in the case of Olive "Lulu" Feruzi. However, Vera's alleged link to the matter was but one of several troubling factors prompting administrators to expand their investigation. Especially difficult for church officials to overlook was the fact that at the time of her alleged affair with Samwil, Etheldrea was engaged to another man. Fellow congregant Godson Mwaimu had asked for Etheldrea's hand two years previously, but the pair delayed their marriage at the behest of her father, who cited her young age as the chief reason to wait.[36] Perhaps even more troubling to administrators was the rumor that it was Godson, Etheldrea's fiancé, who forced Samwil, Etheldrea's lover, to give her the abortifacient.[37] This was in fact highly plausible because in East African communities, it was often the lover or boyfriend who was responsible for securing the abortion.[38]

The priest hoped the accusations brought against Etheldrea were "quite untrue"; however, the suggestions alone would have been enough for Samwil's family to call off the wedding and for church officials to expel Etheldrea from school, kick her off the *shamba*, and excommunicate her. With such high stakes, the priests-in-charge launched an investigation. Present at the public *baraza* (community meeting) were Etheldrea's mother, Grace; Etheldrea's grandmother, *Bibi* Helen; Bibi Helen's friend and neighbor, Fatima *binti* Ali; the *mkunga*, Mama Mwajuma; Etheldrea's fiancé, Godson Mwaimu; an African teacher named Mwalimu Evalyna; and the African priest-in-charge or "padre." It is not clear whether Etheldrea attended, but she was sure to have known about the gathering. The records of the *baraza* are scant, but sources suggest that gossip and hearsay predominated. For example, it appears that Etheldrea's grandmother had first heard about Etheldrea's pregnancy from her friend Fatima *binti* Ali, who had heard the news from her husband, who in turn had heard it from a neighbor. About the extended he-said-she-said, the priest-in-charge quipped it was all "quite useless." Eventually, however, the attendees managed to reach a consensus: they conceded that although Etheldrea "probably . . . had *mimba*" (pregnancy), they were absolutely certain that she had not "*haribu*ed the *mimba*" (destroyed the pregnancy).

Attendees offered two pieces of evidence to support their argument that Etheldrea had not had an abortion. First, Etheldrea had not been ill prior to her suspected miscarriage. Attendees argued that both Olive "Lulu" Feruzi and another young *shamba* woman named Rebekah Hamisi had "taken *dawa*" (medicine) to end pregnancies and grew severely ill before their deaths. (Until this *baraza*, church officials could only guess that these women had taken abortifacients; similar *mabaraza* after each case failed to uncover any incriminating evidence.) Second, the attendees argued, Etheldrea's *mimba* was "only 2 or 3 months" along, an inherently tenuous gestational age at which a spontaneous miscarriage would not have been entirely uncommon. Regardless, her supporters agreed, to intentionally destroy a pregnancy would have been "quite a sinfully [*sic*] matter."[39]

Despite the congregants' presentation of "evidence" and their public disavowal of abortion as a sin, the matter was far from settled. The nagging suspicion remained, at least in the minds of the missionaries, that the congregants' repeated denials of abortion were little more than an attempt to conceal behavior they knew missionaries would find reprehensible and to curry favor with church administrators. There was, of course, the nurses' testimony, circumstantial evidence, sophisticated local knowledge about abortion, and a long history of abortion in the region that led missionaries to question the congregants' position. And they likely knew that despite what *baraza* attendees told the missionaries, congregants were very likely to have had a different outlook on the issue of abortion than British officials.

Far from the anomaly that the church officials believed these cases to be, abortion was just one strategy within a long-standing repertoire from which precolonial Africans drew when dealing with socially dangerous pregnancies. In many communities, people believed that only pregnancies conceived by bodies properly prepared for procreation were "legitimate."[40] In some areas, initiation rituals prepared women and men for procreation; in other areas, marriage rituals and exchanges did this work.[41] Well into the colonial period, people living in East Africa believed that a being conceived before such rituals occurred was not a proper person. Rather, it was a "creature of ill-omen" that had the capacity to bring about misfortune in the form of drought, famine, or other disasters. The Meru, who live in what is today central Kenya, for example, believed that children were a link between themselves and their ancestors; ancestors cursed children conceived by improperly prepared women in order to express their anger at those involved.[42]

Abortion—and when that failed, infanticide—was one of precolonial Africans' "most common remedies for curbing the destructive potential" of pregnancies illegitimately conceived, of dealing with "social relations gone awry," and of "amending mistakes and avoiding public scrutiny."[43] The Zigua, for example, believed that the circumstances under which a child was conceived, carried to term, or born could have disastrous effects on the health and perpetuity of the community.[44] Children conceived by uninitiated Ngulu girls were slain for these reasons, and among the Chagga of Tanzania uninitiated couples found to have conceived were taken to the forest and made to lie on top of one another before their bodies were pierced through with a stake.[45] A Chagga woman who put her household to shame by "growing" two children at once (conceiving before an older child was weaned) may have been forced to drink the juices of certain herbs or to insert the midrib of a leaf into her body (through the vagina into the uterus) to terminate the pregnancy.[46]

Ethnographies and other scholarship about ethnolinguistic communities from which Mbweni congregants hailed suggest that abortion was, and in fact remains, a socially acceptable option for dealing with extramarital and other "illegitimate" pregnancies, events that communities often found to be deeply disgraceful or socially devastating.[47] In many African communities, abortion was seen as a "necessary action taken to avoid social ostracism" and, in some cases, death.[48] The nature of and rationale for East Africans' widespread use of abortion is important to understand: it suggests that the social health and integrity of the community—the public good, as it were—often superseded that of a single individual.[49] In other words, internal logic suggested that it was more important to ensure the durability and perpetuity of the community as a whole than to save a single life that had been improperly conceived and therefore might potentially threaten the health and well-being of the entire community.

The crucial role that abortion played in ensuring the health and perpetuity of the entire community is precisely why young women at Mbweni would have known about it. Faced with a pre- or extramarital pregnancy that threatened a family's place within the congregation or promised to ignite the ire of the local missionaries, individuals would have drawn on a wealth of inherited knowledge to find solutions. Elsewhere in East Africa, it was women of the grandmothers' generation and older women specialists who were responsible for maintaining and disseminating information about sex and reproduction. Through a wide range of female initiation rituals, conducted formally and informally, privately and in small groups, older women taught young women through song, dance, and play about sexuality, sensuality, marriage, and procreation.[50] Abortion and techniques known to induce miscarriage were part of this repertoire, and were long shared intergenerationally. As we have seen, marriages and foster relationships in the mission were composed across ethnic lines. Families lived in close proximity, and news and knowledge traveled quickly. While there is no direct evidence from the UMCA sources to tell us how young women themselves learned about abortion, we can imagine that when it came to protecting the congregation against the threat of an improperly conceived or ill-timed pregnancy, women from a range of ethnic backgrounds would have offered suggestions and advice. Knowledge particular to an elderly refugee's place of origin or a technology known to derive from a particular ethnic group would have added options and alternatives for the young woman, rather than presented a barrier to use, given the stakes. Young women would themselves have shared knowledge and information, seeking help or assistance from trusted elders when needed.

Despite the widespread and powerful ideas about abortion, the participants in the *baraza* knew that the missionaries found pre- and extramarital sex, pre- and extramarital pregnancies, and abortion above all to be sins. Indeed, they had likely heard missionaries articulate well-formulated theological justifications to this effect. At home in Britain in the early twentieth century, abortion was perceived as a working-class phenomenon. To many, abortion was by its very nature a rejection of women's traditional role of childbearing, and thus antithetical to civilization because of the threat it posed to the hierarchical family structure. Medical professionals and clerics referred to abortion as a "grievously sinful attempt to destroy the life which God has given, from which the conscience of every woman ought to turn away in horror," and a "hideous excrescence of civilization." According to one British Anglican bishop, women who engaged in abortions—either by procuring or performing them—had "instincts worse than savages."[51] While by the turn of the century the crime of abortion was largely "looked on in fashionable circles as no crime at all," and many British mothers seemed "not to understand that self-induced abortion was illegal," the Anglican Communion continued to argue well into the 1930s against birth control of any kind.[52] It was not until the 1930 Lambeth Conference, in fact, that the bishops relented on their view that procreation was the primary purpose of "sexual union" in marriage, and would give but "grudging authorization to the practice of birth control in marriage, under the dictates of the individual conscience and medical supervision."[53] Officials of the colonial government agreed with missionary officials that abortion was abhorrent, but as we have seen, they offered different grounds for their objections.

The congregants were well aware that church administrators did not want "savages" for mothers of this Christian community, and were savvy enough to use this knowledge to advance their argument of Etheldrea's innocence. By arguing the case in the missionaries' own terms, the congregants illustrated their willingness to participate in the missionaries' moral community and reaffirmed to the administrators the role of Christianity in their lives—a calculated move for tenuous times. While the *baraza* and the anonymous letter illuminated the extent of abortion at Mbweni, the growing scandal also revealed the competing moral registers at play among various constituencies on the *shamba*. What we know of East African communities in this period suggests that abortion and what missionaries thought of as "premarital" pregnancy were not at all unusual. Congregants were keenly aware that church officials would see these events differently than they did; therefore, they sought to hide these transgressions from administrators. The *baraza* revealed to administrators, seemingly for the first time, that congregants had conspired to conceal from them several "premarital" pregnancies and abortion attempts.

Missionaries' lingering suspicions about Etheldrea's guilt and congregants' conspiracy to conceal her and other girls' transgressions did not sit well with church officials. The African padre confronted the adults at the end of mass the next Sunday about "the case." He told the congregants that if the "facts as stated were true," a grave sin had been committed. The priest was explicit in his condemnation and called the sinners out by name: he said that, as a result of their investigations, it was now clear that Etheldrea, Lulu, and Rebekah had "taken *dawa*." Worse was the administrators' discovery that these sins were "fairly common." Not only did people seem "to think nothing of it," but "nearly everyone on the *shamba* had talked about it" while lacking "the courage" to stop the abortions or to discuss them with church officials. On the other hand, if someone had falsely accused Etheldrea, Denys, Samwil, and Etheldrea's family of plotting the abortion, that was also "an unutterabl[e] . . . sin." Either way, the transgressions implicated the entire community, and the entire community would be punished. Due to the "extreme seriousness" of these matters, the padre declared that "until further notice, there would be no more sermons in church, no more work and no more school."[54]

The rationale behind the padre's temporary sanctions was likely twofold. Religiously, Tractarian philosophy indicated that learning and the observance of sacraments were the cornerstones of Christianity. Tractarians idealized ceremonial practice and strict observance of fasts and festivals as not only fundamental to proper worship but central to Christian identity.[55] According to one UMCA bishop, access to the sacraments was central to the "high privilege it is to be a Christian"; it was a priest's job to "keep prominently before the people . . . what a calamity it is if, through their willful sins, they should be cut off from sharing in the blessings of community of the Church. To forbid a man to receive the Holy Eucharist is the greatest penalty we can give." Thus in such cases of "open defiance of any plain law of Christian living," the sinner would face temporary or permanent excommunication.[56] Descendants of freed slaves and immigrants to the island, the African Christians did not have well-established kin ties or other ties of obligation on Zanzibar to draw on in times of need. Without the ability to identify as Christians, and without access to the practices and institutions that gave congregants both social legitimacy and economic stability, the congregants were left with few prospects.

At church the following Sunday, the padre expressed the administrators' alarm through a lesson on Isaiah 1.[57] The Book of Isaiah recounts the story of the rebirth of Zion through the return of God's chosen people. It is ultimately a redemptive story of a church that rises from its trials "cleansed, glorified, and blissful." What congregants heard that Sunday were not stories about a church renewed, however, but rather tales of a church laid waste by the people's hypocrisy and sin.[58] Known as "The Great Arraignment," the opening chapter of Isaiah describes God's damning condemnation for the sins of His chosen people:

> I have nourished and brought up children, and they have rebelled against me . . . Ah, sinful nation, a people laden with iniquity, a seed of evildoers, children that are corrupters: they have forsaken the Lord, they have provoked the Holy One of Israel unto anger, they are gone away backward.[59]

Here Isaiah, and by proxy the Mbweni church officials, laments the "apostasy, ingratitude, and deep depravity" of the chosen people of God.[60] According to Isaiah, most damning among their sins was that the Jews "kept up the appearance of religion" while their "services of God [remained] so false and hollow." In short, they were deeply hypocritical. Isaiah urges his sinful nation to "turn from their sins, and to seek God" anew. Should they fail to repent, he warns, "heavier judgments should come upon them than they had yet experienced." Indeed, excommunication and the closing of Mbweni awaited congregants if they failed to atone for their sins.

Bibi Mildred's "Sale" of Susan Faraji

In October 1929, eight years after Etheldrea's troubles but by no means for the first time since, Mbweni officials found themselves embroiled in another sex scandal. Rumors of the sexual exploitation of young Susan Faraji by her grandmother Bibi Mildred were part of what church officials must have considered to be a rash of immoral behavior on the *shamba*: in a letter that someone later pasted into the logbook, the diocesan treasurer noted no fewer than three scandalous events in one month. In the first case, the treasurer revealed that Hilda, Owen's mother (whom we met above), was not the only one dispensing questionable marital advice. The advice that newly married men take a mistress to avoid "going mad" was, according to the treasurer, "usually given to young men by the old Mbweni women."[61] In the second case, the treasurer reported that two of the mission's African teachers, Barbara Abdallah and Danieli Taabu, had been living together secretly, unmarried, for more than a year.[62] If living together unmarried were not scandal enough, Danieli was known "to be a person of loose morals" who already had a son out of wedlock.[63] Rather than face ridicule or ostracism from their fellow congregants, however, it seems that the *wazee* (community elders) and "all the other people" knew of their situation and, once again, said nothing.[64]

The third case seemed the most troubling for the treasurer. He reported that Susan Faraji had "been sold" by her Bibi Mildred to a neighbor, and that she had since been "at the disposal" of a "Moslem" (*sic*) man for two years.[65] While under his care, she allegedly "had relations with Arabs"—"relations" that, although not explicitly stated, it is safe to assume were sexual. When they learned of the arrangement, missionaries attempted to persuade the neighbor to let Susan return home. He ultimately agreed to "give her up," citing as the deciding factor her alleged affairs with several "other men." But much to the missionaries' dismay, Bibi Mildred returned Susan to the neighbor that very same evening in an attempt to "persuade him to take her back." The entry does not tell us how Mildred's attempts at reconciliation ended.

As in Etheldrea's case, it seems that Bibi Mildred and Susan were not the only congregants to know about the affair. Officials speculated that Susan's mother, Mariane Salama, "must certainly have known about it," although it is unclear whether she, too, received payment for the transfer of the girl. Inquiries into the case shed "light on the characters of some of the other girls," causing missionaries to suspect that "some of the other grandmothers do the same with girls in their charge." Once again, church officials had on their hands a case of what they would have considered to be gross immorality, and a congregation of individuals who chose, for one reason or another, to hide these events from the missionaries.

Of course, within the context of the UMCA's abolitionism, any transaction that resembled a "sale" would have troubled missionaries. Even worse was a presumed "sale" of an African woman to a "Moslem" or "Arab" man. Echoing what they thought they knew about the past, missionaries cast these individuals as if actors in a role, imagining their congregants playing out the very same racial stereotypes that had brought the missionaries to Africa in the first place. To see the "Arab slave trade" enacted on mission lands, among individuals professing to be Christians, with the explicit intention to deceive officials, was more than they could tolerate. In his letter, the treasurer wrote that he suspected the bishop would be equally horrified and that he would give the treasurer his "permission to *tenga*" (excommunicate) Bibi Mildred "at once." The treasurer also posted a notice in the church that informed the congregation of three points: (1) there would be no mass at Mbweni until the bishop returned from his travels and "dealt with the matter" himself; (2) the Mbweni school should also be closed until his return, because "all the teachers and girls have been in on the secret"; and (3) the names of "certain people" would be sent to the bishop immediately so that he could "consider censure or excommunication."

In addition to these now familiar sanctions, the priest-in-charge once again used Sunday mass as a moment for censure. This time, the padre preached on the text "God can from these stones raise up children unto Abraham," part of a speech from John the Baptist.[66] The passage is a scathing tale of repentance and a warning of judgments to come, the meaning of which was not likely to have been lost on the Mbweni congregants.[67] Upon emerging from ascetic life, John told the waiting crowds that, despite what they had been led to believe, God had not reserved a special place for the Jews in heaven merely because they were children of Abraham; rather, God would only save those who were pure of faith and heart, and who had undergone moral purification through baptism. Yet when facing the crowds, John saw a godless, hypocritical nation.[68] They must repent, he said, because God did not need hypocrites or sinners among his followers.[69] Nor did the UMCA need liars or charlatans among its flocks, the padre seemed to be saying to his congregants, when there was an entire continent of others waiting to be saved.

The missionaries' readings of these events were shaped by their understanding of the history of the Indian Ocean world and the trade it produced, the history of the so-called Arab slave trade, and the Bible. But theirs is not the only way to interpret what happened to Susan Faraji and other young *shamba* women in the late 1920s. Congregants had their own reasons for the choices they made. They also had their own reasons for keeping those choices secret from church officials—or, less nefariously, for failing to include church officials in their considerations. It is clear from missionary outrage and congregants' decisions to hide these events that there were varying definitions of "acceptable" and "deviant" behavior at play in the late 1920s on the Mbweni *shamba*. The scandal in which Susan and her bibi were embroiled—a scandal of presumed sexual exploitation—also illuminates debates about what it meant to be a UMCA Christian, and how to define the community's borders. This scandal, however, also suggests that in 1920s Zanzibar, the question of belonging to the UMCA community was as much a racial question as it was a religious one. Long-standing local discourses about race and rhetoric imported by Western abolitionists became bound up with church members' concerns about community reproduction and perpetuity and underwrote church members' attempts to build a durable community.

The stark racial and religious distinction that the treasurer drew between "Moslem" and "Arab" on the one hand and "Christian" and "African" on the other is based on a myth that presumes deeply rooted divisions between Arab and African in this part of the world. These divisions have little to do with the actual history of Arab trade and settlement on the Swahili Coast, however. Individuals who believed themselves to be "Arab" were either of actual Omani or other Arab descent, or they claimed to be *Shirazi*, a term referring to distant (and largely fictive) Middle Eastern ancestry and identifying largely Swahili-speaking patrician families. These self-proclaimed "Arabs" believed, and in turn taught Westerners, a myth of Arab conquest that held that they "came in the thousands from Arabia [to East Africa], conquered the land in bloody wars and settled themselves in it." In Europeans' racial stereotypes then, an "Arab" might be any urban, upper-class, or aristocratic Muslim, even if he was born in Africa and spoke little to no Arabic. Westerners also assumed that to be "Arab," one must also lack slave ancestry and possess wealth and power derived in part from the possession of slaves.[70] Contrary to what missionaries believed about the racialized history of "Arab slavery," not all masters or slave traders were of Middle Eastern descent.[71]

Further, rather than fixed, the boundaries between "African" and "Arab" were in actuality "assimilative and flexible, based on a 'concept of belonging that is truly liberal'" and can "shift according to situation and generation."[72] Despite this, rhetoric that assumed a natural or primordial basis to racial identity permeated missionaries' assumptions about the history of the slave trade, underwrote mission propaganda in Britain and Africa, shaped daily interactions with congregants, and ultimately surfaced as anti-Arab propaganda in abolitionist mission education.[73] Unlike their secular counterparts, who believed the slave trade needed to be stopped because it "impeded what otherwise might have been the Arabs' fuller civilizing influence on the 'more backward, more passive' peoples of Africa," evangelical abolitionists in Zanzibar did not believe that slave status equaled an "ancestral background of barbarism" and that Arab "civilization" was something to which one should aspire. On the contrary, evangelical abolitionists—UMCA Tractarians included—crafted narratives demonizing Arabs and their religion as "baneful influences."[74] African Christians, both mainland immigrants and those from Zanzibar, would have had few reasons to aspire to, or make claims on, Arab identity. There were a host of complicated historical and contemporary reasons that "Arabs" were "perceived as exploiters and not as a category of persons one would want to emulate or claim as one's own."[75]

The administrators thus categorized Susan's alleged paramours as "Moslem" and "Arab," ignoring racial descriptions that were at the time indistinguishable to the European eye. But it does not yet explain why Bibi Mildred would have been willing to arrange what missionaries understood to be a "sale" of her granddaughter to one of these men, given the presumed history of racial animus between former slaves and local "Arabs." We can never know for sure what motivated Bibi Mildred, but an examination of two possible options demonstrates the disconnect between the administrators' understandings of their congregants' lives, and the way in which their congregants actually lived. Further, the complex relationship between marriage and slavery in late nineteenth- and early twentieth-century Zanzibar illustrates the capacity of the UMCA's female congregants to improvise unique solutions designed to intrude more forcibly into the UMCA community, to enhance their own security, and to shape the racial and civilizational boundaries of the community.

To be sure, the history of racial thought along the Swahili Coast described above suggests a healthy skepticism in the missionaries' depiction of the situation. Both Western rhetoric and local usages conflated complex, fluid identities into discrete categories, pitting the "Arab" against the "African." The men with whom Bibi Mildred negotiated an understanding about Susan Faraji were perhaps no more former slaveholders who could claim blood descent from the Middle East than they were some of the many former slaves who in the early twentieth century claimed "Arab" identity in order to make claims on resources the British administration deemed as being for Arabs only. Former slaves in early twentieth-century Zanzibar did what coastal residents had done for centuries, which was to "define themselves in ways that allowed them to make claims on resources controlled by the widest range of social actors."[76] This they did by pragmatically claiming to belong to the ethnic groups determined by the state to be "deserving" of special benefits through their consumptive habits, their public profession of Islam, and their performance of certain rituals and habits that allowed them to identify as "Arab."

In the early twentieth century, for example, many former slaves began to identify as freeborn "Swahili," a historically open ethnonym that was particularly suitable for former slaves, many of whom "were on the move in the period after abolition and hoping to assert a new social identity distinct from their servile pasts." Then in the 1920s, former slaves—who by then understood the importance of ethnic classifications to British authorities—began to identify as indigenous Zanzibaris rather than Swahili in order to rightfully claim the land on which they had established homes and farms over the previous decades. Between 1924 and 1931, Zanzibaris who could lay claim to a "racial" classification of Arab—either by virtue of genealogy, education, cultural "refinement," marriage, patronage, property, or color—did so as a response to different decrees from the British administration that aimed to "protect" the "real" Arabs from those with "but 'a drop of blue blood' whose actions and habits 'besmirch the reputation of the true Arab.'" These actions increased the number of individuals identifying themselves to census enumerators as Arabs by nearly 80 percent. For many former slaves and other island residents, asserting a particular racial or ethnic identity at any given moment "was more about demanding respect as a citizen than about articulating a fundamental shift in self-perception regarding one's race."[77]

Bibi Mildred's perception of her neighbors' "race" thus may have been significantly different from the identity that missionaries assigned to them, opening a whole range of possibilities for the type of arrangement that Mildred negotiated between the "Moslem" and her granddaughter. And this transfer, too, was perhaps no more a "sale" than an instance of one of a host of arrangements that clients negotiated with patrons, in both the precolonial and contemporary periods. Indeed, it is unlikely that there was, as the missionary logs indicate, a simple cash exchange for Susan's services as a "domestic" slave, concubine, or wife. Such a "sale" would have gone against local practices, precluding the development of the political, social, and kinship alliances cultivated in the context of a marriage.

Perhaps what the treasurer interpreted as a "sale" was in reality an installment of bridewealth, in which Bibi Mildred was acting as the de facto lineage head.[78] To the missionaries' mind this scenario was inconceivable, because a marriage between Susan and a "Moslem" or "Arab" man would have meant that Mildred—a former slave herself—was willing to overlook what the missionaries saw as stark racial and religious differences.[79] But the mutable nature of race on early twentieth-century Zanzibar meant, as we have seen, that these distinctions were stronger in missionary rhetoric than they were in the minds of congregants in the 1920s. Mildred might just as easily have been negotiating a marriage between an urban, aristocratic Muslim neighbor and her granddaughter, or between her granddaughter and a former slave who had happened to adopt Islam (rather than Christianity) in a bid to make claims on resources rationed by the state, and status controlled by the Arab elite.

As *wamisheni*, the UMCA congregants did not have the same ability to manipulate ethnic and racial categories as a means of making claims on resources controlled by the British administration, or on status ascribed by historical understandings of *ustaarabu* and urban Swahili culture. Rather, their affiliation with the mission was predicated on the fact that they were former slaves—migrants from the mainland—and, by their very presence on the island, *not* freeborn Swahili, indigenous Zanzibari, or any variation of "Arab." To be sure, the surnames of many Mbweni residents betray their slave pasts—the church would not have changed surnames such as "Faraji," "Ramadhani," "Ambali," "Malisawa," for example, after a slave was freed or redeemed; new Christian first names would have been given, however, to mark their incorporation into the Christian flock. Surnames notwithstanding, members of the UMCA community were invariably and immutably "African."

Rather than adopt physical, sartorial, or performative characteristics that would allow them to assert a new social identity distinct from their servile pasts, if the UMCA's inherently "African" Christians wished to remain affiliated with the church, they had to imagine new ways to lay claim to resources increasingly controlled by British administrators and the racial and ethnic communities they deemed "deserving" at any particular time. Negotiating a marriage between her granddaughter and a landholding, perhaps educated, culturally refined—albeit Muslim—neighbor would have granted Mildred access to these resources; it would also have allowed Mildred to hedge her bets, as it were, affording her membership in two communities and, consequently, extra stability in a time of rapid social and political change. Cultivating political, economic, and social ties with an otherwise "distant" family or community in the hopes of increasing security would not have been a new concept but part of a much longer-standing process of expansion and security building in which families negotiated political, economic, and social ties through negotiating marriages among couples of distant communities.

Another possibility is that Mildred arranged for Susan Faraji a more temporary situation, something that provided Mildred with some cash or other financial resources without losing access to her granddaughter and without—at least until missionaries became aware—jeopardizing Susan Faraji's place in the UMCA community. This option, one that anthropologists call "redeemable pawnship," was a widely practiced social institution in precolonial Africa. In pawnship, all of the rights to a person—including a woman's sexual and reproductive capacities—were temporarily transferred to another individual or lineage. If a female pawn married, the creditor lineage, rather than her own lineage, received the bridewealth and the right of permanently affiliating her children.[80] In coastal Kenya and the northeastern region of Tanzania, the home regions of many of the UMCA's first generations of freed slaves, pawns were at times exchanged as compensation for a crime or injury, though more often it was a "resort during droughts and food shortages, when hungry people surrendered pawns for food."[81] In the precolonial period, lineages were often able to collect the pawn after satisfying some debt. Scholars have argued that this changed in the late nineteenth century, however, particularly in areas affected by the increased demand for plantation labor on the coast and the widespread instability and warring that accompanied the advance of the ivory and slaving frontiers into the interior. In the minds of pawnholders, "the distinction between pawnship and slavery tended to disappear as the coast became part of the East African slave trade," and "pawnship was subsumed within slavery as one mechanism that generated new slaves for the expanding economy."[82] Indeed, this may have been the route by which Bibi Mildred herself arrived at the mission.

In arranging a short-term pawnship situation, Bibi Mildred might have imagined several scenarios for herself and her granddaughter. It is possible that Mildred was not having her needs met while living at the station. The mission provided land and a small stipend to lay congregants, but many sought additional income-generating activities. Some cultivated and sold the surplus to the mission or outside; some took small jobs offered by the mission; and others worked in town. If Bibi Mildred had in fact pawned Susan, she might have done so in exchange for cash or some other form of capital that she could invest in a small food, tailoring, or *pombe* (local brew) business outside the purview of the church to help provide for additional security, luxury wants, or other felt needs. This "pawn" would in effect function as a loan to be paid back over time. In this, Mildred would have been in line with many of her female Zanzibari contemporaries who, as the early nineteenth century progressed and the influence of the British administration was more thoroughly felt, found it increasingly difficult to procure waged jobs in town. Those who did manage to find work suffered wage discrimination, typically earning "only one-half to two-thirds of the wage paid to their male counterparts."[83] Women in Zanzibar were at this time also facing a gradual elimination of their property rights under Islamic law.[84] Marginalized from work in the public sector, many Zanzibar women sought more "respectable" and independent forms of employment that were "historically associated with free Swahili women, such as trade, entertainment, or the production and sale of food and crafts." Trade and home-based manufacturing gave many women more control over their days, allowing them to incorporate household, childcare, and social obligations with income-generating activities. The profits from such enterprises may have been marginal, but they "nonetheless contributed to women's growing sense of economic and personal empowerment." Extra income and business connections would have, once again, provided Mildred with increased stability in her rapidly changing world. Never sure about the long-term viability of the church community, and threatened time and again with the church's closure, Mildred would have been smart to seek out ways to shore up her own personal wealth.

As for Susan Faraji's "relations with Arabs," some sexual services may have been part of a pawnship arrangement from the beginning. Alternatively, Susan may have had romantic affairs with boys or men the missionaries identified as "Arab" while under the charge of the "Moslem." This, of course, the missionaries would have been loath to consider, but any racial or moral differences between Susan Faraji and her paramour would have been more easily surmountable in their eyes than in the missionaries'. Finally, Susan's alleged dalliances may have been something that the neighbor fabricated in an attempt to extract himself from the relationship when he saw how much trouble it was causing. Whatever the situation, any children born to Susan Faraji while she was a pawn under the patronage of the "Moslem" would have legally been of his lineage and remained his property when she left. The children, known to be of mixed racial and religious heritage, would not have returned with Susan Faraji to complicate or possibly contaminate the nature of the community defined as growing from former slaves.

If Susan Faraji's "affair" was indeed a pawnship transfer, any potential offspring would have remained with the neighbor's family. Bearing a child with the neighbor might have made Susan a more desirable partner in future years, however, for it would have "proven her fertility" without introducing a child into the community.[85] A pawnship arrangement would have allowed Bibi Mildred to build a more secure foundation for herself and her granddaughter without risking the intrusion of a non-Christian child or a child of mixed racial heritage into the African spiritual community—a community that was becoming increasingly defined by race. This was important because we have seen that by virtue of their status as UMCA Christians on Zanzibar, Bibi Mildred and Susan Faraji were immutably African, and were therefore not able to claim a different ethnic or racial status in order to secure resources in tumultuous times. Their gender also limited their capacity to direct change in any official capacity. Rather, they had to act surreptitiously by controlling sexuality and reproduction, passion and lust (or, alternatively, fear and disgust), shame and pride in ways that would allow them to intrude more forcibly into the evangelical community, to shore up their resources, and to gain increased security. Looking to romantic and sexual affairs, and to female lay evangelists' attempts to control them, we see one of the many ways in which the UMCA's female lay evangelists could, at particular moments, manage the future and nature of the spiritual community.

Ultimately it is impossible to know Bibi Mildred's motivations regarding her granddaughter Susan Faraji.[86] Perhaps what is more important than the hypothetical question of whether the affair was a strategic marriage or a form of slavery is that this story illuminates tensions between British missionary understandings of local practice and East African ways of understanding the relationship between slavery and marriage to which women improvised unique solutions designed to intrude more forcibly into the UMCA community, to enhance their own security, and to shape the boundaries of the community.[87] UMCA administrators understood marriage and slavery to be distinct, and perhaps even diametrically opposed. They had delivered their congregants from the grip of slavery into the (theoretical) equality of a companionate marriage. However, the lines between marriage, pawnship, concubinage, and slavery were not nearly as clear in the minds of East Africans in the late nineteenth and early twentieth centuries. We have seen that women were exceptionally vulnerable in nineteenth-century East African societies and they thus developed a range of strategies to enhance their security. Female slaves, for example, could become the concubine of a powerful man. If their union produced a son, the woman could lose much of the stigma of slavery and gain the "prestige and protection of having mothered a free person." She might even become his wife, earning manumission. Such a path to upward mobility was not certain, however, and depended on the whims of masters, mistresses, and other wives.[88] Further, with marriage a woman would become wholly dependent on her husband.

The range of options available to former female slaves living on mission stations in the early twentieth century were much more open and varied than British administrators would have been able to imagine. Women drew from these options in myriad ways to shape their realities and the world around them. Women like Bibi Mildred and Etheldrea's family and advocates used quotidian, embodied performance of certain civilizational values as a way to hem the community and to protect its borders, while simultaneously ensuring their continued membership in the community. Etheldrea and her family performed a version of the companionate, monogamous bride-to-be for missionaries and the community at large, hiding Etheldrea's more transgressive behavior as a way to resist excommunication. The other women who sought abortions controlled their own fertility as a way to remain engaged in the church community, but did so in a way that drew from much longer-standing practices in order to make sense of and control changing circumstances. The scandals discussed arose from emotions that were produced by an ideological tension between members' notions of how best to regulate the ideological, social, and biological institutions of reproduction—institutions that lie at the center of the community-building process—and thus how best to manage the future of the community itself. And, for female lay evangelists in 1920s Zanzibar, the community in their minds was one that was diverse, encompassing, and increasingly defined by race.

■ ■ ■

By the first decades of the twentieth century, UMCA congregants had come to see themselves as part of a broad spiritual community, one that cut across and superseded the affinities of ethnicity, colonies, and civil organizations. Congregants did not articulate their concerns within the paradigm of "resistance" or "oppression" that scholars often attribute to nationalism's political innovators, but instead they focused—at least in the evidence they left behind—on composing a community attuned to the creation of a specific brand of African "civilization," defined by the values of Christian modernity, supra-tribal unity, and racial exclusivity. To be sure, the UMCA was not the only organization or community concerned with the shape and nature of an "African civilization," or seeking to define "civilization" for themselves. Civilizational change was at the heart of British and European evangelical missions across the continent—across the world, in fact—and Africans engaged with this process to varying degrees.

Scholars have shown that throughout the first half of the twentieth century, East African men used women's fertility and sexual morality as a language to debate community composition, the boundaries of racial communities, and African "civilization." In interwar Tanzania and Zanzibar, for example, African male intellectuals tied women's sexual behavior (or purported sexual behavior) to the health and future of African civilization. In later years, Tanzanians focused on the miniskirt and on women's public comportment as a way to enforce racial and civilizational boundaries.[89] Luo men in eastern Africa's cities fussed over independent women's threat to the civil order, and Tanzanians in the 1960s sought to identify, enumerate, and contain women, equating their conduct with the future of the socialist project.[90]

Yet, scholars have been silent on the intellectual contributions of women to this discussion. As the case studies above illustrate, women also engaged in these debates by attending to and cultivating their own fertility. By aborting ill-timed pregnancies, the UMCA's sisters in spirit made decisions about the types of relationships and offspring suitable for the moral community. Out of sight of church administrators, congregants defined for themselves what constituted an improperly conceived being and hemmed the boundaries of the community. Disagreements over the definition and fluidity of marriage and over the definition and fluidity of race played out on women's bodies and in their embodied, daily performance of Christian living. Racial and civilizational boundaries were created not just through discourse, but through women's embodied acts. These case studies illustrate that in interwar East Africa, women were not just the subject of men's racial discourse, but they were active and involved participants in the creation of community and of racial and civilizational boundaries. By regulating reproduction through a range of affective relationships, female congregants contributed to the intellectual lineages and modes of thought that shaped the spiritual community.

CHAPTER SIX

I Am a Spiritual Mother

Affect, Celibacy, and Social Reproduction, 1920–1970

In 1926, Stella Mwenyipembe declared her intention to join six British nuns as the first "little sister" of the UMCA's religious order for women. As a novice at the Community of the Sacred Passion (CSP) convent in Magila, a central station in northeastern Tanzania, Stella would have been tasked—in addition to studying for Holy Orders—with working with some of the 180 pupils in the girls' school, in one of the local hospitals, or with local women in the district.[1] This work would have been something with which Stella was well acquainted, having grown up around the CSP Sisters—as their student, patient, and fellow parishioner. Further, as the daughter of an African priest, Stella had firsthand knowledge of the religious life. Her father, Samwil Mwenyipembe, was in fact well known for his heroics as a sort of priest-turned-Renaissance-man during the First World War. Living with his family at an outstation near Magila when the war began, Mwenyipembe remained alone at the station after his colleagues either fled or were imprisoned. For several years Mwenyipembe assumed his colleagues' responsibilities, tending singlehandedly to the spiritual and physical needs of a community that stretched several days' walk in all directions: he performed services, repaired and maintained church buildings and farms, mediated between German officials and imprisoned church staff, allocated increasingly scarce resources to congregants and other remaining staff, maintained the print shop, and was granted limited permission to perform marriage ceremonies, a rite usually reserved for the British members of staff.[2] Thus it was likely with a clear understanding of the demands of the religious life that Stella Mwenyipembe entered the CSP in 1926.

Yet, despite this comprehensive understanding of the commitment she was about to undertake, Stella quit the order before taking permanent vows. In fact, Stella was not alone in her decision to leave the order: motivated by a range of complicated factors, African women repeatedly made what British church officials saw as "very brave attempt[s] in the face of enormous opposition" to join the order. Until Stella joined as a "little sister," the CSP had been the exclusive purview of British women. Founded in 1911 by the UMCA's Bishop Weston, the order was a response to the very Tractarian desire of some of the mission's administrators and female workers to offer the opportunity for aspirants to formally pledge themselves to a life of poverty, prayer, chastity, and service in Africa. The order's founder and earliest sisters had high hopes (though low expectations) that the community would eventually incorporate African women. And indeed, it was not until 1946 that an African woman was able to persist in her quest to take Holy Orders.[3]

A celibate religious order was in many ways the logical outgrowth of the values of religious asceticism, monasticism, and retirement at the heart of Tractarianism. Attending to emotions and affects such as fear and discontent, striving and aspiration, faith and self-sacrifice, we see that a religious order has long served as an opportunity for Christian African women to forge a unique subjectivity. Not only did novices form intimate, affective spiritual relationships among themselves, but they also became evangelists for the UMCA's affective spiritual community writ large. Profession also allowed aspirants to embed themselves more firmly within the church community, and granted them opportunities to assert more control over the nature of the burgeoning spiritual community. In so doing, women from what became Chama cha Mariamu Mtakatifu (CMM) deployed longer-standing values in order to build a new type of community.

Tractarianism and the Religious Life in Britain

Historians of Tractarianism have noted the appeal of the revival movement to British women in particular—indeed, women were overrepresented among lay Anglo-Catholics generally, numbering between approximately 66 and 82 percent of all London-area congregations.[4] Contemporary Anglo-Catholics recognized the paradox implicit in this gendered appeal: one commentator remarked, "Men wrote the tracts for the Times . . . but it was women who first carried all this theory into practice."[5] Critics of the movement derided the imbalance among the laity as one of the movement's many faults. The rector of Saint Mary-le-Port, Bristol, for example, lamented that the Anglo-Catholic priest "rules with despotic sway over ever so many young ladies, not a few old ones, some sentimental young gentlemen, and one or two old men in their dotage."[6] Other critics (and there were many) even went so far as to claim that the movement was a conspiracy driven by women: "The Ritual movement is a lay movement," said a disgruntled curate in Paddington, "but it is more than that; it is a female movement . . . The Ritualistic clergyman is led, or rather misled, by a few ladies, who have time and taste for ornamental work, for embroidering coloured stoles, chasubles, &c., and they allow themselves no rest until they have persuaded him to wear these things . . . to the intense gratification of a few zealots and the unbounded annoyance of many sensible people."[7] Dissenters derided female Tractarians as simpletons who found "one of the sweetest pleasures of their life in decorating chancels, and working vestments, and helping to make the service of the altar as splendid as they know how."[8] While the movement's detractors often trivialized the involvement of women for their own political purposes, new religious movements, such as evangelical and middle-of-the-road Anglicanism, did tend to attract proportionately more women than men. While Anglo-Catholic churches may have served more than their share of women, the disproportion was little more than an exaggeration of a contemporary trend.[9]

The particular allure of Anglo-Catholicism for Victorian British women is a hard thing to parse with much confidence, given the sources and nature of an inquiry into the fraught realm of "intention." Despite what its detractors believed, Tractarianism had more to offer women than an opportunity to perfect their embroidery. To be sure, women without families could find refuge in Anglo-Catholic congregations as a *femme dévote*, losing themselves in what was virtually full-time employment pursuing "a variety of activities useful and (in their own terms) important" to the functioning of the church.[10] The sociologist John Shelton Reed suggests that the ritualism of the service and the strength of Anglo-Catholic clerics may have been appealing to some unmarried women because it offered "authoritative dicta from clerical 'fathers.'" Yet even if they were drawn in primarily by Tractarianism's ritualism and authority, most women would not have characterized their positions within the church in terms as simple as their detractors did—as what one Oxfordshire magistrate termed "clerical trammels."[11] While some women may have found in ritualism a sort of patriarchal authority missing in their own lives, many more were likely to have seen it as a challenge to the established patriarchy. For example, ritualists in England advocated for the separation of genders at worship. Not only was this move anti-class and anti-hierarchical, as it removed private and closed (for-purchase/by-donation) pews from the nave, but it was also thought to reduce "personal domestic feelings" as part of the worship experience. Fathers of families would no longer be recognized as such, and the range of social classes, gender, and other forms of privilege in the congregation melded into an "undifferentiated mass of worshipers."[12] Finally, mainline Protestants argued that the ritual of confession was an affront to Victorian family ideology because of its association with sins of the flesh. Priests were, according to popular opinion, "preparing themselves, by the study of filthy and obscene literature, to pollute the purity of our wives, daughters, and little children, by questions and suggestions on the most indecent of subjects"; the ritual's "symbolic, if not actual, threat to domestic authority" might have in fact been attractive to women.[13]

It is far more likely, however, that a complex amalgam of theological, political, and personal concerns drove British women to join the Tractarian revival in such great numbers. Perhaps nowhere was the allure of Anglo-Catholicism to women (and corresponding popular outrage) stronger than in the institutionalization of the celibate, monastic ideal. As early as the 1840s, and as a direct result of the Oxford Movement's return to catholic values, Tractarians began to establish (or reestablish, as they saw it) the very sort of religious communities that the Church of England had done away with during the Reformation.[14] While reformers had initially hoped that orders for both genders would flourish, the revival of sisterhoods was particularly successful.[15] The first reformers to resurrect the idea of the sisterhood imagined that they would operate as a "refuge and resource: places of refuge for unmarried women and as sources of charitable relief and trained nurses to ameliorate the suffering of the poor."[16] In fact, the Oxford Movement's own John Henry Newman wrote in 1835 that sisterhoods could "give dignity and independence to the position of women in society." Affiliation with a convent could also, he believed, provide "a refuge for 'redundant' females, since, 'as matters stand, marriage is the sole shelter which a defenseless portion of the community has against the rude world.'"[17] The Oxford Movement's Anglo-Catholics were not the only Protestants looking to expand the role of women in the church in the 1830s and 1840s. Quakers and other Nonconformist women, inspired by their liberal faith, were some of the first to speak out for women's equality; at the same time, the Lutheran Pastor Fliedner opened a house for religious women in Kaiserwerth, Germany (later made famous by the work of Florence Nightingale), and also in 1837, Dom Prosper Gueranger inaugurated a new phase of the history of Benedictine life in France.[18]

Despite a broader interest in the religious life for Protestant women in Britain and Europe, the movement's advocates faced considerable opposition to the idea. To be sure, contemporaries in the Church of England had long opposed the Tractarian revival movement. As John Shelton Reed argues, "Many of the practices championed by Anglo-Catholics were symbolic affronts—and in a few cases actual threats—to central values of Victorian middle-class culture. The movement's opponents were right to be offended. To some extent, they were *meant* to be offended."[19] The ideal of religious life was not fundamentally different in this sense from the movement as a whole; it is, by definition, a withdrawal from and a protest against the standards and habits of the world.[20] Indeed, the rise of sisterhoods must be seen as part of Tractarianism's "silent rebellion" against the restrictions placed on women by Victorian society. As Reed points out, "Sisterhood life took women out of their homes. It gave them important work and sometimes great responsibility. It replaced their ties to fathers, husbands, and brothers by loyalties to church and sisterhood. It demonstrated that there were callings for women of the upper and middle classes other than those of wife, daughter, and 'charitable spinster.' And it at least suggested that the religious life was the higher calling."[21] This was precisely what the movement's detractors found so repulsive. At a time when society emphasized the sanctity of family life, a life of celibacy was "inevitably suspected as casting some slur on marriage, or at least as representing what was believed to be a higher way."[22] Indeed, few outside Anglo-Catholic circles saw the allure of sisterhoods, and even fewer believed that the religious life was truly a more noble and more desirable life than that of marriage and motherhood. Some went so far as to argue that women's aspirations toward the celibate life were "going against nature."[23] To anticipate my argument, these motivations to join and the near-inevitable objections that followed were not entirely dissimilar from those leveled by the families, friends, and neighbors of early African aspirants.

The few non-Tractarians who did see value in sisterhoods in the first half of the nineteenth century tended to see their value as largely secular. The more socially minded among the critics did concede some benefit to what was, to their minds, an otherwise pathetic trend. Given the appalling conditions of the poor, one of the more ambivalent onlookers wondered, was it not wise "to set aside our dislike of clerical pretensions and of the eccentricities of devout women, and to encourage the vast body of unmarried Englishwomen to come forward to the relief of the destitute on their own terms?"[24] Not coincidentally, the first orders were decidedly philanthropic in nature, the ultimate justification for which stemmed from the scriptural encounter and was amplified by social context.[25] The Community of Saint John the Baptist, Clewer, is one early example. Founded in 1852, Clewer was initially established as a refuge for prostitutes who wanted to leave the streets.[26] Rather than send the women he encountered who were "given over to evil living" to a penitentiary for reform, as was popular at the time, the then-rector of Clewer argued that "the task of reclaiming these women was not one for paid workers, but could only be undertaken in a spirit of devotion and service."[27] As such, a "community of devoted women" was formed, an order that served as a model for many early communities. Significantly, it was the same community at Clewer, which had started as an alternative to a penitentiary for "outcasts of society," that hosted Blandina Limo and others of Mbweni's pupil-teachers when they were in England.[28] The relationship between the UMCA and Clewer illuminates something of contemporary Britons' perceptions of their African counterparts. It is not clear if, in visiting the school, Blandina and her colleagues were shadowing the British sisters to learn to work in service of "the relief of the destitute"—heathens in Africa—or if they themselves were seen as akin to the prostitutes, streetwalkers, and other women of ill repute the sisters served. Regardless, given the long history of paternalism and campaigns of moral uplift that plagued Britain's relationship with Africa, there is a degree of irony in the UMCA's relationship with Clewer as a training site for their female African congregants.

As for the Tractarians' early female aspirants, many factors merged in their decision to join a sisterhood—for some it was a religious calling, for others it was a longing to help the poor or a desire for a career, whereas others were disinclined toward marriage or harbored an interest in living with other women.[29] Like Anglo-Catholicism in general, life in a sisterhood was seen to give an unmarried woman "new and meaningful things to do" and a privileged space within which she could develop a career of service.[30] Sisterhoods also "offered an alternative to a life of idleness or drudgery—exotic, but safely exotic, and cloaked in the respectability of religion."[31] For some, an ability to live openly and intimately with other women heightened the allure of religious sisterhoods. Communities put few restrictions on "emotional friendships"—often called "particular friendships"—between members. Clewer, for example, held such intimacies to be a positive force in the community.

The order's founder saw intimacy as integral to the mission of the community. She "would not have love [between members] crushed out but wisely directed" toward God above all. To a sister who was "very much attached to herself" she wrote: "I do not think you need to trouble yourself because you love me. As a fact you do. All efforts to think or feel otherwise will only be unreal and lead to no good. All you need strive for is to love God more . . . Love is of God; it is a Divine gift; do not seek to crush it."[32]

Ultimately the factors influencing aspirants were many and varied, and must not be conflated with our perceptions of modern-day celibates. Women today who join such groups "are invariably seen as being deeply devout: after all, the caring professions and communal living arrangements mean that women who wish to live with other women and work among the disadvantaged do not need to join sisterhoods to carry out these desires." But for women in nineteenth-century Britain, such was not the case; women joined sisterhoods "who today would not dream of making such a choice, and we would be wrong in assuming that all Victorian sisters were profoundly religious."[33] As we move forward, we must keep the same in mind for the women who aspired to enter religious life as a member of the UMCA's sisterhood, the Community of the Sacred Passion. And indeed, the same must be seen to apply to the first generations of African aspirants—their motivations were mixed, and not easily disentangled from the host of other familial, social, and cultural changes that swept across East Africa at the time.

Religious Life in East Africa: The Early Years

Inspired by Tractarians' revived interest in religious communities in England, Bishop Frank Weston sought the establishment of both a sister- and a brotherhood in service of the UMCA's African mission. Before Weston's term as bishop began, there was an attempt at opening a branch of the already-established Saint Raphael's Sisters of Charity within the UMCA at Zanzibar, but the order withdrew.[34] A short-lived Society of the Sacred Mission emerged for men, but in a reflection of broader trends, that society did not last; Weston's efforts toward a sisterhood were more popular and longer-lived. In 1908, when Weston assumed the bishopric of the UMCA, he began the process of establishing a religious community for British women to work in service of the mission. In this early, whites-only version of a UMCA sisterhood, women who volunteered in Britain to join the order would receive training and a passport to a life of service overseas. The Community of the Holy Name at Malvern agreed to train novices for the CSP, and the first novice was clothed in July 1908. Novice Honor Mary had previously worked at Magila with the UMCA, as had several of the order's other early members.[35] By May 1910 there were seven novices, all clothed, trained, and ready to sail for East Africa.

On May 29 the UMCA's newest British sisters arrived at Zanzibar, sobered by the words of Frank Weston, who urged them to remember

> the greatness of the responsibility which lies upon you. We have not only to found in the Diocese the Religious Life: we have to justify ourselves to the rest of the workers, who will probably regard the experiment with something akin to alert criticism!: Everyone is anxious to be kind: you will have the prayers and sympathy of all: but it is only human to regard with critical eyes a movement within a society which separates some members from the rest, and implies a claim to a very close walk with God . . . The new life will be very difficult to you all, removed as you will be from the influence of the Malvern house; but God will be with you.[36]

On August 7, 1911, Sisters Margarita, Mabel, Frances, Elise, Marjorie, and Honor Mary knelt before Frank Weston, bishop of Zanzibar, and took a vow dedicating themselves to God for life, in the service of His African people.[37] Additionally, the CSP also added an order of "companion-sisters," a community for British women who were drawn by God to "desire a life consecrated under definite rule, and feel themselves specially attracted to a life of sacrifice in the spirit of the sacred passion." These "companion-sisters" would not take lifetime vows, but would take annual vows only, so that "women who cannot give up their home duties or leave their present avocations, may find in this order just that way of consecration they have long been seeking." Some, were they prepared, would go to Africa for a short time to offer their special training and experiences.[38] Aside from this and to a large extent, the history of the CSP falls out of the scope of this chapter, except as it relates to the development of the CMM.

When the community was founded, it was with the expectation that if African women ever expressed a desire to enter the religious life, they would join the CSP itself. Yet, repeated attempts by African women to join the order ended in failure. Two years after Stella's aborted attempt to join the order, for example, a young woman named Esta declared her intention to join. Her road was not easy either. Novice Esta spent ten months at Kigongoi, a small village accessible by a very steep road from the equally small village of Maramba, a good distance from the central station at Magila, preparing for Holy Orders. Upon leaving home after a short vacation from study, Esta faced physical intimidation, harassment, and abuse from her resistive patrilineal kin. Esta's mother and aunts followed her to the convent, taunting her the whole way. After she had arrived at Msalabani, settled in, and gone to bed, hammering at the gate awakened Esta and the entire compound. The night guard found Esta's father, a local teacher, at the gate in distress; when the mother superior awoke and descended the stairs to see what was happening, he "rushed at her, brandishing his stick." As the mother retreated upstairs toward safety, Lorenzo "rushed round to the other door which was shut, demanding that his daughter be returned to him." He then "threatened to break down the doors, hammering and shouting all the time that he would take her by force, until the whole Convent was awake." A sister rang the church bell to rouse assistance from the village, and summoned Padre Timotheo, a nearby priest. Timotheo struggled to pacify Esta's father, who "continued to threaten and shout that Novice Esta should be returned to him."[39] Esta's family evidently felt entitled to the rights-in-person that Esta represented, and to the social and economic potential that she embodied, and they were unrelenting. Not five weeks later, Esta's father stalked her and some companions as they were walking a lonely stretch of road and "threatened violence." The intimidation was more than Esta could stand, and she summarily quit the order and returned to her family.[40]

The urge that Esta, Stella, and several other women felt to join a religious order was not particularly unique. Indeed, a substantial literature has shown that African women have long found new avenues to status, power, and independence in the spiritual realm. Celibate religious orders of the early twentieth century were thus no exception to a longer-standing pattern, and such orders attracted women throughout the continent. In East Africa alone, Catholic Fipa women living in northwestern Tanzania desired to emulate their European counterparts, seeking out opportunities to join their mission's religious community. Haya women in Tanzania joined their white sisters, successfully organizing into a semiautonomous religious community in the 1910s.[41]

And to be sure, women's church organizations in general, especially those that did not require a life profession and vows of celibacy and poverty, were popular throughout Africa. Organizations such as Manyanos and Ruwadzano in southern Africa, Chita chaMaria, and the Mothers' Union (MU) in Anglican dioceses throughout Africa were an easier sell for women, their families, and the church. The MU was a popular organization among UMCA adherents for which no particular vows were required. Founded in Britain in 1876 by Mary Sumner, the MU operated on the philosophy that mothering was in and of itself a spiritual act, one that carried wide-ranging implications for society at large.[42] The organization claimed that "female spirituality connected women's familial function with a higher purpose of stabilizing the larger Christian community," and held that prayer and devotional practices have significant social and political importance. As an institution, the MU placed a "high priority on female spirituality as the foundation of family, church, and national life, and accordingly garnered a wide reputation as strengthening the moral and spiritual foundation of the state."[43]

UMCA missionaries opened the first chapter of the MU in Tanganyika Territory in 1922.[44] By 1938, *Central Africa* reported six MU branches in different parts of the diocese, with twenty-six African members and fifteen English-speaking members, and about sixty probationers.[45] European MU leaders trained their African protégées in much the same way that African teachers and clerics' wives had been trained—with classroom work and on-the job training. By 1949 the MU had produced many "keen and capable leaders" who, according to the local bishop, "more and more . . . are taking over the work of leadership in the various branches."[46] Sensing the evangelical value in the work, Africans took the initiative and founded branches autonomously. In many cases, word of the MU's work preceded it, and it was not just African women who clamored for the same work to be done in their own parishes. Men and elders also saw value in bringing a branch of the MU to their villages to teach the values of Christian motherhood, baby-craft, and domestic sciences as a way to convert more Africans and to spread Christianity in their village. In the Fiwila district of Tanzania, for example, male teachers lobbied the organization for a chapter to be run by their wives. In short order the wives founded two branches in the region.[47] Despite a wellspring of support from men, African women were the primary drivers of MU growth in UMCA dioceses. Women used the MU as a means to introduce Christianity to non-Christian villages.[48] In order to help women raise their children in "a Christian way," African MU leaders frequently visited young wives and mothers to illustrate ways to bridge the gap between local "heathen" traditions and Christian living. In Kota in the 1950s, for example, older MU members illustrated ways to make a transition from traditional practices to Christian living by illustrating "tribal customs in relation to Christian teaching." These women instructed newly married couples on a successful Christian marriage and served in an advisory capacity to "help, where they can, a wife who is not agreeing with her husband." MU leaders also brought Christian practices to the childbirth process by participating in the local instructional classes that preceded a woman's first birth.[49]

Scholars have argued that organizations such as the MU performed a number of social functions for their members and the people around them. More instrumental interpretations suggest that in a rapidly urbanizing and industrializing context, these organizations gave female migrants in particular an opportunity "to create a new identity by moving away from traditional kinship structure, to organize social security like funeral arrangements and health care and also to find new norms for educating children."[50] Other scholars see widespread female interest in Christian organizations as an issue of social or cultural liberation, an active response to "religious and social change, which Christianity and a new economic order brought about."[51] Southern African women "created a space for themselves within Methodism because they had distinctly different needs than African men. Non-elite women were not concerned with attaining power, but with using it to persevere. Their domestic responsibilities forced them to concentrate on daily survival strategies."[52] More extreme views suggest that these organizations "defined and defended a new Christian morality in an environment which was widely considered to be immoral," offering a degree of autonomy to women from their "colonial and traditional patriarchal authorities."[53] The movement of women to mission organizations was often "an expression of their refusal to be pawns" in broader social negotiations of their "attempts to resist."[54] When faced with opposition, faithful women in southern Africa "held on to a distinctive and fervent female group solidarity which helped to sustain them in times of personal and community upheaval."[55] And, of course, other strands of scholarship find within the range of priorities and aspirations that drew women to church organizations a distinct desire for spiritual communion. In church organizations, women had an opportunity to elaborate their unique expression of Christianity and to "put their own stamp on Christianity."[56]

If attraction to such organizations was not unique, failure and resistance were not either. While African women today constitute the majority of sisters in Congo, in the early decades of the church's work, missionary efforts to recruit local women were "almost entirely a failed enterprise." Indeed, a high failure rate was common to orders throughout the continent. While resistance to baptizing daughters in the church and to Christian marriages was strong, the loss of a young woman to religious profession was inconceivable. Many regarded the vow of celibacy to be unnatural and a rejection of social obligations, saw the vow of poverty as unreasonable, and the "vow of obedience an irreparable loss."[57] Such ideas were so foreign that in the lower Congo, the mistress of novices struggled "to create equivalent words in Kikongo for celibacy and to state the condition of poverty in a positive sense. In Congo-Brazzaville, stories of family resistance to girls entering the novitiate were 'folkloriques' in their prevalence, repetition, and embellishment."[58]

Frustrated by this repeated cycle of aspiration and failure, arrival and absconding among UMCA postulants, when it came time to provisionally admit postulants Lusi and Thekla to the CSP in 1939, the order's British sisters and mission administrators changed their tack. The only way the religious life would be possible for Africans, contemporary administrators believed, would be to allow African aspirants to "have their own ménage, entirely on African lines."[59] Thus instead of adapting CSP to fit the needs of its African aspirants, the UMCA clothed Lusi and Thekla as novices under a new order, the Community of Saint Mary, or in Kiswahili, "Chama cha Mariamu Mtakatifu" (CMM).[60] The community later added to this title ". . . of Nazareth and Calvary," by which name it is known today. No other attempt was made to incorporate African female adherents into CSP.[61]

An Imperfect Understanding of the Celibate Life?

According to recollections of the administrative staff, the decision to found an order for African postulants was a matter of practicality. "I think it was very much the wish of everyone that African women, when they were found to have vocation to the religious life, might be admitted to CSP itself, but it just did not work," said the bishop of Zanzibar.[62] And, indeed, before African aspirants were given their own "ménage," the attrition rate of postulants was near perfect. What was it about the nature of the all-white CSP that turned African women off from professing? And, why did no women commit to the religious life until the African order was formed? Administrators offered several justifications for these high rates, chief among them the "considerable culture shock" women experienced when making a change to eating English food and "sharing her life with three English Novices, and so had many adjustments to make."[63] Administrators also believed African postulants' tribal differences rendered them unable to live together—women from the south of Tanzania, for example, were thought to struggle when they moved to a convent in the colder, wetter northwest of the country—a line of thinking that was in direct contradiction to earlier mission rhetoric. Perhaps most important, however, church administrators also argued that the "religious life is, even now, very imperfectly understood among the Africans."[64]

The answer is, of course, far more complicated than the explanation provided by CSP, which was that the African novices had an "imperfect" understanding of celibate life.[65] While the reality of convent life might have been different from the initial expectations of some women, it was not as if the UMCA's African women were completely unfamiliar with the order and its ideals. The CSP was fundamental to the UMCA's communities both on Zanzibar and on the mainland, and the sisters were highly visible, well-respected figures in the communities where they worked. At one time or another, almost all African adherents would have had contact with the European sisters through their work as teachers in classrooms throughout the dioceses, nurses in dispensaries, "mothers" in orphanages, and ministers to inquirers and parishioners outside of church. Attributing aspirants' consistent defections to an "imperfect" understanding of the celibate life, as the European sisters did, also underestimates African congregants' understanding of, and engagement with, long-standing religious and social underpinnings of the mission. Such a perspective also assumes that congregants were unseeing and uncritical bystanders, rather than attentive, engaged, and invested members of their own community who worked actively to maintain moral order and to control its borders.

Indeed, administrators argued that the "chief stumbling block" for African women and their families was "the unmarried state" sisters were expected to maintain.[66] Assuming that congregants simply misunderstood the expectations of celibacy and the religious life also assumes that Africans agreed that celibacy was the single most important definition of a religious life. The idea that the postulants would remain celibate was indeed perplexing to many community members, Christian and non-Christian alike. Children constituted valuable social currency for African women in many societies, making motherhood a highly valued institution. For postulants to intentionally forego the opportunity to pursue biological motherhood was often a sure-fire way to ignite the confusion and ire of family members, friends, community members, and other observers. Yet, there were many reasons to join a religious order and many aspects of life in an order, and postulants may not have seen celibacy as a necessarily defining characteristic of their lives in the religious order. To be sure, marriage in the precolonial African context was a process rather than a moment, something that could be tried and tested before it was accepted. Even after they were brokered, such unions were rarely as permanent as they were considered to be within the Victorian Christian context, and sexual access was negotiated within a range of potentialities, such as we saw in chapter 5. Such testing would not have been understood or permitted, much less articulated as such in the mission records.

Attributing attrition to an "imperfect" understanding of the religious life, particularly as it relates to celibacy, also elides the strong and persistent influence of family, extended kin, and social networks on the girls' decisions and behavior. Parents, kin, and other community members often felt a great sense of loss when their daughters joined the community. One British missionary explained in 1928, "African fathers and mothers were ready to admire the religious life for Europeans, but to give up their own daughters was a different matter."[67] Indeed, a daughter's pledge of religious celibacy forced parents to relinquish, without compensation, certain rights to, and benefits from, their daughters. Indeed, in entering a religious community and taking a vow of celibacy, the young postulant technically forewent marriage and the possibility for biological children. She denied her father the bridewealth payments that might have, in earlier times, compensated for her lost productive and reproductive capacity. A young postulant's removal to a community would also have denied her lineage the potential for the web of social ties that marriage and heirs might have helped to create, at least in the ways that they had been traditionally imagined. Relinquishing rights-in-person to a daughter not only undermined others' potential wealth and access to labor, but it also introduced a level of individualism into a complex decision-making process that was intended to guard and protect the health and perpetuity of the lineage. Such a move also shaped the lineage into a new kind of social entity, one in which the desires of an autonomous individual could outweigh the desires of the lineage. In such a situation, individuals and entire families risked severing ties to ancestors and compromised the transmission of knowledge and skills from clan to clan, from generation to generation.

Resistance, meddling, and the pressure of kin, friends, and community members often fueled postulants' defections. For many, their family's displeasure was too much to bear and they acquiesced to the harassment leveled against them. For those that remained, the sense of loneliness, guilt, and dislocation did not end once they were behind the convent's main gates. The choice between family and the convent was often absolute: one African sister explained about her pledge of celibacy, "If you do this thing, you become an enemy to your family."[68] For novices in Fipa, Tanzania, this trauma of separation and disappointment was a flashpoint that "brought to the forefront a succession of doubts, uncertainties, and resentments that most students carried with them throughout their training."[69] These feelings were often exacerbated by an order's internal dynamics and particularities.

And among the UMCA, the salient internal dynamics were likely those of race and difference, especially for African postulants who were alone among British sisters. Generally less educated than their Mbweni counterparts and even mainland clerics' wives like those at Saint Cyprian's, African postulants from rural outstations may not have had a firm command of English or even Kiswahili, or much confidence in communicating as peers with British sisters. Once in the UMCA's formerly whites-only order, however, the "little sisters" of the CSP like Stella and Esta had to negotiate a hierarchy in which their British "superiors" considered them to be of "backward cultures and . . . low in moral fiber." This social hierarchy based on race was common when white missions accepted African members. Not long after establishing an order in Congo, for example, female missionaries declared their higher status in a memo that stated, "The native sisters can never be on the same footing as Europeans in regard to clothing, food, and lodging."[70] In the Fipa Catholic community, the earliest African sisters were held to a lower standard than their European counterparts. The nascent state of Christianity in the region, officials believed, dictated "a more lenient approach to the vows and lifestyle required of the first African sisters." They were allowed to "participate in Fipa wedding celebrations and funerals, to drink small amounts of beer, and even to brew beer themselves . . . the first African sisters made promises (*ahadi*) not vows for fear that the vows would be difficult to keep."[71] While the UMCA's commitment to developing a Native Clergy may have assuaged some of the patronizing rhetoric that shaped interactions in the convents cited above, the "little sisters" of the CSP were not on an equal footing with their British counterparts.

Yet, it is important to consider that this internal hierarchy, which formed along the lines of race and an assumption of ranked cultural development, may have been a useful tool for the order's African postulants. We cannot know the intentions of the "little sisters," but it is possible they knew of the British officials' perceptions of them as "backward" and ignorant of the nuances of the celibate life, and used those assumptions to their advantage. Did they cultivate this sense of themselves as unsophisticated participants in the religious life in order to have a way out, and to keep their options open? As we have seen, Africans often considered sexual relationships—which in the context of a religious order would have been defined by a strict *lack* of sex—to be temporary. They were entered into not with the pretense of exclusivity or permanency, but more often as part of a negotiated social contract: pawns served as domestic slaves for the length of a loan; women looked to a husband's brother or cousin to resolve infertility in a marriage; children engaged in sex play until puberty; lovers engaged in extramarital affairs precisely because love and sexual passion were not valued as a solid foundation for marriage.[72] As such, one's abstinence or one's lack of sexual engagement—particularly a decision that was freely entered into—likely appeared to postulants and their families as negotiable, flexible, and temporary as any other sexual relationships a woman or her extended family might negotiate.

Thus, did the "little sisters" cultivate or perpetuate a "backward" or unsophisticated demeanor in order to engage with the religious life on their own terms? Did the "little sisters" take advantage of the British officials' views of them to experiment with celibacy and the religious life, to try it on and to test it out for a period of time, knowing that their "low moral fiber" could serve as an excuse should they decide to call it quits? Or, perhaps the "little sisters'" decisions not to join the CSP were a sign of dissatisfaction with the hierarchy itself. Rather than "failing" to fit into their British sisters' routines and to fully appreciate the demands of the religious life, perhaps they refused to be under the thumb of their white sisters. Perhaps they yearned instead for a separate space, where they could pursue their own vision of a religious life away from British control. It may be that repeated refusals to join the CSP were a method of gaining more control over the ideals of ethnic diversity and racial exclusivity that underwrote the UMCA.

Further, administrators did not consider the possibility that Africans' dissatisfaction with the life they found in the CSP was the result of their inability to forge the types of affective spiritual relationships with their fellow sisters with congregants that they desired. The racial and power dynamics between African and British novices were not even, and as such the African "little sisters" were not given equal voice in the development of the community. Nor, for that matter, were they encouraged to invest in relationships with their "big sisters" as they might have with African sisters. As such it is possible, as we will see below, to understand the development and founding of the CMM as a new form of subjectivity and organization forged by Africans themselves in an attempt to create a place to pursue on their own terms affective spiritual relationships with fellow sisters, with congregants, and with other community members.

Growth of the Chama cha Mariamu Mtakatifu (CMM)

Settled under a new name, the community grew more quickly in the next several decades. Two additional women, Mariamu and Agnes, both from the Zigua ethnic group, expressed a desire for the religious life and joined the fledgling CMM in 1940. They were made postulants and, concerned as the British staff were with the presumed determinism of one's tribal background, sent to live in a *msonge* (noted in the sources as a "round Zigua-type house") that was built adjacent to the CSP Mother House. There they could live together in a situation the missionaries believed was more appropriately suited to the needs of Africans. By April 1941, Novice Thekla and a new postulant had left the order, and Novice Lusi was sent to join Mariamu and Agnes. Lusi, too, returned home after only a few months. Missionaries chalked Lusi's departure up to the difficulties she must have experienced as "the only southerner" in a "remote part" of the colony, "as tribal customs, food and housing were all very different."[73] These recurrent arrivals and departures continued apace, with perhaps two women arriving and two departing per year. By 1946, however, two novices took annual vows at Kwa Mkono, one in the complex of mission villages of which Msalabani, Magila, Maramba, and Kigongoi were also a part; after another four and a half years the same women became the first professed Sisters of CMM. Three more postulants joined Novices Mariamu and Helena to complete the proper founding of the community in 1946. The first three novices made their First Profession on February 18, 1949, at Kwa Mkono, and Sisters May Elizabeth, Jessie, and Fieda all remained with the order to take life vows as sisters on December 30, 1957.

In 1960, aspirants began arriving from southwestern Tanzania to the sisters' house at Kwa Mkono. Just as in years before, many did not persist, although enough did to enable the community to grow. CMM opened a branch house at Msalabani, on the hill above the village of Magila. Women there and at the mother house at Kwa Mkono taught school, worked as matrons and headmistresses at the girls' schools, worked as nurses, and were employed in wafer making and bookbinding. When I visited a CMM convent in Dar es Salaam in 2013, the *masista* told me they were still engaged in many of the same activities.[74] They were proud to be using one of the mission's first wafer presses, just as they had for nearly a century. The press sits in a small room where orphaned children under the care of the convent, chickens, and dogs run between the nuns' legs, picking scraps of unleavened bread off of the ground to serve as a toy or snack.

UNDATED PHOTOGRAPH, FROM COMMUNITY OF THE SACRED PASSION, *THE COMMUNITY OF THE MISSION SISTERS OF THE SACRED PASSION OF JESUS*, N.D.

FIGURE 14. The convent at Msalabani.

CMM became officially independent of CSP in 1968, at which time Sister May Elizabeth was installed as the first African mother superior of the CMM. In 1974, CMM acquired the last of CSP's houses, this one in Newala, as the last of the British sisters returned to England. Today, nearly a century after Stella joined the CSP, an entirely separate order of African sisters is flourishing, with 150 women—including postulants and novices—living together in eleven houses in Tanzania and one in Zambia.[75] Attending to their professions of chastity, sacrifice, and submission illustrates that *masista* pursued alternative paths toward adult womanhood that allowed them a stake in community development and to monitor the boundaries and nature of the community. Attending to emotions and affects such as fear and discontent, striving and aspiration, faith and self-sacrifice, we also see that a religious order has long served as an opportunity for the UMCA's African women to forge a unique subjectivity.

Once the experiences of African women in the CSP tailored the religious order into something that fit their own needs and demands, they began to realize some of these same benefits that Tractarian women in Victorian Britain had discovered. For example, they derived dignity and independence from the important work and responsibilities sisterhoods offered them outside of the home and out from under their fathers' or brothers' thumbs. Religious orders offered women a viable and increasingly respected alternative to marriage. They also allowed faithful women to pursue a religious calling not otherwise offered in the church structure. Finally, sisterhoods allowed women to live intimately with other women.

Membership in the CMM also offered women and their families a host of material and instrumental benefits. For many families, the mission offered "an alternative structure for achieving subsistence and, ultimately, the health and longevity of one's offspring."[76] Indeed, some women hailed from situations in which the people around them calculated the postulants' choices in terms of their association with the mission. Parents might have imagined that their daughter's confession was a way to become more firmly embedded in the local Christian community. The convent and its affiliate institutions—hospitals, schools, and the church at large—constituted a new web of social, economic, and political networks into which the parents of newly professed postulates could tap. The thought of knowing personally a nurse at the local dispensary or hospital, or the headmistress at a girls' secondary school, probably offered some parents both hope for access and special treatment, and solace in that their daughter's choice could pay all manner of dividends. In its later iteration as the CMM, the organization prided itself on self-reliance and produced crops and goods for themselves as well as surpluses that they could also sell or give away to those in need—families might have imagined themselves as first in line for these riches, and for the advice and political arbitration that the sisters were known for offering. Although the order would probably protest, Sister Martha provided an interesting response to the question of how her people benefit from her affiliation with CMM when I interviewed her in 2008. When asked if they receive "direct help," she replied, "Yes. Like giving financial assistance. My salvation is their everything."[77]

CMM also offered the possibility to forge networks of extended kin, similar to those forged in the context of marriage, that was likely attractive to women and their families. The church, as a theoretical marriage partner, offered families and lineages certain social and economic benefits not available elsewhere. Negotiating a marriage with the mission, as it were, also allowed families to extend their social circle, and to increase the numbers and types of individuals and institutions on which they could rely in tough times. Further, these mission marriages reduced the possibility that a daughter could enter a "bad" marriage. With a mission marriage there was no risk of incurring a son-in-law who would default on his bridewealth

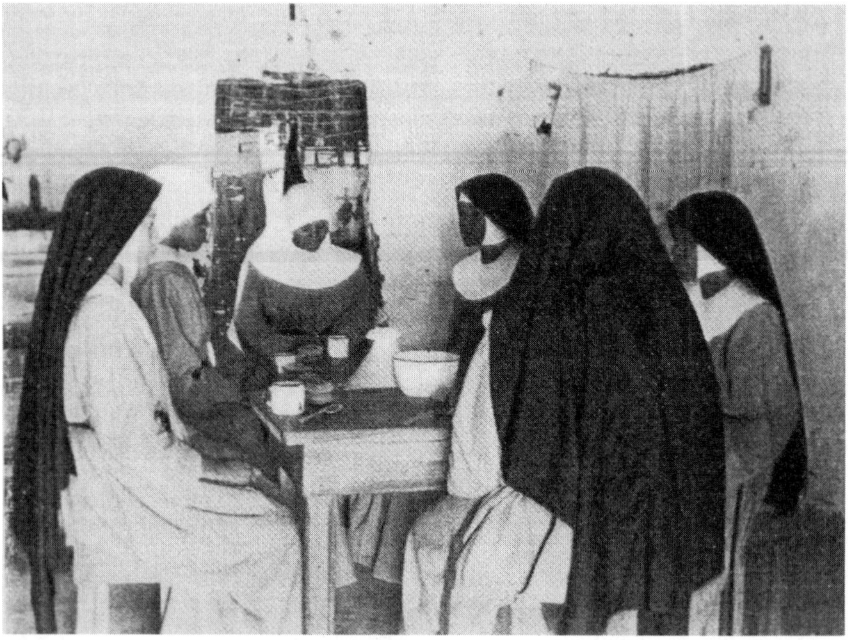

UNDATED PHOTOGRAPH, FROM "FROM LIBERIA TO MSALABANI," *CENTRAL AFRICA* 81, NO. 971 (NOVEMBER 1963).

FIGURE 15. CMM sisters in the Refectory at Msalabani.

UNDATED PHOTOGRAPH, FROM "THE COMMUNITY OF ST. MARY OF NAZARETH AND CALVARY," *CENTRAL AFRICA* 76, NO. 901 (FEBRUARY 1958).

FIGURE 16. CMM sisters, circa 1957.

payments, or of becoming saddled with in-laws who did not reciprocate in social exchanges. A mission was perhaps a more financially and socially reliable partner for a devout young woman, a partner who would offer a daughter—and, theoretically, her family—access to hugely expanded social networks, a profession, and financial stability. Forging bonds of affective spirituality with a church, or with Jesus himself, rather than with a companionate partner of the opposite sex, also allowed women to negotiate a long-term partnership arrangement that still permitted her to act autonomously as an evangelist within the church.

For the especially devout, a daughter pursuing the religious life might have confirmed her parents' own investments in their daughter's spiritual development, affirmed their own social identity as Christians, and perhaps offered family and friends the comfort of knowing they would have a personal intercessor in both church and spiritual affairs. And for some among those, the call of God was not theirs to judge: Sister Jesse's mother, for example, explained her support by saying, "I am God's creature. Who am I to resist His will in this matter?"[78] And, according to a mission publication (admittedly prone to the occasional exaggeration), the family of an Islamic convert was similarly swayed by their faith in the religious payoffs of their daughter's choice. When church officials explained to a father that if his daughter entered the community she could not marry and he would receive no bridewealth, he replied, "When I give my daughter to God, I do not expect any payment for her."[79] Decades later, CMM sisters have similar responses. When asked if her family benefits from her affiliation with CMM, Sister Merina responded, "Maybe the way it benefits is through my prayers now. When I pray for them so much and I go home they say 'now we see we are truly being blessed, even though there was a disturbing issue, it is not there any more, we are therefore thankful for the prayers.'"[80] Sister Ethel added, "I help them through prayer in their endeavors so they can do well and prosper in their life."[81]

The order offered a host of personal and professional options that were either alternative pathways to opportunities available in their home communities, or were opportunities for advancement within the context of the UMCA community that did not exist at home. Anecdotal evidence suggests that many religious women understood the convent as a place to turn to when faced with limited choices in their community. Marginalized or otherwise disadvantaged women often saw in the convent an opportunity for a lifetime of support; she might envision herself as part of a community and a family, and dream of the opportunities for education and career training. Among aspirants in the 1960s, CSP complained, was the idea that "if you become a Sister, you will get the chance of an education (and maybe even the training) that your parents had been unable or unwilling to provide." Education, the sister continued, "is the means of a job and a salary which will then provide for the numerous younger members of the family, so a great many of the aspirants to CMM in those years, arrived less for the sake of the Religious Life, than for the chance of getting an education. One even came under the impression that if she could get as far as training and a salaried job, she would then be allowed to send at least half her salary for the support of her family."[82] While this may not have been the ideal route to the religious life in the minds of the church administration, it was a viable and productive pathway for postulants and their families.

Religious Celibacy, Adult Womanhood, and Affective Spirituality

Perhaps most significantly, the order offered women an alternative path toward adult womanhood through which novices could shape and control the nature of the burgeoning spiritual community, much the same as their colleagues did when they began radiating out from Mbweni and establishing stations on the mainland. To be sure, in choosing to join the UMCA's celibate religious order, African female congregants were not deviating fundamentally from African ideals of adult womanhood, which are often described by scholars as bound to the experience of motherhood. Yet, biological motherhood was only one of the possible routes to adulthood in the precolonial period—and not a guaranteed route at that. Indeed, in parts of precolonial Africa, motherhood was both a social institution and an ideology that was not strictly defined by the biological act of reproduction.[83] Scholars have distinguished between what the "social category of mother" and the "biological event of giving birth."[84] In order to achieve the social status of mother in precolonial North Nyanza, "a woman should do more than conceive and give birth: she should do these in a specified and socially recognized context."[85] Indeed, female bodies needed to be properly prepared—through circumcision, initiation, or other rites and rituals—to conceive. Girls from central Kenya who gave birth before initiation, for example, were not recognized as either mothers or adult women by the community, but were instead seen as socially dangerous beings with the capacity to cause potentially widespread devastation. Yet, just as biological reproduction was not in itself sufficient for a woman to be a mother, biological reproduction within the context of marriage was only the *most common*, not the only, route into the social category of mother—and adult womanhood. In other words, for those for whom biological motherhood or marriage was neither possible nor desirable, there existed alternative pathways to achieve the status of social motherhood, and of socially recognized adult womanhood. Religious specialists, for example, gained "status, respect, social and economic security in precolonial society because they provided necessary and important services."[86] In addition to adoption and fostering, North Nyanzan women in a childless marriage in the precolonial period could take advantage of the social institution of **-perekezi*. After accompanying a bride to her new home, the **-perekezi* "could stay with the new wife for a prolonged period and, should she become pregnant by the husband, would become one of his wives. Because of her relationship with the **-perekezi*, the wife could lay some claim to her **-perekezi*'s children if she did not conceive."[87]

By electing to pursue profession and participation in CMM, African congregants were creating yet another new pathway toward adult womanhood, one that was imminently suited to the new status hierarchies and opportunities of a rapidly changing Tanganyika. In so doing, unmarried and childless female African congregants were drawing both on older African practices and on newer Victorian institutions, crafting socially acceptable ways to participate in the UMCA and in the world around them as adult women. As a result, they were able to form intimate relationships of affective spirituality with individuals around them. These relationships resembled in many ways, but were not exactly like, those forged through the institution of biological motherhood. Through these relationships, they were able to act as evangelists—just like their lay counterparts. Quotidian performance of the mission's civilizational values and relationships of affective spirituality allowed celibate women to participate in the social reproduction of the UMCA community and its values.

One sister with whom I spoke in 2013 was keenly aware of her and her colleagues' evangelical power, and of the power of the relationships she forged to serve as a foundation for proselytization and community expansion. She said, "When a teacher teaches in various schools, a student might imitate her behavior. The students might be pleased with the behavior of a sister and take it so that in future it is easy to see the student has this habit. This brings a true blessing . . . that the transformation is done in faith."[88] In this way, the celibacy of the *masista* was both productive and reproductive.

The procreative power of celibacy is evidenced by a quote from another elderly *sista* I spoke with in 2012. She spoke to me in particular about her work with orphaned children, and her role in their spiritual development. Her affective and spiritual relationship with an individual orphan, she argued, was fundamental to building the child's relationship with the church. She said,

> In my work you can pray, but you can [also] be moved to go and help orphaned children somewhere, they are going through this and this . . . On reaching there you find you get deeply moved and hurt because you see things are not right and you get concerned about how you must do something. That is why I say we don't pray so that God descends with answers, oh no, God passes through people with the ability, even in Tanzania. In this world . . . there are people of different abilities. When you pray God touches a particular servant to go and help in a certain place, that is why we live.[89]

Masista live, she continued, "to create awareness through evangelism on how to pray for people or educate people on how to live and free themselves from poverty." Indeed, the bonds of motherhood allow *masista* to build a community of believers. "The children I see out there," one sister told me during the same visit in 2012, "I take them as mine and I am obligated to tend for people's children. They are not mine, but I do it very well."[90]

The careers of contemporary CMM *masista* and their work in the community also suggest that they understand themselves as "spiritual mothers," engaged in relationships of affective spirituality with community members and others around them. Teaching and nursing were the most common career choices for *masista*, just as they have long been for their noncelibate contemporaries. More utilitarian pursuits—such as wafer making and bookbinding, handiwork and cookery—allow them to tend to the needs of a broader population. Says one sister, "We bring people to God by our work, running groups of women and girls, teaching housecraft-domestic science . . . We try to work hard so that we be able to be self-reliant—we do handwork, agriculture, poultry, piggery and we have a few cows, and goats and fish ponds. We support the church by making vestments and wafer making."[91] Indeed, the convent at Masasi seemed to epitomize self-reliance—an impressive bio-gas operation fueled the entire convent and some of the surrounding area with electricity, and their human power produces sesame oil and other garden products for sale. At the CMM convent in Masasi, for example, *masista* are focused in large part on serving the needs of local women, framed as "poorest of the poor." *Masista* at Masasi run a chapter of the Guild of Saint Agnes,

UNDATED PHOTOGRAPH, FROM COMMUNITY OF THE SACRED PASSION, *THE COMMUNITY OF THE MISSION SISTERS OF THE SACRED PASSION OF JESUS*, N.D.

FIGURE 17. CMM sister sewing at the community house at Newala.

an organization for schoolgirls that "helps Christian girls to love God and live pure lives until marriage." They also work with female school-leavers so that they may return and finish, at least through Standard VII; they articulated plans to build an orphanage for young girls on their property "so that we can help some of them in education and bring up that they can grow up well and with faith and be good people in family and the community."[92]

Indeed, the intimate, affective spiritual relationships between CMM *masista* and their congregants were unequivocal, to their eyes and in the eyes of the community. When asked by my research assistant in 2008 if she ever felt like having children or wished she had, one sister replied with a dismissive "I have spiritual children." *Masista* "don't have kids or husbands; our husband is Jesus Christ," said another. "We were called to serve others and pray for those who need our prayers," she continued.[93] Mothers, another nun argued, run the risk of great emotional burdens: "Married people lose their children . . . and others give birth without plan." In a poignant tribute to the number of HIV orphans in contemporary Tanzania, she continued, "Better the womb which does not conceive than children bringing you hopeless grandchildren as they die."[94]

Yet, *masista* and their congregants also engaged in relationships of affective spirituality that were collective, aimed at the broader community. African Catholic sisters in Congo explained their motive for becoming members of the religious congregation in terms of a maternity that makes them "mothers for all the people." Their choice is presented as more of an "affirmation than a denial of the basic matrifocal Congo valuation of women in terms of motherhood."[95] Congo sisters were women who "themselves have come to see their chosen life as a kind of 'alternative motherhood' for the whole of the society; they explain their celibacy not so much as a relinquishing of physical maternity for their own clan (*mama mitu*), but much more as a call to nurture and foster life for all in an unbounded, universal maternity (*mama moyo*)."[96] And indeed, although CMM *masista* did not reproduce the church community through biological reproduction, they centered the nation-state as the recipient of their pedagogical, emotional, and spiritual labors. Explained one CMM sister, "When we are praying we don't select a certain group of people to pray for but rather we pray for the entire Tanzanian community."[97] They offer advice and counsel, and do so without discrimination, another told me: "People depend on the CMM, [because] they offer help with problems and counseling. It doesn't matter if they are Muslim or Christian."[98]

Finally, the relationships of affective spirituality *masista* forged with the outside community would not have been possible without strong relationships inside the community itself. I argue it was a combination of subjects' desire for a female group solidarity and a distinct desire for spiritual communion, such as we saw above, that binds CMM *masista* together. Earlier, we saw that the ability to live openly and intimately with other women heightened the allure of religious sisterhoods for British Tractarian women. At Clewer, the institution that provided much of the training of the UMCA's British sisters held intimacies or "particular friendships" between its members to be not only a positive force in the community but also integral to the mission of the community. Sisters who found themselves in this position were encouraged only to strive to love God more.[99] While I do not wish to speculate on the existence or nature of intimate, same-sex relationships between the CMM's members, the point is that the range of intimacies—from friendships, to sisterhoods, to ties that resemble those between a mother and a daughter, and even to romantic relationships—can be seen to be a unifying force within the community.

Modern-day *masista* have intimate ties of affective spirituality between them. One nun characterized the nature of the relationships among sisters of different generations as resembling that of biological mothers and daughters. When asked if she regretted passing up the opportunity to have children, one sister replied: "I can't say. I have young nuns who handle me like their mother. I am already a mother and I don't think I miss it." Such connections were the bonds that held the community together. As Sister Angela told me in 2008, "Groups are helpful in church because if you do not belong to a certain group it becomes hard to receive help in times of trouble, but if you belong to one, you are helped without a problem."[100] Another sister wrote about a "shared prayer" group, likely reminiscent of the prayers embraced by members of the Guild of the Good Shepherd or the Guild of All Saints, in which they focused on the work of the Holy Spirit. The women were "gradually growing into it, and we certainly feel drawn together by the experience, and hope it will develop into something deeply spiritual."[101]

Ultimately, *masista* amplified and expanded upon the multigenerational network that clerics' wives and teachers, daughters and protégées, Mbweni's young lovers and their elders, and other sisters in spirit helped to create. They can be thought of as parallel, and at times overlapping, with the movements of the UMCA's other sisters in spirit. The innermost ring of what can be thought of as concentric circles is the *masista* themselves, and the relationships of affective spirituality their lives together forged. A larger ring consists of *masista* moving out into the community, working with students, congregants, and inquirers, in the ways described above. One sister explained in 2008 that, just like priests and clerics' wives, nuns "also visit patients or older people as well as visiting children in Sunday schools to teach them." This expansion, as we have seen above, was vital to evangelism and the growth of the community.

Masista who moved from their homes to new regions of the country to join the convent also tied disparate and discontiguous stations together, just as the sisters in spirit who preceded them did for nearly a century. Physically, their travel from home to their convent, and back for holidays and vacations, tied the community together. And, just as their colleague sisters in spirit had done, several of the first generation of CMM *masista* traveled to England for study and to help forge relationships with their transnational communion. In what appears to have been the mid-1960s, Sisters May Elizabeth and Jessie went to England for three months. They spent much of their time at the CSP convent in East Hanningfield, and traveled to other religious communities in Britain. Perhaps they also visited with the CSP companion sisters we met earlier in this chapter. Sisters Magdalen and Naomi followed not long after, having been accepted into a domestic science course at Seaford College of Education. Upon their return, each took up a headmistress position in Tanzania's freshly nationalized schools. And today, just as their predecessors had done nearly a century before, modern-day *masista* relish in the movement that their positions permit them. Several women told me that their lives as *masista* allowed them to travel the country, and in fact the world, in ways they never would have imagined possible. Sister Ethel, for example, explained the ways in which the religious life offered her opportunities to evangelize: "I can tour and go from province to province, or I can shift from here to Njombe; after Njombe maybe I can go somewhere else. If I could be outside this place [not a CMM member] maybe I could not be able to reach, say Mtwara, Musasi, name it. So I go to all this places but it is because I am in this lifestyle and I am acquainted to many different people and the like. Maybe I couldn't have met such people if I could be in the outside life but here I am able to meet them, I speak to different people."[102] The networks that they forged reinforced and added to the existing connections, strengthening the foundation of the community and extending its spiritual ties.

But it was the prayers of the *masista* that held the community together spiritually. Nuns speak of the power of prayer to change the lives of those around them, and far away at home. Several nuns spoke of this power as a privilege and responsibility: "I get the chance to uplift my younger [family members] and others. Creating salvation in others; it teaches how to love . . . I could not have achieved these when I was outside [the community]. My family would not be stable like now."[103] Sister Lucy argued that her life in the convent and her position in the church offered her family "advice and the blessings," and Sister Mariam explained that "the responsibility of the celibates is to pray for the people of the world." It is "the main responsibility" of a celibate, she continued, "to pray for the people of the world. The way many deaths occur, a lot of chaos, vehicles on roads—we need to pray for the travelers to reach their homes, to escort their goods where they are going in the morning. When there is an accident you need to be keen when saying the place and confess it is because of us or because of me that this happened. When sickness breaks out, families become sick in many places it is my time to ask God and pray so that these things don't happen. That is the main work of a celibate to do."[104]

■ ■ ■

While British church administrators initially heralded the establishment of a separate community for African aspirants, later generations of church officials came to regret this decision. In 1959, for example, at a moment when the colony was transitioning to self-rule, development, and "nonracial" politics, some among a new generation of missionaries questioned their predecessors' decision to form a separate African spiritual order. In a letter to his then-bishop, the UMCA's general secretary wrote:

> Some of us have always wished that African women, when they were found to have a vocation to the Religious Life, might have been admitted to CSP itself . . . On the face of it, to have separate communities is a species of colour discrimination, and would seem to militate against the unity of the church and of Christian life in Christ. Is it fantastic to suggest that eventually a community with its Mother House in Africa should have an African Mother Superior? I have a feeling that Frank Weston himself would have rejoiced at the idea.[105]

Other missionaries saw the continued separation between the CMM and the CSP as a manifestation of a much more serious problem within the UMCA, which was the mission's failure to keep up with a rapidly changing Tanganyika.[106] "Bluntly," an anonymous former Newala District officer wrote in a letter to his friend Sister Magdalene, the UMCA "is falling behind its environment." The "UMCA is still working on the assumption that Africans are unable to take over their own affairs for a long time yet, and still need a very permanent guiding hand on top," he lectured. But things were "moving so fast, that these assumptions—as assumptions, are unrealistic."[107] The former district officer concluded, "Anyway, however much those inside may be unable to comprehend, from outside people think CSP/CMM is an example of colour-bar, and in a place like Tanganyika in 1960 this is dynamite."[108]

Indeed, for a mission trying to stay relevant in a rapidly changing Tanganyika, it was imperative to embrace the rhetoric of "multiracialism," or even "nonracialism," that the pragmatic Nyerere espoused. Church officials lamented their predecessors' inability to successfully integrate the spiritual order, and they were also profoundly embarrassed by the continued racial segregation within the church.[109] Indeed, the mission's general secretary summed up the widespread feeling when he wrote, "Some of us have always wished that African women, when they were found to have a vocation to the Religious Life, might have been admitted to CSP itself."[110]

The establishment of separate religious orders within the UMCA—one for British sisters and one for their African counterparts—was not an instance of UMCA officials blindly applying a policy derived from the ideal of the "Native Church" to the African aspirants. Rather, the development of the CMM as a racially segregated order was the result of African congregants' initiatives to engage more fully in shaping the nature of the UMCA community and its rhetoric. In particular, African congregants' pursuits of the religious life were the result of a reformulation of longer-standing African institutions that permitted multiple pathways to adult womanhood, and a translation of the Victorian Tractarian ideal of the sisterhood into terms that were useful for them. Female congregants' attempts to join the CSP were ultimately a strategy to assert more control over the rhetoric of pan-ethnic unity, Christian modernity, and in particular racial exclusivity, as full adult members of the church community. Also, the UMCA's African sisters oriented their pedagogical, spiritual, and emotional attentions toward new and emerging, explicitly political, communities. Indeed, CMM *masista*, steeped in the values of Christian modernity, supra-ethnic unity, and racial exclusivity began to engage with new discourses and ways of thinking about and categorizing the world that emerged in the 1930s, '40s, and '50s. In particular, *masista* were faced with new modes of racial thought, with international discourses, such as Pan-Africanism and anticolonial nationalism, and with the increased politicization of African civil service and labor organizations. In looking to make sense of these new ideas and to reconcile the shifting political landscape, *masista* applied inherited values to new circumstances. Far from "retired" from the world, the UMCA's *masista* embodied and performed the UMCA's rhetoric of Christian modernity, supra-ethnic unity, and racial exclusivity in churches, in schools, in hospitals, and in local communities.

CHAPTER SEVEN

The Intimacies of National Belonging

Community Building in Post-Independence Tanzania, 1960–1970

After independence, questions of community building and concerns about the nature and boundaries of the spiritual community remained an important consideration in the self-identification of many UMCA-educated individuals. But like many of their compatriots, they were also engaged in the project of defining how best to move forward as an independent nation, and of how best to knit together the various strands of anticolonial nationalism, ideas about national belonging, and values of the affective spiritual community. Deviating from the ideals of racial purity and virtue that underwrote TANU in the 1950s, President Nyerere brought with him to office a vision of a nonracial Tanganyika that rested on the principle of equality. In the months preceding independence, for example, debates about the Tanganyika Citizenship Bill turned on the relationship between race and citizenship. If "we in Tanganyika are going to divorce citizenship from loyalty and marry it to color," Nyerere said in a speech to African legislators, "we won't stop there . . . A day will come when we will say all people are created equal except the Masai, except the Wagogo, except the Waha, except the polygamists, except the Muslims, etc."[1] Looking toward this future, congregants did as they had done so many times before and drew from a repertoire of beliefs and values to imagine ways they could continue to live as Christians and expand their affective spiritual community while at the same time undertake the work of becoming Tanganyikan.

Take, for instance, two young adults, Gideon Furahani and Rose Limo, both of whom were raised in UMCA congregations outside of Magila, in northeastern Tanzania. Rose and Gideon came of age during the struggle for and transition to independence, and identified with the nation's quest for independence and self-determination. Distantly related, the pair met in December 1961. A letter from Gideon written just days after their first meeting, on New Year's Day of 1962, when they were both young and still in secondary school, marks the start of a correspondence that would stretch over eight years.[2] Typed at the dawn of Tanganyika's first full year of independence (whether by an amanuensis or by his own hand is not clear), Gideon's inaugural letter is imbued with the same mix of excitement, expectation, anticipation, and ambivalence with which Tanganyikans throughout the new nation greeted *Uhuru*. Gideon opens the English-language letter by acknowledging the date not just as the beginning of "a year of complete Independence," but also with school exams, career decisions, and family responsibilities on the horizon, as the beginning of a personally consequential year in "which both of us can not play about." Appealing to what he imagined to be Rose's shared sense of responsibility for shaping their personal and collective futures, Gideon wrote:

> I am sorry that we did not get acquainted for a long time but it is no fault of ours as our parents did not introduce us to each other . . . But now the door is open. We are the future leaders of the clan so we must know each other.[3]

Considering the distance between their boarding schools and the limited fraternization allowed between male and female students in 1960s Tanganyika, Gideon reasoned that written correspondence was the best way to cultivate their relationship. After advising Rose to "put me down at [*sic*] your Headmistress's list as one of your correspondents," the pair commenced a long epistolary exchange. Over the years that followed, while Rose and Gideon attended separate boarding schools, took employment at a distance, and Gideon pursued theological training abroad, their friendship blossomed into romance. The personal and often very intimate letters—of which nearly one hundred remain—became the pair's most important means of communication, constituting the main platform for their friendship, courtship, engagement, and early years of marriage.

As scholars working with intimate epistolary exchanges have shown, letters generally, and love letters in particular, are rarely "simple" exchanges but hold the potential to shed light on broader concerns, such as the relationship between public and private spheres, the power and meaning of literacy, and the development of individualized selves.[4] The Furahanis' love letters reveal that as lovers, as young adults, and as expectant citizens, Gideon—and even more so, Rose—were deeply ambivalent about the years that lay before them. Facing adulthood at a moment of immense political and social transition, the pair used their correspondence as an opportunity to sort through these changes, to negotiate the demands of new and inherited discourses, and to imagine and experiment with new ways of being and forms of personhood. Written in the eight years immediately following *Uhuru*, the pair's letters were infused with much the same rhetoric of "modernity," "progress," and "civilization" that energized political nationalists in the victorious Tanganyika African National Union (TANU). While on the one hand Rose and Gideon appear to have identified with the nationalist quest for these values, on the other hand the discourses of community composition and nation building with which they engaged as lovers, as clan mates, as Bondei, and as Anglican modernizers from congregations of the UMCA also suffused and gave structure to their correspondence. Uniting their unfolding discussions about what defined a person—and consequently, love, marriage, family, spiritual community, and nation—as suitably "Christian," "civilized," and "modern" was a complex social tradition about the centrality of marriage to community building that was deeply seated in the African past. In this, the letters reflect an interweaving of discourses of the UMCA's affective spirituality and of national and community belonging, which played out in two individuals' efforts to compose their own and their communities' futures.

Earlier chapters illustrated that a low labor-to-land ratio caused precolonial Africans to invest in people as the basis of wealth. In the wealth-in-people model, communities sought out and valued individuals for their potential to add to the community in some unique way, be it through their knowledge, their talents, their social ties, or their inherited gifts and abilities. At the heart of precolonial Africans' attempts to build communities, then, were strategic compositional processes and deliberate coalition building. Marriage was a particularly common and effective means of strategically composing communities, of forging new social networks, of procuring access to new resources, and of complementing an individual's or a community's particular capacities or knowledge. Families also negotiated marriages with an eye toward communal durability and collective prosperity. Forming affective relationships was also a strategy women (and others) employed to embed more forcibly into the expanding spiritual community.

As sources that have the capacity to shed light on the relationship of the public to the private sphere, Rose and Gideon's letters confirm that marriage remained central to Africans' attempts to compose communities well into the latter half of the twentieth century. At the same time, they also reveal some fundamental innovations in the nature and process of these negotiations. Both lovers saw the health, modernity, and morality of their individual selves and of their marriage as intimately tied to that of the new Tanganyikan nation, and they approached the relationship as an opportunity to contribute personally to President Nyerere's nation-building project. The pair's strivings, debates, and negotiations illustrate the entanglement of longer-standing discourses of affective spirituality, about the community-building function of marriage, and newer ideals about Christian companionate marriage, the autonomous individual, and the identity of the "modern" or "progressive" nation-state. Rose and Gideon's relationship was based in part on the "modern," "progressive" Christian values of love, mutual attraction, and companionate marriage, and in part on the desire to cement political alliances and attend to the composition of the community. As private citizens unassociated with any formal political institutions, Rose and Gideon offer an opportunity to explore the rich and varied process of national imagination from the perspective of the intimate and the quotidian.[5] Rather than "standing separate from" state authority, or striving to achieve their own versions of self-reliance and security, individuals imagined the family and their affective spiritual community as an alternate site for cultivating and composing the nation.[6] They also illustrate that the nation, such as it was in 1960s Tanzania, was not the only, or necessarily the most important, affinity.

Gideon's Tin Trunk Archive

The personal papers of the late Reverend Gideon Furahani are carefully arranged in a glass-fronted cabinet in the library of a small archive outside of Dar es Salaam. The documents remain as Gideon must have left them, meticulously organized in two-ring, hard-cover binders, filed chronologically and by subject, and bound in neat packages with string. The materials that fill the binders include lined blue note cards, white typing paper, and airmail stationery; collected pamphlets, university theological and political science exams, lecture notes, handwritten book excerpts, religious tracts; and seemingly endless amounts of personal and professional correspondence, extending from Rev. Furahani's days in secondary school in the 1960s until his emigration to the United Kingdom in the 1980s. That Gideon, a well-educated church official, wrote profusely is not surprising; that he seems to have hoarded his personal texts, carried them with him from college to university, abroad and back, assiduously cultivating an extensive private archive, is remarkable.

Such projects of personal archiving were surprisingly common in many parts of colonial Anglophone Africa. Literacy often marked status in colonial Africa, and as Karin Barber has explained, participating in cultures of literacy offered individuals the capacity "to enhance personal and social existence and create a particular kind of civilized and civic community."[7] As part of this process, literates, such as teachers, clerks, and rural preachers, as well as some migrant workers and traders—people like Gideon—seem to have been particularly fond of cultivating "archives" of personal ephemera.[8] "Tin trunk archives" have proven to be rich sources for exploring the determined efforts of individuals to imagine new forms of personhood and new categories of self-expression. Such sources laid bare the desire of aspiring elites like Rose and Gideon to, in Barber's words, "assemble and investigate a personal self and to create a repository of values, the crystallized tokens and products of 'civilization,' 'progress,' 'enlightenment,' and 'modernity.'"[9] Gideon's propensity to curate, and the archive's constituent elements—drama club meeting minutes, science lecture notes, hand-copied texts of sermons—are thus evidence of his attempts to mark himself as a literate, well-educated individual armed to participate in "modern" society.

Further, like their contemporaries, Rose and Gideon understood that someone—a teacher, family member, friend, or letter carrier—might intercept and read their exchanges. As Lynn Thomas has shown for students engaged in pregnancy-compensation cases in colonial Kenya, young people were well aware that "rather than being a confidential correspondence between two young people seeking to sort out their own personal problems, these letters were embedded in webs of peer, familial, and institutional relations and could easily be put to instrumental ends."[10] As with the letters in Thomas's pregnancy-compensation cases, the fact that Rose and Gideon's letters only "*appeared* to enable discreet communication between two people" and in actuality provided a stage for personal publicity seems to have been an encouragement to write or perhaps even the very purpose of producing them in the first place.[11] When read in its entirety, then, Gideon's archive reveals as much about Rose and Gideon as individuals as it does about their self-positioning and aspirations.

The Early Years: Self-Fashioning and Pools of Love

In the first eighteen months of their correspondence—from January 1962 until August 1963—Rose and Gideon exchanged letters only periodically. During this time, Gideon was a student at Minaki College, a secondary school originally founded as a UMCA mission school at the Kiungani campus on Zanzibar in 1869 and moved by the mission in 1925 to Kisarawe, where it was established in the quiet hills just outside of Dar es Salaam as Saint Andrews College. Standard XI and XII were gradually added to the teacher-training school, making it a fully functional secondary school by 1947.[12] Significantly, with the expansion of courses and curriculum and the simultaneous opening of additional UMCA colleges in other parts of the territory drawing Anglican men away from Kiungani, space became available for non-Anglican students at Minaki. Christians and Muslims alike came from mission and government schools throughout the territory, attracted by Minaki's reputation as the oldest and most well-respected school in the territory. They quickly filled the openings and solidified Minaki as a nondenominational, religiously and culturally diverse, truly territorial school. A student body coached in the ideas of supra-ethnic unity that attended UMCA education, coupled with a headmaster considered more liberal than his predecessors, created an environment in which students were acutely aware of the rapid political change unfolding around them—something that would become visible in Gideon's letters to Rose. The school was unique in its tolerance of teachers' and students' expressions of desires for self-government: in 1953, for example, the then-schoolteacher Julius Nyerere visited from the neighboring Pugu School to speak to the students about transitioning the African Association (TANU's predecessor) "from tea party ideas to a political movement." According to students and mission officials, the school's principal, Canon Nash, ran the school with a more liberal hand than many of his predecessors when responding to changes in school demographics, governmental policy, and the overriding political tenor of the student body. Specifically, Nash chose to "guide" rather than suppress "nationalistic feelings among the students." Students also recall that he "encouraged his boys to think independently and debate issues of national and international interest."[13] Contrary to the experience of African teachers at government schools, Nash allowed his teachers to both participate in and take leadership positions in TANU.[14] In Bonde and at Minaki, Gideon and his colleagues had front-row seats to the final years of Tanganyika Territory.

Inspired by the momentousness of *Uhuru*, and with the characteristic optimism of Tanganyika's newest citizens, it appears that Gideon began to craft an "inward" self that referenced broader discourses of "modernity," "civilization," and "progress." The written ephemera that remains in Gideon's archive suggests that Gideon was involved in an all-encompassing and multifaceted process of self-fashioning, one that included both external cues, such as dress, speech, and affiliations, and internal refashionings. While at Minaki, Gideon began amassing a considerable archive of personal papers that included, among other items, minutes from dramatic society meetings, records of activities of the Christian Student Union, texts of lectures attended, coursework, and theological and economics exams. The contents of this collection present Gideon as a man poised to take advantage of the opportunities he imagined independence afforded.

By 1963, Gideon had completed his Higher School Certificate and enrolled at Makerere University in Uganda, where he studied broadly in economics, biology, and religious studies, before selecting religious studies as the single subject for his degree.[15] Although Rose's national exam scores were not good enough to allow her to enter Form Five, she managed to matriculate in a geography and history credential course at a teachers' training college in Mpwapwa.[16] Slowing the courtship further was the fact that even though she had secured permission for the correspondence from her father and the TTC headmistress, their letters were sometimes intercepted.[17] The pair's lack of urgency during Gideon's time at Minaki and early Makerere years was likely due in part to the fact that both were busy students and neither of them initially sought to commence an intimate epistolary love affair.

The casualness of their correspondence is evident in the tenor of their early letters. Through a light and friendly back-and-forth, in which they addressed each other as "cousin" or "brother"/"sister," they slowly got to know each other by exchanging news of home, friends, and challenges and achievements in school. Rose shared with Gideon her first "teaching lesson practice" and tales of an exam so hard she thought it was not in English but in "Double Dutch," while Gideon engaged Rose intellectually with riddles, algebraic equations, and phrases in Latin, Greek, and Spanish, and sent her books he thought she would enjoy. He also sent photographs and newspapers from the places he traveled, such as Kampala and

Nairobi. They traded news of the weather, which, to Rose's chagrin, was "too dusty due to lack of rain" in Mpwapwa and uncomfortable because "sometimes it is very gloomy and cold for three continuous days and sometimes very bright and hot."[18] For two people who frequently insisted they had "not any new things to tell you," the ten extant letters from those first eighteen months somehow managed to say quite a lot.[19]

Indeed, by August of 1963 Rose and Gideon had built an amiable friendship in which each seemed quite invested. The letters had grown in length from a single page to several, and the pair exchanged increasingly personal details and photographs—the latter a sign, even in contemporary Tanzania, of an intimate friendship. There is no indication from the archive that the pair had seen each other more than once since their initial meeting; however, their correspondence demonstrates a building, though evidently uneven, flirtation.

Rose appears to have been the first to acknowledge this shift, when—after what the archive records as nine months of silence—she responded to what she seems to have found a discomfortingly intimate letter. She wrote:

> If you at all remember writing in one of your past letters while I was still at home in the December holiday "I feel responsible for you . . . ," well this had been troubling me ever since . . . I have been asking myself many times to why you feel responsible for me but could not find the answer. Perhaps you can give me the correct answer.

Perhaps hoping to avert a romantic advance, Rose concluded, "Do write letters to me but please do not cross the boundary."[20]

Undeterred, Gideon responded:

> Rose: you may not know how strongly I feel about you and although I had promised to tell you nothing till we meet in December, I feel I must tell you now. I have fallen in love with you Rose, and I cannot hide this from you any longer. This may be "crossing the boundary" as you said in one of your letters but I think I must tell you the truth. Since the days of my long vacation I was dreaming about you and now I can hardly spend a dose of sleep without lovely Rose coming unto me. Rose! Let us swim in the pool of love gracefully together and let there be no mud to hinder our diving into the sweet waters.

He signed the letter, "*Gideon H. Furahani* . . . 'yours in the pool of LOVE.'"[21]

Clearly, Gideon was smitten. This deeply emotional confession was a marked departure from even the increasingly personal letters of the past few months. His honesty, intensity, and passion, and the dramatic change in the nature of their relationship, startled Rose. Several more weeks elapsed before she replied in English:

> Thanks very much for your letter I received not very long ago. Really I was thinking how exactly I would answer it. That's why it may be late [*sic*] than you expected it. Really your letter gave me a sort of a shock. I read and reread it I don't know how many times but I don't come to a decision. To say the truth I find this situation very difficult.

In Kiswahili she added, "*Je kwani wewe umesahau kuwa sisi tuko waudugu?*" ("Have you forgotten that we are relations?") She signed the letter, "Yours ever, cousin Rose."[22]

Kinship, Marriage, and Communal Perpetuity

In reminding Gideon that "*sisi tuko waudugu*" ("we are relations"), Rose—who struggled with Kiswahili elsewhere—most likely meant "*ndugu*," the plural of a Kiswahili word with a meaning that encompasses relationships of familiarity and/or commonality, such as relative, kin, sibling, cousin, close friend, comrade, or fellow tribesman or citizen. Although the exact nature of their relationship—blood or otherwise—is not clear from the evidence that remains, in merely *suggesting* a proximate blood relationship, Rose invoked long-standing marriage prohibitions that had long sought to promote communal health, well-being, fertility, prosperity, and perpetuity. In this region, families often aimed to ensure that marriages and reproduction occurred between individuals with a certain degree of consanguinity. Bondei seem to have permitted second-cousin marriage but long proscribed first-cousin marriage; the UMCA had a similar tolerance of distant consanguinity in marriage, although the nature of African families often confused their attempts at enforcement.[23]

Of course we cannot know for sure why Rose sought refuge in the idea of kin; indeed, at times the pair's letters seem to raise as many questions as they answer. It is possible that the two were either too closely related to permit a "proper" marriage, or their families were on opposite sides of the often deep social and political cleavages in Bondei society. It is also possible that Rose may have invoked their kinship ties as a way to sidestep the fact that she was not interested in Gideon. It is perhaps just as likely, however, that Rose used the ambiguity of their kinship ties to distance herself from Gideon just enough to allow her to "play the field" and entertain other suitors. As Rose herself would suggest years later when wondering whether Gideon's periodic silence while in the United States meant he might have been seeing "an American woman," such was not out of the realm of possibility.[24]

In the long history of courtship and marriage in East Africa, multiple and concurrent partnerships were often tolerated, expected, and sometimes even encouraged before a "marriage" was complete. What Caroline Bledsoe has called "conjugal testing," a process in which partners and families work "cautiously toward more stable unions," often stretched over months or years, and was, thus, often a time during which individuals would try out relationships with other partners. Indeed, the occurrence of nonpenetrative sexual play in many areas—such as *ngweko* in central Kenya or what is translated as "thigh sex" elsewhere—suggests that youthful courtship had long included relations and experimentation with multiple partners.[25] The epistolary form of the love letters seems to have stretched these existing practices of courtship in new directions by allowing them to unfold over hundreds or even thousands of miles. The expanded temporal and geographic distances permitted by letters may, in fact, have made it easier for individuals to be involved in more than one courtship at the same time. Correspondence also enhanced the possibilities of conveying carefully crafted selves, and obfuscating other relationships and intentions. This seems to have been the case for our young lovers: Gideon's near-obsessive letter-tracking system reveals no trace of other female (or intimate male) correspondents, much less lovers, thus giving his exchange with Rose a singular and almost teleological quality. If Gideon had kept all of the personal letters he sent and received over those eight years, his archive might tell a very different story. Given this and Rose's growing ambivalence, it would have been surprising if neither had other romantic or sexual relations over the eight years.

By choosing the language of "kin" to mark the match as untenable to both herself and any potential reading public, she asserted her investment in a "properly sanctioned" marriage and her aspirations in contemporary Anglican society. Rose's protestations can be read as a way to prove to herself and others that she sought a marriage that supported local (Christian, Bondei, and emergent nationalist) attempts at communal perpetuity. Their blood relationship was all that was standing in the way of the "modern" ideal—a monogamous, companionate marriage between two well-educated, upwardly mobile, autonomous Christians. In other words, Rose's protestations became a mark of her modernity, of her civility, and of her desire to participate in a strategically composed, well-formed community. Beyond marking a fundamental shift in the pair's relationship, Rose's recourse to the idea of "*waudugu*" and the values and institutions that it entails was a strategic choice that offered her a level of control in crafting her relationship with Gideon, and her reputation.

In many ways, Rose and Gideon's debates about marriage resembled those that prefigured the great Marriage Debate of 1970–71, public and official conversations that accompanied the first successful overhaul of colonial-era marriage law in the British Commonwealth. As Andrew Ivaska has shown, reform of the United Law of Marriage was the state's attempt to "at once . . . mark a break from the colonial by eliminating the hierarchy that privileged Christian marriage under the British code and to cast that break as one befitting Tanzania's status as a modern, progressive nation on the world stage." The cultural ferment that characterized urban Tanzania's "long sixties moment," argues Ivaska, saw colonial officials and elite African nationalists alike "working to rearticulate notions of tradition that would be at once authentic and modern."[26] Rose and Gideon's project, however, was less about trying to make the "traditional" "modern" than about trying to draw from a vast cultural repertoire—some of which was explicitly "traditional" and some of which was explicitly "modern"—in a way that made the most sense for their own strivings to be "modern" individuals. This process of constantly reaching back into a vast repertoire of values to compose a marriage, a family, and a community that would be socially healthy and viable replicated what their ancestors had done for generations.

The Language of Intimacy

Rose's abrupt and isolated switch to Kiswahili, particularly her recourse in Kiswahili to the idea of *waudugu*, is notable: in part because of its singularity—being the first use of Kiswahili in those first eighteen months and the last for nearly another year; and also because neither Rose nor Gideon tended to switch languages "midstream," even in later letters when Kiswahili became the "matrix" language into which they embedded full Kibondei and English sentences.[27] Their language of choice, English, was also the official language of the Tanganyika Territory and Zanzibar during the colonial period, and by the 1960s English had come to be associated primarily with "progress, advancement, and social mobility," whereas Kiswahili was seen as "a 'second-class' language."[28] English was the medium of instruction in secondary schools and higher education, and many students educated in English-language schools felt that what they perceived to be the comparatively low quality of secondary-school materials and teachers proved Kiswahili's inferiority to English.[29] Popular culture, with its glossy English-language magazines and cinemas in English and Asian languages, further increased the popular prestige of English.[30] Despite the elite connotations of English, however, there was no socioeconomic group in the 1960s, including mission-educated students like Rose and Gideon, who operated exclusively in English.[31] It is also possible to read political meaning into Rose's use of the Kiswahili "*waudugu*" in her otherwise English letters. For multilinguals like Rose and Gideon, using two or more languages in a single event (such as a conversation or letter) is a common way to negotiate social identities, an instrumental choice from, as Monica Heller has argued, a "range of linguistic practices . . . use[d] to establish social goals."[32] With English as the standard or "matrix" language, Kiswahili became the "embedded" language used to express the desire for, or the actual existence of, a social sanction against their marriage.[33]

Rose's language choices seem to confirm other scholars' interpretation that Tanzanian multilinguals of the 1960s reserved Kiswahili and other African languages for topics that were more intimate, more personal, than those discussed in English.[34] A survey of multilanguage speakers in Dar es Salaam in the mid-1960s among people who would have been Rose and Gideon's contemporaries in education and age suggested that for "younger and more detribalized speakers" the roles of Kiswahili and the vernacular were often blurred, and Kiswahili dominated in situations where older speakers might otherwise have used the vernacular, such as intimate or familial settings.

The pair's use of language suggests much about their relationship, including the nature of Rose's ambivalence and, as the relationship progressed, their increased intimacy and expanded entanglement with the Tanzanian national project. (It may seem strange that Rose would become at once more ambivalent about the relationship yet more heavily invested in it, but such relationships are complicated.) This shift is reflected in the pair's transition from English to Kiswahili late in 1963, on the heels of Gideon's matriculation at Makerere. Although Rose and Gideon provide no explanation, it is possible that the pair switched to Kiswahili and Kibondei to acknowledge both the increasing intimacy of their relationship and the increasing politicization of Kiswahili as the language of Tanganyikan independence and national unity. Gideon and Rose's use of Kiswahili as a "matrix" language suggests an attempt to align themselves with the nation-building efforts of Nyerere's government.

Since before *Uhuru*, Kiswahili had been the language of TANU, making Bondeis, Zanakis, Digos, and many others into participants in the same imagined community, associating it, as Farouk Topan has argued, "with national identity, integration and development." As "the vanguard of nation building," Kiswahili challenged English as a preferred language in many circles, and between 1964 and 1970, English became "somewhat stigmatized . . . as not friendly to African socialism and the idea of nation building."[35] Nyerere's fluency in English and preference for Kiswahili—neither of which was his mother tongue—were widely considered the "linguistic ideal of a Tanzanian" and may have inspired Gideon and Rose to emulate his example.[36] The pair's preference for Kiswahili was common in the new nation, as one's ability to operate in Kiswahili became, as Abdulaziz Mkilifi suggests, "a mark of national pride, even though it may not mean that one operates it any more efficiently than previously."[37] Rose's use of Kiswahili, then, despite some obvious difficulties with the language, reinforces the sense that she and Gideon understood their projects of creating themselves and creating a national subjectivity as being intimately related.

By contrast, the vernacular could act as an intergroup language of "ethno-cultural identification and solidarity," as Mkilifi's study cited above suggests. This is because for individuals in increasingly urban-focused, nationally minded, well-educated communities, the distinction between the "vernacular"—in this case, Kibondei—and Kiswahili was blurred; the "true" vernacular (Kibondei) was often abandoned for the "native" or "indigenous" language (Kiswahili) that could provide community solidarity. Among Rose and Gideon's young, relatively well-educated, multilingual contemporaries in the 1960s, Kiswahili, rather than English or their "true" vernacular, was often the choice for "affective socialization."[38] Kiswahili thus represented for the pair an opportunity to express more intimate feelings in a manner that was in keeping with their attention to the construction of the nation.

Rose and Gideon's "affective socialization" took place against a backdrop of their increasingly cosmopolitan lives. By early 1964, Gideon was settling in at Makerere and becoming actively involved in campus life. Perhaps inspired by his 1962 participation in the All African Christian Youth Assembly in Nairobi, he was a member of the Makerere Student Christian Union and of the Guild of Saint Augustine (a body of young Christians considering ordination); he also found time to serve as president of the dramatic society (an engagement that is perhaps not surprising given the effusiveness with which he often wrote to Rose).[39] A capable scholar, Gideon was selected in his second year to pursue an honors degree in religious studies. Even before graduation he was "promised possibilities," which included ordination, a lectureship in Makerere's Department of Religious Studies, and support to pursue an MA or a PhD at Cambridge or Oxford. After "a lot of soul searching," Gideon decided he "would be better to serve as a priest" than a lecturer, and he postponed the MA/PhD option indefinitely (there is no record of his reasons for this decision).[40] By 1963, Rose had nearly completed her teacher-training course and was doing a teaching practicum in history, geography, and Kiswahili at a secondary school in northern Tanzania when the 1963–64 academic year began.[41] Rose seems to have taken opportunities to travel during this time, visiting Dodoma, Ngorongoro, and Dar es Salaam for school, work, and pleasure, including to a neighboring school "to dance 'country dance' and for a netball competition."[42] Although the letters give no hint of concern, Rose's new mobility may have made Gideon suspicious about her investment in the relationship; indeed, when the pair eventually entered into formal marriage discussions, Rose would become defensive about this period of her life.

Perhaps it was exactly this newfound freedom and sense of independence that prompted Rose to finally articulate her ambivalence to Gideon. In so doing, Rose invoked a discourse she knew well, and one that she likely knew Gideon would understand: that of Christian ethics. Publicly abdicating responsibility for her future and relying instead on God's will, Rose asked, "*Je, unaweza kujua Mungu aliyoyapanga?*" ("Can you know what [things, matters, troubles] God has planned?")[43] With her often imprecise Kiswahili, it is possible that Rose meant to ask "*alivyoyapanga*" (how God planned them) or even "*alivyowapangia*" ("how God planned for them"). Regardless, in insisting on Kiswahili for what appears to be a rough translation of Jeremiah 29:11, "For I know the plans I have for you," Rose employed yet another moral discourse to distance herself from a relationship with Gideon. As we will see again below, Christianity was not always a coherent ideology, but something that Rose—and individuals in communities throughout Tanzania and elsewhere—struggled to interpret in their own lives. Indeed, Gideon too sought refuge in the rhetoric of Christianity, albeit invoking it to opposing ends. In a draft penned in October 1964, Gideon wrote, in English:

> Rose, love is inexpressable [*sic*] in paper and ink but I need your assurance ~~I greatly miss your company~~. When we meet, ~~when you are in Dar~~ in Dar probably, we will

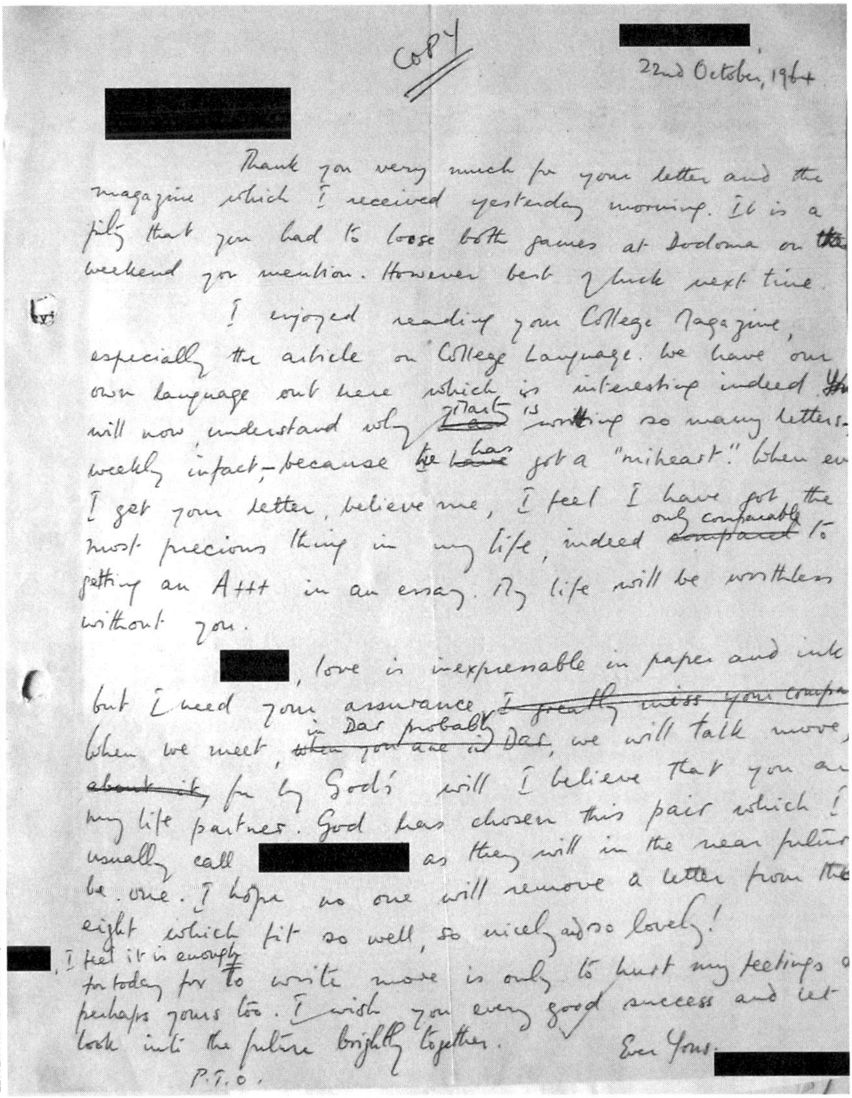

COPY

22nd October, 1964.

Thank you very much for your letter and the magazine which I received yesterday morning. It is a pity that you had to loose both games at Dodoma on the weekend you mention. However best of luck next time.

I enjoyed reading your College Magazine, especially the article on College Language. We have our own language out here which is interesting indeed. You will now understand why [illegible] is writing so many letters — weekly in fact — because he has got a "miheart." When ever I get your letter, believe me, I feel I have got the most precious thing in my life, indeed only comparable to getting an A+++ in an essay. My life will be worthless without you.

, love is inexpressable in paper and ink but I need your assurance. ~~I greatly miss your compa~~ When we meet, in Dar probably, we will talk more, for by God's will I believe that you are my life partner. God has chosen this pair which I usually call as they will in the near future be one. I hope no one will remove a letter from the eight which fit so well, so nicely and so lovely!

, I feel it is enough for today for to write more is only to hurt my feelings and perhaps yours too. I wish you every good success and let us look into the future brightly together.

Ever Yours.

P.T.O.

"LETTER FROM G. FURAHANI," 22 OCTOEER 1964, NEW HALL, PPGF, LSMATC. PHOTOGRAPH BY AUTHOR.

FIGURE 18. Of Gideon's letters included in the archive, most were carbon copies or drafts such as the one above, dated October 1964. After receipt of most of Rose's letters, Gideon added substantive marginalia, such as "sent," "received," and "replied on" dates.

> talk more ~~about it~~, for by God's will I believe that you are my life partner. God has chosen this pair which I usually call "ROSEGIDE" as they will in the near future be one. I hope no one will remove a letter from the eight which fit so well, so nicely and so lovely! Rose, I feel it is enough for today for to write more is only to hurt my feelings and perhaps yours, too. I wish you every good success and let us look into the future brightly together.[44]

Unfortunately, there is no record of what was just the first of many formal marriage proposals that seem to have followed.

We do know, however, that Rose refused Gideon's first proposal. Her response seemingly was intended to buy her more time: "I have understood all that you have said and I sense that you are serious about your proposal," she wrote, "but please don't tell the elders about it because until now I haven't decided what I want to do after this. Maybe I will let you know once I have made up my mind later on."[45] Even after two years, at the end of 1967, Rose had not yet "made up her mind." Each excuse Rose offered for not accepting Gideon's proposal seems to reinforce the possibility that she had other romantic interests, and that she was weighing an engagement to Gideon as one of several options. When Gideon pressed the issue of marriage in 1966, before his departure for a three-year course in the United States, Rose responded, "I don't want to be married and after two months I am left alone for three years. You wouldn't like that either if you were in my shoes."[46] Were she committed and pursuing Gideon exclusively, being "alone" during Gideon's absence might not have weighed so heavily on Rose; by being unengaged during his absence, however, Rose would have much more freedom.

Rose also attributed her lack of commitment to the impending marriage to ill health. Toward the end of 1966, Rose reported to Gideon that she had become unwell. Her complaints took the form of general malaise and lethargy, anxiety, and other moderate ailments. At first mention, she blamed her poor health on a death in the family:

> Honestly, I am writing this letter but I am not happy with life. My physical health is weak these days. No so many days ago we had a funeral for my brother's child. The story of that child is too long, I can't write it down. I will tell you when you come back during leave; that is, if you find me alive. The death of that child really affected me and that is why I am feeling this way now. I am not doing any kitchen work—all I do is to eat food and take medication.[47]

Depression and ill health continued throughout the following two years, a now chronic situation that Rose argued was made even worse by her prolonged separation from Gideon. In 1967, she wrote:

> You might be wondering why you are not receiving letters regularly from Rose but these days, my dear, I am very disturbed. I am not happy most of the time and, in short, I am having rather a difficult time. My laughter is sometimes pretend, for I do not want other people to notice how unhappy I am. I don't know why I am like this. Plus, the fact that you are very far away causes me to lose hope of seeing you again. I don't know what to do.[48]

Rose reiterated time and again that "the longer Gideon stays abroad, the more Rose suffers."[49]

Rose's "suffering" was physical, not just emotional. As she wrote in a Kiswahili letter dated February 1968:

> These days I am becoming not so perfect and I won't hide anything from you. Currently I can't even carry a bucket full of water and I haven't even practiced because tap water is available in the back. Secondly, I haven't mastered cooking a pot of food for ten people. Thirdly, I don't collect bundles of firewood anymore because firewood is for sale these days.
>
> So my love, please think twice. If you can handle all of that, then it's all very well. If you can't handle that don't hesitate to inform me. I won't just hang on to you so that you will suffer later on.
>
> That's how the situation is. I will be waiting for your response.[50]

The prolonged illness had left her *mbovubovu* (rotten, spoiled, unwell), she stated, and unable to perform what were then fundamental housekeeping and wifely duties. Although after they married they did go on to have several children, Rose may also have feared—or simply wanted Gideon to believe—that she would be unable to have children. Her health eventually got so poor that she transferred from secondary-school teaching to the apparently less stressful primary-school environment.[51] A medical examination, however, "did not reveal any abnormalities except for tachycardia," which may have explained her general malaise. Despite this, the doctor continued, "I cannot convince myself that she is organically sick. On interrogation it became more and more obvious, that she is tense, has her difficulties with other teachers, and is emotionally unstable . . . some tranquilizing treatment would probably do her good."[52] While she does appear to have been physically ill, Rose's self-diagnosis of lovesickness is questionable in light of the rest of the archive.

Over time, Rose clearly wanted to convince Gideon, and potential readers of her letters—and maybe even herself—that she was deeply in love. And perhaps she was. But her letters also suggest that her expressions of love did not necessarily translate into a desire for an exclusive, long-term relationship with Gideon. The tension between Rose's expressions of love and her apparent disinterest in marriage is particularly clear in 1966, when Rose employed an amanuensis. The use of amanuenses or other assistant writers, including trained secretaries, typists, scribes, and less formal personal-letter writers, was common among nonliterates and well-educated literati alike in colonial Africa. Individuals relied on skilled letter writers even when they were able to write, because letter writers offered, as Catherine Burns describes in relation to the South African herbalist Louisa Mvemve's attempts to maintain the image of a highly educated woman in her public correspondence, a "form of eloquence" that "seems to have demanded the efforts of more than one individual."[53] Gideon, for example, seems to have employed a periodic amanuensis, perhaps hoping to signal to himself and others that he was a sophisticated, well-educated man of means. Rose's one-off decision to employ an amanuensis, however, seems to stem less from aspirations to "modernity" or elite standing than from a desire to convince Gideon of her affection.

Apparently too distraught to put pen to paper, Rose dictated her sentiments to a friend, who wrote in Kiswahili:

> I was depressed when I heard that you wouldn't arrive like you had promised. So, the illness is back.
>
> Ahh, I should wait for you for three years? How? Am I an angel? I say that because currently I am suffering a lot and partly this is because of you . . . I am sorry this handwriting is not mine but worry not. The person who "wrote" this is me and I am the one who wrote this . . . NB: Still ill.[54]

Rose's declaration that she is not "an angel" is by far her most suggestive statement of the existence of other lovers, especially when read within the context of the pair's eventual marriage negotiations. Rather than having the intention of revealing other relationships to Gideon, however, it seems that Rose hoped to use the amanuensis as a witness to her intense "suffering," and thus to her presumptive faithfulness and fidelity during the couple's three-year separation. Making another person complicit in her lovesickness had the added benefit of providing preemptive support to Rose's claims of fidelity and mental stability in any investigative rituals that might precede marriage. And just over a year later, such an occasion did indeed arise.

Debates over Marriage and Community

In the face of Rose's protestations against marriage, Gideon remained undeterred. Immediately before his return to Tanzania from the United States, Gideon made the first recorded move to open formal marriage negotiations with Rose's family. Gideon tells Rose that he will send his brothers to her family with a "payment."[55] With the immediately surrounding letters missing, Gideon's meaning remains cryptic: whether the payment was intended as an installment of bridewealth or truly as an *ugoni* (a fine for committing adultery), as Gideon states, is not clear. Not once did Gideon or Rose mention explicitly the existence of a fiancé or husband, or refer to the need for a divorce. Indeed, Rose's general ambivalence seems to have been the only impediment to marriage. After this first, ambiguous mention of a premarital payment, Gideon was more explicit, indicating in August 1968 that he would send *wajumbe* (messengers) to Rose to perform a *kuchunguliana*. Remembered today as a ritual to check the virginity of a bride-to-be, the word *kuchunguliana*, the reciprocal form of *kuchungua* (to check, examine, or to look at carefully), implies mutuality to the ritual.[56] As such, a *kuchunguliana* was not simply an investigation of virginity, a practice common in the region, but rather was a mutual inquiry by both families for evidence of disease, madness, debt, entanglement in disputes, and other troubling circumstances.[57]

In a letter to Gideon, Rose articulated her resistance to the idea of a *kuchunguliana*. Perhaps unsurprising given her preceding letters, Rose explained that she was not against *kuchunguliana* because it was an outmoded, "traditional," or non-Christian practice, but because she "didn't know" if she would be able to pass the examination. In response to Gideon's suggestion that the *kuchunguliana* would help "ascertain whether she had a *doa* or not" (literally, a stain, spot, or blemish; more broadly, a defect, fault, flaw, shortcoming, or scar), Rose distinguished between *mashaka yangu ya afya* (her health troubles) and another type of *doa*. Regarding the first, she explained that because Gideon was well acquainted with her health problems and that they had come to "an understanding" about them, there was no reason to open the matter to further questioning. Regarding the second, she wrote that "the way I see it I don't have a *doa*":

> [My chastity and faithfulness] may be hard for you to believe because you were not around for a long time, and Rose travelled to Tabora, Mpwapwa, Moshi, Arusha, Dar-es-Salaam, and Tanga alone. If you still don't believe me you can bring your messengers over, but I hate such accusations. I hope I have explained myself well enough, even though there are things that I have left out which you would find hard to believe. But only God knows my honesty.[58]

Indeed, given this explanation, the couple's repeated reference to *doa* in letters without any further elaboration reads as a euphemism for Rose's transgressions. Although it appears that Rose traveled with friends and for work or school, such independence and mobility in and of themselves seemingly raised questions about her faithfulness and chastity.[59] Likely hoping that her response would chastise Gideon into calling off the *kuchunguliana*, Rose begrudgingly agreed to the examination.

Rose's response to the proposed *kuchunguliana* highlights an important intersection between the discourse of "modern," companionate marriage and longer-standing African understandings of the political capacity of marriage. Whatever their impetus, Rose's adamant declarations of love and her protestations over the potential enforcement of *kuchunguliana* posit Rose as a virtuous Christian woman who, as deeply in love with Gideon as she claimed to be, would neither need a "tribal custom" to sanctify her union nor be expected to live up to the dictates of premarital celibacy. In Rose's estimation, *kuchunguliana* was unnecessary, as their new, companionate love was enough to consecrate the marriage. While Gideon agreed that *kuchunguliana* was one of the *mambo ya kikabila* (tribal things/customs) that "no longer have any importance in the lives of people," the decision was not theirs alone to make.[60]

■ ■ ■

In August 1968, Gideon returned to Rose with more news of the *kuchunguliana*. "You might be pleased to hear the following piece of news," he wrote, which was that his family

> agreed that there will be no "*kuchunguliana*." They will agree to my judgment and they have agreed to wait for my report, which I haven't told them yet. Since you

> already told me, I hope that their joy will be great when I affirm it. However, before we play about with the whole process I will wait for the decision from your side, as we must make sure that we please both sides. I have no doubt this too will be done with respect and kindness without any bad feelings to either side. (I was so pleased when the decision came yesterday and I was informed of it.)[61]

Rose and her family seem to have agreed with Gideon's family's decision, for the matter of *kuchunguliana* was dropped without another mention, and Rose and Gideon married in 1968.

The families' debates about *kuchunguliana* reveal some fundamental innovations in the practices and processes of marriage composition, which were permitted in part by Rose and Gideon's status as school-educated, aspiring elites. In particular, the debate highlights the newfound authority of such youth vis-à-vis their elders. Gideon's (and presumably Rose's) family's decision to "to wait for my report" suggests that young people with advanced schooling had more power to negotiate with elders than their parents or grandparents would have had. By deferring to Gideon's judgment, his family also seems to have recognized the new forms of knowledge, wealth, and status conferred by higher education and travel abroad, and the value of those achievements and experiences to composing strong families and communities.

That Rose and Gideon could "play about with the whole process" of *kuchunguliana* by letter, rather than in person or through messengers, marks yet another innovation to practices of courtship and marriage in East Africa during the 1960s. In addition to allowing young people more autonomy in contracting marriages, the epistolary form of their courtship allowed it to unfold over a greater distance and duration. As we saw above, young people used letters to initiate relationships and romantic affairs outside the purview of families and relatives. Letters also enabled young lovers to carry out relationships at greater distances and over longer periods of time than ever before, mirroring the increase in mobility and independence generally afforded by school education. In so doing, correspondence provided young people with additional venues in which to develop and test new relationships, potentially balancing more than one lover at a time. Such machinations could allow the letter writers greater space to craft varying public personas.

Indeed, Rose and Gideon's rejection of *kuchunguliana* signals a complex process of cultural and ideological continuity and change. The families' concession to bypass *kuchunguliana* and their willingness to accept other innovations to the process of marriage does not mark what Neil Kodesh refers to as the "seemingly moribund fate of African tradition during the colonial period"; rather, it highlights the continuity of much longer-standing ideas about community composition.[62] While the practice of *kuchunguliana* may have been in the process of becoming passé, it was, in fact, only one element in a broader repertoire of traditional practices dedicated to ensuring that children born of marriages were "properly" conceived and carried. In African societies that valued wealth-in-people, marriages were central because of their capacity to produce, both biologically and socially, the next generation of community members.[63] While Rose and Gideon may have been resistant to the practice of *kuchunguliana* itself, the remainder of their archive suggests that they were anything but resistant to the idea of participating in the construction of properly ordered communities. In fact, Rose and Gideon's emphasis on love, affection, morality, civility, and Christianity suggests their desire to perpetuate communities—both spiritual and social, local and national—that would be ordered by those very ideals. Rose and Gideon's discussion of *kuchunguliana* thus reveals that while in the late nineteenth and early twentieth centuries, the process, content, and definition of some African marriages changed, the sociopolitical function of marriage as a fulcrum around which various communities were constructed and composed remained relatively stable.

■ ■ ■

Rose and Gideon's correspondence suggests that when seen through marriage's long-standing position as the key to community composition, the affective spiritual community could be an alternate site of national imagination. Our young lovers understood their marriage as an explicitly political act of community building and cast themselves as characters in a national drama. Just as their language choices, self-presentation, and campaigns of self-documentation suggest, Gideon's first hint of a formal proposal confirms how closely he and Rose tied their own identities and futures to that of the emergent nation: responding to yet another of Rose's concerns, this time about the cost of wedding bands, Gideon wrote, "Don't worry about anything. I think a ring made out of wood will be fine; how can we afford the expensive ones while we have decided to work for the nation?"[64] Through negotiating their twentieth-century marriage, Rose and Gideon became political innovators, selecting, producing, and testing the content and boundaries of their country.

Further, while the written record of Rose and Gideon's love affair confirms what others have established—that individuals did engage with anticolonial nationalism in ways that were beyond the control of TANU intellectuals—it also provides evidence of the uneven, diffuse, and extremely personal ways that school-educated individuals participated in President Nyerere's nation-building project. Indeed, both Rose and Gideon drew on ideas at the heart of the UMCA's affective spiritual community, and they realized that their personal future depended on the proper use of a variety of discourses and ideologies. What Ivaska has shown for officials' attempts to articulate national culture—that "traditionalist and modernizationist imperatives often existed alongside one another and were mutually constitutive"—is true, too, for the personal and the quotidian.[65] These lovers moved between the scales of affective spirituality, emotional intimacy, modern marriage, generational politics, clan solidarity, and national citizenship with ease, and without any sense of contradiction. To imagine their individual and collective futures, Rose and Gideon, like many Tanganyikans, drew from spiritual, intellectual, and moral repositories that were much broader and more varied that those privileged by victorious nationalist leaders and organizations. In particular, of course, these lovers drew from the ideals developed and spread by a network of female lay evangelists, core values of the UMCA such as Christian modernity, supra-ethnic unity, and racial exclusivity. They embodied these values, performed them, and struggled with them, ultimately applying them to new and explicitly political circumstances. This intimate and yet highly political engagement with the nation-building project suggests that "the church," "the nation," "the family," "the self," and "the private" are not separate or distinct realms, but are in fact blurred and overlapping.

Epilogue

On a dry day at the start of the long rains of 2008, just before the road from Tanga became impassible, my research assistant Tom and I set out to make what was becoming a familiar drive to the village of Maramba. Together with the neighboring villages of Kigongoi and Magila, Maramba hosted bustling UMCA mission stations—which included churches, schools, a convent, and health centers—for approximately a century, until the formal UMCA mission organization pulled out of Tanzania in the 1960s. The history of the UMCA in the area dates back to the Reverend C. A. Arlington's first visit to the Usambara Mountains in 1867, not long before the UMCA's female lay evangelists turned this area of what is today northeastern Tanzania into a major node in the UMCA's evangelical network. It was, in fact, where Blandina and Petro Limo settled to do their work after they departed from Zanzibar, where the nuns made their first start on the mainland, and where Rose and Gideon Furahani were born and raised. Today local residents speak fondly of the past, and lament that a declining economy and scant government support has forced younger generations to make their lives outside of the valley entirely. They scoff at the irony that the government's single recent investment, a paved road intended to ease travel up the steep road from Maramba to Kigongoi, came without funds for maintenance. The road has since buckled, rendering it impassable even in the dry season and with four-wheel drive, thus leaving Maramba and Kigongoi both increasingly isolated. Fortunately for us, Tom and I were only going to Maramba that day, and not further down the treacherous road; we had plans to visit Padre Luke and Mama Olivia Dunia, Maramba's patriarch and matriarch.

Padre Luke and Mama Olivia were venerated by their parishioners, beloved by former students, and esteemed by many others within UMCA congregations, even in circles that extended far beyond Maramba. Well before visiting the lush valley with the deep red soil for the first time, I heard about the Dunias from priests in Dar es Salaam, congregants in Zanzibar, former pupils in Tanga, and nuns in Masasi. During their long lives, they, and their reputations, had traveled far and wide throughout the spiritual community. Thus when I finally arrived in Maramba to conduct historical research, most residents were willing to participate . . . with a caveat. Congregants would be happy to share their individual stories, they said, but they were adamant that I speak with Mama Olivia first. Only Mama had the complete history of the village, and no story, not even their own, would be complete without her input. Luckily, I had met Mama Dunia on my very first trip to the village.

On this particular afternoon in 2008, I had come to talk not with members of the wider spiritual community to whom she ministered, but with Mama Dunia herself. After Tom and I climbed the steep hill to the Dunias' *shamba* and enjoyed chai and *maandazi* (spiced doughnuts) in the breeze on the porch, Mama and I settled down in the back room to talk. The bedroom was dark and cool, the large windows shaded by the pomelo trees growing on the farm. I sat on a squat loveseat, and Mama perched on the side of the bed that she had shared with her now-ailing husband since their wedding day in 1940. From the time of his stroke and paralysis in 1987, Mama Olivia had maintained a near-constant vigil at the bedside of the former priest, nursing an affliction she believed would kill him if left unattended for too long. She had explained when we spoke previously that she used the few hours of relief that her friends' and family's daily assistance afforded her to complete routine domestic tasks and the surprisingly large number of other small *shamba* chores she could still manage at the age of eighty-seven. To sell their produce in town, to maintain their home, to do the hard work on the *shamba*, and to procure basic necessities, the Dunias relied on the kindness of their grown daughter (a teacher in Maramba) and son (a banker in nearby Tanga), and on the countless people with whom they had cultivated relationships over the decades spent ministering to the people of the valley, and farther afield. This number included the Dunias' neighbors, former parishioners, and the extended family of children Mwalimu Olivia had raised in the classroom.

Mama Dunia was a charismatic, energetic, and warm woman, and it had been immediately clear to me upon our first meeting why she was so adored by villagers, parishioners, and former pupils alike. Beyond that, however, it was evident that the relationships of affective spirituality that Dunia had cultivated with fellow congregants, students, and inquirers alike were paying dividends in the couple's old age, continuing to undergird the community and its members both spiritually and physically.

Sitting across from Mama Dunia as she stroked her husband's hand, I wanted to know what she thought about the life that had made her into the beloved village matriarch to whom neighbors sent supplies and for whom their children labored in the fields. What did she think about the community that she and the Padre had helped build, and the networks they had helped to strengthen? To her mind, what was the most valuable outcome of years spent teaching and ministering, I wondered? What was the contemporary relevance of the faith she and Padre Luke had planted through their relationships with others, their daily work, and their embodied, quotidian performances (albeit phrased in not so many words)?

Mama Dunia's pride was clearly visible when she spoke of her role in the Maramba church. She told me that community members had long ago changed her name to "Mama Mwalimu." The title, she explained in English, meant "Mother Teacher." The name stuck even after she retired, she said, because she continued to care for the spiritual and physical well-being of her pupils. She boasted that she had never let a student go hungry. "Have you eaten?" she would ask. "Did you get drinking water?" Familiar enough with a student's circumstances to know that a "yes" was not always the truth, she would fill the child with maandazi and chai and send her on her way.[1] For Dunia, the line between teaching, ministering, and parenting was nonexistent—in each case, the job was to "love them physically and spiritually." Dunia saw her investment in the health, well-being, and spiritual development of an individual child as an investment in the welfare of the entire community. "I didn't want a person staggering in school," she said, "so that the community will benefit."[2]

Much of what Dunia said to me that day about her role in the spiritual community would have resonated with women like Beatrice Kilekwa and Rose Matula, whom we met in this book's introduction. The day-to-day work of female lay evangelists in 1896 and in 2008 was, in fact, similar in many ways: all of these women taught in small, rural schools; they forged enduring relationships with students and protégées, introducing Christianity among new cohorts and new generations; they visited homes of inquirers and congregants, treating village children as their own; and they did the hard quotidian work of Christian living in public. They established long-term, companionate, and (theoretically) monogamous relationships; they raised Christian children in full view of their parishioners; and they adopted the domestic habits and rituals of "practical" or "civilized" Christianity.[3] While Beatrice, Rose, and their friends Amy and Mabel were unlikely, at least at first, to speak the same languages as their congregants or to know much about local customs, Dunia's evangelism was rooted in the community in which she was born. The networks they forged, and the intimate friendships that sustained them physically and spiritually across disparate and discontiguous stations, however, were nearly identical. So too was their social position. Indeed, the social positions of all the women we have met in this book were similar: they all used a sophisticated evangelical repertoire—a shared emotional and spiritual subjectivity; daily, embodied performance of a set of commonly held, though always negotiated, values; and constant movement between mission stations—to build a community on Zanzibar and the adjacent mainland over the course of nearly 150 years.

There were other aspects of Dunia's life, however, that at first glance may not have been as easily recognizable to her sisters in spirit of nearly a century and a half ago. Perhaps most significant was the "community" at the heart of Dunia's work. Rather than focus simply on the former UMCA spiritual community, Dunia's attentions were attuned to a much broader community. She considered her work to have an explicitly national component. Teachers' and clerics' wives, she said, "should love everyone, should have good intentions of raising the nation . . . [of] advancing the nation." Ultimately, she said, "I want development . . . my intention is progress, and not just for my family. No, my country has to [progress]."[4] In her description of the role of a cleric's wife and teacher, Dunia defined the nation-state of Tanzania as one of the central objects of her and her contemporary colleagues' pedagogical, spiritual, and emotional labors. In so doing, she deliberately situated herself, her fellow clerics' wives and teachers, and her community in a relationship to the Tanzanian nation-state.

To be sure, it is possible that my own status as an outsider and a trained historian may have shaped the way Dunia characterized her work. She may have assumed, as has been argued for respondents in rural Njombe, Tanzania, that I valued "stories of development, modernization, and nation-building" over, for example, the "private, intimate sphere of family and neighbors" in which interlocutors were the most comfortable operating.[5] In the context of different "interview" settings, proddings elicited different results. In settings elders deemed more "appropriate for turning their memories into instruction," they "placed their accounts of the past not in the historians' state-dominated chronology, but in a private, intimate sphere of family and neighbours." The grand narratives of colonialism, nationalism, and independence figured little in their stories, but instead they told stories about individuals and set them in the context of family relationships.[6] UMCA congregants, however, explicitly addressed the private, affective, intimate sphere in our conversations, and in the historical sources. Dunia and her colleagues actively placed their accounts of the past within a state-dominated chronology that intersected and overlapped with the private, intimate spheres of family and neighbors. They spoke, unprompted, about the grand developments of colonialism, nationalism, independence, and collective action. But they also spoke about their intimate relationships. Indeed, it was within the context of discussing emotional and spiritual bonds that they chose to comment on the grand narratives of nation and nationalism. Their affective spiritual relationships were the foundation through which they understood, conceptualized, and contributed to the nation in the first place.

Although in 2008 Dunia argued that the beneficiary of her and her colleagues' labors was the nation-state of Tanzania, if I had asked Dunia in the late 1930s or early 1940s how she conceived of her responsibilities as a cleric's wife and teacher, it is likely that Mama Dunia would have responded differently. In the 1930s and '40s, when Mama Dunia was completing her teacher training and preparing to marry Padre Luke, neither the term "nation-state" nor the way of imagining the political space it represented were in circulation among rural Africans. Territorial nationalism and the modular unit of the nation-state—which is the most common form of sovereignty in the world today—are concepts that only gained currency in Africa after the Second World War. Indeed, Africans' aspirations for political sovereignty in the form of the nation-state were largely the result of experiences during and around World War II. Soldiers returning from war proffered new ideas about democracy and equality, and shared stories of anticolonial independence movements. Expanding literacies and technologies of communication introduced new ways of conceptualizing political space. The experiences of strike actions and unionism led to new forms of solidarity. Finally, engagement with intellectual discourses from abroad offered new models of unity and aspirations for independence.

A mere two decades earlier, however, Africans coming of age between the world wars, including the young Mama Dunia, were living in a very different world. Theirs was one in which other forms of political unity, such as Pan-Islamism, Pan-Africanism, Pan-Asianism, forms of diasporic unity, such as Christian humanitarianism and proletarian internationalism, offered equally viable and exciting paths toward the future.[7] The earlier forms of deterritorialized identity, which included the UMCA's diverse affective spiritual community, shaped the realities, expectations, and aspirations of interwar Africans, and vied at turns with more locally rooted identities. Even in the late 1950s, when some had begun to rally behind an anticolonial nationalism and to agitate for decolonization, the nation-state was not the only political community the majority of East Africans imagined. The world of colonial Africans was complex and cosmopolitan, offering a host of affiliations, forms of political solidarity, and transterritorial or deterritorialized networks from which to choose. Elsewhere, Luo, Haya, Toro, Ganda, and Gikuyu people were concerned not with solidifying an independent nation for Kenya, Tanganyika, or Uganda, but rather with constructing a *patria*, or fatherland, "rooting people in place as inheritors of their ancestors' instructive customs and traditions." Ethnic patriots were in fact explicitly opposed to the idea of the nation-state, which "threw people together without discrimination, undermining the institutions that protected moral order," and "severing the young from the instruction that history could provide."[8] Converts of the East African Revival, a Christian conversion movement that began in the mid-1930s in Rwanda and spread to Kenya, Tanganyika, and Uganda, were similarly unmotivated by the idea of the nation-state, for they imagined themselves as pilgrims on the road toward their future home in Heaven. They were cosmopolitans drawn together into a large, transcontinental community of confession, conversion, and Christian revival.[9] Other groups, such as the continent's Pan-Africanists, focused on the solidarity of Africans worldwide, and on the uplift of the "civilization" or "race" as a whole. Still others were adamantly opposed to political independence for Britain's East African colonies, attempting instead to reform and restructure the imperial unit to give Africans more influence over their own affairs.[10] The speed and finality with which decolonization came in the early 1960s surprised East Africans and their British colonizers alike. Until then, there had been no reason to believe that among the myriad forms of political organization and moral discourses available, the nation-state would become the fate of African colonies across the continent. It was the "contingent outcome of a variety of other aspirations."[11]

Thus if Mama Dunia had been asked in the 1930s or 1940s to imagine her role as a cleric's wife and teacher, it is unlikely that she would have responded as she did when I asked her in 2008: by centering the nation-state as the recipient of her pedagogical, emotional, and spiritual labors. Rather, she and her colleagues likely would have imagined the beneficiary of those efforts to be the UMCA's deterritorialized affective spiritual community—a community held together by the constant pilgrimages of congregants, by intimate relationships of affective spirituality, and by a set of commonly held, though always negotiated, values. As we saw in the latter half of this book, by the 1930s UMCA congregants had come to see themselves as part of a diverse and encompassing spiritual community that cut across colonies, ethnic associations, and civil organizations with little attention to the paradigm of "resistance" or "oppression" that scholars often attribute to nationalism's political innovators.[12] Instead, UMCA congregants were concerned with composing a community attuned to the values of Christian modernity, supra-tribal unity, and racial exclusivity, and they actively worked to maintain and enforce the boundaries of this community.

Over the course of the 1930s through the 1950s, however, UMCA congregants became entangled with new ideas and new forms of political organization, such as those described above, and mapped the longer-standing social, cultural, and religious ideals of the UMCA onto new and emerging, explicitly political, communities. Yet, all the while they refused to lose sight of the outlines of the spiritual community. Perhaps in this way, then, Dunia's articulation of the aims of her labor were not fundamentally different from the way her sisters in spirit understood their work 150 years earlier. Dunia's work remained about using affective spiritual relationships as the basis for spreading the Gospel and the civilizational tenets particular to the UMCA community. Rather than supplanting or replacing the concerns of individual Africans, nationalism and the nation-state became incorporated into the way that Dunia and other members of the former UMCA's spiritual community understood their evangelical mission. The nation-state was, in other words, one of the concerns of UMCA congregants' efforts, but by no means their sole interest.

Attending to affect and to the affective dimensions of the lives of the UMCA's female evangelists highlights the perils of attempting to read these stories backward, through the teleological lens of nationalism that has held historians of Tanzania, among others, in its grip. Instead, attending to affect, emotions, and in particular to the relationships of affective spirituality of the UMCA's sisters in spirit, opens up a range of new insights about the past. For one, we can see the formation of new subjectivities and of new forms of affinity and affiliation, such as the female lay evangelists whose embodied performances of Christian values potentiated a unique, inclusive spiritual community that crosscut and superseded ethnic and national affiliations. We have seen that rather than identify as Yao, Nyamwezi, Bondei, Makua, or Digo, congregants prioritized their affective spiritual ties/bonds, illustrating that the term and the study of cultural nationalisms can incorporate more than the study of ethnicity and race, but can also encompass communities of religion and belief. Taking affect and belief seriously, and as acting in the realm of the real, we can see community forms that the voices, actions, and writings of men and cultural organizations cannot express. It allows us, as was the case for therapeutic networks in Buganda, to see past "'what [was] left' in the organizational repertoire" when ethnographers composed the earliest descriptions of African communities.[13] For many scholars of Christianity and nationalism in Africa, this "what was left" was ethnicity and ethnic cultural nationalisms, and it has been the taken-for-granted form of organization, affiliation, and expression that motivated Africans in Tanzania and beyond. Attending thusly to quotidian performance, affect, and belief, we obviate the problematic theoretical assumption that ethnicity was the single or most salient outcome of Africans' engagement with the vernacular Bible and mission Christianity. We uncover instead a new realm in which discourse about morality, civilization, and culture unfolded, one that includes congregants from distinct ethnicities and backgrounds, and that spread across disparate lands.

Further, attending to the quotidian, embodied performance of sisters in spirit over a century and a half—clerics' wives and teachers, nurses and nuns, mothers and daughters—demands we change our definitions of "intellectual" and of "politics." The daily lives of these women illustrate that intellectual history can be accessed through the domestic realms of the past. It is not merely written or spoken, but is embodied and performed. Recognizing this will provide us access to new intellectual networks, and allow us to better understand how intimate lives, feelings, and actions influenced institutional action. We can also see the gendered aspects of the increasingly robust intellectual history of Africa, and access the modes of thinking of newly forged social categories and subjectivities.[14] The dreams and aspirations of contingent and gendered subjectivities will emerge from the shadows when we attend to affects, emotions, embodied performance, and the domestic.

Finally, attending to affect and emotions allows us access to marginalized and contingent historical actors such as women and other subalterns. Listening to these stories can help us better understand the unfolding of broader processes of the long twentieth century—specifically, they allow us to see that not all efforts of colonial subjects were directed toward forms of community and groupness that were "inherently inclusive and liberating," but were rather hemmed by individuals and ways of thinking that acted to police and circumscribe the boundaries of community.[15] We see also radical and unique forms of affinity that were eclipsed by the victorious, male-centric, anticolonial nationalism of organizations such as TANU, and others that inherited the colonial state and its institutions. Taken together, this allows us to hear stories of Africans on their own terms, rather than on those that a small group of nationalists or their Western biographers and historians choose to tell about them. It allows us to see their lives in greater relief—their raw and complicated emotions, their aspirations and strivings, their loves and their losses, their faith and their failures—and to write a much richer version of the past.

A Note on Sources

The documents on which this story is based come from a range of national, organizational, "shadow," and "tin trunk" archives, as well as from several personal collections. I started my search for documents, as many historians of Tanzania do, at the Tanzania National Archives (TNA). Even the main TNA building in Dar es Salaam is a far cry from the grandeur many would imagine for a "national" archive; the regional depots are another case entirely. Years of underfunding and neglect wreaked havoc on what was once a well-organized, efficient system. After numerous failed attempts to find several sets of documents relating to UMCA education in the main document repository, a sympathetic archivist eventually donned a lab coat and dust mask to search through the TNA's "back room"—an un-air-conditioned storage shed that contained piles of discarded and unlabeled cardboard boxes. To quiet my inquiries, the archivist allowed me to accompany him. Even if I had been allowed to take photographs with my then-rudimentary cell phone camera, I could not have captured the chaos. It was the stuff of historians' nightmares. If the physical state of the postcolonial national archives govern access to the precolonial- and colonial-era past, so too do the modern-day social and cultural norms of the institution itself. Rarely discussed in theoretical assessments of the archives are the ways in which local norms of gender, seniority, and status regulate a researcher's experience in the archives, and the documents she is permitted to read. Unable to access nearly half of the documents I requested from the listing guides, I made an appointment with the director of the TNA to discuss the missing documents. As a young (and young-looking) female graduate student researcher, I experienced markedly different treatment and subsequently received even more limited access than my male contemporaries and older male colleagues who had met with the same director.

If the TNA suffers from the same fragmentation and disorganization as other postcolonial national archives, the Zanzibar National Archives (ZNA) have largely remained immune. The ZNA is well-organized and efficient; it contains diaries, journals, and a host of other records from the UMCA's stations in Mbweni, as well as on education and schooling more generally. British missionaries kept diaries of their daily work, and administrators at each mission station maintained some form of a log or diary, into which they entered notes about events large, small, and seemingly insignificant. Noteworthy events or moments that caught the attention of mission staff would garner paragraphs or pages of notes; less exciting times, workers noted the coming and going of the mail ship or a dead camel in the streets.

The "shadow archives" of the British presence in Tanzania were also refreshingly abundant.[1] Archives at small former UMCA parishes were fruitful; baptismal, marriage, and death records often remain in the possession of the churches. When I visited St. John's Church at Mbweni, Zanzibar, the groundskeeper produced for me record books nearly 150 years old, which he kept locked in a wooden and glass sideboard in the side entrance of the church. Like many documents from "tin trunk archives,"[2] these were in surprisingly good shape considering the circumstances in which they were stored. A small storage closet at St. Nicholas Church in Buguruni contains registers, school diaries, and other materials from several decades at St. Andrew's College (now Minaki and formerly Kiungani). Similar collections are retained in the cathedral complex in Masasi and at St. Nicholas Church in Dar es Salaam, among other locations. In England, the British Library contains information on the UMCA and on British evangelism in East Africa. Rhodes House at Oxford College holds letters of British mission officials, unaffiliated colonial officials, as well as several sets of letters from Africans—many, but not all, of which have been microfilmed and are available through the CAMP microfilm series on the UMCA/USPG. A small library in Shropshire, England, contains newspaper clippings relevant to a female medical missionary, May Allen. The Mother House of the Community of the Sacred Passion in Shoreham-by-Sea maintains nearly all of the extant records of the order, as well as many school logs and material about schools they ran and administered in the Tanga region. Joining the sisters for silent lunch and tea-time conversation was a highlight of my fieldwork in England.

As Karin Barber and Derek Peterson have illustrated, Africans were also curators. "Native preachers" produced their own documents, including mission station diaries and logs written in both English and Kiswahili. The library at the University of Dar es Salaam has what is probably the largest collection of records from African agents of the UMCA. Africans' contributions to the official record of the UMCA do not end at the staid and formulaic dated entries in lined record books; they also produced letters, autobiographies, sermons, marriage certificates, diaries, logs, and other ephemera. African-authored letters regarding church business, as well as letters written by British mission administrators, are maintained at Rhodes House and are available in part through the CAMP collection at the University of Chicago. The now-Bishop William Mndolwa was a librarian at St. Mark's Theological College in Buguruni, Dar es Salaam, when I was conducting my fieldwork. He undertook the responsibility of collecting, cataloging, and preserving documents from the UMCA-era that remained in small, dispersed archives throughout the country. He personally financed trips to remote areas of Tanzania to collect personal papers, church archives, and Mothers' Union materials, and has curated a small collection at St. Mark's. These materials included a trove of one hundred love letters exchanged between an African priest and his fiancée, and their amorous exchanges provided perhaps the first clues that it would be possible to tell a story through the lens of affect.

Beyond the practical questions of physical access to these documents, which was often difficult, are broader theoretical questions about transparency, the ontological shaping of the archives, and document "accessibility."[3] A substantial literature, spurred in large part by scholars of South and Southeast Asian history, has theorized the nature of the colonial archive as it was constituted by the imperial state and the "access" that these structures grant. Africanists have in large part considered the biases of the colonial archive a "methodological given" and have instead turned to seeking out and developing alternative kinds of evidence.[4] Oral traditions, life histories, the histories of words and things provided insights into the past, and historians learned to read against and along the grain. Historians of Africa, perhaps because of the relative dearth of African voices in the colonial historical record, seem to privilege oral sources above all others. Some historians, Jonathon Glassman has pointed out, even go so far as to "question any account that omits them."[5] When conceiving this study, I planned to supplement the archival "silences" with interviews, seeking out stories and memories handed down to descendants of the first generations of UMCA adherents. In the end, I conducted over eighty interviews with elderly UMCA congregants and clerics, descendants of UMCA congregants, current Anglican Church of Tanzania members and clergy, local historians and former UMCA stakeholders, members of the Mothers' Union, African and British nuns of orders established by the UMCA, teachers (both current and former) at schools once affiliated with the UMCA, and others familiar with the UMCA. I also benefited from informal conversations with Tanzanian, Zanzibari, and British interlocutors about the UMCA, its work, and its congregants, as well as about many other aspects of Tanzanian and mission history.

Throughout these conversations, however, I learned less that had direct application to my queries than I had initially (and perhaps naively) hoped. When I asked elderly adherents of former UMCA churches about their parents' or grandparents' generations, for example, they had little to share, other than general facts. When pressed about parents' or grandparents' experiences in school, their elders' views on religion or other esoteric beliefs, how their parents viewed the colonial or evangelical experience, how their parents met, or what their grandparents' relationships were like with their friends and classmates, for example, most interlocutors had very little to share. Perhaps they did not trust me, or feel that I had any right to these memories; yet that seems unlikely, considering how forthcoming many of them were with other types of information. More likely is that the questions I was asking required children to have spoken with their parents and grandparents about topics that did not often occupy young children, and which may have been far from the minds of older generations as well.

Some information I solicited, such as family histories of slavery, was more problematic. Silences, omissions, or alternative versions of this history were easier for me to anticipate and account for. Active forgetting has also played a role in the way that parishioners of churches that once belonged to the UMCA now understand their past. For example, in 2008 I spoke with Mzee Nyangi, an elderly congregant of St. Paul's Church at Mbweni, the very place where Beatrice and Petro were married some 110 years earlier.[6] During the second time we met, in the nave of the church, Mzee Nyangi narrated his family history to me. Out of wooden armoires in the breezeway he pulled dusty, moth-eaten church registers. In an old, crumbling log we found the entry for the marriage of his paternal grandparents—September 3, 1876, in the chapel at Kiungani School. Nyangi told me his version of his grandparents' early lives together, which were spent working for the church. Curious about their "conversion story," I asked him how his grandparents had come to be congregants at the mission. Were they slaves, I asked? His grandmother, he said, never spoke about her story. But his grandfather's family, he said, "*hawalikuwa kwa watumwa*" (was not of slave heritage). Nyangi was emphatic. How had he come to Mbweni? I asked. "Well, he just came," he said, "probably looking for a job. And when he came here, he was taken as a catechist. He was one of the first catechists . . . No, no, no, he didn't come as a slave."[7] Nyangi is from one of the oldest and best-known families in the church, and it seems impossible that he did not know this important fact about his own family. I did not raise the point with Nyangi, but a list of children under the patronage of the UMCA published in 1878 includes his grandfather, George Nyangi. Records indicate that he arrived on the HMS *Daphne* on November 28, 1868, and was believed to have been of Yao descent. Nyangi was right, then, that his paternal grandfather came from the area near Masasi; but he had not come on his own volition, looking for a job. Nyangi was vehemently invested in "forgetting" this point of history, in spite of the available evidence.[8]

Stories like Nyangi's are not the only challenges to working with oral sources, as a vast literature on the subject has shown.[9] Ultimately, the interviews that had the most utility for me, and the interviews on which I relied most heavily in the subsequent narrative, were from congregants—most now elderly—who lived and/or worked in UMCA and former-UMCA communities during the 1940s, 1950s, and 1960s. I found the interviews with elderly African nuns to be the most illustrative, and the most rewarding. Their personal memories have been shaped by a wide variety of forces, and I have remained attentive to the resulting biases in their contributions to this book.

Notes

INTRODUCTION

1. Beatrice was reported as "13 or 14" in 1893. "Beatrice of Mbweni," *African Tidings* 6, no. 91 (May 1897): 54.
2. This was a common fate for East African women. See, for example, Edward Alpers, "The Story of Swema: Female Vulnerability in Nineteenth-Century East Africa," in *Women and Slavery in Africa*, ed. Clare Robertson and Martin Klein (Madison: University of Wisconsin Press, 1983), 85–219; Marcia Wright, *Strategies of Slaves and Women: Life-Stories from East/Central Africa* (New York: Lilian Barber Press, 1992).
3. "Beatrice of Mbweni," 54.
4. There is some discrepancy regarding the Kilekwas' movements. In his autobiography, which was written in 1937, Petro Kilekwa writes, "After my marriage I did not want to go back to Masasi, for after many talks with Nyasa students, I felt strongly drawn to Nyasaland." The memoir does not include any reference to the Kilekwas' work in Masasi after their marriage. However, several mission sources authored at the time of the events indicate that the Kilekwas spent a short time in Masasi working with the Mtaulas before going to Nyasaland. It is very possible that this stint was short and unremarkable, and did not fit with Kilekwa's carefully crafted narrative of himself, so he left it out of the book. The mission-authored sources are clear, however, to place Beatrice and Rose

together in Masasi, and to track the Kilekwas' journey through Lindi to Masasi, and then onward to Likoma. Perhaps the missionary writing about Beatrice was confused, but the preponderance of evidence suggests that their stint at Masasi was short-lived, a stopover on the way to Nyasaland. Petro Kilekwa, *Slave Boy to Priest: The Autobiography of Padre Petro Kilekwa* (London: Universities' Mission to Central Africa, 1937).

5. "Beatrice of Mbweni," 54.
6. "Census at Easter 1898," *Central Africa* 7, no. 192 (December 1898): 191–92.
7. Caroline Thackeray, "Our Native Female Teachers," *Central Africa* 14, no. 168 (December 1896): 204.
8. Ibid.
9. "Beatrice of Mbweni," 54.
10. Ibid.
11. "Our African Mail: A Sad Fact," *African Tidings* 17, no. 228 (October 1908): 117.
12. The missionary's description of the "race" under construction—of a "race of intellectual Christians"—is one of a community defined by a shared culture rather than by geographical origin or biological heredity, as it is regarded today. This missionary's statement was in line with UMCA thought specifically and with nineteenth-century British thought more generally, and represents but a single moment in the long history of racial thought. Race, as Jonathon Glassman argues, was neither "invariably hierarchical nor invariably built around a core of biological theory." Far more influential in the construction of racial thought, he argues, "was the anthropological concept of clearly bounded 'cultural monads,'" a concept that refers to the insurmountability of cultural differences. This belief in cultural differences was most expressed in terms of "'barbarism' and its foil, 'civilization,' from which modern race thinkers inherited the project of comparing all humanity according to a single, universal standard." Jonathon Glassman and James Brennan discuss this transformation at length, but essentially it wasn't until the 1920s in East Africa when "race" began to suggest geographical origin rather than culture. By the 1920s, however, racial thought in colonial Tanganyika and Zanzibar began to shift, contributing to the development of an understanding of "civilization" and "race" that was based on geographical origins rather than on culture. Race, we now know, much like nation and ethnicity, is a mode of thought in which groups are "subjectively presumed to be authentic cultural wholes that define themselves by metaphors of shared descent." Indeed, as we will see in subsequent chapters, the racial category "African" is a mode of thought rather than a fixed element of social structure. As such, the racial category "African" has a history. See especially the introduction in Jonathon Glassman, *War of Words, War of Stones: Racial Thought and Violence in Colonial Zanzibar*

(Bloomington: University of Indiana Press, 2011); James R. Brennan, *Taifa: Making Nation and Race in Urban Tanzania* (Athens: Ohio University Press, 2012), 1.

13. Thackeray, "Our Native Female Teachers," 207. Emphasis mine.
14. Kilekwa, *Slave Boy to Priest*, 30.
15. Kenda Mutongi, *Worries of the Heart: Widows, Family, and Community in Kenya* (Chicago: University of Chicago Press, 2007).
16. Caroline Thackeray, "The African Woman of the Future," *Central Africa* 28, no. 330 (June 1910): 151.
17. Kilekwa, *Slave Boy to Priest*, 43–45.
18. Ibid., 46–47.
19. Wendy Urban-Mead, *The Gender of Piety: Family, Faith, and Colonial Rule in Matabeleland, Zimbabwe* (Athens: Ohio University Press, 2015), 11.
20. John Iliffe, *A Modern History of Tanganyika* (New York: Cambridge University Press, 1979), 216–17; Marcia Wright, *German Missions in Tanganyika, 1891–1941: Lutherans and Moravians in the Southern Highlands* (Oxford: Clarendon Press, 1971).
21. H.D.M. Spence-Jones, *The Pulpit Commentary*, vol. 1 (Grand Rapids, MI: Wm. B. Eerdmans Publishing Co., 1883), 217; H.D.M. Spence-Jones, *The Pulpit Commentary*, vol. 2 (Grand Rapids, MI: Wm. B. Eerdmans Publishing Co., 1883), 404; C. Orelli, *The Prophecies of Isaiah* (Edinburgh: T&T Clark, 1889), 197.
22. Steven Feierman, *Peasant Intellectuals: Anthropology and History in Tanzania* (Madison: University of Wisconsin Press, 1990).
23. Ibid.
24. Kathryn de Luna has illustrated that attending to affect allows us to probe the boundary between individual and collective affective subjectivities. De Luna's analysis of the debates about the meaning of one of the best-known Bantu reconstructions, *-kúmú, for example, suggests ways to conceptualize collective affective subjectivity. She illustrates that matters of the emotion of honor, which Jan Vansina has described as something granted to the person experiencing it, "concerned not only individuals, but also the wider family or other social group." Defilements and conveyances of one's honor thus "activated emotional subjectivity to all members of that individual's group." Honor that followers granted to the *-kúmú was "honor experienced by all members of his following." Kathryn de Luna, "Affect and Society in Precolonial Africa," *International Journal of African Historical Studies* 46, no. 1 (2013): 139.
25. Dorothy Ko, *Teachers of the Inner Chambers: Women and Culture in Seventeenth-Century China* (Palo Alto, CA: Stanford University Press, 1995).
26. Benedict Anderson, *Imagined Communities: Reflections on the Origin and Spread of*

Nationalism (New York: Verso, 1983), 54.

27. There was, of course, what Anderson has called "a double aspect to the choreography" of the UMCA's religious pilgrimages: evangelism was focused on a seemingly infinite number of non-Christians, of which only a small number would ever inquire about, or affiliate with, the UMCA and eventually become integrated in the sacred geography of the mission; the work itself was undertaken by a much smaller number of "native" evangelists who embodied and performed Christianity, forging a community through their shared definition of Christianity, their emotive and real ties to each other and to Zanzibar, and their movement between stations. Anderson, *Imagined Communities*, 54.
28. John Kelly and Martha Kaplan, *Represented Communities: Fiji and World Decolonization* (Chicago: University of Chicago Press, 2001), 4.
29. Lynn Thomas and Jennifer Cole's collection on love in Africa, and Meaghan Vaughan's exploration of the history of romantic love in sub-Saharan Africa were published in 2009, just as I was writing an article for the *Journal of African History* thinking through a wonderful cache of love letters between an African priest and his UMCA-trained fiancée. Jennifer Cole and Lynn Thomas, eds., *Love in Africa* (Chicago: University of Chicago Press, 2009). Kathryn de Luna and Nancy Rose Hunt have covered much of this literature in recent review articles: de Luna, "Affect and Society in Precolonial Africa"; Nancy Rose Hunt, "The Affective, the Intellectual, and Gender History," *Journal of African History* 55 (2014): 331–45; Megan Vaughan, "The History of Romantic Love in Sub-Saharan Africa: Between Interest and Emotion," *Proceedings of the British Academy* 167 (2009).
30. Nancy Rose Hunt, "An Acoustic Register, Tenacious Images, and Congolese Scenes of Rape and Repetition," *Cultural Anthropology* 23, no. 2 (May 2008): 220–53.
31. Silvan S. Tomkins, *Affect, Imagery, Consciousness*, vol. 2, *The Negative Affects* (New York: Springer Publishing, 1962); Clare Hemmings, "Invoking Affect: Cultural Theory and the Ontological Turn," *Cultural Studies* 19, no. 5 (September 2005): 548–67.
32. Stephen Shoemaker, "Mary at the Cross, East and West: Maternal Compassion and Affective Piety in the Earliest Life of the Virgin and the High Middle Ages," *Journal of Theological Studies* 62 (October 2011): 570.
33. Susan C. Karant-Nunn, *The Reformation of Feeling: Shaping the Religious Emotions in Early Modern Germany* (Oxford: Oxford University Press, 2010).
34. Barbara Rosenwein, "Worrying about Emotions in History," *American Historical Review* 107, no. 3 (June 2002): 842.
35. Peter B. Nockles, *The Oxford Movement in Context: Anglican High Churchmanship, 1760–1857* (Cambridge: Cambridge University Press, 1994), 190–98; R. W. Church, *The Oxford Movement: Twelve Years, 1833–1845* (Chicago: University of Chicago Press, 1970), xv.

36. J. B. Peires, *The Dead Will Arise: Nongqawuse and the Great Xhosa Cattle-Killing Movement of 1856–7* (Bloomington: Indiana University Press, 1989); Douglas Thomas, *African Traditional Religion in the Modern World: An Introduction* (Jefferson, NC: McFarland, 2005).
37. Bruce Berman and John Lonsdale, *Unhappy Valley: Conflict in Kenya and Africa* (Athens: Ohio University Press, 1992), 267.
38. Both scholarly and popular histories argue that it was the work of these men in formal governmental, social, and cultural institutions that developed and spread the social norms of bourgeois respectability, "supra-tribal" unity, and Christian modernity, cultural values that underlaid the earliest expressions of modern nationalist political culture in Tanzania. John Iliffe's characterization of the underlying tenets of nationalist expression in Tanzania is generally accepted by historians of Tanzania. Iliffe, *A Modern History of Tanganyika*.
39. Jean Marie Allman, "The Disappearing of Hannah Kudjoe: Nationalism, Feminism, and the Tyrannies of History," *Journal of Women's History* 21, no. 3 (Fall 2009); Susan Geiger, *TANU Women: Gender and Culture in the Making of Tanganyikan Nationalism, 1955–1965* (Portsmouth, NH: Heinemann, 1997).
40. Thackeray, "The African Woman of the Future," 151.
41. Allman, "The Disappearing of Hannah Kudjoe," 15. While Susan Geiger's monograph on TANU women does chart the contributions of Muslim women, it does so within the framework of an established anticolonial nationalist organization. Monographs by Gracia Clark and Elizabeth Schmidt, for example, showcase the contributions of women to nationalism, but do not explore how everyday work and embodied performance generate discourses and modes of thought that were adopted and improvised upon by later generations of political innovators. Gracia Clark, *Onions Are My Husband* (Chicago: University of Chicago Press, 1994); Elizabeth Schmidt, *Mobilizing the Masses: Gender, Ethnicity, and Class in the Nationalist Movement in Guinea, 1939–1958* (Portsmouth, NH: Heinemann, 2005).
42. This is well documented in the existing literature on the connection between archives and colonial or state epistemologies. See also Laura Ann Stoler, *Along the Archival Grain: Epistemic Anxieties and Colonial Common Sense* (Princeton, NJ: Princeton University Press, 2010); Achille Mbembe, "The Power of the Archive and Its Limits," in *Refiguring the Archive*, ed. Carolyn Hamilton (Cape Town: Springer, 2002), 19–27; Derek R. Peterson, *Ethnic Patriotism and the East African Revival: A History of Dissent, c. 1935–1972* (New York: Cambridge University Press, 2012), 27.
43. Paul Landau usefully interrogates the use of the term and category "religion" in the

pre-Christian context in Africa. Paul Landau, "'Religion' and Christian Conversion in African History: A New Model," *Journal of Religious History* 23, no. 1 (1999): 8–30.

44. Stoler, *Along the Archival Grain*, 1.
45. A small literature traces the way British missionaries shaped the life stories and "recaptive" narratives of Africans they incorporated into their mission. For East Africa, see in particular Gareth Griffiths, "'Trained to Tell the Truth': Missionaries, Converts, and Narration," in *Missions and Empire*, ed. Norman Etherington (Oxford: Oxford University Press, 2005), 153–72; Wright, *Strategies of Slaves and Women*.
46. The Tanzanian National Archives is notoriously underfunded, understaffed, and unorganized. Leander Schneider, "The Tanzanian National Archives," *History in Africa* 30 (2003): 447–54.
47. Jean Allman, "Phantoms of the Archive: Kwame Nkrumah, a Nazi Pilot Named Hanna, and the Contingencies of Postcolonial History-Writing," *American Historical Review* 118, no. 1 (February 2013): 104–29.
48. Ibid. See also Priya Lal, *African Socialism in Postcolonial Tanzania: Between the Village and the World* (Cambridge: Cambridge University Press, 2015), 35.
49. Iliffe, *A Modern History of Tanganyika*; Ann-Marie Stoner-Eby, "African Leaders Engage Mission Christianity: Anglicans in Christianity, 1876–1926" (PhD diss., University of Pennsylvania, 2003); Justin Willis, "The Makings of a Tribe: Bondei Identities and Histories," *Journal of African History* 33, no. 2 (1992): 191–208; Justin Willis, "The Nature of a Mission Community: The Universities' Mission to Central Africa in Bonde," *Past & Present*, no. 140 (August 1993): 127–54.
50. Allman, "Phantoms of the Archive"; Karin Barber, ed., *Africa's Hidden Histories: Everyday Literacy and Making the Self* (Bloomington: Indiana University Press, 2006).
51. A broad literature deals with the complexities of oral sources in the African context alone. For an example, see Luise White, Stephan F. Miescher, and David William Cohen, *African Words, African Voices: Critical Practices in Oral History* (Bloomington: Indiana University Press, 2001).
52. James L. Giblin, *A History of the Excluded: Making Family a Refuge from State in Twentieth-Century Tanzania* (Athens: Ohio University Press, 2005).
53. Scholars studying precolonial Africa have sought to understand emotions as a way to bridge the experiences of their subjects and their audience. This empathetic approach, Kathryn de Luna has argued, often "project[s] our modern, Western sensibilities onto the experiences of our subjects," and "pays little attention to the culturally variable emotional standards that might have shaped relationships and actions of past peoples." To better understand emotional and affective registers of the past, precolonial historians

have attended to the long histories and shifting meanings of words, oral traditions, and archeological and climatological data, all of which "resonate with affectivity." Work on early Africa has further illustrated that the emotional and material are connected, that people experience great emotions through inanimate things. Circulating objects also helps to create affective bonds. De Luna, "Affect and Society in Precolonial Africa." For affective histories of the more recent past, historians have turned toward a wide complement of written sources, as well as toward the "semiotic and performative," toward understanding figures, objects, and symbols as "meaning-making apparatuses in their own right," whether in newspaper columns, songs, dress, or cinema. Work on letter writing and letter writers has been crucial to the development of work on the affective, and allows historians to consider the intellectual lives of their subjects. Barber, *Africa's Hidden Histories*. The collection of emotionally vivid letters in Shula Mark's *Not Either an Experimental Doll* was one of the first to assert the benefits of foregrounding the affective lives of Africans. Shula Marks, *Not Either an Experimental Doll: The Separate Worlds of Three South African Women* (Bloomington: Indiana University Press, 1987). Recently, Wendy Urban-Mead used contextualized life histories to parse gendered piety in a mission community in Zimbabwe. Urban-Mead, *The Gender of Piety*.

54. Hunt, "The Affective, the Intellectual, and Gender History," 343.
55. Giblin, *A History of the Excluded*.
56. Tanzanianists, such as Jim Brennan, Kelly Askew, and Mohamed Said, have begun the process of looking to history's "losers" in an attempt to avoid the teleology of earlier literature. Largely revisions of Iliffe's narrative, however, these approaches work within the boundaries of Tanganyika Territory and aim to show how "women, peasants, and other marginal groups experienced and participated in the making of Tanganyika's nationalism." Peterson, *Ethnic Patriotism and the East African Revival*, 153. See also Allman, "The Disappearing of Hannah Kudjoe"; Brennan, *Taifa*; Kelly Askew, *Performing the Nation: Swahili Music and Cultural Politics in Tanzania* (Chicago: University of Chicago Press, 2002); Mohamed Said, *The Life and Times of Abdulwahid Sykes (1924–1968): The Untold Story of the Muslim Struggle against British Colonialism in Tanganyika* (Richmond, VA: Minerva Press, 1998); Geiger, *TANU Women*.
57. J. D. Y. Peel, *Religious Encounter and the Making of the Yoruba* (Bloomington: Indiana University Press, 2000), 280.
58. Ibid., 281.
59. Ibid., 282.
60. Fred Morton, *Children of Ham: Freed Slaves and Fugitive Slaves on the Kenya Coast, 1873–1907* (Boulder, CO: Westview Press, 1990).

61. The LMS worked among the Xhosa and Namaqua in southern Africa, and the Lutherans worked explicitly in Zululand. See Elizabeth Elbourne, *Blood Ground: Colonialism, Missions, and the Contest for Christianity in the Cape Colony and Britain, 1799–1853* (Montreal: McGill-Queen's University Press, 2002).
62. The UMCA was not the only mission organization to focus on ex-slaves, a population that was often quite ethnically diverse. For example, Yorubaland recaptives in Sierra Leone and the congregation at the CMS Freretown Mission in Kenya were ex-slaves. Peel, *Religious Encounter and the Making of the Yoruba*; Morton, *Children of Ham*.
63. The UMCA missionaries' embrace of Kiswahili was in stark contrast to other mission organizations in Tanganyika, which "considered the supra-tribal language of Swahili as a threat to their own efforts to Christianize individual ethnic groups." Kiswahili was useful to the UMCA because it was a single language that had the theoretical power to strip adherents of a belief in the supremacy of their old identities and to create new means of unification. African clerics and others who adopted Christianity through Kiswahili used it, rather than any single ethnically linked vernacular, as the language of mission on Zanzibar and the mainland. Adding to the homogenizing influence of Kiswahili was the fact that the mission's first cohorts of adherents at Zanzibar, particularly the young *mateka* ("captives" or "booty," slaves freed from dhows), were already unmoored from whatever social organization (ethnic or tribal) gave birth to them, and thus were socially impressionable. Frieder Ludwig, *Church and State in Tanzania* (Boston: Brill, 1999), 21.
64. Kelly Askew makes a similar argument about the performance of Swahili music and cultural forms in *Performing the Nation: Swahili Music and Cultural Politics in Tanzania*.
65. This is not to say that UMCA missionaries' efforts to translate scripture into Yao or Kibondei were not decisive in the development of a Yao or Bondei identity, for indeed they were. Rather, the missionaries' ultimate preference for Kiswahili and English, and their calling to rebuild Zion in East Africa contributed to adherents' sense of a supra-ethnic identity.
66. Hunt, "The Affective, the Intellectual, and Gender History," 331–45.
67. Ibid., 339.
68. Hunt is not the only scholar to lament the lack of attention to women's thought and thinking, and to gender equity in intellectual histories of Africa. Judith Byfield, for example, has observed that the contributions of black women in Africa or the diaspora to intellectual histories, their thoughts, and their writings and intellectual ideas are rarely considered. Byfield, "Finding Voice, Giving Voice: Gender, Politics, and Social Change," *South Atlantic Quarterly* 109, no. 2 (Spring 2010): 362. This, of course, is not

a lacuna restricted exclusively to women of color. Hilda Smith noted in the *Journal of Women's History* that in emphasizing the importance of women's bodies to their pasts, scholars have consistently framed those bodies "from the shoulders down." This is especially true of women from non-Western regions of the world, Smith continues, because the study of them has been tied to Western or elitist postcolonial and subaltern theorists; the core of those theories emerged from male theorists "little concerned with women, whose insights have had to be reformulated to include gender." Smith's analysis of why intellectual histories of women or women's organizations exist is damning, suggesting that this derives not from a "purposeful avoidance" or lack of interest in women's intellectual history, but rather from a set of assumptions that include the idea that "women have not offered fundamental and lasting analyses of broad social, intellectual, and political phenomena that characterized an age or a society." Hilda L. Smith, "Women's History as Intellectual History: A Perspective on the Journal of Women's History," *Journal of Women's History* 20, no. 1 (Spring 2008): 26.

69. Indeed, as Susan Z. Andrade has argued, the domestic "offers as sharp an analytic perspective on collectivity and national politics as does the arena of public political action." Susan Z. Andrade, *The Nation Writ Small: African Fictions and Feminisms, 1958–1988* (Durham, NC: Duke University Press, 2011), 1.
70. Previous scholarship has traced the development of racial thought through more traditionally "intellectual" venues, such as newspapers and textbooks, books published by evangelical presses and revivalists' testimonies and autobiographies, and the cartographies and spatial demographics of urban Dar es Salaam. I am thinking here especially of Glassman, *War of Words, War of Stones*; and Brennan, *Taifa*.
71. Peterson, *Ethnic Patriotism and the East African Revival*; Brennan, *Taifa*; Emily Callaci, "Dancehall Politics: Mobility, Sexuality, and Spectacles of Racial Respectability in Late Colonial Tanganyika, 1930s–1961," *Journal of African History* 52, no. 3 (November 2011): 365–84; Andrew Ivaska, *Cultured States: Youth, Gender, and Modern Style in 1960s Dar es Salaam* (Durham, NC: Duke University Press, 2011).
72. Paul Landau has shaped much of the conversation about this broader issue with his important research on the nuances of religion, Christian "conversion," and translation. David Maxwell's historical study of Pentecostalism, as well as the work of Birgit Meyer have integrated the religious into the instrumental motivations. Paul Landau, "'Religion' and Christian Conversion in African History: A New Model," *Journal of Religious History* 23, no. 1 (1999): 8–30; David Maxwell, *African Gifts of the Spirit: Pentecostalism and the Rise of a Zimbabwean Transnational Religious Movement* (Athens: Ohio University Press, 2007); Birgit Meyer, "Commodities and the Power of Prayer: Pentecostalist Attitudes

towards Consumption in Contemporary Ghana," *Development and Change* 29, no. 4 (October 1998): 751–76.

73. Urban-Mead, *The Gender of Piety*, 12.
74. David Gordon, *Invisible Agents* (Athens: Ohio University Press, 2012).
75. David Gordon argues that the bias toward the symbolic study of religion is not evident in all scholarship. Given the clear role of missionary Christian discourses in creating colonial hegemonies, many scholars have discussed them as sources of power. Jean and John Comaroff, J. D. Y. Peel, Elizabeth Elbourne, and Paul S. Landau, for example, engage the influence and African appropriations of colonial Christian missionary discourses, "although they generally conceive of power in a Foucauldian disciplinary sense. Efforts to discuss spirits, Christian or otherwise, as sources of power have not been as frequently or as effectively carried out." Gordon, *Invisible Agents*, 5.
76. See, for example, Peires, *The Dead Will Arise*; John Thornton, *The Kongolese Saint Anthony: Dona Beatriz Kimpa Vita and the Antonian Movement, 1684–1706* (Cambridge: Cambridge University Press, 1998).
77. The work of Karen Fields is an obvious exception, as well as that of Ellis and ter Haar, and Keller and Iyob. Karen Fields, *Revival and Rebellion in Colonial Central Africa* (Princeton, NJ: Princeton University Press, 1985); Stephen Ellis and Gerrie ter Haar, *Worlds of Power: Religious Thought and Political Practice in Africa* (Oxford: Oxford University Press, 2004); Edmond Keller and Ruth Iyob, *Religious Ideas and Institutions: Transitions to Democracy in Africa* (Pretoria, South Africa: Unisa Press, 2012). Derek Peterson also engages these ideas in *Ethnic Patriotism and the East African Revival.* Other important explorations of African Christianity include T. O. Ranger and Isaria Kimambo, *Historical Study of African Religion* (Berkeley: University of California Press, 1972); and Gerhardus C. Oosthuizen, M. C. Kitshoff, and S. W. D. Dube, eds., *Afro-Christianity at the Grassroots: Its Dynamics and Strategies* (New York: Brill Academic Publishers, 1994).
78. T. O. Ranger, "Protestant Missions in Africa: The Dialectic of Conversion in the American Methodist Episcopal Church in Eastern Zimbabwe, 1900–1950," in *Religion in Africa: Experience and Expression*, ed. T. D. Blakeley et al. (London: James Currey, 1994), 275–313.
79. Several exceptions are Urban-Mead, *The Gender of Piety*; M. Louise Pirouet, *Black Evangelists: The Spread of Christianity in Uganda, 1891–1914* (London: Africa Book Centre Ltd, 1978); Galawdewos, *The Life and Struggles of Our Mother Walatta Petros: A Seventeenth-Century African Biography of an Ethiopian Woman*, trans. Wendy Laura Belcher and Michael Kleiner (Princeton, NJ: Princeton University Press, 2015); Barbara M. Cooper, *Evangelical Christians in the Muslim Sahel* (Bloomington: Indiana University Press, 2010); Phyllis M. Martin, *Catholic Women of Congo-Brazzaville: Mothers and Sisters*

in Troubled Times (Bloomington: Indiana University Press, 2009).

80. Brennan, *Taifa*; Geiger, *TANU Women*; Iliffe, *A Modern History of Tanganyika*.

CHAPTER 1. TRACTARIAN BEGINNINGS: THEOLOGY AND SOCIETY IN BRITAIN AND EAST AFRICA, 1830–1865

1. C. Brad Faught, *The Oxford Movement: A Thematic History of the Tractarians and Their Times* (University Park, PA: Penn State University Press, 2003), 44, 132–33, 135–38.
2. Elizabeth Elbourne, *Blood Ground: Colonialism, Missions, and the Contest for Christianity in the Cape Colony and Britain, 1799–1853* (Montreal: McGill-Queen's University Press, 2002), 62.
3. Jean Comaroff and John Comaroff, *Of Revelation and Revolution*, vol. 1, *Christianity, Colonialism, and Consciousness in South Africa* (Chicago: University of Chicago Press, 1991), 43; Elbourne, *Blood Ground*, 62.
4. Comaroff and Comaroff, *Of Revelation and Revolution*, 1:84.
5. Ibid.
6. As contemporary thinking went, "It was not enough to send a missionary into the country to teach him [the African] that he was a child of God. It was also necessary that they be taught to trade. He would sell human bodies until he learnt how to use those bodies in selling something else. He must therefore be shown how to farm according to the best methods, how to grow crops like cotton or coffee of which Europe had need." Owen Chadwick, *Mackenzie's Grave* (Eugene, OR: Wipf & Stock, 2009), 15.
7. Ibid., 31.
8. Comaroff and Comaroff, *Of Revelation and Revolution*, 1:84.
9. Ibid.
10. Adrian Hastings, *The Church in Africa, 1450–1950* (Oxford: Oxford University Press, 1996), 283.
11. Nancy Rose Hunt, *A Colonial Lexicon of Birth Ritual, Medicalizaiton, and Mobility in the Congo* (Durham, NC: Duke University Press, 1999), 131.
12. Comaroff and Comaroff, *Of Revelation and Revolution*, 1:43.
13. Karen Tranberg Hansen, *African Encounters with Domesticity* (New Brunswick, NJ: Rutgers University Press, 1992), 3.
14. Hastings, *The Church in Africa*, 283–86.
15. David Livingstone, *Missionary Travels and Researches in South Africa* (London: John Murray, 1857), 447.
16. Steven Feierman, "A Century of Ironies in East Africa," in *African History: From Earliest*

Times to Independence, ed. Philip D. Curtin et al., 2nd ed. (London: Longman, 1995), 352.

17. Ibid., 353.
18. Jonathon Glassman, *Feasts and Riot: Revelry, Rebellion, and Popular Consciousness on the Swahili Coast, 1856–1888* (Portsmouth, NH: Heinemann, 1995), 29.
19. Ibid., 80.
20. Ibid.
21. Jonathon Glassman argues "it is misleading to descrie as a coherent system something so fraught with conflict and change as the relationships between masters and slaves . . . slavery was "absorptive" only in those instances where masters lacked the interest or the ability to whole-heartedly resist those demands, where masters failed to put into practice their ideal vision of the slave as a permanent outsider." Ibid., 81.
22. Feierman, "A Century of Ironies in East Africa," 352–54.
23. Glassman, *Feasts and Riot*, 55–78.
24. For more on the effects of the advance of the ivory frontier, see Feierman, "A Century of Ironies in East Africa," 356–61; Glassman, *Feasts and Riot*, 55–78. For monograph-length works, see Abdul M. H. Sheriff, *Slaves, Spices and Ivory in Zanzibar* (Athens: Ohio University Press, 1987); Edward Alpers, *Ivory and Slaves: Changing Patterns of International Trade in East Central Africa to the Later Nineteenth Century* (Berkeley: University of California Press, 1975); and Frederick Cooper, *Plantation Slavery on the East Coast of Africa* (New Haven, CT: Yale University Press, 1977).
25. Glassman, *Feasts and Riot*, 82.
26. William Monk, *Dr. Livingstone's Cambridge Lectures* (Cambridge: Deighton, Bell, 1858), 22.
27. Ibid., 22–23.
28. Anne Elizabeth Mary Anderson-Morshead, *The History of the Universities' Mission to Central Africa, 1859–1898*, vol. 1 (London: Office of the Universities' Mission to Central Africa, 1905), 3.
29. H. L. Sidney Lear, *Life of Robert Gray: Bishop of Cape Town and Metropolitan of Africa*, vol. 1 (London: Rivingtons, 1876), 467.
30. "Appeal to the Members of the University of Oxford on Behalf of the Oxford and Cambridge Mission to Central Africa" (Oxford: Baxter Printer, n.d.), 1.
31. Chadwick, *Mackenzie's Grave*, 20.
32. Ibid., 22.
33. Faught, *The Oxford Movement*, 33; R. W. Church, *The Oxford Movement: Twelve Years, 1833–1845* (Chicago: University of Chicago Press, 1970), xv.
34. Kenneth Hylson-Smith, *High Churchmanship in the Church of England: From the Sixteenth*

Century to the Late Twentieth Century (Edinburgh: T&T Clark, 1993), 123–24.

35. Faught, *The Oxford Movement*, 33.
36. Ibid., 36–37.
37. Church, *The Oxford Movement: Twelve Years*, xv.
38. Hylson-Smith, *High Churchmanship*, 123–25.
39. Faught, *The Oxford Movement*, 135–37.
40. Peter B. Nockles, *The Oxford Movement in Context: Anglican High Churchmanship, 1760–1857* (Cambridge: Cambridge University Press, 1994), 178–79, 84.
41. Nockles, *The Oxford Movement in Context*, 190–98; Church, *The Oxford Movement: Twelve Years*, xv.
42. Owen Chadwick, *The Spirit of the Oxford Movement* (New York: Cambridge University Press, 1990), 26.
43. Nockles, *The Oxford Movement in Context*, 198.
44. Chadwick, *The Spirit of the Oxford Movement*, 138.
45. Nockles, *The Oxford Movement in Context*, 202.
46. Chadwick, *The Spirit of the Oxford Movement*, 27.
47. Nockles, *The Oxford Movement in Context*, 203.
48. Ibid., 207.
49. Faught, *The Oxford Movement*, 44, 132–33, 135–38.
50. Andrew Porter, "An Overview, 1700–1914," in *Missions and Empire*, ed. Norman Etherington (Oxford: Oxford University Press, 2005), 55.
51. Philip D. Curtin, *The Image of Africa: British Ideas and Action, 1780–1850* (London: Macmillan, 1965), 260.
52. Ibid., 89.
53. Elbourne, *Blood Ground*, 26.
54. Curtin, *The Image of Africa*, 52–54, 281.
55. George Augustus Selwyn, *The Work of Christ in the World: Four Sermons Preached before the University of Cambridge* (Cambridge: Macmillan, 1855), 38–41.
56. Faught, *The Oxford Movement*, 127, 38.
57. "Conference at Likoma: The Bishop's Address," *Central Africa* 17, no. 201 (September 1899): 157.
58. H. M. Smith, *Frank, Bishop of Zanzibar: Life of Frank Weston, D.D., 1871–1924* (London: Macmillan, 1926), 30. By 1860 many among the High Church Anglican congregations at home and abroad were becoming disillusioned by the extravagance of what was required to maintain the European "civilized" lifestyle overseas, especially in the face of falling worldwide enrollment of missionaries and proselytes alike. Even David Livingstone, the

man whose very name is synonymous with British exploration in central and southern Africa, began to question the wisdom of formally linking Christianity and civilization: the Tswana, he admitted, were nomads and "retailers of news" who lived lives that were "very favourable to the spread of the Gospel, although . . . opposed to the spread of civilization." Porter, "An Overview," 54.

59. Fred Morton, *Children of Ham: Freed Slaves and Fugitive Slaves on the Kenya Coast, 1873–1907* (Boulder, CO: Westview Press, 1990), 55.
60. Paul Landau, *Realm of the Word: Language, Gender, and Christianity in a Southern African Kingdom* (Portsmouth, NH: Heinemann, 1995), xxi.
61. John Iliffe, *A Modern History of Tanganyika* (New York: Cambridge University Press, 1979), 219.
62. Ibid., 218.
63. Justin Willis, "The Nature of a Mission Community: The Universities' Mission to Central Africa in Bonde," *Past and Present* 140 (August 1993): 138.
64. Morton, *Children of Ham*, 61.
65. For more on this, see specifically G. W. Mallendar, "Journal of G. W. Mallendar, UMCA Printer in Africa, 1888–1895," n.d., Reel 13, Folio 29 [hereafter noted as R13, F29], Archives of the Universities' Mission to Central Africa from the Archives of the United Society for the Propagation of the Gospel "A" Series, Center for Research Libraries CAMP Microfilm [hereafter AUMCA].
66. Mallendar, "Journal."
67. Nockles, *The Oxford Movement in Context*, 203.
68. Selwyn, *The Work of Christ in the World*, 45; "Sermon of the Archbishop of Canterbury: Preached in St. Paul's Cathedral on the Twenty-Eighth Anniversary of the Mission," *Central Africa* 7, no. 79 (July 1889): 106.
69. C. Orelli, *The Prophecies of Isaiah* (Edinburgh: T&T Clark, 1895), 8. Commentaries cited here and below are all of an Anglican persuasion, and were published at the time of the mission's work by the same publishing houses that published the UMCA's recruitment and devotional materials in Oxford, Cambridge, and London. Further, they fall under the category of "widely read" as described by Nigel Cameron, *Biblical Higher Criticism and the Defense of Infallibilism in 19th Century Britain* (New York: Mellon, 1987), ch. 6 (especially).
70. Orelli, *The Prophecies*, 9, 319.
71. Ibid., 192–95; H. D. M. Spence-Jones, *The Pulpit Commentary* (Grand Rapids, MI: Wm. B. Eerdmans Publishing Co., 1980–1983), 569.
72. Orelli, *The Prophecies*, 10, 320.
73. "Sermon of the Archbishop of Canterbury," 107.

74. Ibid., 109.
75. Spence-Jones, *The Pulpit Commentary*, 1:217 and 2:404; Orelli, *The Prophecies*, 197.
76. "Sermon of the Archbishop of Canterbury," 105.
77. Orelli, *The Prophecies*, 217; Spence-Jones, *The Pulpit Commentary*, 2:404.
78. "Sermon of the Archbishop of Canterbury," 105–6
79. Faught, *The Oxford Movement*, 136.
80. H. Goodwin, *Memoir of Bishop Mackenzie* (Cambridge: Deighton, Bell, 1864), 2–6.
81. Faught, *The Oxford Movement*, 136.
82. Society for Promoting Christian Knowledge (SPCK), *Mission Heroes* (London: Society for Promoting Christian Knowledge, 1895), 8–9.
83. SPCK, *Mission Heroes*, 9.
84. Faught, *The Oxford Movement*, 137.
85. Tim Jeal, *Livingstone* (New Haven, CT: Yale University Press, 2001), 224. The bishop's deacon, Henry Rowley, was an intellectually intimidating and hard-working man who tended toward needless combativeness. Lovell Procter and Horace Waller, both twenty-seven years old, were traveling outside England for the first time. Both Procter and Waller were spirited romantics—one for the cause itself, and the other for young women. Waller fell in love on the passage from England and was engaged to be married even before his feet hit dry land again. Finally, there was the Reverend H. C. Scudamore. Records do not detail Scudamore's role in the mission, and he was unique among the party for not keeping a diary. He was, apparently, exceedingly calm and was most popular with the UMCA's African dependents. There was Alfred Adams, listed as an agricultural laborer; we know little else about him. Sources differ on whether the bishop's devoted spinster sister Anne left England with the rest of the party. She would have been one of but a handful of European women to travel to the African mission field to date; although it appears that she had intentions to join the party at some point, she never made it past the Cape. Landeg White, *Magomero: Portrait of an African Village* (New York: Cambridge University Press, 1987), 10–15.
86. Faught, *The Oxford Movement*, 311.
87. SPCK, *Mission Heroes*, 12.
88. White, *Magomero*, 12.
89. Ibid., 14.
90. For the most comprehensive coverage, see White, *Magomero*.
91. Ibid., 64.
92. Ibid., ch. 1.
93. Anderson-Morshead, *The History of the Universities' Mission to Central Africa*, 1:33.

94. White, *Magomero*, 67.
95. Bishop Tozer, *"Mbweni Logbook," Letter of Bishop Tozer* (Cape Town, 1864), CB1 Group [hereafter CB] 1B, 18 July 1864, Universities' Mission to Central Africa [hereafter UMCA], Zanzibar National Archives [hereafter ZNA].
96. "Speech Delivered by Bishop Steere at Oxford," August 1875, R10, F825, AUMCA.
97. Bishop Tozer, entry for 10 October 1864, "Bishop Tozer's Letters and Journals, Book IV," CB1–1C, ZNA, UMCA.
98. G. H. Wilson, *The History of the Universities' Mission to Central Africa* (Westminster: Universities' Mission to Central Africa, 1936), 84.
99. Dora S. Yarton Mills, *Where We Live and What We Do* (London: Office of Universities' Mission to Central Africa, 1909), 148.
100. Ibid., 148.

CHAPTER 2. FROM SLAVES TO CHRISTIAN MOTHERS: DEVELOPING A DOCTRINE OF FEMALE EVANGELISM, 1863–1877

1. "Mama Kate. An African Saint," *African Tidings* 17, no. 225 (July 1908): 225.
2. George Augustus Selwyn, *The Work of Christ in the World: Four Sermons Preached before the University of Cambridge* (Cambridge: Macmillan, 1855), 63; Boyd Hilton, "1807 and All That: Why Britain Outlawed Her Slave Trade," in *Abolitionism and Imperialism in Britain, Africa, and the Atlantic*, ed. Derek Peterson (Athens, OH: Swallow Press, 2010).
3. Jonathon Glassman, "The Bondsman's New Clothes," *Journal of African History* 32, no. 2 (1991): 286; Glassman, *Feasts and Riot: Revelry, Rebellion, and Popular Consciousness on the Swahili Coast, 1856–1888* (Portsmouth, NH: Heinemann, 1995), 106–8.
4. Marcia Wright, *Strategies of Slaves and Women: Life-Stories from East/Central Africa* (New York: Lilian Barber Press, 1993), introduction.
5. Edward Steere, "MA Extracts from Reports about Released Slaves: Parly Papers Appendix B, Zanzibar University Mission, signed Edward Steere," 15 January 1873, Reel 8, Folio 68 [hereafter noted as R8, F68], Archives of the Universities' Mission to Central Africa from the Archives of the United Society for the Propagation of the Gospel "A" Series, Center for Research Libraries CAMP Microfilm [hereafter AUMCA].
6. "First Quarterly Statement of Bishop Steere," August 1875, R10, F815, AUMCA.
7. Ibid.
8. Robert Marshall Heanley, *A Memoir of Edward Steere, D.D., L.L.D.: Third Missionary Bishop in Central Africa* (London: George Bell & Sons, 1888), 124.
9. "Extract of Dr. Kirk's Dispatch of 22 September 1871; Sent to the Bishop of Winchester,"

"CB1–4: Bishop Tozer and Steere," CB1 Collection, number 4, Zanzibar National Archives [hereafter CB1–4].

10. Ibid.
11. Ibid.
12. John Iliffe, *A Modern History of Tanganyika* (New York: Cambridge University Press, 1979).
13. Glassman, *Feasts and Riot*, 109–12.
14. Ibid., 107–9.
15. R. M. Githige, "The Issue of Slavery: Relations between the CMS and the State on the East African Coast Prior to 1895," *Journal of Religion in Africa* 16, no. 3 (October 1986): 209.
16. Fred Morton, *Children of Ham: Freed Slaves and Fugitive Slaves on the Kenya Coast, 1873–1907* (Boulder, CO: Westview Press, 1990).
17. Letter of Edward Steere, 2 June 1875, R9, F39, AUMCA.
18. Ibid.; Letter of Edward Steere, 19 October 1881, R9, F558, AUMCA.
19. Steven Feierman, "A Century of Ironies in East Africa," in *African History: From Earliest Times to Independence*, ed. Steven Feierman and Phil Curtin, 2nd ed. (New York: Pearson, 1995); "Slaves Rescued by the Mbweni People," *African Tidings* 3 (1894): 90–92.
20. Wright, *Strategies of Slaves and Women*, 25–26; Edward Alpers, "The Story of Swema: Female Vulnerability in Nineteenth-Century East Africa," in *Women and Slavery in Africa*, ed. Clare Robertson and Martin Klein (Madison: University of Wisconsin Press, 1983), 85–219.
21. Letter of Edward Steere, 19 October 1881, R9, F558, AUMCA.
22. In addition to providing productive and reproductive labor, slaves also functioned as material commodities. Particularly in the status-conscious culture of nineteenth-century Zanzibar, East Africa historian Jeremy Prestholdt tells us, slaves were socially valuable "for their ability to represent the interests of those who sought to control them." For slavers and redeemers alike, slaves were "symbolic social capital" who functioned as "screens onto which concepts of civilization were projected." Jeremy Prestholdt, *Domesticating the World: African Consumerism and the Genealogies of Globalization* (Berkeley: University of California Press, 2008), 116–18.
23. Glassman, *Feasts and Riot*, 58–59.
24. Given that Kate was given to the UMCA in the Seychelles, she may well have come to the coast through the southern route to Kilwa or Lindi, rather than the central route depicted above. The central routes were known for their high degree of Arab control, however, and had a close association with the routes that terminated at ports directly opposite Zanzibar. Glassman, *Feasts and Riot*, 56.
25. Gareth Griffiths, "'Trained to Tell the Truth': Missionaries, Converts, and Narration," in

Missions and Empire, ed. Norman Etherington (New York: Oxford University Press, 2005), 163–65.

26. Morton, *Children of Ham*; Wright, *Strategies of Slaves and Women*; Alpers, "The Story of Swema."
27. "The Story of Fayida," *African Tidings* 7, no. 99 (January 1898): 99.
28. Griffiths analyzes Panya's particular story in depth as an example of the "process by which the paradigmatic narratives of the tracts were produced through a controlled transmission of story from 'subject' to 'author.'" While Panya's life story printed in *African Tidings* was certainly not an unmediated "true" account, it does offer certain facts about Panya's life that we can take as true, or true enough for the purposes of this analysis, in that they reinforce general trends of the period. To Griffiths, and despite the mediation of the translator, transcriber, and amanuensis—the UMCA's missionary Alice Foxley—Panya's is "one of the most revealing accounts of the personal life and narrative of an African convert and of the processes by which it was recorded." Griffiths, "Trained to Tell the Truth," 163–65.
29. Indeed, although the horrors of the long-distance trade that brought slaves, such as Fayida, Panya, and Kate, from the interior are well documented, it is important to remember here and elsewhere that the accounts of their journeys were animated by abolitionist zeal and are naturally subject to exaggeration. In addition to the sources cited here, see Alpers, "The Story of Swema," 185–99; Wright, *Strategies of Slaves and Women*.
30. "First Quarterly Statement of Bishop Steere," 11.
31. Glassman, *Feasts and Riot*, 106–8; Prestholdt, *Domesticating the World*, 125.
32. Justin Willis makes a similar argument for the first cohorts of Christians becoming integrated into the UMCA community at Bonde. Justin Willis, "The Nature of a Mission Community: The Universities' Mission to Central Africa in Bonde," *Past & Present*, no. 140 (August 1993): 127–54.
33. Glassman, "The Bondsman's New Clothes," 286; Glassman, *Feasts and Riot*, 106–8.
34. Wright, *Strategies of Slaves and Women*, 25.
35. Ibid., 43.
36. Wright, *Strategies of Slaves and Women*, introduction.
37. Bishop Tozer, entry for 1 September 1864, "Bishop Tozer's Letters and Journals, Book IV," CB1–1C, ZNA, UMCA.
38. Abdul Sheriff, *History and Conservation of Zanzibar Stone Town* (Athens: Ohio University Press, 1995), 2–8.
39. Prestholdt, *Domesticating the World*, 96.

40. Ibid., 122.
41. Ibid.
42. "Speech delivered by Bishop Steere at Oxford," August 1875, R10, F815, AUMCA.
43. Margaret Dewey, *The Messengers: A Concise History of the United Society for the Propagation of the Gospel* (London: Mowbray, 1975), 60.
44. "Annual Reports of the U.M.C.A. 1890–91," in N. J. Small, "U.M.C.A. (Universities' Mission to Central Africa): The Early Work in Education, 1876–1905," *Tanzania Notes and Records* 86/87 (1980): 35–54.
45. Patricia Grimshaw, "Faith, Missionary Life, and the Family," in *Gender and Empire*, ed. Philippa Levine (Oxford: Oxford University Press, 2004), 266.
46. Patricia Grimshaw, "Women and Cultural Exchanges," in *Missions and Empire*, ed. Norman Etherington (Oxford: Oxford University Press, 2005), 179.
47. Susan Thorne, *Congregational Missions and the Making of an Imperial Culture in Nineteenth-Century England* (Stanford, CA: Stanford University Press, 1999), 95.
48. Thorne, *Congregational Missions*, 95. See also Grimshaw, "Women and Cultural Exchanges," 178–81; and Grimshaw, "Faith, Missionary Life, and the Family," 266.
49. Rhonda A. Semple, *Missionary Women: Gender, Professionalism, and the Victorian Idea of Christian Mission* (Rochester, NY: Boydell, 2003), 3. See also Elizabeth Prevost, *The Communion of Women: Missions and Gender in Colonial Africa and the British Metropole* (New York: Oxford University Press, 2010), 2.
50. Prevost, *The Communion of Women*, 2.
51. Grimshaw, "Women and Cultural Exchanges," 178–81.
52. Semple, *Missionary Women*, 187.
53. "Woman Workers in the UMCA," *Central Africa* 17, no. 193 (January 1899): 7.
54. "Woman Workers," 7.
55. M. B., "Ladies Needed for Mbweni," *Central Africa* 14, no. 157 (January 1896): 16.
56. "Woman Workers," 7.
57. "Training House for Women Missionaries," *Central Africa* 15, no. 170 (October 1897): 165.
58. Sister Violet, CSP, *Preparation for Service in Africa* (Westminster: Universities' Mission to Central Africa, n.d.), 11.
59. Dewey, *The Messengers*, 62.
60. "Woman Workers," 8.
61. "Letter of Bishop Frank Weston," 13 December 1899, AI (XVII) A, Papers of the Universities' Mission to Central Africa: Papers of the United Society for the Propagation of the Gospel [hereafter UMCA/USPG], Rhodes House, Oxford [hereafter Rhodes].
62. C. Thackeray, "The African Woman of the Future," *Central Africa* 28, no. 330 (June 1910):

153. Emphasis in original.

63. Dora S. Yarton Mills, *Where We Live and What We Do* (London: Office of Universities' Mission to Central Africa, 1909), 224–27.
64. Thackeray, "The African Woman of the Future."
65. "'Women's Work': Addresses by Mrs. Creighton and Miss Thackeray, Delivered at the Women's Meeting Held in St. Martin's Town Hall on Thursday, June 12, 1898," *Central Africa* 16, no. 188 (August 1898): 133.
66. Thackeray, "The African Woman of the Future," 158.
67. Letter of Caroline Thackeray, Mbweni, 26 September 1887, R16, F775, AUMCA.
68. Caroline Thackeray, "Blandina Limo: An African Priest's Wife," *Central Africa* 32, no. 380 (August 1914): 202–6.
69. F. Klamborowski, "Likoma Girls' School," *Central Africa* 50, no. 589 (January 1932): 25.
70. "Sister Agnes," *Central Africa* 13, no. 148 (April 1895): 60.
71. Letter of M. Forbes Capel, 5 April 1877, R11, F85, AUMCA.
72. Letter of M. Forbes Capel, 2 May 1877, R11, F69, AUMCA.
73. Heanley, *A Memoir of Edward Steere*, 111.
74. "Leaflet No. 2: Present Work," R10, F810, AUMCA.
75. "Leaflet No. 2: Present Work"; "First Quarterly Statement of Bishop Steere."
76. "First Quarterly Statement of Bishop Steere."
77. Ibid.
78. Grimshaw, "Faith, Missionary Life, and the Family," 264.
79. Thorne, *Congregational Missions*, 95.
80. Steere, "MA Extracts from Reports about Released Slaves."

CHAPTER 3. INDUSTRIALS AND SCHOOLGIRLS: BONDS OF PERSONAL DEPENDENCY AND THE MBWENI GIRLS' SCHOOL, 1877–1890

1. The same rate of growth, though due less to the spoils of the slave trade than to intentional expansion on the mainland, could be seen elsewhere in the mission. By 1880, the mission had expanded to several stations on the mainland, including Magila, in the Usambara Mountains of northeastern Tanzania, and Masasi, in southern Tanzania. The UMCA also had several stations on Zanzibar itself, including the Christ Church cathedral, a hospital, the main mission house, and a small school in a quarter of Stone Town called Mkunazini, the settlement at Mbweni, a seminary at Kiungani, and a boys' school at Kilimani. "The Universities' Mission to Central Africa: Present Work," dated "Lady Day" (25 March) 1881, R10, F809, AUMCA.

2. Ibid.; *Central African Mission Diary, 1888–1908*, CB1–6, ZNA. Indeed, some scholars would argue that these patterns of illicit trading continue today. See Benjamin Lawrance and Richard Roberts, eds., *Trafficking in Slavery's Wake: Law and the Experience of Women and Children in Africa* (Athens: Ohio University Press, 2012); Steven Feierman, "A Century of Ironies in East Africa (c. 1780–1890)," in *African History: From Earliest Times to Independence*, ed. Steven Feierman and Phil Curtin, 2nd ed. (New York: Pearson, 1995), 353. For more on these broader trends, see ch. 2.
3. Personal communication of N. Forbes Capel, 26 March 1877 (Mbweni, Zanzibar), R11, F79, AUMCA.
4. Ibid.
5. Personal communication of N. Forbes Capel, 2 March 1877 (Mbweni, Zanzibar), R11, F69, AUMCA.
6. Personal communication of N. Forbes Capel, 30 January 1877 (Mbweni, Zanzibar), R11, F60, AUMCA; Jonathon Glassman, *Feasts and Riot: Revelry, Rebellion, and Popular Consciousness on the Swahili Coast, 1856–1888* (Portsmouth, NH: Heinemann, 1995), 108.
7. Fred Morton, *Children of Ham: Freed Slaves and Fugitive Slaves on the Kenya Coast, 1873–1907* (Boulder, CO: Westview Press, 1990), 65.
8. Ibid., 63.
9. Iliffe, *A Modern History of Tanganyika*, 84–85. See also Landeg White, *Magomero: Portrait of an African Village* (New York: Cambridge University Press), 1987.
10. Iliffe, *A Modern History of Tanganyika*, 211–12.
11. Personal communication of E. Randolph, 7 April 1877, R11, F145, AUMCA; Personal communication of E. Steere, 8 February 1878, R9, F457, AUMCA.
12. Personal communication of M. Allen, 24 August 1877, R11, F167, AUMCA.
13. Personal communication of N. Forbes Capel, 5 April 1877 (Mbweni, Zanzibar), R11, F85, AUMCA.
14. Personal communication of N. Forbes Capel, 6 February 1877 (Mbweni, Zanzibar), R11, F65, AUMCA.
15. "1876," *Central African Mission Reports*, CB1–6, ZNA, 1; Personal communication of N. Forbes Capel, 20 January 1877 (Mbweni, Zanzibar), R11, F60, AUMCA.
16. Personal communication of D. M. Thackeray, 2 June 1881, R11, F425, AUMCA.
17. "1878," *Central African Mission Reports*, CB1–6, ZNA, 23.
18. Personal communication of N. Forbes Capel, 30 January 1877 (Mbweni, Zanzibar), R11, F60, AUMCA.
19. Personal communication of N. Forbes Capel, 2 March 1877 (Mbweni, Zanzibar), R11, F69, AUMCA.

20. Steere was architect of much of what constituted the mission, including the now-famous Cathedral Church of Christ in Mkunazini—the altar of which is thought to have been built on the very site of the old slave whipping post. Missionaries claimed that the high altar of the "Slave Market Church" was erected on the very spot where the market's whipping post had once stood. As Jonathon Glassman points out, this placement draws an "eloquent analogy between the sufferings of the slaves and those of 'He . . . by Whose stripes we are healed.'" (Indeed, missionaries frequently drew such analogies between their congregants and God's chosen people.) It seems that in this case, however, the analogy has been taken too far. It seems unlikely that slaves were publicly flogged before sale, or that slave children were randomly killed, "their throats slit where the church's baptismal font now stands." Among other absurdities, as Glassman argues, it "flies in the face of logic to imagine businessmen routinely destroying most of their merchandise in this way." If that were not enough, few of the historic slave chamber narratives dating to the years before the church's construction so much as hint at the kinds of details later abolitionists claim, and there is not one mention of a whipping post. Jonathon Glassman, "Echoes of Abolition in Twentieth-Century Zanzibar," in *Abolitionism and Imperialism in Britain, Africa, and the Atlantic*, ed. Derek Peterson (Athens: Ohio University Press, 2010), 178–79.
21. For more on the mission in Bonde, see Justin Willis, "The Nature of a Mission Community: The Universities' Mission to Central Africa in Bonde," *Past & Present*, no. 140 (August 1993): 127–54; Justin Willis, "The Makings of a Tribe: Bondei Identities and Histories," *Journal of African History* 33, no. 2 (1992): 191–208.
22. The same rate of growth, though due less to the spoils of the slave trade than to intentional expansion on the mainland, could be seen elsewhere in the mission. By 1880, the mission had expanded to several stations on the mainland, including Magila, in the Usambara mountains of northeastern Tanzania, and Masasi, in southern Tanzania. The UMCA also had several stations on Zanzibar itself, including the Christ Church cathedral, a hospital, the main mission house, and a small school in a quarter of Stone Town called Mkunazini, the settlement at Mbweni, a seminary at Kiungani, and a boys' school at Kilimani. "The Universities' Mission to Central Africa: Present Work," dated "Lady Day" (25 March) 1881, R10, F809, AUMCA.
23. "The Children's Corner: A Letter from Miss Thackeray," *Central Africa* 3, no. 34 (October 1885): 143.
24. C. Alan, "A Letter from the Bishop," *Central Africa* 3, no. 33 (September 1885): 127.
25. As Smythies understood it, among Africans "the women are the menials, and among the natives are kept in a very subordinate position, not eating with their husbands, or even

in some cases sitting down with them in public." Therefore, he said, "in educating our girls we need [to take] the greatest care, as having been more educated perhaps than their husbands, and having been the object of the ladies' care for so long, they are apt to be conceited, and not to give their husbands that obedience which is the custom here to exact from them." African women needed to be married, missionaries argued, because it kept them from "innumerable and nameless mischiefs," and because the nuclear families that marriages produced were the bedrock of the mission's evangelical model. Alan, "A Letter from the Bishop."

26. Personal communication of N. Forbes Capel, 2 March 1877, R11, F60, AUMCA.
27. The Bishop, "Our African Post Bag," *Central Africa* 2, no. 17 (May 1884): 89–93.
28. Laura Fair, *Pastimes and Politics: Culture, Community, and Identity in Post-Abolition Urban Zanzibar, 1890–1945* (Athens: Ohio University Press, 2001), 16.
29. Alan, "A Letter from the Bishop."
30. Ibid.
31. The Bishop, "Our African Post Bag."
32. Personal communication of C. D. M. Thackeray, 11 May 1885 (Mbweni, Zanzibar), R16, F 761, AUMCA.
33. Ibid., 8.
34. Community of Saint John Baptist, *The Founders of Clewer: A Short Account of the Rev. T. T. Carter and Harriet Monsell to Celebrate the Centenary of the Community of St. John Baptist in 1952* (London: Mowbray, 1952), 19–22.
35. Personal communication of C. D. M. Thackeray, 26 September 1887 (Mbweni, Zanzibar), R16, F775, AUMCA.
36. Michelle Liebst, "African Workers and the Universities' Mission to Central Africa in Zanzibar, 1864–1900," *Journal of Eastern African Studies* 8, no. 3 (2014): 366.
37. Ibid., 371.
38. Ibid., 371–72.
39. Boyd Hilton, "1807 and All That: Why Britain Outlawed Her Slave Trade," in *Abolitionism and Imperialism in Britain, Africa, and the Atlantic*, ed. Derek R. Peterson (Athens: Ohio University Press, 2010), 63–83.
40. Liebst, "African Workers," 369.
41. Ibid., 373.
42. Glassman, *Feasts and Riot*, 108.
43. Ibid.
44. John Iliffe, *A Modern History of Tanganyika* (New York: Cambridge University Press, 1979), 84–85.

45. Glassman, *Feasts and Riot*, 108.
46. Liebst, "African Workers," 375.
47. Caroline Bledsoe and Uche Isiugo-Abanihe, "Strategies of Child-Fosterage among Mende Grannies in Sierra Leone," in *Reproduction and Social Organization in Sub-Saharan Africa*, ed. Ron J. Lesthaeghe (Berkeley: University of California Press, 1989), 443–44. On fosterage in sub-Saharan African more broadly, see Uche Isiugo-Abanihe, "Child Fosterage in West Africa," *Population and Development Review* 11, no. 1 (1985); Caroline Bledsoe, "'No Success without Struggle': Social Mobility and Hardship for Foster Children in Sierra Leone," *Man* 25, no. 1 (1990).
48. Bledsoe, "No Success without Struggle," 70–73.
49. Misty L. Bastian, "Young Converts: Christian Missions, Gender and Youth in Onitsha, Nigeria, 1880–1929," *Anthropological Quarterly* 73, no. 3 (2000): 151.
50. "J. D.," "Miss Jones' Girls," *African Tidings* 16, no. 207 (January 1907): 18.
51. "J. Zanzibar," "In Memoriam: Kate Mabruki," *Central Africa* 26, no. 306 (June 1908): 143.
52. 17 March 1919, CB1–8, ZNA.
53. 4 May 1919, CB1–8, ZNA.
54. 2 June 1919, CB1–8, ZNA. Though the groom's name suggests he was Muslim, he was likely a Christian freed slave who kept his name, or a convert without a Christian name—it would have been uncharacteristic for the church to have invested so many resources in preparing Fibi for marriage, only to turn her over to an unknown Muslim man.
55. 21 August 1918, CB1–8, ZNA.
56. Saint Augustine's, a theological college started by the Society for the Propagation of the Gospel (SPG) in Foreign Parts, was a college intended to "train men for service in the mission field." It opened in 1848 to the students of the SPG-sponsored schools throughout the world and was soon sending out "a stream of ordinands of many races." See Rev. H. P. Thompson, *Into All Lands: The History of the Society for the Propagation of the Gospel in Foreign Parts, 1701–1950* (London: SPCK, 1951), 112–13. At the time of the Industrial Wing dedication, Cecil was a deacon, working at Mbweni before departing for England. Cecil had previously been living at Chitangali, near Masasi in southern Tanzania, at a station he had planted and managed almost alone—except, that is, for the help his wife could offer when she was not tending to their three small children.
57. "Mbweni Girls' School: The New Industrial Wing," *Central Africa* 6, no. 63 (March 1888): 39–40.
58. J. M. Neale and R. F. Littledale, *A Commentary on the Psalms*, vol. 2 (London: Joseph Masters, 1868), 321–26.
59. Ibid.

60. Iliffe, *A Modern History of Tanganyika*, 90–116.
61. "Fayida," *African Tidings* 7, no. 100 (February 1898): 13–16.
62. Laura Philipps, "The Girls' Home at Mbweni," *African Tidings* 6 (1897): 16.
63. Personal communication of C. D. M. Thackeray, 26 September 1887 (Mbweni, Zanzibar), R16, F775, AUMCA.
64. Kenda Mutongi, *Worries of the Heart: Widows, Family, and Community in Kenya* (Chicago: University of Chicago Press, 2007), 47.
65. "Conference at Likoma: The Bishop's Address," *Central Africa* 17, no. 201 (September 1899): 157.
66. Nancy Hunt, "Colonial Fairy Tales and the Knife and Fork Doctrine," in *African Encounters with Domesticity*, ed. Karen Tranberg Hansen (New Brunswick, NJ: Rutgers University Press, 1992), 143.
67. Elizabeth Elbourne, *Blood Ground: Colonialism, Missions, and the Contest for Christianity in the Cape Colony and Britain, 1799–1853* (Montreal: McGill-Queen's University Press, 2002), 214.
68. Hunt, "Colonial Fairy Tales and the Knife and Fork Doctrine," 146.
69. Philipps, "The Girls' Home at Mbweni."
70. Untitled, *African Tidings* 1, no. 38 (December 1892): 94.
71. Philipps, "The Girls' Home at Mbweni."
72. Pat Thane, "Women and the Poor Law in Victorian and Edwardian England," *History Workshop*, no. 6 (Autumn 1978): 38.
73. Alan Kidd, *State, Society and the Poor in Nineteenth-Century England* (New York: Palgrave Macmillan, 1999), 47.
74. Ibid., 50.
75. Gertrude Himmelfarb, *Poverty and Compassion: The Moral Imagination of the Late Victorians* (New York: Vintage, 1991).
76. George Augustus Selwyn, *The Work of Christ in the World: Four Sermons Preached before the University of Cambridge* (Cambridge: Macmillan & Co., 1855), 38–41.
77. Edward Higgs, "Domestic Servants and Households in Victorian England," *Social History* 8, no. 2 (May 1983); F. K. Prochaska, "Female Philanthropy and Domestic Service in Victorian England," *Bulletin of the Institute of Historical Research* 54 (1981); Lucy Lethbridge, *Servants: A Downstairs History of Britain from the Nineteenth Century to Modern Times* (New York: Norton, 2013); Nancy Hunt, "Domesticity and Colonialism in Belgian Africa: Usumbura's Foyer Social, 1946–1960," *Signs: Journal of Women in Culture and Society* (1990): 449–50.
78. Kathleen's childhood home was along one of the oldest trading routes on the mainland,

which stretched inland from Kilwa to the dense populations around Lake Nyasa. In the sixteenth century, Portuguese and Yao traders began using a regional trading network to move gold, ivory, and cloth between the coast and the hinterland. As the plantation economies of the Mascarenes and in the New World became more significant in the eighteenth century, demand for slaves from the region began to rise. In the late 1770s the French began to export great numbers of slaves acquired by Yao traders along this route. A century later, slave exports through Zanzibar continued at an estimated 20,000 per year. Most still came from the south, where Kilwa's exports increased between 1862–63 and 1866–67 from 18,500 to 22,038. Although Sultan Barghash's 1876 decree against the transport of slaves overland stifled some of this trade, both smuggling and an overland trade to northern coastal ports flourished for several years. Illicit slaving dhows kept British cruisers, and by extension the mission, busy for decades. These patterns meant that many of the UMCA's Zanzibar congregants had lived in this area prior to being kidnapped or otherwise enslaved. In fact, this is the very same area to which fifty former Mbweni slaves were repatriated in 1876 as part of the mission's efforts to establish a second mainland mission station. Iliffe, *A Modern History of Tanganyika*, 49.

79. "Central African Mission List of Children: January 1878," CB1–5, ZNA, UMCA.
80. "Report of the Mbweni Girls' School," *Central Africa* 5, no. 50 (February 1887): 25–26.
81. L. P., "'Skumshun' at Mbweni," *African Tidings* 10, no. 145 (November 1901): 131.
82. "Report of the Mbweni Girls' School"; Caroline Thackeray, "Our Native Female Teachers," *Central Africa* 14, no. 168 (December 1896): 203–8.
83. "Beatrice of Mbweni," *African Tidings* 6, no. 91 (May 1897): 54.
84. "'Women's Work': Addresses by Mrs. Creighton and Miss Thackeray, Delivered at the Women's Meeting Held in St. Martin's Town Hall on Thursday, June 13, 1898," *Central Africa* 16, no. 188 (August 1898): 125–37.
85. "Miss Jones' Girls," *African Tidings* 16, no. 208 (February 1907): 208.
86. "Mama Kate. An African Saint," *African Tidings* 17, no. 225 (July 1908): 75–78.
87. "To Patrons of Our Girls," *Central Africa* 3, no. 28 (April 1885): 58.
88. "Women's Work," 125–37. It is not clear from the sources why Rome was a destination for African pupil-teachers and their European escorts, but it is likely because exposure to church history and culture was an important component of the girls' education. Other sources suggest that the furloughs on which pupil-teachers accompanied European teachers were mixed with vacations to such places as the Italian seaside; Rome may have been part of a learning vacation for the girls.
89. "Mama Kate," 75–78; "In Memoriam: Kate Mabruki," 143.
90. Dorothy Ko, *Teachers of the Inner Chambers: Women and Culture in Seventeenth-Century*

China (Palo Alto, CA: Stanford University Press, 1995), 12–13.

91. Profession of holy orders was not in the late 1800s an option for the UMCA's African women, nor would it be until 1926. Devoted spinsterhood was also something that missionaries frowned upon, believing that the "native" was bound for moral ruin if he or she remained single.
92. Ko, *Teachers of the Inner Chambers*, 12–13.
93. "Fayida," 13–16.
94. Personal communication of G. W. Mallendar, in "Journal of G. W. Mallendar, U.M.C.A. Printer in Africa, 1888–1895," R13, F29, AUMCA.
95. Robert Marshall Heanley, *A Memoir of Edward Steere, D.D., L.L.D.: Third Missionary Bishop in Central Africa* (London: George Bell & Sons, 1888).
96. "Women's Work," 133.
97. "Central African Mission List of Children: January 1878," CB1–5, ZNA, UMCA.
98. Ibid.
99. The deep red hills still host a vibrant, welcoming Anglican community today, and villagers swear that, if well equipped with a four-wheel drive in the dry season, you can ascend to the top of one of the ridges that provides shade to the crops and see Mount Kilimanjaro in the distance.
100. Thackeray, "Our Native Female Teachers," 206.
101. P. L. Jones-Bateman, "The Children's Corner," *Central Africa* 4, no. 48 (December 1886): 189.
102. A. E. M. Anderson-Morshead, *The History of the Universities' Mission to Central Africa, 1859–1898*, vol. 1 (London: Office of the Universities' Mission to Central Africa, 1905), 182.
103. "Post Bag," *Central Africa* 15, no. 174 (June 1897): 92–93.
104. Untitled, *African Tidings* 1, no. 38 (December 1892): 93.
105. "1878," *Central African Mission Reports*, CB1–6, ZNA.

CHAPTER 4. NETWORKS OF AFFECTIVE SPIRITUALITY: EVANGELISM AND EXPANSION, 1890–1930

1. Mission sources refer to Limo interchangeably as "Petro" and as "Peter." To distinguish Petro Limo from Petro Kilekwa, who appeared in this book's introduction, I will refer to Limo as "Peter" from this point forward.
2. Justin Willis, "The Nature of a Mission Community: The Universities' Mission to Central Africa in Bonde," *Past & Present* 140 (August 1993): 149.
3. Justin Willis argues that Limo's near-meteoric rise within the church in Bonde was due

to the fact that as a young boy, Petro lacked patrilineal kin; in the context of complicated local politics, his "lack of alternatives" led him to devote himself wholly to the mission, eschewing other communities and patrons. Mission officials rewarded this singular devotion to the church with a quick ascendance through the ecclesiastical hierarchy. Alternatively, early converts who were eager to maintain claims on several communities found themselves subject to public humiliation by church officials and stagnation in the church hierarchy. Willis, "The Nature of a Mission Community," 149.

4. "C.D.M.T.," "Blandina Limo: An African Priest's Wife," *Central Africa* 32, no. 380 (August 1914): 155. This article, presumably written by Caroline Thackeray, is an obituary published in the mission's monthly circular. Of course any obituaries, but particularly in the colonial/missionary context, are besetting sources. In her analysis of the rhetoric of nineteenth-century female evangelical obituaries, Cheryl M. Cassidy argues that readers at home were captivated by obituaries of missionaries and their "heathen" converts. Obituaries were part of the rhetoric or propaganda of missionary life, "glorifying and eulogizing lives spent fruitfully." Despite "similar salvific achievements," Cassidy continues, "missionary and heathen convert deaths were reported differently." The obituaries of "converts" served to validate "not the dying person but the missionary purpose." Obituaries of missionaries, on the other hand, were "extended eulogies to service, duty, and self-sacrifice, repositioning the missionary with an essentialist model of womanhood." In other cases, obituaries served a romanticized ideal of mission life. As sources, however, they are often one of the only ways to get at particular biographical information, and offer a unique lens into the nature of the memories certain individuals left. Cheryl Cassidy, "Dying in the Light: The Rhetoric of Nineteenth-Century Female Evangelical Obituaries," *Victorian Periodicals Review* 35, no. 3 (Fall 2002): 206–7.
5. "C.D.M.T.," "Blandina Limo," 203.
6. "The Ordination to the Priesthood of the Rev. P. Limo," *Central Africa* 12, no. 136 (April 1894): 71–72.
7. B. Limo, "A Letter from Blandina Limo," *Central Africa* 13, no. 148 (April 1895): 60–62.
8. Ibid., 62.
9. "C.D.M.T.," "Blandina Limo," 204.
10. "Obituary," *African Tidings* 30, no. 380 (June 1921).
11. "Kwa Kibai," *Central Africa* 12, no. 138 (June 1894): 88.
12. "C.D.M.T.," "Blandina Limo," 204.
13. Limo, "A Letter from Blandina Limo," 60–61.
14. Ibid.
15. Thank you to Alecia Shannon for the biblical reference here.

16. Limo, "A Letter from Blandina Limo," 62.
17. Willis, "The Nature of a Mission Community," 150.
18. Limo, "A Letter from Blandina Limo," 62.
19. C. Thackeray, "Our Native Female Teachers: A Letter from Miss Thackeray," *Central Africa* 14, no. 168 (December 1896): 205.
20. For letter writing as a form of affective community building in Atlantic Moravian missions, see Jacqueline van Gent, "Sarah and Her Sister: Letters, Emotions, and Colonial Identities in the Early Modern Atlantic World," *Journal of Religious History* 38, no. 1 (March 2014). For other forms of affective community building, see Jane Haggis and M. Allen, "Imperial Emotions: Affective Communities of Mission in British Protestant Women's Missionary Publications c. 1880–1920," *Journal of Social History* (Spring 2008).
21. Barbara Rosenwein, "Worrying about Emotions in History," review essay, *American Historical Review* 107, no. 3 (2002): 842.
22. Ibid.
23. Neil Kodesh, "Networks of Knowledge: Clanship and Collective Well-Being in Buganda," *Journal of African History* 49, no. 2 (July 2008): 200.
24. Ibid., 215.
25. Susan Matt, "You Can't Go Home Again: Homesickness and Nostalgia in U.S. History," *Journal of American History* (September 2007): 469. See also Susan Matt, *Homesickness: An American History* (New York: Oxford University Press, 2010).
26. Judith Rowbotham, "'Soldiers of Christ'? Images of Female Missionaries in Late Nineteenth-Century Britain: Issues of Heroism and Martyrdom," *Gender & History* 12, no. 1 (April 2000): 96, 98.
27. Cassidy, "Dying in the Light," 206–7.
28. Matt, "You Can't Go Home Again," 470–71.
29. Gareth Griffiths, "'Trained to Tell the Truth': Missionaries, Converts, and Narration," in *Missions and Empire*, ed. Norman Etherington (New York: Oxford University Press, 2005), 159.
30. Griffiths, "Trained to Tell the Truth," 155.
31. Matt, "You Can't Go Home Again," 475.
32. Ibid., 480.
33. Rowbotham, "Soldiers of Christ," 88.
34. Matt, "You Can't Go Home Again," 480.
35. John Iliffe, *A Modern History of Tanganyika* (New York: Cambridge University Press, 1979), 119.
36. Ibid., 120–21.

37. Ibid., 125.
38. Ibid., 231.
39. Ibid.
40. The German Defense Force included 218 Europeans and 2,542 *askari* (African soldiers), as well as more than two thousand police and countless potential African recruits. The force's reputation worried the British missionaries, especially now that the Germans found themselves surrounded by likely enemies. More than two thousand *askari* in Kenya, Uganda, and Nyasaland; an equal number of European civilians; and eight hundred police in Northern Rhodesia constituted the British King's African Rifles (KAR). Troops potentially sympathetic to Britain were also stationed nearby in the Belgian Congo and Mozambique, although their allegiances were fickle. Iliffe, *A Modern History of Tanganyika*, 240–41.
41. Iliffe, *A Modern History of Tanganyika*, 249.
42. "Samwil Mwenyipembe's Journal (English translation) with a note by Archdeacon Woodward dated 6 December 1917," Box D1(2), Folios 316–75, Universities' Mission to Central Africa [hereafter UMCA], Papers of the United Society for the Propagation of the Gospel [hereafter USPG Collection], Bodleian Library of Commonwealth and African Studies, Rhodes House, Oxford University Library Services [hereafter Rhodes], 1–5.
43. Ibid., 4.
44. Ibid., 12.
45. Iliffe, *A Modern History of Tanganyika*, 255; Personal communication of Peter Limo, 2 April 1922, Box A5, UMCA/USPG Collection, Rhodes.
46. "Samwil Mwenyipembe's Journal," 16–17.
47. Iliffe, *A Modern History of Tanganyika*, 257.
48. "Samwil Mwenyipembe's Journal," 5.
49. Ibid., 16.
50. Iliffe, *A Modern History of Tanganyika*, 234; Alice Foxley, "The Livingstone Jubilee Meeting," *Central Africa* 26, no. 301 (January 1908): 35.
51. "R.B.," "The Guild of the Good Shepherd for the Mbweni Teachers," *Central Africa* 14, no. 162 (June 1896): 103–6.
52. "E.M.B.," "The Guild of the Good Shepherd," *African Tidings* 2, no. 45 (July 1893): 55.
53. "R.B.," "The Guild of the Good Shepherd," 103–6.
54. Caroline Thackeray, "The African Woman of the Future," *Central Africa* 28, no. 330 (June 1910): 158.
55. Personal communication of Caroline Thackeray, 28 September 1885 (Mbweni, Zanzibar), Reel 16, Folio 766, [hereafter noted as R16, F766], Archives of the Universities' Mission to

Central Africa from the Archives of the United Society for the Propagation of the Gospel "A" Series, Center for Research Libraries CAMP Microfilm [hereafter AUMCA].

56. "R.B.," "The Guild of the Good Shepherd," 103.
57. "'Women's Work': Addresses by Mrs. Creighton and Miss Thackeray, Delivered at the Women's Meeting Held in St. Martin's Town Hall on Thursday, June 12, 1898," *Central Africa* (1898): 125–37.
58. Arthur Gordon Blood, *The History of the Universities' Mission to Central Africa*, vol. 2 (London: Industrial Press, 1957), 230.
59. Ibid., 160.
60. "D.J.H.," "Theological Wives," *Central Africa* 50, no. 591 (March 1932): 46–47.
61. Entry for 1 December 1938, *Logbook of St. Cyprian's Theological College, 1910–1953* [hereafter *St. Cyprian's Log*], Diocesan Secretary's Office at St. Nicholas Church, Buguruni, Dar es Salaam, Tanzania [hereafter StNC]. For examples of religious instruction, see Entry for 22 November, *St. Cyprian's Log*, StNC; Entry for 1 December 1941, *St. Cyprian's Log*, StNC; Entry for 7 December 1941, *St. Cyprian's Log*, StNC. For examples of instruction and coursework, see Entry for 25 May 1945, *St. Cyprian's Log*, StNC; Entry for 18 June 1931, *St. Cyprian's Log*, StNC.
62. Entry for 21 April 1932, *St. Cyprian's Log*, StNC; Entry for 18 June 1931, *St. Cyprian's Log*, StNC.
63. For "Miss Wisdom," see Entry for 1 December 1938, *St. Cyprian's Log*, StNC; Entry for 1 December 1941, *St. Cyprian's Log*, StNC; Entry for 7 December 1941, *St. Cyprian's Log*, StNC; Entry for 25 May 1945, *St. Cyprian's Log*, StNC; Entry for 27 May 1945, *St. Cyprian's Log*, StNC.
64. "R.G.P.L.," "St. Cyprian's College, Tunduru," *Central Africa* 63, no. 747 (March 1945): 28.
65. For "Quiet Days" and retreats, see Entry for 8 August 1932, *St. Cyprian's Log*, StNC; Entry for 30 October 1940, *St. Cyprian's Log*, StNC; Entry for 22 November 1941, *St. Cyprian's Log*, StNC; Entry for 22 November 1941, *St. Cyprian's Log*, StNC.
66. Entry for 28 April 1932, *St. Cyprian's Log*, StNC.
67. For "*rashia*," see Entry for 22 December 1932, *St. Cyprian's Log*, StNC; for the shipment from Chidya, see Entry for 24 December 1932, *St. Cyprian's Log*, StNC; for "mudding," see Entry for 27 February 1931, *St. Cyprian's Log*, StNC.
68. Entry for 3 June 1938, *St. Cyprian's Log*, StNC.
69. Entry for 28 February 1932, *St. Cyprian's Log*, StNC.
70. "D.J.H.," "Theological Wives, II," *Central Africa* 50, no. 592 (April 1932): 66.
71. Matt, "You Can't Go Home Again," 487.
72. Elizabeth Prevost, *The Communion of Women: Missions and Gender in Colonial Africa and*

the British Metropole (New York: Oxford University Press, 2010), 36.

73. Ibid., 39.
74. "Our African Mail: Kathleen," *African Tidings* 17, no. 222 (April 1908): 44.
75. "H.M.," "Mama Amwalimu Kathleen," *Central Africa* 52, no. 624 (December 1934): 257.
76. P. B. Nockles, *The Oxford Movement in Context: Anglican High Churchmanship, 1760–1857* (Cambridge: Cambridge University Press, 1994), 202.
77. Kelly Askew, *Performing the Nation: Swahili Music and Cultural Politics in Tanzania* (Chicago: University of Chicago Press, 2002), 10.
78. Thackeray, "Our Native Female Teachers," 204.
79. "H.M.," "Mama Amwalimu Kathleen," 257–58; F. Klamborowski, "Likoma Girls' School," *Central Africa* 50, no. 590 (February 1932): 24.
80. G. Palmer, "How We Kept School at Likoma," *African Tidings* 4, no. 74 (December 1895): 119–22.
81. "H.M.," "Mama Amwalimu Kathleen," 257.
82. Ibid., 258.
83. "H.M.," "Women's Work at Likoma," *Central Africa* 24, no. 281 (May 1906): 127.
84. "H.M.," "Mama Amwalimu Kathleen," 257.
85. Klamborowski, "Likoma Girls' School," 24.
86. "H.M.," "Mama Amwalimu Kathleen," 257–58.
87. Klamborowski, "Likoma Girls' School," 24.
88. Ibid., 25.
89. Thackeray, "Our Native Female Teachers," 204.
90. J. Russell and N. Pollock, *News from Masasi* (Vienna: Veroffentlichungen der Institute fur Afrikanistik und Agyptologie dur Universitat Wien, 1993), 23.
91. Ibid., 47–48.
92. Ibid., 47.
93. The extant letters, which are in Kiswahili and in translation, are deposited at Rhodes House. The letters appear to have been dictated by Agnes in Kiswahili to an amanuensis, who then translated the letters into English. "Letters from Africans," Box A5, UMCA/USPG Collection, Rhodes.
94. Personal communication of Cecil Majaliwa, 22 August 1895, letter no. 25 (Chitangali, Tanzania), UMCA, Rhodes, Box A5; Personal communication signed Canon, 13 September 1897, letter no. 35 (Masasi, Tanzania), Box A5, UMCA, Rhodes.
95. Russell and Pollock, *News from Masasi*, 51; Personal communication of Margret Woodward, 16 February 1900, letter no. 35, Box A5, UMCA, Rhodes.
96. Russell and Pollock, *News from Masasi*, 51.

97. Personal communication of Agnes Achitinao (Ajanjuili), 15 March 1898, letter no. 31 (Chiwata, Tanzania), Box A5, UMCA, Rhodes; Russell and Pollock, *News from Masasi*, 51.
98. Personal communication of Agnes Sapuli, 14 September 1909, letter no. 119 (Mwiti, Tanzania), Box A5, UMCA, Rhodes.
99. Personal communication of Agnes and Francis Sapuli, 20 September 1912, letter no. 71 (Luwatala, Tanzania), Box A5, UMCA, Rhodes.
100. Personal communication of Agnes and Francis Sapuli, 20 September 1912, letter no. 71 (Luwatala, Tanzania), Box A5, UMCA, Rhodes.
101. Benedict Anderson, *Imagined Communities: Reflections on the Origin and Spread of Nationalism* (New York: Verso, 1983), 56.
102. Personal communication of Agnes Sapuli, 14 September 1909, letter no. 119 (Mwiti, Tanzania), Box A5, UMCA, Rhodes.
103. Prevost, *The Communion of Women*, 1.
104. Prevost, *The Communion of Women*, 4.
105. Elizabeth Prevost has explored this community at length in *The Communion of Women*. The monograph offers a compelling analysis of the global Mothers' Union organization, which is outside the scope of this book.
106. Personal communication of Agnes Sapuli, 2 December 1911, letter no. 115 (Chilimba, Tanzania), Box A5, UMCA, Rhodes; Personal communication of Francis Sapuli, 16 October 1919, letter no. 99 (Chilimba, Tanzania), Box A5, UMCA, Rhodes.
107. It may have been Augustino's skill as a footballer and his status as a head teacher at Kiungani that allowed him to build a reputation as the head of the Zanzibari Christian community, and from there to be appointed to head the Zanzibar branch of the AA. "REB," "Mbweni Girls' School: The New Industrial Wing," *Central Africa* (1888). As Laura Fair argues, football skill allowed Zanzibari men to "build their personal reputations and to become recognized as important team, neighbourhood and nationalist leaders." Sports in general, but football in particular, also provided a field for the political conflict and for the expression of "class and neighborhood rivalries and for strengthening communal identities" and was thus an incredibly influential facet of life. Laura Fair, "Kickin' It: Leisure, Politics and Football in Colonial Zanzibar, 1900s–1950s," *Africa: Journal of the International African Institute* 67, no. 2 (1997).

CHAPTER 5. OF MARRIAGES AND *MIMBAS*: MINDING THE BORDERS OF THE CHRISTIAN COMMUNITY, 1910–1930

1. "Report for 1879–1880," in "Central Africa Mission Diary: 1888–1908," CB1 Collection, number 6, Zanzibar National Archives [hereafter CB1–6].
2. "W," "Likoma Girls' School," *African Tidings* 3, no. 61 (November 1894): 85.
3. The most significant of these is Paul Landau, "'Religion' and Christian Conversion in African History: A New Model," *Journal of Religious History* 23, no. 1 (1999): 8–30. See also Paul Landau, "Hegemony and History in Jean and John L. Comaroff's 'Of Revelation and Revolution,'" *Africa* 70, no. 3 (2000): 501–19; Pier M. Larson, "'Capacities and Modes of Thinking': Intellectual Engagements and Subaltern Hegemony in the Early History of Malagasy Christianity," *American Historical Review* 102, no. 4 (1997): 969–1002; and Jean Comaroff and John Comaroff, *Of Revelation and Revolution*, vols. 1–2 (Chicago: University of Chicago Press, 1991).
4. "Conference at Likoma: The Bishop's Address," *Central Africa* 17, no. 201 (September 1899): 157.
5. "F.M.K.," "X-girls," *Central Africa* 45, no. 539 (November 1927): 231–33.
6. Because of the intimate nature of this story, I have used pseudonyms and changed immediately identifying details. In all cases, I have tried to remain faithful to the original nature of the names and have drawn replacements from those commonly used in the Universities' Mission to Central Africa communities during the period.
7. Personal communication of the Treasurer, Zanzibar Diocese, 10 October 1929, "Central Africa Mission Diary: 1922–1932," CB1 Collection, number 9, Zanzibar National Archives.
8. Derek Peterson, "Morality Plays: Marriage, Church Courts, and Colonial Agency in Central Tanganyika, ca. 1876–1928," *American Historical Review* 111, no. 4 (October 2006): 988.
9. Laura Fair, *Pastimes and Politics: Culture, Community, and Identity in Post-Abolition Urban Zanzibar, 1890–1945* (Athens: Ohio University Press, 2001), 18, 27. They did so in part, as Laura Fair and Jonathon Glassman have argued, by not only engaging in the performance of typically "Swahili" cultural forms of public rituals, song, and dance societies, but in reformulating urban popular culture "in ways that granted them a more central place in performance." Jonathon Glassman, *Feasts and Riot: Revelry, Rebellion, and Popular Consciousness on the Swahili Coast, 1856–1888* (Portsmouth, NH: Heinemann, 1995).
10. Brett Shadle, *"Girl Cases": Marriage and Colonialism in Gusiiland, Kenya, 1890–1970* (Portsmouth, NH: Heinemann, 2006), xxvi.
11. Indirect rule was intended to preserve social stability and increase administrative efficiency by integrating the "traditional" indigenous political system into the colonial

apparatus so that there would be only one set of rulers. The policy was based on a historical fallacy, however: that there was something that resembled a "traditional" indigenous political system. Britain's official stance was that ethnicity, tribe, and race were fixed categories with discrete customs and beliefs that endured, relatively unchanged, to the contemporary period, and that ritual chiefs led these "traditional" communities.

12. Shadle, *"Girl Cases,"* xxvi, xxxi.
13. Lynn M. Thomas, *Politics of the Womb: Women, Reproduction, and the State in Kenya* (Berkeley: University of California Press, 2003), 27.
14. Fair, *Pastimes*, 27.
15. In the early 1900s in Gusiiland, Kenya, for example, men who discussed and wrote about the trend of women eloping or otherwise avoiding marriage completely ignored the women's motivations. Their language "often denied women any role in illicit unions whatsoever. Women did not elope but were carried off, senior men insisted; they did not desert their husbands, but were caused to desert. Runaway wives, in turn, explained why their marriages were illegitimate." Rather than go through accepted channels of complaint, women simply took matters into their own hands, forging their own (albeit informal) marriages. Shadle has argued that the prevailing literature has attributed too much explanatory power to male conflict, intergenerational and otherwise, and has inadvertently put scholars in a position of denying women agency. Women, he argues, "sometimes appear only as things over which men fought." Shadle, *"Girl Cases,"* xxvi, xxx.
16. Peterson, "Morality Plays," 984–85, 1005–6.
17. Peter Pels, "Creolisation in Secret: The Birth of Nationalism in Late Colonial Uluguru, Tanzania," *Africa: Journal of the International African Institute* 72, no. 1 (2002): 18.
18. Luise White, *Speaking with Vampires: Rumor and History in Colonial Africa* (Berkeley: University of California Press, 2000).
19. Entry for 3 August 1918, "Central Africa Mission Diary: 1918–1922," CB1 Collection, number 8, Zanzibar National Archives.
20. Logbooks of the Community of the Sacred Passion, The Convent of the Sacred Passion, Shoreham-by-Sea, England, vol. 1, Mbweni (hereafter CSP Mbweni), 2 January 1917.
21. Shadle, *"Girl Cases,"* xviii.
22. Scholars have observed that missionaries' compulsive need to keep records was a method of gaining control over adherents' conduct. By maintaining "catalogues of decisions made, sins disavowed, and judgments rendered," the authors of record books "reached outside the archives' walls and reformed Africans' real-life relationships." The entries in church registers, diaries, and logbooks served as evidence of the promises that

parishioners had made to the church, and as a means to call "errant parishioners before the [church] courts, asking them to live up to the promises they had made on paper." With this evidence, church officials "invited adherents to conform their lives to the book, to orient their behavior to accord with the mode portrayed in the record." And Africans often played into Europeans' archetypes, signing their names to registers and confessing sins. They also recast their characters when they used the very legal categories missionary judges had authorized in order to reframe arguments about property, marriage, or work to their own advantage. Just as often, however, Africans jettisoned this theater altogether and sought to keep their private affairs out of reach of the arm of the church. Pels, "Creolisation in Secret," 18.

23. Entry for 9 August 1918, "Central Africa Mission Diary: 1918–1922."
24. Entry for 6–10 April 1948, "Central African Mission Diary: July 1946–January 1953."
25. In 1905 Miss Stevens took over from Miss Mills at Kilimani. Though the letter that provides evidence of this scandal did not include the year in which it was written, the chronology arranged by the UMCA archivist Ian Pearson indicates that it was written on 4 October of 1908 or 1909. He indicates that folios 477–98 (this letter is numbered f. 495) were from 1908–1909. Ian Pearson, "Guide to the Archives of the Universities' Mission to Central Africa from the Archives of the United Society for the Propagation of the Gospel," available from the Center for Research Libraries; accompanies UMCA microfilm series. A. E. M. Anderson-Morshead, *The History of the Universities' Mission to Central Africa, 1859–1898*, vol. 1 (London: Office of the Universities' Mission to Central Africa, 1905).
26. Letter of William, Bishop of Zanzibar, Zanzibar, 4 October, no year given (likely 1908/1909). AI (XVII) A, Papers of the Universities' Mission to Central Africa: Papers of the United Society for the Propagation of the Gospel [hereafter UMCA/USPG], Rhodes House, Oxford [hereafter Rhodes].
27. Entry for 30 July 1919, "Central Africa Mission Diary: 1918–1922."
28. Entry for 12 April 1919, "Central Africa Mission Diary: 1918–1922."
29. Entry for 16 July 1919, "Central Africa Mission Diary: 1918–1922."
30. Entry for 4 August 191, "Central Africa Mission Diary: 1918–1922."
31. Entry for 23 November 1921, "Central Africa Mission Diary: 1918–1922."
32. Entry for 4 June 1921, "Central Africa Mission Diary: 1918–1922."
33. The payment of *mahari* here is one example of the ways in which the church tolerated the incorporation of longer-standing African practices into the practice of Christianity. Entry for 13 June 1921, "Central Africa Mission Diary: 1918–1922."
34. Entry for 23 November 1921, "Central Africa Mission Diary: 1918–1922."
35. Entry for 24 November 1921, "Central Africa Mission Diary: 1918–1922."

36. Entry for 27 June 1919, "Central Africa Mission Diary: 1918–1922."
37. Entry for 25 November 1921, "Central Africa Mission Diary: 1918–1922."
38. Further, in 1920s Kenya, for example, if a *muthaka* (circumcised, unmarried Meru man) got a girl pregnant, he was expected to arrange the abortion. Thomas, *Politics of the Womb*, 123–28.
39. Entry for 25 November 1921, "Central Africa Mission Diary: 1918–1922."
40. There is little evidence on the "success" rates for abortions in general, much less for the precolonial period in Africa. Abortions are rarely public events, and the procedure, as well as the events that led to the abortion, are controversial and subject to moral debate. In contemporary Tanzania abortion is illegal and punishable by fourteen years in prison for the person administering the abortion, seven for the woman receiving the abortion, and three for anyone who knowingly supplied materials. Therefore, today—in a period in which records exist and interviews can be conducted—abortion rates remain only "best guess" calculations. Hospital admission records exist only for women with complications resulting from incomplete abortions, such as hemorrhage and sepsis. In nonhospital settings women often underreport induced abortion for fear of disapproval, or legal or religious sanctions. Precolonial abortion techniques were both dangerous and of unpredictable efficacy; the techniques that remain today, however, have likely been maintained because they provide a moderate rate of success. M. L. Plummer et al., "Abortion and Suspending Pregnancy in Rural Tanzania: An Ethnography of Young People's Beliefs and Practices," *Studies in Family Planning* 39, no. 4 (December 2008): 281–82.
41. For a comprehensive explanation of this, see Thomas, *Politics of the Womb*, chapter 1. For abortion as a tool to deal with a pre- or extramarital pregnancy, see von Waldow as cited in Lloyd W. Swantz, *The Zaramo of Tanzania: An Ethnographic Study* (Syracuse, NY: Syracuse University Press, 1956), 65; Charles William Hobley, *Ethnology of a-Kamba and Other East African Tribes* (Cambridge: University of Cambridge Press, 1910). Schapera also notes that in the latter half of the nineteenth century, children born as a result of premarital pregnancies "were often killed to avoid their bringing evil upon the community." Isaac Schapera, "Premarital Pregnancy and Native Opinion: A Note on Social Change," *Africa* 6, no. 1 (1933). For abortion as a means to deal with pregnancies understood to have the potential to harm the well-being of the community, see Emil Torday and Thomas Joyce, "Notes on the Ethnography of the Ba-Huana," *Journal of the Royal Anthropological Institute of Great Britain and Ireland* 36 (1906): 288, 92; H. S. Stannus, "Notes on Some Tribes of British Central Africa," *Journal of the Royal Anthropological Institute of Great Britain and Ireland* 40 (1910): 285–335; John Caldwell

and Pat Caldwell, "Marital Status and Abortion in Sub-Saharan Africa," in *Nuptiality in Sub-Saharan Africa: Contemporary Anthropological and Demographic Perspectives*, ed. Caroline Bledsoe and Gilles Pison (Oxford: Clarendon, 1994), 279; T. O. Beidelman, *The Matrilineal Peoples of Eastern Tanzania* (*Zaramo, Luguru, Kaguru, Ngulu, etc.*), Ethnographic Survey of Africa (London: International African Institute, 1967), 70; Charles Dundas, "Native Laws of Some Bantu Tribes of East Africa," *Journal of the Royal Anthropological Institute of Great Britain and Ireland* 51 (1921); Anthony Mochiwa, *Habari Za Wazigua* (London: Macmillan, 1954). Similarly, Rhiannon Stephens has suggested that as far back as the second half of the first millennium, speakers of proto–North Nyanza sought to control reproduction in a variety of ways. Rhiannon Stephens, *A History of African Motherhood: The Case of Uganda, 700–1900* (Cambridge: Cambridge University Press, 2013).

42. Thomas, *Politics of the Womb*, 33.
43. Amy Stambach, "Kutoa Mimba: Debates about Schoolgirl Abortions in Machame, Tanzania," in *The Sociocultural and Political Aspects of Abortion: Global Perspectives*, ed. Alaka Malwade Basu (Westport, CT: Praeger, 2003), 83.
44. Beidelman, *The Matrilineal Peoples*, 70.
45. Beidelman, *The Matrilineal Peoples*, 65; Stambach, "Kutoa Mimba," 83–85.
46. Stambach, "Kutoa Mimba."
47. For the Akamba, see Hobley, *Ethnology of a-Kamba*, 58. For Ngulu, see Beidelman, *The Matrilineal Peoples*, 65. Among the Usambara, Upare, and neighbors, see Dundas, "Native Laws of Some Bantu Tribes of East Africa," 217–78; and Godfrey Dale, "An Account of the Principal Customs and Habits of the Natives Inhabiting the Bondei Country, Compiled Mainly for the Use of European Missionaries in the Country," *Journal of the Anthropological Institute of Great Britain and Ireland* 25 (1896): 181–239. For the Nyamwezi, see Dundas, "Native Laws"; Stephen Rockel, "Enterprising Partners: Caravan Women in Nineteenth Century Tanzania," *Canadian Journal of African Studies/Revue Canadienne des Etudes Africaines* 34, no. 3 (2000): 748–78; Otto Friedrich Raum, "German East Africa: Changes in African Tribal Life under German Administration, 1892–1914," in *History of East Africa*, ed. Vincent Harlow and E. M. Chilver (Oxford: Oxford University Press, 1965). For examples from the southern regions, see Crawford Angus, "A Year in Azimba and Chipitaland: The Customs and Superstitions of the People," *Journal of the Royal Anthropological Institute of Great Britain and Ireland* 27 (1898): 316–25.
48. Stambach, "Kutoa Mimba," 84.
49. Even today, East African women continue to employ abortifacients to deal with undesirable pregnancies. They procure *dawa* from local herbalists; they attempt to

convince medical students-in-training to perform free or lower-cost abortions; they self-administer concoctions of strong black tea, soda bicarbonate, wood ashes in solution, high doses of chloroquine, a solution of the laundry detergent "Blue," aspirin, and/or antibiotics as abortifacients; and they attempt to induce abortions manually. Abortion also remains an option in family planning across the continent, and it continues to be a tool used by women and couples throughout Africa seeking to negotiate socially tenuous situations. For example, Amy Stambach has found, perhaps unsurprisingly, that women in the Chagga region of Tanzania often resort to abortion in order to remain in school. They do so, however, not solely because of the burden of raising a child or the challenges it poses to their ability to continue their educations, but because they are seen to have deviated from expected processes of social development. Women also seek abortions—and make decisions about their partner's involvement in the procedure—based on an idealized future relationship with the father. By helping to procure and fund an abortion, men assert their intentions for a future relationship with the woman, and declare a stake in her reproductive future. Stambach, "Kutoa Mimba."

50. Laura Fair, "Making Love in the Indian Ocean: Hindi Films, Zanzibari Audiences, and the Construction of Romance in the 1950s and the 1960s," in *Love in Africa*, ed. Jennifer Cole and Lynn Thomas (Chicago: University of Chicago Press, 2009), 68; Sarah Mirza and Margaret Strobel, *Three Swahili Women: Life Histories from Mombasa, Kenya* (Bloomington: Indiana University Press, 1979).
51. Patricia Knight, "Women and Abortion in Victorian and Edwardian England," *History Workshop Journal* 4 (Autumn 1977): 57–68.
52. James Owen Drife, "Historical Perspective on Induced Abortion through the Ages and Links with Maternal Mortality," *Best Practice & Research Clinical Obstetrics & Gynaecology* 24, no. 4 (August 2012): 435.
53. Christina Hauck, "Abortion and the Individual Talent," *ELH* 70, no. 1 (Spring 2003): 228.
54. Entry for 27 November 1921, "Central Africa Mission Diary: 1918–1922."
55. P. B. Nockles, *The Oxford Movement in Context: Anglican High Churchmanship, 1760–1857* (Cambridge: Cambridge University Press, 1994), 209.
56. "Conference at Likoma: The Bishop's Address," 158–59.
57. Entry for 6 December 1921, "Central Africa Mission Diary: 1918–1922."
58. H. D. M. Spence-Jones, *The Pulpit Commentary* (Grand Rapids, MI: Wm. B. Eerdmans Publishing Co., 1980–1983), 1:217, 2:404; C. Orelli, *The Prophecies of Isaiah* (Edinburgh: T&T Clark, 1895), 197; Albert Barnes, *Notes, Critical, Explanatory, and Practical, on the Book of the Prophet Isaiah*, vol. 1 (London: Routledge, 1866), 74.
59. Isaiah 1:4, King James Bible.

60. Barnes, *Notes*, 76.
61. Letter of Treasurer, Zanzibar Diocese, 10 October 1929, "Central Africa Mission Diary: 1922–1932."
62. Entry for 10 October 1929, "Central Africa Mission Diary: 1922–1932."
63. It is not evident from the administrators' records what views, if any, the African congregants held of Danieli's "illegitimate" children. It may well be that Danieli suffered little in the minds of the African congregants; women, more than men, suffered harm to their reputations as a result of out-of-wedlock pregnancies. This is another point on which the church administrators and congregants may have disagreed. Entry for 12 August 1929, "Central Africa Mission Diary: 1922–1932."
64. Entry for 10 October 1929, "Central Africa Mission Diary: 1922–1932."
65. Susan's age at the time of the alleged "sale" is unknown, but we can presume from the circumstances that she was in her early teens.
66. Entry for 10 October 1929, "Central Africa Mission Diary: 1922–1932." The records merely indicate that the priest-in-charge spoke on "God can from these stones to raise up children unto Abraham," which is a verse that appears in Matthew 3:9 and Luke 3:8, both of which are recitations of John the Baptist preaching to the Jews in Jordan. Although the record of John the Baptist's preaching is nearly identical to Matthew 3:7–12, contemporary theologians held that the version of the speech recorded in Matthew "seems to be nearer to the original source." Because of their similarities, and because of contemporary theologians' faith in the version from Matthew, I have chosen here to focus on that version. Alfred Plummer, *An Exegetical Commentary on the Gospel According to St. Matthew* (London: Elliot Stock, 1909), 28.
67. Entry for 10 October 1929, "Central Africa Mission Diary: 1922–1932." Not only is John the Baptist's message clear, but the Gospel of Saint Matthew would have been familiar to many among the congregants at Mbweni because missionaries taught it frequently. Thackeray, "Our Native Female Teachers: A Letter from Miss Thackeray," *Central Africa* 14 (December 1896): 207–8; Michael Sadler, *The Gospel According to St. Matthew, with Notes Critical and Practical* (London: George Bell & Sons, 1890), 32.
68. James Morison, *A Practical Commentary on the Gospel According to St. Matthew* (London: Hodder and Stoughton, 1895), 26–27, 33.
69. Scholars imagine John pointing to the stones of shingle that lined the banks of the Jordan and saying, "Do not delude yourselves with the idea that God needs you," for "out of the most unpromising material He could make subjects who in the Kingdom would be equal to the children of Abraham." Plummer, *An Exegetical Commentary on the Gospel According to St. Matthew*, 21; Morison, *A Practical Commentary*, 35.

70. Conversely, Glassman argues, "slave status connoted an ancestral background of barbarism, which is to say ancestral origins in the African interior, outside the world of Islam." Glassman, "Racial Violence," 187.
71. Ibid., 178, 187.
72. Illustrating the fluidity of these racial concepts is *ustaarabu*, the Swahili word for "civilization," which literally connotes the *process* of becoming like an Arab. Glassman, *War of Words, War of Stones*, 4–5.
73. UMCA missionaries shared in a general set of assumptions that motivated Western abolitionism in East Africa in the second half of the nineteenth century. Both secular and evangelical abolitionists believed that humanity is naturally broken into "peoples," "races," or "nations" that remain more or less discrete over time. Behind the contemporary adage "Three C's," or "commerce, Christianity, and civilization," was the idea that "civilization" must be spread by supposedly "advanced" nations or races to those that are less so. Both variants—the secular and the evangelical—held that "abolition was a necessary step in the direction of moral and economic progress" in Africa. Ibid., 17.
74. Glassman, "Racial Violence," 185.
75. Fair, *Pastimes*, 54.
76. Ibid.
77. Ibid., 32–52.
78. As an extensive literature on bridewealth payments or exchanges in much of precolonial Africa illustrates, bridewealth was not a "sale" but rather a transfer in resources that was intended to symbolically compensate the bride's lineage for the labor, knowledge, and unique individual capacities they lost upon her marriage.
79. Memories of the period of slavery were fresh in the minds of Mbweni's Christians, many of whom had once been slaves themselves or were descendants of freed slaves, and the abolitionist rhetoric promulgated by the Western evangelicals by whom many adherents were taught perpetuated these differences. As one woman recalled in 2007, her childhood playtimes on the Mbweni *shamba* were often overshadowed by warnings from elders who urged her and her playmates to stay close to home lest Arabs waiting in the bush should "steal" them, and who reprimanded bad behavior with threats to sell children to Arabs. *Bibi* Miriam, interview with the author, 10 January 2008, Zanzibar.
80. As the classical study on slavery in Africa explains, however, "If the debt was never paid, the pawn remained permanently and totally transferred to the creditors. The pawn was not a hostage to insure good behavior but an object of equivalent value to the loan, and the whole transaction was a pecuniary one." Suzanne Miers and Igor Kopytoff, *Slavery in Africa: Historical and Anthropological Perspectives* (Madison: University of Wisconsin

Press, 1977), 10.

81. James L. Giblin, *The Politics of Environmental Control in Northeastern Tanzania, 1840–1940* (Philadelphia: University of Philadelphia Press, 1992), 44.
82. Fred Morton, *Children of Ham: Freed Slaves and Fugitive Slaves on the Kenya Coast, 1873–1907* (Boulder, CO: Westview Press, 1990), 27.
83. Fair, *Pastimes*, 33.
84. Ibid., 201.
85. Elisabeth McMahon has argued that former slave women in nineteenth and twentieth century Unguja and Pemba were more likely to be able to remarry if she had proven her fertility by bearing children. Elisabeth McMahon, "The Value of a Marriage: Missionaries, Ex-Slaves, and the Legal Debates over Marriage in Colonial Pemba Island," in *Gendered Lives in the Western Indian Ocean: Islam, Marriage, and Sexuality on the Swahili Coast*, ed. Erin Stiles and Katrina Daly Thompson (Athens: Ohio University Press, 2015).
86. Thank you to Emily Callaci for helping to clarify my thinking here.
87. Many former female slaves living on neighboring Pemba at the turn of the century sought to overcome similar vulnerability with a range of strategies that improvised upon this inherent slippage in East Africans' conceptions of marriage and slavery. These refugees and ex-slaves used a serial-marriage pattern to secure their daily existence. Women generally viewed marriage as a temporary enterprise that allowed them access to social and material capital. On both Unguja and Pemba, women were found to have "had little compunction about leaving husbands if they found a suitor whom they liked better or who could better fill their needs." Emancipation offered women the opportunity to control their sexuality and to reduce their vulnerability through a choice of marital partners, but it did not fundamentally alter their view of marriage. As we saw earlier, tensions thus arose between Christian missionaries, who advocated long-term companionate marriages between autonomous individuals of the same religious faith, and their former-slave congregants. McMahon, "The Value of a Marriage."
88. Glassman, *Feasts and Riot*, 90. Sarah Mirza and Margaret Strobel have also discussed marriage among slaves, as has Laura Fair; Patricia W. Romero has discussed concubines. Mirza and Strobel, *Three Swahili Women*; Patricia W. Romero, *Lamu: History, Society, and Family in an East African Port City* (Princeton, NJ: Markus Wiener, 1997); Fair, "Making Love in the Indian Ocean."
89. Andrew M. Ivaska, *Cultured States: Youth, Gender, and Modern Style in 1960s Dar es Salaam* (Durham, NC: Duke University Press, 2011).
90. Derek R. Peterson, *Ethnic Patriotism and the East African Revival: A History of Dissent, c. 1935–1972* (New York: Cambridge University Press, 2012).

CHAPTER 6. I AM A SPIRITUAL MOTHER: AFFECT, CELIBACY, AND SOCIAL REPRODUCTION, 1920–1970

1. Letter of Bishop Weston, 24 January n.d., Folio no. 38, CSP A2-A3, Papers of the Universities' Mission to Central Africa: Papers of the United Society for the Propagation of the Gospel [hereafter UMCA/USPG], Rhodes House, Oxford [hereafter Rhodes].
2. Concerned that their unmarried girls would be conscripted into manual labor or worse, congregants had begun to arrange marriages under "heathen rites." In December 1915, for example, a young girl named Masingano caught the eye of a German official stationed locally. Afraid of Herr Fischer, her relatives acquiesced and allowed him to pay 80 rupees in exchange for her. She remained with Fischer until he fled at the end of the war. "Samwil Mwenyipembe's Journal (English translation) with a note by Archdeacon Woodward dated 6 December 1917," Box D1(2), Folios 316–75, UMCA/USPG, Rhodes, 5, 16.
3. Sister Mary Stella, CSP, *She Won't Say No: The History of the Community of the Sacred Passion* (n.p.: no imprint, n.d.), 14, 25, 110.
4. John Shelton Reed, "'A Female Movement': The Feminization of Nineteenth-Century Anglo-Catholicism," *Anglican and Episcopal History* 57, no. 2 (June 1988): 204.
5. Mary Frances Cusack, "Woman's Place in the Economy of Creation," *Fraser's Magazine* 9 (1874): 202, as cited in Susan Mumm, *Stolen Daughters, Virgin Mothers: Anglican Sisterhoods in Victorian Britain* (London: Bloomsbury, T&T Clark, 2001).
6. Samuel Abraham Walker, "Priestcraft," in *Tracts against Treason* (London: Hamilton, Adams & Co., 1874), 14, as cited in Reed, "A Female Movement," 201–2.
7. Reed, "A Female Movement," 203.
8. Ibid., 206, 208.
9. Ibid., 204.
10. Ibid., 209–10.
11. Ibid., 209.
12. Ibid., 216.
13. Ibid., 217, 225.
14. Ibid., 226.
15. Most estimates calculate that there were between 3,000 and 4,000 members in 1900, living in around sixty communities. Mumm, *Stolen Daughters, Virgin Mothers*, 1.
16. Ibid.
17. Ibid., 131.
18. Gail Malmgreen, *Religion in the Lives of English Women, 1760–1930* (Bloomington: Indiana University Press, 1986), 66; A. M. Allchin, *The Silent Rebellion: Anglican Religious Communities, 1845–1900* (London: SCM Press, 1958), 50.

19. Reed, "A Female Movement," 200.
20. Allchin, *The Silent Rebellion*, 69.
21. Reed, "A Female Movement," 229–30.
22. Allchin, *The Silent Rebellion*, 78.
23. Reed, "A Female Movement."
24. Ibid., 228.
25. Mumm, *Stolen Daughters, Virgin Mothers*, 100.
26. Ibid., 8.
27. Community of St John Baptist, *The Founders of Clewer: A Short Account of the Rev. T. T. Carter and Harriet Monsell to Celebrate the Centenary of the Community of St John Baptist in 1952* (London: Mowbray, 1952), 19–22.
28. Ibid., 19.
29. Mumm, *Stolen Daughters, Virgin Mothers*, 13, 75.
30. Reed, "A Female Movement," 227.
31. Ibid., 231.
32. Mumm, *Stolen Daughters, Virgin Mothers*, 13, 75.
33. Ibid., 13.
34. Sister Mary Stella, CSP, *She Won't Say No*, 3.
35. Ibid., 1, 3.
36. Ibid., 5.
37. Ibid., 7.
38. Letter of Bishop Weston, Rhodes.
39. Sister Mary Stella, CSP, *She Won't Say No*, 109–10.
40. Ibid.
41. Birgitta Larsson, "Conversion to Greater Freedom? Women, Church and Social Change in Northwestern Tanzania under Colonial Rule," *Canadian Journal of African Studies* 27, no. 1 (1993): 75.
42. For more on the Mothers' Union, particularly in the UMCA, see Elizabeth Prevost, *The Communion of Women: Missions and Gender in Colonial Africa and the British Metropole* (New York: Oxford University Press, 2010).
43. Ibid., 383.
44. Despite the relatively late date at which the MU came to the UMCA, the idea of a mothers' organization was certainly not new to the African women workers in the UMCA. In 1878, just thirteen years after the first girls came to the mission, British missionary May Allen began a Mothers' Meeting for the first time in Zanzibar; in 1896 a similar program started in Likoma. In 1911 a delegation of British MU members

approached Caroline Thackeray and Sister Mabel, CSP about establishing a branch of the Mothers' Union in Zanzibar. Sister Mabel was not optimistic about the success of a branch of the MU because, she believed, "our African women are very far back in many ways." Despite the successes of the informal groups of women that had formed across the dioceses, the bishop agreed that the MU was "not at all suited to the circumstances of our Christians in Zanzibar and East Africa." When the issue was raised in the UMCA's Nyasaland Diocese in 1921, the answer was much the same. The first formal chapter of the MU finally opened in Sphinxhaden, Nyasaland, in either 1922 or 1923, followed by a chapter in Tanga Diocese in 1933, and in Zanzibar Diocese in 1940. Ibid.; also Anne Elizabeth Mary Anderson-Morshead, *The History of the Universities' Mission to Central Africa, 1859–1898*, vol. 1 (London: Office of the Universities' Mission to Central Africa, 1905). Thank you to Elizabeth Prevost for sharing copies of letters and other ephemera relating to the MU she gathered at the Mary Sumner House and at Rhodes House [hereafter Prevost personal file]; Letter of Nurse Alica Rees, location unspecified, 23 April 1896, E.2 papers, F. 842, Rhodes House (Prevost personal file); Letter of Mabel CSP, "Mkwein," Zanzibar, 6 November 1910 (Prevost personal file); Letter of Bishop Frank Weston of Zanzibar, Oxford, 23 May, year uncertain (Prevost personal file); Letter of Olive M. Wilkes, Sphinxhaden, Nyasaland, 14 January 1923 (Prevost personal file); "A Little Heaven: Work of the Mothers' Union," *Central Africa* (1938): 66; Arthur Gordon Blood, *The History of the Universities' Mission to Central Africa*, vol. 3, *1933–1957* (London: Industrial Press, 1957), 20.

45. "A Little Heaven: Work of the Mothers' Union," 66.
46. Blood, *The History of the Universities' Mission to Central Africa*, 3:197.
47. "Gleaning after the Review," *African Tidings* 51 (1942): 91.
48. "Hopes and Visions: Work of the Mothers' Union," *Central Africa* 58, no. 692 (August 1940): 131.
49. *M.U. with UMCA in Africa* (Westminster: The Universities' Mission to Central Africa, 1956), 13–14.
50. Marja Hinfelaar, *Respectable and Responsible Women: Methodist and Roman Catholic Women's Organisations in Harare, Zimbabwe (1919–1985)* (Zoetermeer, Netherlands: Boekencentrum, 2001), 14.
51. Larsson, "Conversion to Greater Freedom," 15.
52. Barbara Moss, "'And the Bones Come Together': Women's Religious Expectations in Southern Africa, c. 1900–1945," *Journal of Religious History* 23, no. 1 (February 1999): 109–10.
53. Hinfelaar, *Respectable and Responsible Women*, 14.

54. Larsson, "Conversion to Greater Freedom," 86.
55. Deborah Gaitskell, "'Praying and Preaching': The Distinctive Spirituality of African Women's Church Organizations," in *Missions and Christianity in South African History*, ed. Henry Bredekamp and Robert Ross (Johannesburg: Witwatersrand University Press, 1995), 211–12.
56. Ibid.
57. Phyllis Martin, *Catholic Women of Congo-Brazzaville: Mothers and Sisters in Troubled Times* (Bloomington: Indiana University Press, 2009), 93.
58. Ibid.
59. Sister Mary Stella, CSP, *She Won't Say No*, 110.
60. Ibid.
61. Ibid.
62. Letter of William, Bishop of Zanzibar, Hegongo, 11 September 1959, SF no. 79–80, UMCA/USPG Collection, Rhodes House, Oxford.
63. Sister Mary Stella, CSP, *She Won't Say No*, 109.
64. Ibid., 113.
65. Ibid.
66. Ibid.
67. Ibid., 114.
68. Ibid., 113.
69. Kathleen Smythe, *Fipa Families: Reproduction and Catholic Evangelization in Nkansi, Ufipa, 1880–1960* (Portsmouth, NH: Heinemann, 2006), 109.
70. Martin, *Catholic Women of Congo-Brazzaville*, 108.
71. Smythe, *Fipa Families*, 94.
72. Jennifer Cole and Lynn M. Thomas, eds., *Love in Africa* (Chicago: University of Chicago Press, 2009), 7.
73. Sister Mary Stella, CSP, *She Won't Say No*, 111.
74. The CMM is a small, relatively closed community. To my knowledge, no documents that record women's experiences exist from the order's early years, nor do interviews. I have had to rely on interviews conducted in 2008 and 2013, many with elderly informants who joined the order in the 1950s, to contextualize and give meaning to much of the information that I gathered from British-authored documents and from diaries and logbooks.
75. Letter of Sister Magdelene, July 2006, Masasi, Tanzania. Original in author's possession.
76. Smythe, *Fipa Families*, 95.
77. Sister Martha, CMM, interview with the author, June 2012, Dar es Salaam. Original in

Swahili.

78. Miss M. O'Shea, "In God's Service," *Central Africa* 76, no. 903 (April 1958): 51–52.
79. "The Community of Saint Mary," *UMCA Annual Review* (1947): 5.
80. Sister Merina, CMM, interview with the author, June 2012, Dar es Salaam.
81. Sister Ethel, CMM, interview with the author, June 2012, Dar es Salaam.
82. Sister Mary Stella, CSP, *She Won't Say No*, 114.
83. Rhiannon Stephens, *A History of African Motherhood: The Case of Uganda, 700–1900* (Cambridge: Cambridge University Press, 2013), 2.
84. Ibid., 39.
85. Ibid.
86. Moss, "And the Bones Come Together," 108.
87. Stephens, *A History of African Motherhood*, 51.
88. Several of the *masista* with whom I spoke wished to remain anonymous, citing a recent scuffle with the Mother House as the reason. Rather than assign pseudonyms, I have kept them entirely anonymous. Anonymous CMM, interview with the author, June 2012. Original in Swahili.
89. Ibid.
90. Ibid.
91. Sister Magdelene, CSP, interview with the author, July 2006, Masasi, Tanzania.
92. Letter of Sister Magdelene, July 2006, Masasi, Tanzania.
93. Sister Magdelene, CMM, interview with the author, July 2006, Masasi, Tanzania. Original in English.
94. CSP Sisters, group interview with the author, 20 April 2008, Magila, Tanzania.
95. Joan F. Burke, "Celibacy and the Metaphor of Maternity," in *These Catholic Sisters Are All Mamas! Towards the Inculturation of the Sisterhood in Africa, an Ethnographic Study*, Studies of Religion in Africa (Leiden, Netherlands: Brill Academic Publishers, 2001), 257; see also Martin, *Catholic Women of Congo-Brazzaville*.
96. Burke, *These Catholic Sisters Are All Mamas*, 263.
97. CSP Sisters, group interview with the author, 20 April 2008, Magila, Tanzania.
98. Ibid.
99. Mumm, *Stolen Daughters, Virgin Mothers*, 13, 75.
100. Sister Angela CMM, interview with the author, June 2012. Original in Swahili.
101. Letter of Ruby, CSP, 29 April 1975, Msalabani, CMM box, Library of Saint Mark's Anglican Theological College, Dar es Salaam [LSMATC].
102. Sister Ethel CMM, interview with the author, June 2012, Dar es Salaam. Original in Swahili.

103. Anonymous CMM, interview with the author, June 2012. Original in Swahili.
104. Sister Lucy CMM, interview with the author, June 2012, Dar es Salaam. Original in Swahili.
105. Letter, signed General Secretary, 26 August 1959, UMCA/USPG, Rhodes House.
106. Sister Magdalene, CSP, untitled document, 5 April 1960, The Convent of the Sacred Passion, Shoreham-by-Sea, England, UK.
107. Ibid.
108. Ibid.
109. Letter, signed General Secretary. 26 August 1959.
110. Ibid.

CHAPTER 7. THE INTIMACIES OF NATIONAL BELONGING: COMMUNITY BUILDING IN POST-INDEPENDENCE TANZANIA, 1960–1970

1. Of course, this view was later tempered by Nyerere and TANU's insistence that Tanganyika was "primarily African," rather than Asian or European. James Brennan, *Taifa: Making Nation and Race in Urban Tanzania* (Athens: Ohio University Press, 2012), 155–56. For more on the politics of this debate, see especially chapter 4.
2. Because of the intimate nature of this story, I have used pseudonyms and changed immediately identifying details. In all cases, I have tried to remain faithful to the original nature of the names and have drawn replacements from those commonly used in the Universities' Mission to Central African communities during the period. Attempts to contact Rose and her family were futile. G. Furahani, "Curriculum Vitae," 1965, Personal Papers of Gideon Furahani [PPGF], Library of Saint Mark's Anglican Theological College, Dar es Salaam [LSMATC]. Original in English.
3. Letter from G. Furahani, 1 January 1962, Korogwe, PPGF, LSMATC. Original in English.
4. Laura M. Ahearn, *Invitations to Love: Literacy, Love Letters, and Social Change in Nepal* (Ann Arbor: University of Michigan Press, 2001); Karin Barber, ed., *Africa's Hidden Histories: Everyday Literacy and Making the Self* (Bloomington: Indiana University Press, 2006); Keith Breckenridge, "Love Letters and Amanuenses: Beginning the Cultural History of the Working Class Private Sphere in Southern Africa, 1900–1933," *Journal of Southern African Studies* 26, no. 2 (2000): 337–48; Lynn M. Thomas, "Schoolgirl Pregnancies, Letter-Writing, and 'Modern' Persons in Late Colonial East Africa," in Barber, *Africa's Hidden Histories*, 180–207.
5. Scholars' attempts to reconstruct the history of the early postcolonial period from this perspective are well underway. The search for how Africans understood and engaged

with politics and with the idea of the "nation" in the course of their everyday lives has turned scholarly attention toward the family. This is particularly true in Tanzanian historiography, given the emphasis in the postcolonial era on national familyhood or *ujamaa.* Jim Giblin, for example, has argued that rather than seeing their lives as intimately tied to "colonialism, nationalism, or the transition from colonial to postcolonial rule," rural Tanzanians "consciously situate[d] family in relationship to state authority . . . even while standing separate from it." This "standing separate from" the state and politics of national imagination gave "excluded" citizens "room to formulate their own ideas of moral expectation and responsibility, and to act upon them freely." James L. Giblin, *A History of the Excluded: Making Family a Refuge from State in Twentieth-Century Tanzania* (Athens: Ohio University Press, 2005), 7. More recently, Priya Lal has pointed out the creative and highly contingent ways that rural citizens engaged with the *Ujamaa*-era state. In Mtwara, officials "could not control the actual meanings of gender and family on the ground, just as they could not determine how people interpreted and used the concepts of self-reliance and security locally," Lal argues. Thus, rather than seeing the nuclear family as the natural and enduring institution promoted in state rhetoric, individuals in Mtwara often approached family as a "contingent social resource and survival strategy, and formed and dissolved marital and kinship alliances in order to achieve their own versions of self-reliance and security." Priya Lal, "Militants, Mothers, and the National Family: *Ujamaa*, Gender, and Rural Development in Postcolonial Tanzania," *Journal of African History*, 51, no. 1 (2010): 2, 10.

6. Giblin, *A History of the Excluded.*
7. Karin Barber, "Introduction: Hidden Innovators in Africa," in *Africa's Hidden Histories*, ed. Karin Barber, 5. See also Derek Peterson, *Creative Writing: Translation, Bookkeeping, and the Work of Imagination in Colonial Kenya* (Portsmouth, NH: Heinemann, 2004).
8. Barber, *Africa's Hidden Histories.*
9. Barber, "Introduction: Hidden Innovators in Africa," 3; Thomas, "Schoolgirl Pregnancies," 191.
10. At most colonial-era boarding schools, for example, rules governing students' communication with outsiders were strict, and pupils could generally expect school officials to read their letters. Thomas, "Schoolgirl Pregnancies," 191.
11. Lucy Mair, *African Marriage and Social Change* (London: Frank Cass, 1969), 1; Thomas, "Schoolgirl Pregnancies," 190. When they were writing, Rose and Gideon were likely aware that their letters would be read only piecemeal by a headmistress or letter carrier, be it a postal worker, family member, or friend. After Gideon's death, his family donated the letters as part of his personal papers to the Anglican Church of Tanzania.

12. P. M. Libaba, *A History of Minaki* (Morogoro, Tanzania: Mzumbe Book Project, 2000), 45–46.
13. Libaba, *A History of Minaki*, 45.
14. For example, Nyerere himself chose John Keto, then a teacher at Minaki, to stand for election in 1958–59 as Tanga's African representative to the National Executive Committee. John Keto, interview with the author, May 2008, Korogwe, Tanzania. Original in English. John Iliffe, *A Modern History of Tanganyika* (New York: Cambridge University Press, 1979), 560.
15. Furahani, "Curriculum Vitae."
16. Letter from R. Limo, 9 March 1962, Magila, PPGF, LSMATC. Original in English.
17. Letter from R. Limo, 9 December 1962, Muheza, PPGF, LSMATC. Original in English.
18. Letter from R. Limo, 23 May 1963, Mpwapwa, PPGF, LSMATC. Original in English.
19. Letter from R. Limo, 10 January 1963, Mpwapwa, PPGF, LSMATC. Original in English.
20. Letter from R. Limo, 23 August 1963, Mpwapwa, PPGF, LSMATC. Original in English.
21. Letter from G. Furahani, 12 September 1963, Korogwe, PPGF, LSMATC. Original in English.
22. Letter from R. Limo, 21 September 1963, Mpwapwa, PPGF, LSMATC.
23. Godfrey Dale, "An Account of the Principal Customs and Habits of the Natives Inhabiting the Bondei Country, Compiled Mainly for the Use of European Missionaries in the Country," *Journal of the Anthropological Institute of Great Britain and Ireland* 25 (1896): 201; Sister Phillipa, CSP, interview with the author, 5 September 2008, Shoreham-by-Sea, England; Rev. Maimbo Mndolwa, interview with the author, 8 July 2008, Dar es Salaam.
24. Letter from R. Limo, 10 November 1967, Magila, PPGF, LSMATC. Translated from Kiswahili.
25. Jomo Kenyatta, *Facing Mt. Kenya: The Tribal Life of the Gikuyu* (New York: Vintage, 1965).
26. Andrew M. Ivaska, *Cultured States: Youth, Gender, and Modern Style in 1960s Dar es Salaam* (Durham, NC: Duke University Press, 2011), 204, 10.
27. See Carol M. Eastman, "Codeswitching as an Urban Language-Contact Phenomenon," and L. Swigart, "Two Codes or One? The Insiders' View and the Description of Codeswitching in Dakar," in *Codeswitching*, ed. Carol M. Eastman (Philadelphia: Multilingual Matters, 1992), 1–17, 83–102.
28. Farouk Topan, "Tanzania: The Development of Swahili as a National and Official Language," in *Language and National Identity in Africa*, ed. Andrew Simpson (Oxford: Oxford University Press, 2008), 257; W. H. Whiteley, *Swahili: The Rise of a National Language*, reprint (1969; Hampshire, UK: Gregg Revivals, 1993), 61.
29. Whiteley, *Swahili*, 61.

30. Topan, "Tanzania," 257; Whiteley, *Swahili*, 61.
31. M. H. Abdulaziz Mkilifi, "Triglossia and Swahili-English Bilingualism in Tanzania," *Language in Society* 1, no. 2 (1972): 197–213.
32. Eastman, "Codeswitching," 10; Jan Blommaert, *State Ideology and Language in Tanzania* (Cologne, Germany: Rüdiger Köppe Verläg, 1999), 160.
33. Eastman, "Codeswitching," 1–2; Topan, "Tanzania," 258.
34. Mkilifi, "Triglossia," 210; Eastman, "Codeswitching," 5.
35. Topan, "Tanzania," 258; Eastman, "Codeswitching," 5; Whiteley, *Swahili*, 99.
36. Topan, "Tanzania," 257.
37. Letter from R. Limo, 20 April 1966, PPGF, LSMATC. Original in English and Kiswahili; Whiteley, *Swahili*, 99; Topan, "Tanzania," 259. This insistence also held true for people in Mkilifi's study "Triglossia," 203.
38. Mkilifi, "Triglossia," 203.
39. Letter from G. Furahani, 21 December 1962, Korogwe, PPGF, LSMATC. Original in English.
40. Letter from G. Furahani, 22 August 1964, New Hall, PPGF, LSMATC. Original in English.
41. Letter from R. Limo, 1 June 1964, Moshi, PPGF, LSMATC. Original in English.
42. Letter from R. Limo, 30 September 1964, Mpwapwa, PPGF, LSMATC. Translated from Kiswahili.
43. Letter from R. Limo, 29 August 1964, Mpwapwa, PPGF, LSMATC. Original in English.
44. Letter from G. Furahani, 22 October 1964, New Hall, PPGF, LSMATC. As with his other handwritten notes, this appears to be a rough draft with strike-throughs in the original. Original in English.
45. Letter from R. Limo, 17 July 1965, Magila, PPGF, LSMATC. Translated from Kiswahili.
46. Letter from R. Limo, 25 February 1966, Magila, PPGF, LSMATC. Translated from Kiswahili.
47. Letter from R. Limo, 27 October 1965, Muheza, PPGF, LSMATC. Translated from Kiswahili.
48. Letter from R. Limo, 15 December 1967, Muheza, PPGF, LSMATC. Translated from Kiswahili.
49. Letter from R. Limo, 28 March 1968, Korogwe, PPGF, LSMATC. Translated from Kiswahili.
50. Letter from R. Limo, February 1968, Muheza, PPGF, LSMATC.
51. Letter from J. Rwechungura, Regional Education Officer, Tanga Region, 12 February 1968, PF9 UTSK1077, ref. no. 579/UTS/K 1077/20, in Personnel File of Miss R. Limo [PFRL], PPGF, LSMATC. Original in English.
52. Letter from O. Walter, 31 April 1968, Bunbuli Hospital, Lutheran Medical Centre, PFRL, PPGF, LSMATC. For a discussion of anxiety and mental illness in letters, see Shula Marks, *Not Either an Experimental Doll: The Separate Worlds of Three South African Women*

(Bloomington: Indiana University Press, 1987).

53. Catherine Burns, "The Letters of Louisa Mvemve," in Barber, *Africa's Hidden Histories*, 89.
54. Letter from R. Limo, location and date unspecified (from context, likely 1966), PPGF, LSMATC.
55. Letter from G. Furahani, 14 August 1968, PPGF, LSMATC.
56. M. Mndolwa, electronic communication with the author, 26 January 2009; Sister Phillipa, CSP, interview with the author, 7 September 2008, Shoreham-by-Sea, England.
57. Letter from G. Furahani, 11 August 1968, Nyala, PPGF, LSMATC. Translated from Kiswahili.
58. Letter from R. Limo, 1 August 1968, Korogwe, PPGF, LSMATC. Translated from Kiswahili.
59. Colonial officials, African men, and families were often concerned not just about the potentially declining morals of urban, mobile, or educated women, but also that their new roles and mobility would take them out of the home and render them incapable of fulfilling "proper" duties. For more on this, see Lynn M. Thomas, *Politics of the Womb: Women, Reproduction, and the State in Kenya* (Berkeley: University of California Press, 2003); Susan Geiger, *TANU Women: Gender and Culture in the Making of Tanganyikan Nationalism, 1955–1965* (Portsmouth, NH: Heinemann, 1997).
60. Letter from G. Furahani, 11 August 1968, Nyala, PPGF, LSMATC. Translated from Kiswahili.
61. Letter from G. Furahani, 14 August 1968, PPGF, LSMATC. Original in English; parenthetical comment in original.
62. Kodesh refers here to the works of Terence Ranger and others whose scholarship deals with the "invented" nature of ethnicity, language, law, and religion. Neil Kodesh, "Renovating Tradition: The Discourse of Succession in Colonial Buganda," *International Journal of African Historical Studies* 34, no. 3 (2001): 511–12.
63. Thomas, *Politics of the Womb*, 5.
64. Letter from G. Furahani, 21 March 1968, PPGF, LSMATC. Translated from Kiswahili.
65. Ivaska, *Cultured States*, 5.

EPILOGUE

1. Olivia Luke Dunia, interview with the author, 28 April 2008, Maramba, Tanzania. I have used pseudonyms at the request of the "Dunias."
2. Ibid.
3. Kenda Mutongi, *Worries of the Heart: Widows, Family, and Community in Kenya* (Chicago: University of Chicago Press, 2007).

4. Olivia Luke Dunia, interview with the author, 28 April 2008.
5. James L. Giblin, *A History of the Excluded: Making Family a Refuge from State in Twentieth-Century Tanzania* (Athens: Ohio University Press, 2005), 3–4.
6. Ibid., 4.
7. Frederick Cooper, *Colonialism in Question: Theory, Knowledge, History* (Berkeley: University of California Press, 2005), 11.
8. Derek Peterson, *Ethnic Patriotism and the East African Revival: A History of Dissent, c. 1935–1972* (Cambridge: Cambridge University Press, 2012), 4, 251, 293.
9. Peterson, *Ethnic Patriotism*, 4–6.
10. Cooper, *Colonialism in Question*, 11.
11. Ibid., 200.
12. Frederick Cooper, "Conflict and Connection: Rethinking Colonial African History," *American Historical Review* 99, no. 5 (December 1994): 1516–45.
13. Neil Kodesh, "Networks of Knowledge: Clanship and Collective Well-Being in Buganda," *Journal of African History* 49, no. 2 (July 2008): 199.
14. Nancy Rose Hunt, "The Affective, the Intellectual, and Gender History," *Journal of African History* 55 (2014): 331–45.
15. Jonathon Glassman, *War of Words, War of Stones: Racial Thought and Violence in Colonial Zanzibar* (Bloomington: University of Indiana Press, 2011), 12.

A NOTE ON SOURCES

1. Jean Allman, "Phantoms of the Archive: Kwame Nkrumah, a Nazi Pilot Named Hanna, and the Contingencies of Postcolonial History-Writing," *American Historical Review* 118, no. 1 (February 2013): 104–29.
2. Karin Barber, *Africa's Hidden Histories: Everyday Literacy and Making the Self* (Bloomington: Indiana University Press, 2006).
3. Laura Ann Stoler, *Along the Archival Grain: Epistemic Anxieties and Colonial Common Sense* (Princeton, NJ: Princeton University Press, 2010), 9.
4. Allman, "Phantoms of the Archive," 106.
5. Jonathon Glassman, *War of Words, War of Stones: Racial Thought and Violence in Colonial Zanzibar* (Bloomington: University of Indiana Press, 2011), xi.
6. I have used a pseudonym here to respect my interlocutor's identity.
7. "Mzee Nyangi," interview with the author, 22 February 2008, Zanzibar.
8. "Central African Mission List of Children: January 1878," "Central Africa Mission Diary: 1864–1888," CB1 Collection, number 5, Zanzibar National Archives [hereafter CB1–5].

9. To name but a few: Luise White, Stephan F. Miescher, and David William Cohen, *African Words, African Voices: Critical Practices in Oral History* (Bloomington: Indiana University Press, 2001); Luise White, *Speaking with Vampires: Rumor and History in Colonial Africa* (Berkeley: University of California Press, 2000). Jonathon Glassman has some important insights on the utility of oral sources in Glassman, *War of Words, War of Stones*.

Bibliography

ARCHIVES AND UNPUBLISHED SOURCES

British Library, London

Pamphlets and books published by the UMCA, the Society for Promoting Christian Knowledge, the United Society for the Propagation of the Gospel, and the Mothers' Union.

Cooperative Africana Materials Project (CAMP) microfilm collection at the Center for Research Libraries (CRL), Chicago

Microfilm collection titled Archives of the Universities' Mission to Central Africa, from the Archives of the United Society for the Propagation of the Gospel "A" Series.

The Convent of the Sacred Passion, Shoreham-by-Sea, England

Logbooks, diaries, and miscellanea of the Community of the Sacred Passion and of the College of the Holy Cross.

Special Collections, School of Oriental and African Studies, University of London (SOAS)

Assorted UMCA materials, including later volumes of the UMCA journals *Central Africa* and *Msimulizi.*

Bodleian Library of Commonwealth and African Studies, Rhodes House, Oxford University Library Services

UMCA/USPG Collection.

Library of St. Mark's Anglican Theological College, Dar es Salaam, Tanzania

Collected papers from the Dioceses of Zanzibar and Tanga, the Community of the Sacred Passion, Chama cha Mariamu Mtakatifu, and the personal papers of "Gideon H. Furahani."

Diocesan Secretary's Office at St. Nicholas Church, Buguruni, Dar es Salaam, Tanzania

The office of the Diocesan Secretary houses logbooks, mission diaries, and registers of Kiungani College, St. Andrew's College, Minaki, and St. Cyprian's College, as well as miscellaneous logbooks, mission diaries, and registers from St. Nicholas Church and other parish churches in the former UMCA.

Tanzania National Archives

Secretariat Files, Colonial Annual Reports, DO Reports, the Central African Mission Reports (Blue Books), and a range of Accession Files including 16, 61, 249, 301 (AP & PF), 516, 562. Other UMCA materials included logbooks, mission diaries, and registers from Dar es Salaam, Kwamagolne, Korogwe, St. Cyprian's, and St. Mark's Theological College.

East African Collection, University of Dar es Salaam Library

The Library at UDSM has a large collection of logbooks and mission diaries from Masasi stations of the UMCA and other mission paraphernalia, as well as newspapers and BA, master's, and PhD theses.

Zanzibar National Archives

The AB series, BA series, and CB series, the latter including logbooks, diaries, and letters of the Universities' Mission to Central Africa.

Published Primary Sources

African Tidings, Universities' Mission to Central Africa
Central Africa, Universities' Mission to Central Africa
UMCA Annual Review, Universities' Mission to Central Africa
The Citizen
Msimulizi, Universities' Mission to Central Africa
New English Review
Church of England Newspaper

INTERVIEWS

Amani, Margaret, in Dar es Salaam, 10 December 2007
Apiuwa, Joseph, in Zanzibar, 29 February 2008
Baji, Philip, in Korogwe, 20 April 2007
Bendera, Margreth Philipo, in Maramba, 27 April 2008
Carere, Margaret Bartlett, in Dar es Salaam, 10 December and 14 December 2007
Chambai, George, in Mkuzi, 21 April 2008
Chilumba, Margaret, in Dar es Salaam, 28 November 2007
Chilunda, Agatha Joyce, in Dar es Salaam, 14 November 2007
CSP, Christina, in Korogwe, 20 April 2008
CSP, Julia, in Korogwe, 20 April 2008
CSP, Stella in Korogwe, 20 April 2008
Dhahabu, Zainabu, in Korogwe, 22 April 2008
Diwi, Angelina Charles, in Maramba, 28 April 2008
Diwi, Charles, in Maramba, 28 April 2008
George, Edina, in Dar es Salaam, 30 November 2007
Habils, Simon, in Magila, 24 April 2008
Hassani, Matayo, in Maramba, 27 April 2008
Hemedi, Alfred, in Dar es Salaam, 7 December 2007
Hemedi, Cecila, in Dar es Salaam, 16 November 2007
Heri, Agnes Paulina, in Dar es Salaam, 15 December 2007
Kaleza, Leila Henry, in Zanzibar, 26 February and 20 March 2008
Keto, John, in Korogwe, 20 April 2008
Kigo, Mary Rafael, in Maramba, 27 April 2008
Kijazi, Dorcus, in Korogwe, 19 March 2008
Kiondo, Lillian, in Maramba, 27 April 2008

Kwetukia, Tom, in Korogwe, 8 January and 15 April 2008
Livinga, Monica, in Dar es Salaam, 7 November 2007
Lucas, Marion Grace, in Zanzibar, 18 March 2008
Lugendo, Mary Diwi, in Maramba, 27 April 2008
Lutakamale, Prisca Emile, in Dar es Salaam, 8 November 2007
Makala, Steven Chambi, in Maramba, 27 April 2008
Makao, Grace, in Dar es Salaam, 15 November 2007
Mapunda, Joyce Mhando, in Dar es Salaam, 16 November 2007
Masewa, Sophia Herbert, in Zanzibar, 23 February 2008
Mbaruku, Christine, in Korogwe, 20 April 2008
Mcharuru, Frank, in Dar es Salaam, 12 June 2008
Mhina, John, in Magila, 24 April and 29 April 2008
Mhina, Maria Petro, in Maramba, 27 April 2008
Mkate, Basil, in Masasi, June 2006
Mkoka, Irene Bartlett, in Dar es Salaam, 12 December 2007
Mnyambu, John Peter, in Korogwe, 19 April 2008
Mnyambu, Stella, in Korogwe, 20 April 2008
Mokiwa, Judith Atanasio, in Maramba, 27 April 2008
Mselemu, Frank, in Korogwe, 8 January and 18 April 2008
Muhina, Mary, in Tanga, 1 May 2008
Musa, Esta, in Zanzibar, 9 February and 17 February 2008
Mvungi, Mary, in Korogwe, 20 April 2008
Namala, Violet, in Dar es Salaam, 21 November 2007
Njema, Christopher, in Zanzibar, 23 March 2008
Njema, Florence, in Dar es Salaam, 28 November 2007
"Nyangi, Mzee," in Zanzibar, 22 February 2008
Ramadhani, Augustino, in Dar es Salaam, 24 June 2008
Ramadhani, Bridgeth, in Dar es Salaam, 25 June 2008
Ramadhani, John, in Zanzibar, 9 February and 18 March 2008
Salimu, Alice, in Dar es Salaam, 7 December 2007
Sambila, Veronica Milly, in Dar es Salaam, 21 November 2007
Sekomba, Philipo Magembe, in Maramba, 27 April 2008
Sembano, Basil, in Dar es Salaam, 30 June 2008
Semhando, Agatha, in Magila, 9 January, 24 April, and 29 April 2008
Semhando, Harold, in Magila, 9 January, 24 April, and 29 April 2008
Sengano, Elias, in Korogwe, 7 January 2008

Simpindu, Nicholas, in Dar es Salaam, 16 October and 7 December 2007
Sudi, Jane, in Zanzibar, 21 February 2008
Sudi, Peter, in Zanzibar, 22 February and 26 February 2008
Tajiri, Ali Nassur, in Zanzibar, 19 March 2008
Tandau, Alfred, in Dar es Salaam, 14 December 2007
Tandau, Margaret, in Dar es Salaam, 6 November 2007
Waimu, Margaret, in Dar es Salaam, 6 December 2007
Wakati, Josephine, in Zanzibar, 21 February 2008

Several respondents were repeatedly helpful, engaging in conversations on an ongoing basis between October 2007 and August 2008.

Chitemo, Amani, in Dar es Salaam
Kabudi, John, in Dar es Salaam
Mndolwa, William, in Dar es Salaam
Suri, Phoebe, in Zanzibar

Several interviewees did not wish to have their last names published.

"Francis," in Zanzibar, 22 March 2008
"Joyce," in Korogwe, 23 April 2008
"Kate," in Zanzibar, 23 March 2008
"Mariam," in Zanzibar, 4 February and 26 February 2008

Respondents from the Convent of the Chama cha Mariamu Mtakatifu in Dar es Salaam with whom I spoke in June 2012 wished to remain anonymous, as did others I consulted throughout the research period.

PUBLISHED SOURCES

Abrahams, R. G. *The Peoples of Greater Unyamwezi, Tanzania (Nyamwezi, Sukuma, Sumbwa, Kimbu, Konongo)*. Edited by Daryll Forde. Ethnographic Survey of Africa. London: International African Institute, 1967.

Ahearn, Laura M. *Invitations to Love: Literacy, Love Letters, and Social Change in Nepal*. Ann Arbor: University of Michigan Press, 2001.

Allchin, A. M. *The Silent Rebellion: Anglican Religious Communities, 1845–1900*. London: SCM Press, 1958.

Allman, Jean. "The Disappearing of Hannah Kudjoe: Nationalism, Feminism, and the Tyrannies of History." *Journal of Women's History* 21, no. 3 (Fall 2009): 13–35.

———. "Making Mothers: Missionaries, Medical Offices and Women's Work in Colonial Asante, 1924–1945." *History Workshop Journal* 38 (1994): 23–47.

———. "Phantoms of the Archive: Kwame Nkrumah, a Nazi Pilot Named Hanna, and the Contingencies of Postcolonial History-Writing." *American Historical Review* 118, no. 1 (February 2013): 104–29.

Alpers, Edward. *Ivory and Slaves: Changing Patterns of International Trade in East Central Africa to the Later Nineteenth Century*. Berkeley: University of California Press, 1975.

———. "The Story of Swema: Female Vulnerability in Nineteenth-Century East Africa." In *Women and Slavery in Africa*, edited by Clare Robertson and Martin Klein, 185–200. Madison: University of Wisconsin Press, 1983.

Anderson, Benedict. *Imagined Communities: Reflections on the Origin and Spread of Nationalism.* New York: Verso, 1983.

Anderson-Morshead, Anne Elizabeth Mary. *The History of the Universities' Mission to Central Africa, 1859–1898.* Vol. 1. London: Office of the Universities' Mission to Central Africa, 1905.

Andrade, Susan Z. *The Nation-Writ Small: African Fictions and Feminisms, 1958–1988.* Durham, NC: Duke University Press, 2011.

Angus, Crawford. "A Year in Azimba and Chipitaland: The Customs and Superstitions of the People." *Journal of the Royal Anthropological Institute of Great Britain and Ireland* 27 (1898): 316–25.

Askew, Kelly. *Performing the Nation: Swahili Music and Cultural Politics in Tanzania.* Chicago: University of Chicago Press, 2002.

Atkinson, Ronald. "The Evolution of Ethnicity among the Acholi of Uganda: The Precolonial Phase." *Ethnohistory* 36, no. 1 (1989): 19–43.

Barber, Karin, ed. *Africa's Hidden Histories: Everyday Literacy and Making the Self.* Bloomington: Indiana University Press, 2006.

Barnes, Albert. *Notes, Critical, Explanatory, and Practical, on the Book of the Prophet Isaiah 1.* London: George Routledge and Sons, 1866.

Bastian, Misty L. "Young Converts: Christian Missions, Gender and Youth in Onitsha, Nigeria, 1880–1929." *Anthropological Quarterly* 73, no. 3 (2000): 145–58.

Beidelman, T. O. "Altruism and Domesticity: Images of Missionizing Women among the Church Missionary Society in Nineteenth-Century East Africa."

In *Gendered Missions: Women and Men in Missionary Discourse and Practice*, edited by Mary Taylor Huber and Nancy C. Kutkehaus, 113–43. Ann Arbor: University of Michigan Press, 1999.

———. *Colonial Evangelism: A Socio-Historical Study of an East African Mission at the Grassroots*. Bloomington: Indiana University Press, 1982.

———. "Contradictions between the Sacred and the Secular Life: The Church Missionary Society in Ukaguru, Tanzania, East Africa, 1876–1914." *Comparative Studies in Society and History* 23, no. 1 (1981): 73–95.

———. *The Matrilineal Peoples of Eastern Tanzania (Zaramo, Luguru, Kaguru, Ngulu, etc.)*. London: International African Institute, 1967.

Berend, Zsuzsa. "'The Best or None!' Spinsterhood in Nineteenth-Century New England." *Journal of Social History* 33, no. 4 (2000): 935–57.

Berman, Bruce, and John Lonsdale. *Unhappy Valley: Conflict in Kenya and Africa*. Athens: Ohio University Press, 1992.

Birks, Rev. T. R. *Commentary on the Book of Isaiah: Critical, Historical and Prophetical; Including a Revised English Translation*. London: Rivingtons, 1871.

Blakely, Thomas D., Walter E. A. van Beek, and Dennis L. Thompson, eds. *Religion in Africa: Experience and Expression*. London: James Currey, 1994.

Bledsoe, Caroline. *Contingent Lives: Fertility, Time, and Aging in West Africa*. Chicago: University of Chicago Press, 2002.

———. "'No Success without Struggle': Social Mobility and Hardship for Foster Children in Sierra Leone." *Man* 25, no. 1 (1990): 70–88.

———. "Transformations in Sub-Saharan African Marriage and Fertility." *Annals of the American Academy of Political and Social Science* 510 (1990): 115–25.

———. *Women and Marriage in Kpelle Society*. Stanford, CA: Stanford University Press, 1980.

Bledsoe, Caroline, and Barney Cohen. *Social Dynamics of Adolescent Fertility in Sub-Saharan Africa*. Washington, DC: National Academy Press, 1993.

Bledsoe, Caroline, and Uche Isiugo-Abanihe. "Strategies of Child-Fosterage among Mende Grannies in Sierra Leone." In *Reproduction and Social Organization in Sub-Saharan Africa*, edited by Ron J. Lesthaeghe, 442–74. Berkeley: University of California Press, 1989.

Bledsoe, Caroline, and Gilles Pison, eds. *Nuptiality in Sub-Saharan Africa: Contemporary Anthropological and Demographic Perspectives*. Oxford: Clarendon Press, 1994.

Bleek, Wolf. "Did the Akan Resort to Abortion in Pre-Colonial Ghana? Some

Conjectures." *Africa: Journal of the International African Institute* 60, no. 1 (1990): 121–31.

Blommaert, Jan. *State Ideology and Language in Tanzania*. Cologne, Germany: Rüdiger Köppe Verläg, 1999.

Blood, Arthur Gordon. *The History of the Universities' Mission to Central Africa*, vol. 3, 1933–1957. London: Industrial Press, 1957.

Braam, Tamara, and Leila Hessini. "The Power Dynamics Perpetuating Unsafe Abortion in Africa: A Feminist Perspective." *African Journal of Reproductive Health* 8, no. 1 (2004): 43–51.

Brain, Belle M. *Love Stories of Great Missionaries*. London: Fleming H. Revell Co., 1913.

Breckenridge, Keith. "Love Letters and Amanuenses: Beginning the Cultural History of the Working Class Private Sphere in Southern Africa, 1900–1933." *Journal of Southern African Studies* 26, no. 2 (2000): 337–48.

Brennan, James R. "Realizing Civilization through Patrilineal Descent: The Intellectual Making of an African Racial Nationalism in Tanzania, 1920–50." *Social Identities* 12, no. 4 (July 2006): 405–23.

———. *Taifa: Making Nation and Race in Urban Tanzania*. Athens: Ohio University Press.

Buchert, Lene. *Education in the Development of Tanzania: 1919–1990*. London: James Currey Ltd., 1994.

Burke, Joan F. "These Catholic Sisters Are All Mamas! Celibacy and the Metaphor of Maternity." In *Women and Missions: Past and Present: Anthropological and Historical Perceptions*, edited by Fiona Bowie, Deborah Kirkwood, and Shirley Ardener. Providence, RI: Berg, 1993.

———. *These Catholic Sisters Are All Mamas! Towards the Inculturation of the Sisterhood in Africa, an Ethnographic Study*. Leiden, Netherlands: Brill Academic Publishers, 2001.

Burns, Catherine. "The Letters of Louisa Mvemve." In *Africa's Hidden Histories: Everyday Literacy and Making the Self*, edited by Karin Barber, 78–112. Bloomington: Indiana University Press, 2006.

Byfield, Judith. "Finding Voice, Giving Voice: Gender, Politics, and Social Change." *South Atlantic Quarterly* 109, no. 2 (Spring 2010): 357–68.

Caldwell, John, and Pat Caldwell. "Marital Status and Abortion in Sub-Saharan Africa." In *Nuptiality in Sub-Saharan Africa: Contemporary Anthropological and Demographic Perspectives*, edited by Caroline Bledsoe and Gilles Pison, 274–95. Oxford: Clarendon, 1994.

Callaci, Emily. “Dancehall Politics: Mobility, Sexuality, and Spectacles of Racial Respectability in Late Colonial Tanganyika, 1930s–1961.” *Journal of African History* 52, no. 3 (November 2011): 365–84.

Cameron, Nigel. *Biblical Higher Criticism and the Defense of Infallibilism in 19th Century Britain*. New York: Mellon Press, 1987.

Cassidy, Cheryl M. “Dying in the Light: The Rhetoric of Nineteenth-Century Female Evangelical Obituaries.” *Victorian Periodicals Review* 35, no. 3 (Fall 2002): 206–13.

Chadwick, Owen. *Mackenzie's Grave*. Eugene, OR: Wipf & Stock Publishers, 2009.

———. *The Spirit of the Oxford Movement*. New York: Cambridge University Press, 1990.

Chretien, Jean-Pierre. *The Great Lakes of Africa: Two Thousand Years of History*. Translated by Scott Straus. New York: Zone Books, 2003.

Church, R. W. *The Oxford Movement: Twelve Years, 1833–1845*. Chicago: University of Chicago Press, 1970.

Cliffe, Lionel. “From Independence to Self-Reliance.” In *A History of Tanzania*, edited by I. N. Kimambo and A. J. Temu, 239–57. Dar es Salaam: Kapsel Education Publications, 1997.

Cole, Jennifer, and Lynn M. Thomas. *Love in Africa*. Chicago: University of Chicago Press, 2009.

Comaroff, Jean, and John Comaroff. *Of Revelation and Revolution*, vol. 1, *Christianity, Colonialism, and Consciousness in South Africa*. Chicago: University of Chicago Press, 1991.

———. *Of Revelation and Revolution*, vol. 2, *The Dialectics of Modernity on a South African Frontier*. Chicago: University of Chicago Press, 1997.

Comaroff, John L., and Simon Roberts. “Marriage and Extra-Marital Sexuality: The Dialectics of Legal Change among the Kgatla.” *Journal of African Law* 21, no. 1 (1977): 97–123.

Community of the Sacred Passion. *The Community of the Mission Sisters of the Sacred Passion of Jesus*. N.p.: no imprint, n.d.

Community of St John Baptist. *The Founders of Clewer: A Short Account of the Rev. T. T. Carter and Harriet Monsell to Celebrate the Centenary of the Community of St John Baptist in 1952*. London: A.R. Mowbray, 1952.

Cook, F. C., ed. *The Holy Bible, According to the Authorized Version (A.D. 1611), with an Explanatory and Critical Commentary and a Revision of the Translation, by Bishops and Other Clergy of the Anglican Church*. Vol. 5. New York: Charles Scribner's Sons, 1888.

Cooper, Barbara M. *Evangelical Christians in the Muslim Sahel*. Bloomington: Indiana University Press, 2010.

Cooper, Frederick. *Colonialism in Question: Theory, Knowledge, History*. Berkeley: University of California Press, 2005.

———. "Conflict and Connection: Rethinking Colonial African History." *American Historical Review* 99, no. 5 (December 1994): 1516–45.

———. *From Slaves to Squatters: Plantation Labor and Agriculture in Zanzibar and Coastal Kenya, 1890–1925*. New Haven, CT: Yale University Press, 1980.

———. "Islam and Cultural Hegemony: The Ideology of Slaveowners on the East African Coast." In *The Ideology of Slavery in Africa*, edited by Paul E. Lovejoy, 271–307. Beverly Hills, CA: Sage, 1981.

———. *Plantation Slavery on the East Coast of Africa*. New Haven, CT: Yale University Press, 1977.

Cory, Hans. *Sukuma Law and Custom*. London: Oxford University Press, 1953.

Curtin, Patricia Romero. "Laboratory of the Oral History of Slavery: The Island of Lamu on the Kenya Coast." *American Historical Review* 88, no. 4 (1983): 858–82.

Curtin, Philip D. *The Image of Africa: British Ideas and Action, 1780–1850*. London: Macmillan, 1965.

Curtin, Philip, Steven Feierman, Leonard Thompson, and Jan Vansina, eds. *African History: From Earliest Times to Independence*. 2nd ed. New York: Pearson, 1995.

D'Oyly, Rev. George, and Rev. Richard Mant. *The Holy Bible, According to the Authorized Version; with Notes, Explanatory and Practical, Taken Principally from the Most Eminent Writers of the United Church of England and Ireland*. London: Society for Promoting Christian Knowledge, 1856.

Dale, Godfrey. "An Account of the Principal Customs and Habits of the Natives Inhabiting the Bondei Country, Compiled Mainly for the Use of European Missionaries in the Country." *Journal of the Anthropological Institute of Great Britain and Ireland* 25 (1896): 181–239.

Davidoff, Leonore, and Catherine Hall. *Family Fortunes: Men and Women of the English Middle Class, 1780–1850*. Revised edition. London: Routledge, 2002.

Davin, Anna. "Imperialism and Motherhood." *History Workshop Journal* 5 (1978): 9–66.

Decle, Lionel. *Three Years in Savage Africa*. New York: Mansfield, 1898.

DeGregorio, Scott. "Affective Spirituality: Theory and Practice in Bede and Alfred the Great." *Essays in Medieval Studies* 22 (2005): 129–39.

de Luna, Kathryn. "Affect and Society in Precolonial Africa." *International Journal of African Historical Studies* 46, no. 1 (2013): 123–50.

———. "Hunting Reputations: Talent, Individuals, and Community in Precolonial South Central Africa." *Journal of African History* 53, no. 2 (2012): 279–99.

Dewey, Margaret. *The Messengers: A Concise History of the United Society for the Propagation of the Gospel*. London: Mowbray, 1975.

Drife, James Owen. "Historical Perspective on Induced Abortion through the Ages and Links with Maternal Mortality." *Best Practice & Research Clinical Obstetrics & Gynaecology* 24, no. 4 (August 2010): 431–41.

Dundas, Charles. "Native Laws of Some Bantu Tribes of East Africa." *Journal of the Royal Anthropological Institute of Great Britain and Ireland* 51 (1921): 217–78.

Eastman, Carol M. "Codeswitching as an Urban Language-Contact Phenomenon." In *Codeswitching*, edited by Carol M. Eastman, 1–18. Philadelphia: Multilingual Matters, 1992.

Eckert, Andreas. "Cultural Commuters: African Employees in Late Colonial Tanzania." In *Intermediaries, Interpreters, and Clerks: African Employees in the Making of Colonial Africa*, edited by Benjamin N. Lawrance, Emily Lynn Osborn, and Richard L. Roberts, 248–69. Madison: University of Wisconsin Press, 2006.

Elbourne, Elizabeth. *Blood Ground: Colonialism, Missions, and the Contest for Christianity in the Cape Colony and Britain, 1799–1853*. Montreal: McGill-Queen's University Press, 2002.

Ellis, Stephen, and Gerrie ter Haar. *Worlds of Power: Religious Thought and Political Practice in Africa*. Oxford: Oxford University Press, 2004.

Etherington, Norman, ed. *Missions and Empire*. New York: Oxford University Press, 2005.

Fair, Laura. "Dressing Up: Clothing, Class and Gender in Post-Abolition Zanzibar." *Journal of African History* 39 (1998): 63–94.

———. "Kickin' It: Leisure, Politics and Football in Colonial Zanzibar,

1900s–1950s." *Africa: Journal of the International African Institute* 67, no. 2 (1997): 224–51.

———. "Making Love in the Indian Ocean: Hindi Films, Zanzibari Audiences, and the Construction of Romance in the 1950s and the 1960s." In *Love in Africa*, edited by Jennifer Cole and Lynn Thomas, 58–82. Chicago: University of Chicago Press, 2009.

———. *Pastimes and Politics: Culture, Community, and Identity in Post-Abolition Urban Zanzibar, 1890–1945*. Athens: Ohio University Press, 2001.

Farler, J. P. "The Usambara Country in East Africa." *Proceedings of the Royal Geographical Society and Monthly Record of Geography* 1, no. 2 (1879): 81–97.

Faught, C. Brad. *The Oxford Movement: A Thematic History of the Tractarians and Their Times*. University Park, PA: Penn State University Press, 2003.

Feierman, Steven. "A Century of Ironies in East Africa (c. 1780–1890)." In *African History: From Earliest Times to Independence*, edited by Philip Curtin, Steven Feierman, Leonard Thompson, and Jan Vansina, 352–76. 2nd ed. New York: Pearson, 1995.

———. *Peasant Intellectuals: Anthropology and History in Tanzania*. Madison: University of Wisconsin Press, 1990.

———. *The Shambaa Kingdom: A History*. Madison: University of Wisconsin Press, 1974.

Fields, Karen. *Revival and Rebellion in Colonial Central Africa*. Princeton, NJ: Princeton University Press, 1985.

Furley, O. W., and T. Watson. *A History of Education in East Africa*. New York: NOK Publishers, 1978.

Gaitskell, Deborah. "'Praying and Preaching': The Distinctive Spirituality of African Women's Church Organizations." In *Missions and Christianity in South African History*, edited by Henry Bredekamp and Robert Ross, 211–32. Johannesburg: Witwatersrand University Press, 1995.

Galawdewos. *The Life and Struggles of Our Mother Walatta Petros: A Seventeenth-Century African Biography of an Ethiopian Woman*. Translated by Wendy Laura Belcher and Michael Kleiner. Princeton, NJ: Princeton University Press, 2015.

Geiger, Susan. *TANU Women: Gender and Culture in the Making of Tanganyikan Nationalism, 1955–1965*. Portsmouth, NH: Heinemann, 1997.

Gellner, Ernest. *Nations and Nationalism*. Ithaca, NY: Cornell University Press, 1983.

Giblin, James L. *A History of the Excluded: Making Family a Refuge from State in Twentieth-Century Tanzania.* Athens: Ohio University Press, 2005.

———. *The Politics of Environmental Control in Northeastern Tanzania, 1840–1940.* Philadelphia: University of Philadelphia Press, 1992.

Githige, R. M. "The Issue of Slavery: Relations between the CMS and the State on the East African Coast Prior to 1895." *Journal of Religion in Africa* 16, no. 3 (October 1986): 209–25.

Glassman, Jonathon. "The Bondsman's New Clothes: The Contradictory Consciousness of Slave Resistance on the Swahili Coast." *Journal of African History* 32, no. 2 (1991): 277–312.

———. *Feasts and Riot: Revelry, Rebellion, and Popular Consciousness on the Swahili Coast, 1856–1888.* Portsmouth, NH: Heinemann, 1995.

———. "Racial Violence, Universal History, and Echoes of Abolition in Twentieth-Century Zanzibar." In *Abolitionism and Imperialism in Britain, Africa, and the Atlantic*, edited by Derek Peterson, 176–206. Athens: Ohio University Press, 2010.

———. *War of Words, War of Stones: Racial Thought and Violence in Colonial Zanzibar.* Bloomington: University of Indiana Press, 2011.

Glazebrook, M. G. *Studies in the Book of Isaiah.* Oxford: Clarendon Press, 1910.

Goodwin, H. *Memoir of Bishop Mackenzie.* Cambridge: Deighton, Bell and Co., 1864.

Goody, Esther N. *Parenthood and Social Reproduction: Fostering and Occupational Roles in West Africa.* Cambridge: Cambridge University Press, 1982.

Gordon, David. *Invisible Agents.* Athens: Ohio University Press, 2012.

Griffiths, Gareth. "'Trained to Tell the Truth': Missionaries, Converts, and Narration." In *Missions and Empire*, edited by Norman Etherington, 153–72. New York: Oxford University Press, 2005.

Grimshaw, Patricia. "Faith, Missionary Life, and the Family." In *Gender and Empire*, edited by Philippa Levine, 260–80. Oxford: Oxford University Press, 2004.

Grimshaw, Patricia, and Peter Sherlock. "Women and Cultural Exchanges." In *Missions and Empire*, edited by Norman Etherington, 173–93. Oxford: Oxford University Press, 2005.

Guyer, Jane I., and Samuel M. Eno Belinga. "Wealth in People as Wealth in Knowledge: Accumulation and Composition in Equatorial Africa." *Journal of African History* 36, no. 1 (1995): 91–120.

Haggis, Jane, and M. Allen. "Imperial Emotions: Affective Communities of Mission in British Protestant Women's Missionary Publications c. 1880–1920." *Journal of Social History* (Spring 2008): 692–716.

Hansen, Karen Tranberg. *African Encounters with Domesticity*. New Brunswick, NJ: Rutgers University Press, 1992.

Hanson, Holly. *Landed Obligation: The Practice of Power in Buganda*. Portsmouth, NH: Heinemann, 2003.

Hastings, Adrian. *The Church in Africa, 1450–1950*. Oxford: Oxford University Press, 1996.

———. *The Construction of Nationhood: Ethnicity, Religion, and Nationalism*. Cambridge: Cambridge University Press, 1997.

Hauck, Christina. "Abortion and the Individual Talent." *ELH* 70, no. 1 (Spring 2003): 223–66.

Heanley, Robert Marshall. *A Memoir of Edward Steere, D.D., L.L.D.: Third Missionary Bishop in Central Africa*. London: George Bell and Sons, 1888.

Heckel, Benno. *The Yao Tribe; Their Culture and Education* [*by*] *Benno Heckel; Arts and Crafts of the Bemba* [*by*] *Griffith Quick; Being Reports Presented to the Department of Colonial Education in the Institute*. London: Oxford University Press, 1934.

Heller, Monica. "The Politics of Codeswitching and Language Choice." In *Codeswitching*, edited by Carol Eastman, 123–42. Philadelphia: Multilingual Matters, Ltd., 1992.

Herbert, Eugenia W. *Iron, Gender, and Power: Rituals of Transformation in African Societies*. Bloomington: Indiana University Press, 1993.

Hemmings, Clare. "Invoking Affect: Cultural Theory and the Ontological Turn." *Cultural Studies* 19, no. 5 (September 2005): 548–67.

Higgs, Edward. "Domestic Servants and Households in Victorian England." *Social History* 8, no. 2 (May 1983): 201–10.

Hilton, Boyd. "1807 and All That: Why Britain Outlawed Her Slave Trade." In *Abolitionism and Imperialism in Britain, Africa, and the Atlantic*, edited by Derek R. Peterson, 63–83. Athens, OH: Swallow Press, 2010.

Himmelfarb, Gertrude. *Poverty and Compassion: The Moral Imagination of the Late Victorians*. New York: Vintage, 1991.

Hinfelaar, Marja. *Respectable and Responsible Women: Methodist and Roman Catholic Women's Organisations in Harare, Zimbabwe (1919–1985)*. Zoetermeer, Netherlands: Boekencentrum, 2001.

Hobley, Charles William. *Ethnology of a-Kamba and Other East African Tribes*. Cambridge: University of Cambridge Press, 1910.

Hobsbawm, E. J. *Nations and Nationalisms since 1780*. Cambridge: Cambridge University Press, 1990.

Hunt, Nancy Rose. "The Affective, the Intellectual, and Gender History." *Journal of African History* 55 (2014): 331–45.

———. "An Acoustic Register, Tenacious Images, and Congolese Scenes of Rape and Repetition." *Cultural Anthropology* 23, no. 2 (May 2008): 220–253.

———. "Colonial Fairy Tales and the Knife and Fork Doctrine." In *African Encounters with Domesticity*, edited by Karen Tranberg Hansen, 143–71. New Brunswick, NJ: Rutgers University Press, 1992.

———. *A Colonial Lexicon of Birth Ritual, Medicalization, and Mobility in the Congo*. Durham, NC: Duke University Press, 1999.

———. "Domesticity and Colonialism in Belgian Africa: Usumbura's Foyer Social, 1946–1960." *Signs: Journal of Women in Culture and Society* 15, no. 3 (1990): 447–74.

———. "'Le Bébé en Brousse': European Women, African Birth Spacing and Colonial Intervention in Breast Feeding in the Belgian Congo." *International Journal of African Historical Studies* 21, no. 3 (1988): 401–32.

Hylson-Smith, Kenneth. *High Churchmanship in the Church of England: From the Sixteenth Century to the Late Twentieth Century*. Edinburgh: T&T Clark, 1993.

Iliffe, John. *Honour in African History*. Cambridge: Cambridge University Press, 2004.

———. *A Modern History of Tanganyika*. New York: Cambridge University Press, 1979.

———. "The Spokesman: Martin Kayamba." In *Modern Tanzanians: A Volume of Biographies*, edited by John Iliffe, 66–94. Nairobi: East African Publishing House, 1973.

Isiugo-Abanihe, Uche. "Child Fosterage in West Africa." *Population and Development Review* 11, no. 1 (1985): 53–73.

Ivaska, Andrew M. *Cultured States: Youth, Gender, and Modern Style in 1960s Dar es Salaam*. Durham, NC: Duke University Press, 2011.

Jeal, Tim. *Livingstone*. New Haven, CT: Yale University Press, 2001.

Johnson, Frederick. *A Standard Swahili-English Dictionary* (*Founded on Madan's Swahili-English Dictionary*). Dar es Salaam: Oxford University Press, 1939.

Karant-Nunn, Susan. *The Reformation of Feeling: Shaping the Religious Emotions in Early Modern Germany.* Oxford: Oxford University Press, 2010.

Kayamba, Martin. *African Problems.* London: United Society for Christian Literature, 1948.

Keable, Robert. *The Adventures of Paul Kangai: Stories of a Slave-Boy, Illustrating the Universities' Mission to Central Africa.* Westminster: Universities' Mission to Central Africa, 1915.

Keller, Edmond, and Ruth Iyob. *Religious Ideas and Institutions: Transitions to Democracy in Africa.* Pretoria, South Africa: Unisa Press, 2012.

Kelly, John, and Martha Kaplan. *Represented Communities: Fiji and World Decolonization.* Chicago: University of Chicago Press, 2001.

Kenyatta, Jomo. *Facing Mt. Kenya: The Tribal Life of the Gikuyu.* New York: Vintage, 1965.

Kidd, Alan. *State, Society and the Poor in Nineteenth-Century England.* New York: Palgrave Macmillan, 1999.

Kilekwa, Petro. *Slave Boy to Priest: The Autobiography of Padre Petro Kilekwa.* London: Universities' Mission to Central Africa, 1937.

Knight, Patricia. "Women and Abortion in Victorian and Edwardian England." *History Workshop Journal*, no. 4 (Autumn 1977): 57–68.

Ko, Dorothy. *Teachers of the Inner Chambers: Women and Culture in Seventeenth-Century China.* Palo Alto, CA: Stanford University Press, 1995.

Kodesh, Neil. *Beyond the Royal Gaze: Clanship and Public Healing in Buganda.* Charlottesville: University of Virginia Press, 2010.

———. "History from the Healer's Shrine: Genre, Historical Imagination, and Early Ganda History." *Comparative Studies in Society and History* 49, no. 3 (July 2007): 527–52.

———. "Networks of Knowledge: Clanship and Collective Well-Being in Buganda." *Journal of African History* 49, no. 2 (July 2008): 197–216.

———. "Renovating Tradition: The Discourse of Succession in Colonial Buganda." *International Journal of African Historical Studies* 34, no. 3 (2001): 511–41.

Kopytoff, Igor. "The Internal African Frontier: The Making of African Political Culture." In *The African Frontier: The Reproduction of Traditional African Societies*, edited by Igor Kopytoff, 3–86. Bloomington: Indiana University Press, 1987.

Lal, Priya. *African Socialism in Postcolonial Tanzania: Between the Village and the World*. Cambridge: Cambridge University Press, 2015.

———. "Militants, Mothers, and the National Family: *Ujamaa*, Gender, and Rural Development in Postcolonial Tanzania." *Journal of African History* 51, no. 1 (2010): 1–20.

Landau, Paul. "Hegemony and History in Jean and John L. Comaroff's 'Of Revelation and Revolution.'" *Africa* 70, no. 3 (2000): 501–19.

———. *Realm of the Word: Language, Gender, and Christianity in a Southern African Kingdom*. Portsmouth, NH: Heinemann, 1995.

———. "'Religion' and Christian Conversion in African History: A New Model." *Journal of Religious History* 23, no. 1 (1999): 8–30.

Larson, Pier M. "'Capacities and Modes of Thinking': Intellectual Engagements and Subaltern Hegemony in the Early History of Malagasy Christianity." *American Historical Review* 102, no. 4 (1997): 969–1002.

Larsson, Birgitta. "Conversion to Greater Freedom? Women, Church and Social Change in Northwestern Tanzania under Colonial Rule." *Canadian Journal of African Studies* 27, no. 1 (1993): 136–38.

Lawrance, Benjamin, and Richard Roberts, eds. *Trafficking in Slavery's Wake: Law and the Experience of Women and Children in Africa.* Athens: Ohio University Press, 2012.

Lear, H. L. Sidney. *Life of Robert Gray: Bishop of Cape Town and Metropolitan of Africa*. Vol. 1. London: Rivingtons, 1876.

Lesthaeghe, Ron J., ed. *Reproduction and Social Organization in Sub-Saharan Africa*. Berkeley: University of California Press, 1989.

Lethbridge, Lucy. *Servants: A Downstairs History of Britain from the Nineteenth Century to Modern Times*. New York: W.W. Norton, 2013.

Liebst, Michelle. "African Workers and the Universities' Mission to Central Africa in Zanzibar, 1864–1900." *Journal of Eastern African Studies* 8, no. 3 (2014): 366–81.

Libaba, P. M. *A History of Minaki*. Morogoro, Tanzania: Mzumbe Book Project, 2000.

Livingston, Julie. *Debility and the Moral Imagination in Botswana*. Bloomington: Indiana University Press, 2005.

———. "Disgust, Bodily Aesthetics and the Ethic of Being Human in Botswana." *Africa: Journal of the International African Institute* 78, no. 2 (2008): 288–307.

Livingstone, David. *Missionary Travels and Researches in South Africa.* London: John Murray, 1857.

Ludwig, Frieder. *Church and State in Tanzania.* Boston: Brill, 1999.

Mair, Lucy. *African Marriage and Social Change.* London: Frank Cass, 1969.

Malmgreen, Gail. *Religion in the Lives of English Women, 1760–1930.* Bloomington: Indiana University Press, 1986.

Marks, Shula. *Not Either an Experimental Doll: The Separate Worlds of Three South African Women.* Bloomington: Indiana University Press, 1987.

Maroney, Heather Jon. "Embracing Motherhood: New Feminist Theory." In *The Politics of Diversity: Feminism, Marxism and Nationalism,* edited by Roberta Hamilton and Michele Barrett, 40–64. London: Verso, 1986.

Martin, Phyllis. *Catholic Women of Congo-Brazzaville: Mothers and Sisters in Troubled Times.* Bloomington: Indiana University Press, 2009.

Matt, Susan. *Homesickness: An American History.* New York: Oxford University Press, 2010.

———. "You Can't Go Home Again: Homesickness and Nostalgia in U.S. History." *Journal of American History* 94, no. 2 (September 2007): 469–97.

Maxwell, David. *African Gifts of the Spirit: Pentecostalism and the Rise of a Zimbabwean Transnational Religious Movement.* Athens: Ohio University Press, 2007.

Mbembe, Achille. "The Power of the Archive and Its Limits." In *Refiguring the Archive,* edited by Carolyn Hamilton, 19–26. Cape Town: Springer, 2002.

Miers, Suzanne, and Igor Kopytoff. *Slavery in Africa: Historical and Anthropological Perspectives.* Madison: University of Wisconsin Press, 1977.

McMahon, Elisabeth. "The Value of a Marriage: Missionaries, Ex-Slaves, and the Legal Debates over Marriage in Colonial Pemba Island." In *Gendered Lives in the Western Indian Ocean: Islam, Marriage, and Sexuality on the Swahili Coast,* edited by Erin Stiles and Katrina Daly Thompson, 60–84. Athens: Ohio University Press, 2015.

Meyer, Birgit. "Commodities and the Power of Prayer: Pentecostalist Attitudes towards Consumption in Contemporary Ghana." *Development and Change* 29, no. 4 (October 1998): 751–76.

Mirza, Sarah, and Margaret Strobel. *Three Swahili Women: Life Histories from Mombasa, Kenya.* Bloomington: Indiana University Press, 1979.

Mkilifi, M. H. Abdulaziz. "Triglossia and Swahili-English Bilingualism in Tanzania." *Language in Society* 1, no. 2 (1972): 197–213.

Mochiwa, Anthony. *Habari Za Wazigua*. London: Macmillan, 1954.

Monk, William. *Dr. Livingstone's Cambridge Lectures.* Cambridge: Deighton, Bell and Co., 1858.

Morison, James. *A Practical Commentary on the Gospel According to St. Matthew*. London: Hodder and Stoughton, 1895.

Morton, Fred. *Children of Ham: Freed Slaves and Fugitive Slaves on the Kenya Coast, 1873–1907*. Boulder, CO: Westview Press, 1990.

Moser, Rupert R. "Transformation of Southern Tanzania Marriages." In *Transformations in African Marriage*, edited by David Parking and David Nyamwaya, 323–29. Manchester, UK: Manchester University Press, 1987.

Moss, Barbara A. "'And the Bones Come Together': Women's Religious Expectations in Southern Africa, c. 1900–1945." *Journal of Religious History* 23, no. 1 (February 1999): 108–27.

Mumm, Susan. *Stolen Daughters, Virgin Mothers: Anglican Sisterhoods in Victorian Britain.* London: Bloomsbury, T&T Clark, 2001.

M.U. with UMCA in Africa. Westminster: The Universities' Mission to Central Africa, 1956.

Musisi, Nakanyike B. "Colonial and Missionary Education: Women and Domesticity in Uganda, 1900–1945." In *African Encounters with Domesticity*, edited by Karen Tranberg Hansen, 172–94. New Brunswick: Rutgers University Press, 1992.

Mutongi, Kenda. *Worries of the Heart: Widows, Family, and Community in Kenya*. Chicago: University of Chicago Press, 2007.

Neale, J. M., and R. F. Littledale. *A Commentary on the Psalms*. Vol. 2. London: Joseph Masters, 1868.

Newbury, David S. "Understanding Genocide in Rwanda." *African Studies Review* 41, no. 1 (1998): 73–97.

Nkya, Ananilea, and Agoro Anduru. *Always Serving: A Portrait of Thecla Grace Mchauru*. Dar es Salaam: Publishers Association of Tanzania, 1993.

Nockles, P. B. *The Oxford Movement in Context: Anglican High Churchmanship, 1760–1857*. Cambridge: Cambridge University Press, 1994.

Norton, W. A. "Customs of Central and South Africa: Some Notes and Comparisons." *Journal of the Royal African Society* 14, no. 53 (1914): 81–7.

Nurse, Derek, and Thomas J. Hinnebusch. *Swahili and Sabaki: A Linguistic History*. Berkeley: University of California Press, 1993.

Nurse, Derek, and Gerard Philippson. *The Bantu Languages*. New York: Routledge, 2003.

Oosthuizen, Gerhardus C., M. C. Kitshoff, and S. W. D. Dube, eds. *Afro-Christianity at the Grassroots: Its Dynamics and Strategies*. New York: Brill Academic Publishers, 1994.

Orelli, C. *The Prophecies of Isaiah*. Edinburgh: T&T Clark, 1889.

Pearson, Ian. "Guide to the Archives of the Universities' Mission to Central Africa from the Archives of the United Society for the Propagation of the Gospel." Available from the Center for Research Libraries; accompanies UMCA microfilm series, n.d.

Peel, J. D. Y. *Religious Encounter and the Making of the Yoruba*. Bloomington: Indiana University Press, 2000.

Peires, J. B. *The Dead Will Arise: Nongqawuse and the Great Xhosa Cattle-Killing Movement of 1856–7*. Bloomington: Indiana University Press, 1989.

Pels, Peter. "Creolisation in Secret: The Birth of Nationalism in Late Colonial Uluguru, Tanzania." *Africa: Journal of the International African Institute* 72, no. 1 (2002): 1–28.

———. *A Politics of Presence: Contacts between Missionaries and Waluguru in Late Colonial Tanganyika*. Amsterdam: Harwood Academic Publishers, 1999.

Peterson, Derek. *Creative Writing: Translation, Bookkeeping, and the Work of Imagination in Colonial Kenya*. Portsmouth, NH: Heinemann, 2004.

———. *Ethnic Patriotism and the East African Revival: A History of Dissent, c. 1935–1972*. Cambridge: Cambridge University Press, 2012.

———. "Morality Plays: Marriage, Church Courts, and Colonial Agency in Central Tanganyika, ca. 1876–1928." *American Historical Review* 111, no. 4 (October 2006): 983–1010.

Pirouet, M. Louise. *Black Evangelists: The Spread of Christianity in Uganda, 1891–1914*. London: Africa Book Centre Ltd., 1978.

———. "East African Christians and World War I." *Journal of African History* 19, no. 1 (1978): 117–130.

Plummer, Alfred. *An Exegetical Commentary on the Gospel According to St. Matthew*. London: Elliot Stock, 1909.

Plummer, M. L., J. Wamoyi, K. Nyalali, G. Mshana, Z. S. Shigongo, D. A. Ross, and D. Wright. "Abortion and Suspending Pregnancy in Rural Tanzania: An Ethnography of Young People's Beliefs and Practices." *Studies in Family Planning* 39, no. 4 (December 2008): 281–92.

Porter, Andrew. "An Overview, 1700–1914." In *Missions and Empire*, edited by Norman Etherington, 49–63. Oxford: Oxford University Press, 2005.

Prestholdt, Jeremy. *Domesticating the World: African Consumerism and the Genealogies of Globalization*. Berkeley: University of California Press, 2008.

Prevost, Elizabeth. *The Communion of Women: Missions and Gender in Colonial Africa and the British Metropole*. New York: Oxford University Press, 2010.

Prochaska, F. K. "Female Philanthropy and Domestic Service in Victorian England." *Bulletin of the Institute of Historical Research* 54 (1981): 79–85.

Ranger, T. O. "The Invention of Tradition Revisited: The Case of Colonial Africa." In *Legitimacy and the State in Twentieth-Century Africa*, edited by T. O. Ranger, 62–111. London: Macmillan, 1993.

———. "Missionary Adaptation of African Religious Institutions: The Masasi Case." In *The Historical Study of African Religion; with Special Reference to East and Central Africa*, edited by T. O. Ranger and Isaria N. Kimambo, 221–51. London: Heinemann, 1972.

———. "Protestant Missions in Africa: The Dialectic of Conversion in the American Methodist Episcopal Church in Eastern Zimbabwe, 1900–1950." In *Religion in Africa: Experience and Expression*, edited by T. D. Blakeley et al., 275–313. London: James Currey, 1994.

Ranger, T. O., and Isaria Kimambo. *Historical Study of African Religion*. Berkeley: University of California Press, 1972.

Raum, Otto Friedrich. "German East Africa: Changes in African Tribal Life under German Administration, 1892–1914." In *History of East Africa*, edited by Vincent Harlow and E. M. Chilver, 163–207. Oxford: Oxford University Press, 1965.

Reed, John Shelton. "'A Female Movement': The Feminization of Nineteenth-Century Anglo-Catholicism." *Anglican and Episcopal History* 57, no. 2 (June 1988): 199–238.

Robertson, Claire, and Martin Klein, eds. *Women and Slavery in Africa*. Madison: University of Wisconsin Press, 1983.

Rockel, Stephen. "Enterprising Partners: Caravan Women in Nineteenth Century Tanzania." *Canadian Journal of African Studies/Revue Canadienne des Etudes Africaines* 34, no. 3 (2000): 748–78.

Romero, Patricia W. *Lamu: History, Society, and Family in an East African Port City*. Princeton, NJ: Markus Wiener, 1997.

Rosenwein, Barbara. "Worrying about Emotions in History." Review essay. *American Historical Review* 107, no. 3 (2002): 821–45.

Rowbotham, Judith. "'Soldiers of Christ'? Images of Female Missionaries in Late Nineteenth-Century Britain: Issues of Heroism and Martyrdom." *Gender & History* 12, no. 1 (April 2000): 82–106.

Russell, J., and N. Pollock. *News from Masasi.* Vienna: Veroffentlichungen der Institute fur Afrikanistik und Agyptologie dur Universitat Wien, 1993.

Sadler, Michael. *The Gospel According to St. Matthew, with Notes Critical and Practical.* London: George Bell and Sons, 1890.

Said, Mohamed. *The Life and Times of Abdulwahid Sykes (1924–1968): The Untold Story of the Muslim Struggle against British Colonialism in Tanganyika.* Richmond, VA: Minerva Press, 1998.

Schapera, Isaac. "Premarital Pregnancy and Native Opinion: A Note on Social Change." *Africa* 6, no. 1 (1933): 59–89.

Schoenbrun, David L. *A Green Place, a Good Place: Agrarian Change, Gender, and Social Identity in the Great Lakes Region to the 15th Century*. Portsmouth, NH: Heinemann, 1998.

Schneider, Leander. "The Tanzanian National Archives." *History in Africa* 30 (2003): 447–54.

Schwarz, Thomas. "Colonial Disgust: The Colonial Master's Emotion of Superiority." In *German Colonialism, Visual Culture, and Modern Memory*, edited by V. M. Langbehn, 182–96. New York: Routledge, 2010.

Scott, Joan Wallach. *Gender and the Politics of History*. New York: Columbia University Press, 1988.

Selwyn, George Augustus. *The Work of Christ in the World: Four Sermons Preached before the University of Cambridge*. Cambridge: Macmillan & Co., 1855.

Semple, Rhonda A. *Missionary Women: Gender, Professionalism, and the Victorian Idea of Christian Mission*. Rochester, NY: Boydell Press, 2003.

Shadle, Brett. *"Girl Cases": Marriage and Colonialism in Gusiiland, Kenya, 1890–1970*. Portsmouth, NH: Heinemann, 2006.

Sheriff, Abdul. *History and Conservation of Zanzibar Stone Town*. Athens: Ohio University Press, 1995.

Sheriff, Abdul M. H. *Slaves, Spices and Ivory in Zanzibar*. Athens: Ohio University Press, 1987.

Shoemaker, Stephen. "Mary at the Cross, East and West: Maternal Compassion and Affective Piety in the Earliest Life of the Virgin and the High Middle Ages." *Journal of Theological Studies* 62 (October 2011): 570–606.

"Sisterhood Life." In *The Church and the World: Essays on Questions of the Day in 1866*, edited by Orby Shipley, 166–95. London: Longmans, Green, Reader, and Dyer, 1867.

Sister Mary Stella, CSP. *She Won't Say No: The History of the Community of the Sacred Passion*. N.p.: no imprint, n.d.

Sister Violet, CSP. *Preparation for Service in Africa*. Westminster: Universities' Mission to Central Africa, n.d.

Small, N. J. "U.M.C.A. (Universities' Mission to Central Africa): The Early Work in Education, 1876–1905." *Tanzania Notes and Records* 86/87 (1980): 35–55.

Smith, H. M. *Frank, Bishop of Zanzibar: Life of Frank Weston, D.D., 1871–1924*. London: Society for Promoting Christian Knowledge/Macmillan Co., 1926.

Smith, Hilda L. "Women's History as Intellectual History: A Perspective on the Journal of Women's History." *Journal of Women's History* 20, no. 1 (Spring 2008): 26.

Smythe, Kathleen. *Fipa Families: Reproduction and Catholic Evangelization in Nkansi, Ufipa, 1880–1960*. Portsmouth, NH: Heinemann, 2006.

Society for Promoting Christian Knowledge (SPCK). *Mission Heroes*. London: Society for Promoting Christian Knowledge, 1895.

Southall, Aidan. "The Illusion of Tribe." *Journal of Asian and African Studies* 5, no. 12 (1970).

Spence Jones, H. D. M. *The Pulpit Commentary*. Grand Rapids, MI: Wm. B. Eerdmans Publishing Co., 1980–1983. Reprint of 1890s edition.

Stambach, Amy. "Kutoa Mimba: Debates about Schoolgirl Abortions in Machame, Tanzania." In *The Sociocultural and Political Aspects of Abortion: Global Perspectives*, edited by Alaka Malwade Basu, 79–102. Westport, CT: Praeger Publishers, 2003.

Stannus, H. S. "Notes on Some Tribes of British Central Africa." *Journal of the Royal Anthropological Institute of Great Britain and Ireland* 40 (1910): 285–355.

Steere, Edward. *A Handbook of the Swahili Language, as Spoken at Zanzibar*. 3rd ed. London: Society for Promoting Christian Knowledge, 1884.

Stephens, Rhiannon. *A History of African Motherhood: The Case of Uganda, 700–1900*. Cambridge: Cambridge University Press, 2013.

Stiles, Erin, and Katrina Daly Thompson, eds. *Gendered Lives in the Western*

Indian Ocean: Islam, Marriage, and Sexuality on the Swahili Coast. Athens: Ohio University Press, 2015.

Stoler, Laura Ann. *Along the Archival Grain: Epistemic Anxieties and Colonial Common Sense*. Princeton, NJ: Princeton University Press, 2010.

Stoner-Eby, Anne Marie. "African Leaders Engage Mission Christianity: Anglicans in Tanzania, 1876–1926." PhD diss., University of Pennsylvania, 2003.

Strobel, Margaret. *Muslim Women in Mombasa, Kenya, 1890–1973*. New Haven, CT: Yale University Press, 1975.

Strobel, Margaret, and Sarah Mirza. *Wanawake Watatu Wa Kiswahili: Hadithi Za Maisha Kutoka Mombasa, Kenya*. Bloomington: Indiana University Press, 1991.

Summers, Carol. "Intimate Colonialism: The Imperial Production of Reproduction in Uganda, 1907–1925." *Signs* 16, no. 4 (1991): 787–807.

Swantz, Lloyd W. *The Zaramo of Tanzania: An Ethnographic Study*. Syracuse, NY: Syracuse University Press, 1956.

Swigart, L. "Two Codes or One? The Insiders' View and the Description of Codeswitching in Dakar." In *Codeswitching*, edited by Carol M. Eastman, 83–102. Philadelphia: Multilingual Matters, 1992.

Thane, Pat. "Women and the Poor Law in Victorian and Edwardian England." *History Workshop*, no. 6 (Autumn 1978): 29–51.

Thomas, Douglas. *African Traditional Religion in the Modern World: An Introduction*. Jefferson, NC: McFarland, 2005.

Thomas, Lynn M. "Love, Sex, and the Modern Girl in 1930s Southern Africa." In *Love in Africa*, edited by Jennifer Cole and Lynn M. Thomas, 31–57. Chicago: University of Chicago Press, 2009.

———. *Politics of the Womb: Women, Reproduction, and the State in Kenya*. Berkeley: University of California Press, 2003.

———. "Schoolgirl Pregnancies, Letter-Writing, and 'Modern' Persons in Late Colonial East Africa." In *Africa's Hidden Histories: Everyday Literacy and Making the Self*, edited by Karin Barber, 180–207. Bloomington: Indiana University Press, 2006.

Thompson, Rev. H. P. *Into All Lands: The History of the Society for the Propagation of the Gospel in Foreign Parts, 1701–1950*. London: SPCK, 1951.

Thorne, Susan. *Congregational Missions and the Making of an Imperial Culture in Nineteenth-Century England*. Stanford, CA: Stanford University Press, 1999.

Thornton, John. *The Kongolese Saint Anthony: Dona Beatriz Kimpa Vita and the Antonian Movement, 1684–1706*. Cambridge: Cambridge University Press, 1998.

Tomkins, Silvan S. *Affect, Imagery, Consciousness*. Vol. 2, *The Negative Affects*. New York: Springer Publishing, 1962.

Topan, Farouk. "Tanzania: The Development of Swahili as a National and Official Language." In *Language and National Identity in Africa*, edited by Andrew Simpson, 252–66. Oxford: Oxford University Press, 2008.

Torday, Emil, and Thomas Joyce. "Notes on the Ethnography of the Ba-Huana." *Journal of the Royal Anthropological Institute of Great Britain and Ireland* 36 (1906): 272–301.

Tucker, H. W. *Memoir of the Life and Episcopate of George Augustus Selwyn, D.D.* London: William Wells Gardner, 1879.

Taasisi ya Uchuguzi wa Kiswahili (TUKI). *Kamusi Ya Kiswahili-Kiingereza—Swahili-English Dictionary*. Dar es Salaam, Tanzania: Chuo Kikuu cha Dar es Salaam, 2001.

Urban-Mead, Wendy. *The Gender of Piety: Family, Faith, and Colonial Rule in Matabeleland, Zimbabwe*. Athens: Ohio University Press, 2015.

Van Gent, Jacqueline. "Sarah and Her Sister: Letters, Emotions, and Colonial Identities in the Early Modern Atlantic World." *Journal of Religious History* 38, no. 1 (March 2014): 71–90.

Vansina, Jan. *Antecedents to Modern Rwanda: The Nyiginya Kingdom*. Madison: University of Wisconsin Press, 2004.

Vaughan, Megan. "The History of Romantic Love in Sub-Saharan Africa: Between Interest and Emotion." *Proceedings of the British Academy* 167 (2009): 1–23.

White, Landeg. *Magomero: Portrait of an African Village*. New York: Cambridge University Press, 1987.

White, Luise. *Speaking with Vampires: Rumor and History in Colonial Africa*. Berkeley: University of California Press, 2000.

White, Luise, Stephan F. Miescher, and David William Cohen, eds. *African Words, African Voices: Critical Practices in Oral History*. Bloomington: Indiana University Press, 2001.

Whiteley, W. H. *Swahili: The Rise of a National Language*. London: Methuen Young Books, 1969.

Willis, Justin. "The Makings of a Tribe: Bondei Identities and Histories." *Journal of African History* 33, no. 2 (1992): 191–208.

———. "The Nature of a Mission Community: The Universities' Mission to Central Africa in Bonde." *Past & Present*, no. 140 (August 1993): 127–54.

Wilson, G. H. *The History of the Universities' Mission to Central Africa.* Westminster: Universities' Mission to Central Africa, 1936.

Wright, Marcia. *German Missions in Tanganyika, 1891–1941: Lutherans and Moravians in the Southern Highlands*. Oxford: Clarendon Press, 1971.

———. *Strategies of Slaves and Women: Life-Stories from East/Central Africa.* New York: Lilian Barber Press, 1993.

Yarton Mills, Dora S. *Where We Live and What We Do.* London: Office of Universities' Mission to Central Africa, 1909.

Index

N

O

T

U

W

Y

Z